P9-DXK-277

# PassKey EA Review
# Part 1: Individuals

## IRS Enrolled Agent Exam
## Study Guide 2013-2014 Edition

**Authors:**
Collette Szymborski, CPA
Richard Gramkow, EA
Christy Pinheiro, EA ABA®

PassKey Publications
Elk Grove, CA 95758

# Recent Praise for the PassKey EA Review Series

### Kari Hutchens (Canon City, Colorado)

I passed all three exams! Easy to understand and comprehensive. Even from Part 1 of the book (Individuals), I learned so much that I am going to amend two prior year tax returns and get over $1,000 back. Passing all three parts of the EA exam on the first try and getting some extra cash in my pocket gets this book an A+!

### Ken Smith (Chicago, Illinois)

I studied like crazy, night and day, and passed all three parts of the EA exam in just eight days. And I passed on the first try!

### Michael Mirth (North Las Vegas, Nevada)

I am happy to say I am now an enrolled agent. This was the only source I used to study besides some extra practice tests. The way the book presented the materials made it easy to comprehend. If you are looking for a detailed study guide, this one is for you.

### E. Dinetz (Mt. Laurel, New Jersey)

This book is very informative. I have an accounting degree and have done taxes in the past and I learned many new things from this book. I like the fact that after each concept they have a multiple choice quiz/review.

### Oliver Douglass

I found this book to be the least expensive and the best guide around. The tests are on the money and the explanations are so easy to comprehend. Thanks for a great book.

### Baiye Zebulone

Great books. Straight to the point, and very good examples for SEE preparations. I used all three parts to prepare for the SEE and passed Parts 1 and 3 on the first sitting and Part 2 on the second sitting. I will recommend it to anybody who wants to pass the rigorous EA examination.

### Carl Ganster (Wyomissing, Pennsylvania)

I passed all my tests on the first try in five months using the PassKey books. Every topic is covered. It is easy reading, with plenty of examples. I have recommended the books to others who have to take the test. Thanks, PassKey, for writing great test guides. So many of the ones out there are hard to understand.

# Do you want to test yourself?

## Then get the PassKey EA Exam Workbook, newly expanded for tax year 2012!

PassKey EA Review Workbook:
Six Complete Enrolled Agent Practice Exams

Thoroughly revised and updated for tax year 2012, this workbook features **six complete** enrolled agent practice exams, with detailed answers, to accompany the PassKey EA Review study guides. This workbook includes two full exams for each of the three parts of the EA exam: Individuals, Businesses, and Representation.

You can learn by testing yourself on 600 questions, with all of the answers clearly explained in the back of the book.

Test yourself, time yourself, and learn!

Editor: Cynthia Willett Sherwood, EA, MSJ

*PassKey EA Review, Part 1: Individuals, IRS Enrolled Agent Exam Study Guide 2013-2014 Edition*

ISBN: 978-1-935664-22-2

First Printing. PassKey EA Review
PassKey EA Review® is a U.S. Registered Trademark

All Rights Reserved ©2013 PassKey EA Review DBA PassKey Publications. Revised and updated every year to updated IRS EA Exam specifications. United States laws and regulations are public domain and not subject to copyright. The editorial arrangement, analysis, and professional commentary are subject to this copyright notice. No portion of this book may be copied, retransmitted, reposted, duplicated, or otherwise used without the express written approval of the publisher. Questions for this study guide have been taken from previous IRS Special Enrolled Agent examinations and from current IRS publications. The authors have also drafted new questions.

Tammy the Tax Lady® is a trademark of PassKey Publications.

PassKey Publications, PO Box 580465, Elk Grove, CA 95758

www.PassKeyPublications.com

# Part 1: Individuals

**Tammy the Tax Lady®**

Let me get this straight... you only accept cash, and your official job description is "underground pharmaceutical rep?"

# Table of Contents

# Introduction

Congratulations on taking the first step toward becoming an enrolled agent, a widely respected professional tax designation. The Internal Revenue Service licenses enrolled agents, known as EAs, after candidates pass a three-part exam testing their knowledge of federal tax law.

This PassKey study guide is designed to help you study for the EA exam, which is formally called the *IRS Special Enrollment Examination* or *"SEE."* The exam covers all aspects of federal tax law, including the taxation of individuals; corporations, partnerships, and exempt entities; ethics; and IRS collection and audit procedures. This guide is designed for the 2013 to 2014 testing season, which begins May 1, 2013 and closes February 28, 2014. Anyone taking the EA exam during this time period will be tested on 2012 tax law.

## Exam Basics

The EA exam consists of three parts, which candidates typically take on different dates that do not need to be consecutive. The exam is exclusively administered by the testing company Prometric. You can find valuable information and register online at: ***http://www.prometric.com/IRS***

The yearly pass rates for the SEE vary by exam. In the 2011-2012 testing period, an average of more than 80% of test-takers passed Parts 1 and 3. The pass rate for Part 2 was much lower, averaging about 60%.

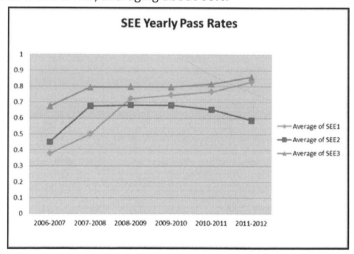

The computerized exam is offered only at Prometric testing centers. The format is multiple choice, with no questions requiring written answers. The length of each part of the exam is 3.5 hours, not including a pre-exam tutorial and post-exam survey.

| Computerized EA Exam Format |
| :-: |
| Part 1 - Individual Taxation-100 Questions |
| Part 2 - Business Taxation-100 Questions |
| Part 3 - Representation, Practice, and Procedures-100 Questions |

# Testing Center Procedures

The testing center is designed to be a secure environment. The following are procedures you'll need to follow on test day:

1. Check in about a half-hour before your appointment time, and bring a current government-issued ID with both a photo and signature. If you don't have valid ID, you'll be turned away and you'll have to pay for a new exam appointment.
2. You'll be given a locker for your wallet, phone, and other personal items. You won't be able to bring any reference materials or other items into the testing room, with the exception of soft earplugs. The center supplies noise-blocking headphones.
3. No food, water, or other beverages are allowed in the testing room.
4. You'll be given scratch paper and a pencil to use, which will be collected after the exam.
5. You'll be able to use an onscreen calculator during the exam, or Prometric will provide you with a handheld calculator. You cannot bring your own.
6. Before going into the testing room, you'll be scanned with a metal detector wand.
7. You'll need to sign in and out every time you leave the testing room. Bathroom breaks are permitted, but the test timer will continue to count down.
8. You're not allowed to talk or communicate with other test-takers in the exam room. Prometric continuously monitors the testing via video, physical walk-throughs, and an observation window.

Violation of any of these procedures may result in the disqualification of your exam. In cases of cheating, the IRS says candidates may be subject to a variety of consequences, including civil and criminal penalties.

Exam-takers who require special accommodations under the Americans with Disabilities Act (ADA) must contact Prometric at 888-226-9406 to obtain an accommodation request form. A language barrier is not considered a disability. [1]

---

[1] *Candidate Information Bulletin* for the Enrolled Agent Special Enrollment Examination.

# Exam Content

The IRS introduces multiple versions of new EA exams each May. If you fail a particular part of the exam and need to retake it, don't expect to see the identical questions the next time.

The IRS no longer releases new test questions and answers, although questions from 2003 to 2005 are available on the IRS website for review. (Be aware that tax law changes every year, so make sure you are familiar with recent updates and don't rely too heavily on these sample questions and answers.) Prometric includes broad exam content outlines for each exam part; however, not all of the topics will appear on the exam and there may be other topics that are included.

Your PassKey study guides present an overview of all the major areas of federal taxation that enrolled agents typically encounter in their practices and that are likely to appear on the exam. Although the PassKey guides are designed to be comprehensive, we suggest you review IRS publications and try to learn as much as you can about tax law in general so that you're well-equipped to take the exam. In addition to this study guide, we highly recommend that all exam candidates read:

- **Publication 17, *Your Federal Income Tax*** (for Part 1 of the exam), and
- **Circular 230, *Regulations Governing the Practice of Attorneys, Certified Public Accountants, Enrolled Agents, Enrolled Actuaries, and Appraisers before the Internal Revenue Service*** (for Part 3 of the exam).

Anyone may download these publications for free from the IRS website.

> **Note:** Some exam candidates take Part 3, *Representation, Practice, and Procedures,* first, rather than taking the tests in order, since the material in Part 3 is considered less complex. The IRS discourages taking the tests out of order by including multiple questions (5% or more at times) of material that relates to taxation of *Individuals* and *Businesses.*

# Exam Strategy

Each multiple choice question provides four choices for an answer. There are several different multiple choice formats used:[2]

---

[2] Candidate Information Bulletin for the Enrolled Agent Special Enrollment Examination.

### Format One- Direct Question

Which of the following entities are required to file Form 709, United States Gift Tax Return?

A. An individual
B. An estate or trust
C. A corporation
D. All of the above

### Format Two-Incomplete sentence

Supplemental wages are compensation paid in addition to an employee's regular wages. They **do not** include payments for_____.

A. Accumulated sick leave
B. Nondeductible moving expenses
C. Vacation pay
D. Travel reimbursements paid at the federal government per diem rate

### Format Three-All of the following EXCEPT

There are five tests which must be met for you to claim an exemption for a dependent. Which of the following is **not** a requirement?

A. Citizen or Resident Test
B. Member of Household or Relationship Test
C. Disability Test
D. Joint Return Test

There may also be a limited number of questions on the exam that have four choices, with three of them incorrect statements or facts and only one that is a correct statement or fact, which you would select as the right answer.[3] All four of these question-and-answer formats appear in your PassKey study guides. During the EA exam, you need to make sure you read each question thoroughly to understand exactly what is being asked.

Your exam may also include some experimental questions that will not be scored. You won't know which ones they are—the IRS uses them to gather statistical information on the questions before they're added to the exam as scored items.

---

[3] 1-31-13: Telephone interview with Larry Orozco, IRS director of competency and standards.

To familiarize yourself with the computerized testing format, there's a tutorial on the Prometric website. If you're not sure of an answer, you may mark it for review and return to it later. Try to eliminate clearly wrong answers of the four possible choices to narrow your odds of selecting the right answer. But be sure to answer every question, even if you have to guess, because all answers left incomplete will be marked as incorrect. Each question is weighted equally.

In the 3.5 hours of the exam, you'll have 210 minutes to answer questions, or slightly more than two minutes per question. Try to answer the questions you're sure about quickly, so you can devote more time to those that include calculations or that you're not as sure about. Remember that the clock doesn't stop for bathroom breaks, so try to allocate your time wisely.

## Scoring

After you finish your exam and submit your answers, you'll learn immediately from a Prometric staff member whether you passed or failed. In either case, you won't receive a printout of the questions you answered correctly or missed.

The IRS determines scaled scores by calculating the number of questions answered correctly from the total number of questions in the examination and converting to a scale that ranges from 40 to 130. The IRS has set the scaled passing score at 105, which corresponds to the minimum level of knowledge deemed acceptable for EAs. Under its testing system, the IRS does not release the percentage of questions that you need to answer correctly in order to pass.

If you pass, you'll receive a score report showing a passing designation, but not your actual score. The IRS considers all candidates who pass as qualified, but does not rank *how* qualified each person may be.

If you fail, you'll receive a scaled score between 40 and 104, so you'll be able to see how close you are to the minimum score of 105. You'll also receive diagnostic information to help you know subject areas you need to focus on when retaking the exam:

- 1: Area of weakness where additional study is necessary. It is important for you to focus on this domain as you prepare to take the test again. You may want to consider taking a course or participating actively in a study group on this topic.
- 2: May need additional study.
- 3: Clearly demonstrated an understanding of subject area.[4]

---

[4] *Candidate Information Bulletin* for the Enrolled Agent Special Enrollment Examination.

If necessary, you may take each part of the exam up to four times during the May 1 and February 28 testing window. You'll need to re-register with Prometric and pay fees for each new time you take an exam part.

You can carry over passing scores for individual parts of the exam up to two years from the date you took them.

## After Passing

Once you've passed the exam, you must apply for enrollment as an EA, which includes an IRS review of your tax compliance history. Failure to timely file or pay personal income taxes can be grounds for denial of enrollment. You may not practice as an EA until the IRS approves your application and issues you a Treasury Card.

Successfully passing the EA exam can launch you into a fulfilling and lucrative new career. The exam requires intense preparation and diligence, but with the help of Passkey's comprehensive *EA Review*, you'll have the tools you need to learn how to become an enrolled agent.

We wish you much success.

# Ten Steps for the IRS EA Exam

## STEP 1-Learn

Learn more about the enrolled agent designation and explore the career opportunities that await you after passing your three-part EA exam. In addition to preparing taxes for individuals and businesses, EAs can represent people before the IRS, just like attorneys and CPAs. Many people who use the PassKey study guides have had no previous experience in preparing taxes, but go on to rewarding new professional careers.

## STEP 2-Gather information

Gather more information before you launch into your studies. The IRS publishes basic information about becoming an EA on its website at www.irs.gov/Tax-Professionals/Enrolled-Agents. You'll also find valuable information about the exam itself on the Prometric testing website at www.prometric.com/see. Be sure to download the *Candidate Information Bulletin*, which takes you step-by-step through the registration and testing process.

## STEP 3-Obtain a PTIN

A PTIN stands for "Preparer Tax Identification Number." Before you can register for your EA exam, you must obtain a PTIN, which is issued by the IRS.[5] The sign-up system can be found at www.irs.gov/ptin. You'll need to create an account, complete an on-line application, and pay a required fee.

## STEP 4-Sign up with Prometric

Once you have your PTIN, you may register for your exam on the Prometric website. After creating an account and paying the required testing fee, you can complete the registration process by clicking on "Scheduling."

## STEP 5-Schedule a time, date, and location

You'll be able to choose a test site and time and date that are convenient for you. Prometric has test centers in most major metropolitan areas of the United States, as well as certain other parts of the world. You may schedule as little as two days in advance—space permitting—through the website or by calling 800-306-3926 Monday through Friday. Be aware that the website and the phone line have different inventory

---

[5] Foreign-based candidates do not need a PTIN to register to take the exam.

of available times and dates, so you may want to check the other source if your preferred date is already full.

### STEP 6-Adopt a study plan

Focus on one exam part at a time, and adopt a study plan that covers all the tax topics on the EA exam. You'll need to develop an individualized study program based on your current level of tax knowledge. For those without prior tax experience, a good rule of thumb is to study at least 60 hours for each of the three exam sections, committing at least 15 hours per week. Start well in advance of the exam date.

### STEP 7-Get plenty of rest, exercise, and good nutrition

Get plenty of rest, exercise, and good nutrition prior to the EA exam. You'll want to be at your best on exam day.

### STEP 8-Test day has arrived!

On test day, make sure you remember your government-issued ID and arrive early at the test site. Prometric advises to arrive at least 30 minutes before your scheduled examination time. If you miss your appointment and are not allowed to test, you'll forfeit your exam fee and have to pay for a new appointment.

### STEP 9-During the exam

This is when your hard work finally pays off. Focus, don't worry if you don't know every question, but make sure you allocate your time appropriately. Give your best answer to every question. All questions left blank will be marked as wrong.

### Step 10-Congratulations. You passed!

After celebrating your success, you need to apply for your EA designation. The quickest way is by filling out Form 23, *Application for Enrollment to Practice Before the Internal Revenue Service*, directly on the IRS website. Once your application is approved, you'll be issued a Treasury card, and you'll be official—a brand new enrolled agent!

# Essential Tax Figures for Tax Year 2012
## Part One: Individuals

Here's a quick summary of all the tax figures for the current exam cycle:

**Income Tax Return Filing Deadline:** April 15, 2013

**The Personal Exemption:** $3,800 (up $100 from 2011)
**\*Note:** In the 2012 tax year, the personal exemption and itemized deductions do not phase out at higher income levels.

**Social Security Taxable Wage Base:** $110,100

**Medicare Taxable Wage Base:** No limit

**Standard Deduction Amounts:**
- Married filing jointly (or qualifying widow/widower) $11,900
- Head of household $8,700
- Single $5,950
- Married filing separately $5,950
- Dependents $950
- Blind taxpayers and senior citizens (over 65) qualify for an increased standard deduction. Additional amounts for 2012 per taxpayer are:
  - $1,450 for single or head of household
  - $1,150 for married filing jointly, married filing separately, or qualifying widow

**Retirement Plan Contribution Limits:** Traditional or Roth IRA: $5,000 ($6,000 for taxpayers age 50 or over by the end of 2012.)

**Roth IRA Phase-out AGI limits:**
- Married filing jointly: $173,000 to $183,000
- Single or head of household: $110,000 to $125,000
- Married filing separately: $0 to $10,000

**Earned Income Credit (EIC) Income Thresholds:**
Earned income and adjusted gross income must each be less than:
- $45,060 ($50,270 MFJ) with three or more qualifying children
- $41,952 ($47,162 MFJ) with two qualifying children
- $36,920 ($42,130 MFJ) with one qualifying child
- $13,980 ($19,190 MFJ) with no qualifying children

**Maximum EIC credit** (for all taxpayers except MFS):
- $5,891 with three or more qualifying children
- $5,236 with two qualifying children
- $3,169 with one qualifying child
- $475 with no qualifying children

Investment income must be $3,200 or less for the year in order to qualify for the EIC.

**Alternative Minimum Tax Exemption (AMT):**
- $78,750 (MFJ or QW)
- $50,600 (Single or HOH)
- $39,375 (MFS)

**Estate and Gift Tax Exclusion Amount:** $5,120,000 (up from $5 million in 2011)

**Gift Tax Annual Exclusion:** $13,000

**Non-Citizen Marital Threshold for Gift Tax:** $139,000

**Kiddie Tax Unearned Income Threshold:** $1,900

**"Nanny Tax" Threshold:** $1,800

**Foreign Earned Income Exclusion**: $95,100

**Child Tax Credit:** $1,000 per child

**Adoption Credit**: $12,650 nonrefundable (credit was refundable in 2011)

**Education Credits and Deductions:**
- Hope/American Opportunity Credit: maximum of $2,500 per student
- Lifetime Learning Credit: maximum of $2,000 per return
- Tuition and fees deduction: maximum of $4,000
- Student loan interest deduction: maximum of $2,500

**Mileage Rates:**
- Business miles: 55.5¢ per mile
- Medical or moving miles: 23¢ per mile
- Charitable purposes: 14¢ per mile

**Section 179 Expense:** $500,000 of qualified expenditures/phase-out at $2 million

# New Tax Law Affecting Individuals

The American Taxpayer Relief Act of 2012 extended a majority of tax cuts already in place. The legislation also made permanent certain other tax provisions that had been temporary. The major changes are as follows:

- **Alternative minimum tax:** The exemption amount on the AMT on individuals is permanently indexed for inflation starting in 2013. The AMT exemption amounts were increased for 2012.
- **Marriage penalty relief:** The increased size of the 15% bracket and the increased standard deduction for married taxpayers filing jointly has been made permanent.
- **Personal exemption phase-out:** This repeals the personal exemption phase-out and the limitation on itemized deductions for taxpayers with adjusted gross income at or below a certain threshold.
- **Reduced rates on capital gains and dividends:** The current maximum tax rate of 15% (or 0% for those below the 25% bracket) has been extended permanently, except that the rate will be 20% for taxpayers above a certain threshold starting in 2013.
- **Child and Dependent Care Credit:** The rules allowing the credit to be calculated based on up to $3,000 for one dependent or up to $6,000 for one has been made permanent.
- **Child Tax Credit:** The $1,000 credit per child was made permanent.
- **American Opportunity Credit:** This credit was extended through 2017.
- **Adoption Tax Credit:** This credit was made permanent. It is nonrefundable for tax year 2012.
- **Education tax relief:** An increase in the annual contribution to Coverdell Education Savings Accounts; an extension of the exclusion for employer-provided educational assistance; and an increase in the phaseout ranges for the student loan interest deduction have all been made permanent.
- **Estate and gift tax:** The estate tax portability election has been made permanent. This is when the surviving spouse's exemption amount is increased by the deceased spouse's unused exemption amount.

**Individual provisions extended retroactively to 2012 include the following:**

Deduction for certain teacher expenses; exclusion from gross income of discharge of qualified principal residence indebtedness; deduction for mortgage insurance; parity for exclusion from income for employer-provided mass transit and parking benefits; deduction of state and local general sales taxes; above-the-line deduction for qualified tuition and related expenses; the credit for energy-efficient existing homes; the credit for two-or-three-wheeled plug-in electric vehicles; and the credit for installing alternative vehicle refueling property in a main home; and in some cases, the American Taxpayer Relief Act of 2012 Act modified certain provisions of these items.

**Also for 2012:**

- Schedule 8812 is now also used for the Additional Child Tax Credit, replacing Form 8812.
- Taxpayers who converted amounts to a Roth IRA or designated Roth account in 2010 must report half of the resulting taxable income on their 2012 returns, unless they reported the full amount on their 2011 returns.
- An employee's W-2 must now report both the employer and employee portion of health care insurance costs for 2012.

# Unit 1: Tax Returns for Individuals

> **More Reading:**
> Publication 17, *Your Federal Income Tax*
> Publication 501, *Exemptions, Standard Deduction, and Filing Information*
> Publication 519, *U.S. Tax Guide for Aliens*
> Publication 552, *Recordkeeping for Individuals*

## Overview of EA Exam Part 1: Individuals

For Part 1 of the enrolled agent exam, you will be expected to know a broad range of information related to preparing tax returns for individual taxpayers. This information includes the basics of filing status, requirements, and due dates; deductions, credits, and adjustments to income; items that affect future returns such as carryover and operating losses; taxable and nontaxable income; retirement income; determining the basis of property; figuring capital gains and losses; rental income; estate and gift taxes, and much more.

Although the focus is on individual taxes, some of the material concerns issues that affect self-employed business persons and deal with business-related income, so there is a degree of overlap with Part 2 of the EA exam: Businesses.

We begin with the preliminary work tax preparers are expected to do in order to prepare accurate tax returns.

## Use of Prior Years' Returns for Comparison

When enrolled agents and other tax professionals prepare tax returns for clients, they are expected to perform due diligence[6] in collecting, verifying, and gathering taxpayer data. EAs are also expected to review prior year tax returns for compliance, accuracy, and completeness.

A tax professional is required by law to notify a taxpayer of an error on his tax return and to notify the taxpayer of the consequences of *not* correcting the error. However, a tax professional is not required to actually correct the error.

The use of prior year returns can help prevent major mathematical errors and alert a tax preparer to issues specific to a particular client. In addition, by reviewing a prior year return, a tax preparer can determine whether there are items that affect the current year's return.

---

[6] The responsibilities of tax preparers are dealt with extensively in Part 3 of the EA exam: Representation, Practices, and Procedures, as detailed in the study guide for PassKey EA Review Part 3.

> **Example**: Janice is an EA with a new client named Terrence who has always prepared his own tax returns. When Terrence makes his tax interview appointment, Janice tells him to bring his prior year Form 1040. At the appointment, Janice notices that Terrence made a large error when calculating his mortgage interest deduction. Janice is required to notify Terrence of the error, as well as the consequences of not correcting the error. She encourages him to file an amended tax return in order to fix the mistake. Terrence declines because he does not want to pay for an amended tax return. Janice notes in her work papers that Terrence has declined to amend his return, even though she has warned him of the consequences. She has therefore fulfilled her professional obligation to notify the taxpayer of the prior year error.

### Taxpayer Biographical Information

Tax preparers are expected to collect essential biographical information from their clients. The following information is required in order to prepare an accurate tax return:

- Legal name
- Date of birth
- Marital status
- Nationality
- Dependents
- Social Security Number or other acceptable Taxpayer Identification Number

Taxpayer biographical information is considered highly sensitive and confidential. Wrongful disclosure of taxpayer information is a criminal offense.

# Recordkeeping for Individuals

Whether a professional tax return preparer is involved or not, a taxpayer is responsible for keeping copies of tax returns and maintaining other records for as long as they may be needed for the "administration of any provision of the Internal Revenue Code."[7] The IRS does not require taxpayers to keep records in any particular way, but says individuals need good records to:

- **Identify sources of income:** Taxpayers receive money or property from a variety of sources. Individuals need this information to separate business from nonbusiness income and taxable from nontaxable income.

---

[7] IRS Publication 552, *Recordkeeping for Individuals.*

- **Keep track of expenses:** Tracking expenses as they occur helps taxpayers identify expenses that can be used to claim deductions.
- **Keep track of the basis of property:** Taxpayers need to retain records showing the original cost or other basis of property they own and any improvements made to them.
- **Prepare tax returns:** Good records help taxpayers, and their preparers, file accurate returns more quickly.
- **Support items reported on tax returns:** If the IRS has questions about items on a return, a taxpayer should have the records to substantiate those items.

Even if a tax professional prepares an individual's tax return, the taxpayer is ultimately responsible for the accuracy of its contents.

The IRS allows taxpayers to maintain records in any way that will help determine the correct tax. A checkbook can serve as a record of income and expenses, along with documents such as receipts and sales slips to help prove particular deductions.

Electronic records are acceptable, so long as a taxpayer can reproduce the records in a legible and readable format. Basic records that everyone should keep include items related to:

- **Income:** Forms W-2, Forms 1099, bank statements, brokerage statements, Forms K-1.
- **Expenses:** Sales slips, invoices, receipts, canceled checks or other proof of payment, written communications from qualified charities, Forms 1098 to support mortgage interest and real estate taxes paid.
- **Home:** Closing statements, purchase and sales invoices, proof of payment, insurance records, receipts for improvement costs.
- **Investments:** Brokerage statements, mutual fund statements, Forms 1099, Forms 2439.

Taxpayers should keep copies of tax returns and records until the statute of limitations runs out for their return.[8]

---

[8] Unit 2, *Tax Rates, Estimates, and Due Dates,* has specific details related to statute of limitations for tax returns and claims for refunds.

# Taxpayer Identification Numbers (TINs)

IRS regulations require that each individual listed on a federal income tax return has a valid Taxpayer Identification Number (TIN).[9] That includes the taxpayer, his or her spouse (if married), and any dependents.

The types of TINs are:

- Social Security Number (SSN)
- Individual Taxpayer Identification Number (ITIN)
- Adoption Taxpayer Identification Number (ATIN)

Although it is not required, the IRS calls it a "best practice"[10] for a preparer to ask to see a Social Security card for each person who will be listed on the return.

Taxpayers who cannot obtain an SSN must apply for an ITIN if they file a U.S. tax return or are listed on a tax return as a spouse or dependent. These taxpayers must file Form W-7, *Application for Individual Taxpayer Identification Number*, and supply documentation that will establish foreign status and true identity.

The issuance of an ITIN also does not confirm an individual's immigration status or give him the right to work in the United States.

> **Example:** Kamala is a U.S. citizen and has a Social Security Number. In January 2012, Kamala marries José Martinez, a citizen of Mexico. José has one daughter from a prior marriage. Kamala decides to file jointly with José in 2012 and also claim her stepdaughter as a dependent. In order to file jointly and claim the child, they must request ITINs for José and his daughter.

An ITIN is also required when a soldier marries a foreign spouse and brings him or her to the United States. In order to file a joint return, the couple would need to request an ITIN for the foreign spouse.

Taxpayers with an ITIN are not eligible to receive Social Security benefits or the Earned Income Credit. In the case of adopted children who do not yet have an SSN, a taxpayer may request an Adoption Taxpayer Identification Number (ATIN) from the IRS if he is adopting a child *and* meets all of the following qualifications:

- The child is placed in the taxpayer's home for legal adoption.
- The adoption is a domestic adoption or the adoption is a legal foreign adoption and the child has a permanent resident alien card or certificate of citizenship.

---

[9] The Preparer Tax Identification Number (PTIN) is also an identifying number, but it is used exclusively by tax preparers to identify themselves on a taxpayer's return. It is not an identifying number for taxpayer use.

[10] http://www.eitc.irs.gov/rptoolkit/faqs/duediligence/.

- The taxpayer cannot obtain the child's existing SSN even though he has made a reasonable attempt to obtain it from the birth parents, the placement agency, and other persons.
- The taxpayer cannot obtain an SSN for other reasons, such as the adoption not yet being final.

The taxpayer needs the ATIN to claim the adopted child as a dependent or to be eligible for a child care credit, but an ATIN cannot be used to obtain the Earned Income Credit. There is *one* narrow exception to the rule that requires all dependents to have an SSN, ITIN, or ATIN. If a child is born *and* dies within the same tax year and is not granted an SSN, the taxpayer may still claim that child as a dependent.

The tax return must be filed on paper and the birth and death certificate attached to the return. The birth certificate must show that the child was born alive, as a stillborn infant does not qualify. The taxpayer enters "DIED" in the space for the dependent's Social Security Number on the tax return.

> **Example:** Alice gave birth to a son on October 1, 2012. The baby had health problems and died within three days. He was issued a death certificate and a birth certificate, but not a Social Security Number. Alice may claim her son as a qualifying child in 2012, even though he only lived a short time.

# Filing Requirements and Thresholds

Not every person is required to file a tax return. A taxpayer is required to file a tax return if his 2012 income exceeds the *combined total* of the standard deduction and personal exemption amounts.[11] Sometimes, a taxpayer is required to file even though none of his income is taxable. To determine whether a person should file a return, a tax preparer must check the taxpayer's Form W-2, and/or Form(s) 1099.

There are different requirements for taxpayers who are self-employed. Generally, a taxpayer is required to file a tax return if he has self-employment earnings of $400 or more. In order to determine whether someone must file a tax return, the tax practitioner must also determine if:

- The person can be claimed as a dependent on another taxpayer's return
- Special taxes might be owed on different types of income
- Some of the taxpayer's income is excludable (or exempt)

The filing requirements listed below apply mainly to wage earners. There will be numerous examples later in the unit in order to demonstrate different filing scenarios. In the case of an individual taxpayer, filing requirements vary based on gross income, age, and filing status.

---

[11] See the tables at the beginning of the book for the standard deduction and personal exemption amounts.

# 2012 Filing Requirements for Most Taxpayers

Here are the 2012 filing requirement thresholds:

- Single: $9,750
- Single, 65 or over: $11,200
- Head of household (HOH): $12,500
- Head of household, 65 or over: $13,950
- Married filing jointly (MFJ): $19,500
    - *Over 65, one spouse (MFJ): $20,650
    - *Over 65, both spouses (MFJ): $21,800
- Married filing separately (MFS): $3,800 (any age)
- Qualifying widow/widower with dependent child: $15,700
    - *65 or over (QW): $16,850[12]

**Example**: Laurel is 36 years old, single, and her gross income was $17,500 last year. She does not have any children. She is required to file a tax return status since her income was over $9,750. She will use the single filing status.

**Example**: Arlene and Marvin are married and plan to file jointly. Frances is 64 and had a gross income of $12,225 for the tax year. Marvin is 66 and his gross income was $6,500 for the year. Since their combined gross income was $18,725, they are not required to file a tax return. The filing requirement threshold for joint filers when one spouse is over 65 is $20,650 in 2012.

**Example:** Wallace is 67 years old and single. No one can claim him as a dependent. His gross income was $11,900 during the tax year. Based only on this information, Wallace is required to file a return because his gross income is over the filing threshold, ($11,200 for 2012) for single taxpayers who are over 65.

**Example**: Rita is 66 years old, married, and had $9,500 of wage income in 2012. Her husband, Roger, also 66, had $10,000 in wage income. They have no dependents. Normally, Roger and Rita would not have a filing requirement because their gross income is under the filing threshold for MFJ taxpayers over 65. However, Rita has decided that she wants to file separately from her husband in 2012. She is therefore required to file a tax return because the filing threshold for MFS is $3,800. Roger must also file a tax return, because his filing status is also MFS by default. Roger cannot choose to file jointly with his wife unless she agrees, since both spouses are required to sign a joint return.

There are special rules for dependents with taxable income, self-employed persons, and nonresident aliens.

A dependent is required to file when he has *any* of the following:

- Unearned income[13] of *more than* $950 (such as interest income)

---

[12] Detailed information about the various filing statuses and who may use them can be found in Unit 3.

- Earned income of *more than* $5,950 (such as wages)
- Gross income of *more than* the larger of:
  - $950, or
  - Earned income (up to $5,650) plus $300

---

**Example:** Cesar is a 16-year-old high school student who is claimed as a dependent on his parents' tax return. He works as a pizza delivery boy ten hours a week and earned $3,200 in wages in 2012. He also had $1,100 of interest income from a certificate of deposit that his grandmother gave him. Cesar is required to file a tax return because his unearned income exceeds $950.

---

**Example:** Taryn is 15 and is claimed as a dependent on her mother's tax return. Taryn babysat full-time over the summer, worked at an ice cream parlor during the school year, and earned a total of $6,100. She had no other income. Taryn must file a tax return because her total earned income is more than $5,950.

---

**Example:** Marc is 20, single, and a full-time college student. Marc's parents claim him on their joint tax return. Marc received $200 in interest income and earned $2,750 in wages from a part-time job. Marc does not have to file a tax return because his total income of $2,950 is below the filing threshold for dependents.

---

Generally, if a dependent child who must file a tax return cannot file it for any reason, such as age, then the parent or other legal guardian must file it on the child's behalf. Not all income is taxable. There are many types of income that are *reportable*, but not taxable, to the recipient. Even if a taxpayer is not legally required to file a tax return, he should—if eligible to receive a refund. Taxpayers should still file tax returns if any of the following are true:

- They had income tax withheld from their pay.
- They made estimated tax payments or had a prior year overpayment.
- They qualify for the Earned Income Credit.
- They qualify for any other refundable tax credits.

---

**Example**: Holly is single, has a four-year-old child, and qualifies for head of household filing status. In 2012, she earns $8,500 in wages and $700 in self-employment income from cleaning houses on the side. Although Holly makes less than the filing threshold for head of household filing status, she is required to file a tax return because her self-employment earnings exceed $400. Even if Holly did not have self-employment earnings, she should still file a tax return, because she likely qualifies for the Earned Income Credit. The EIC is a refundable credit for low income wage earners, which could give Holly a nice refund.

---

[13] Unearned income is all income that is not earned, such as prizes, inheritances, interest income, and dividends. Earned income is money that is earned by the taxpayer, such as wages or self-employment income.

### *Other Odd Filing Requirement Situations*

Sometimes a taxpayer is required to file a tax return when the gross income threshold is not met, such as in the previous example of self-employment earnings of $400 or more. Other examples include the following:

- Church employees who are *exempt* from employers' Social Security and Medicare taxes and have wages of $108.28 or more. (Note: This odd exception has shown up on prior exams.)
- If the taxpayer owes Social Security tax or Medicare tax on tips not reported to his employer.
- If the taxpayer must pay the alternative minimum tax.
- If the taxpayer owes additional tax on a qualified plan, including an IRA, health savings account, or other tax-favored health plan.
- If the taxpayer received Medicare Advantage MSA or health savings account distributions.
- If the taxpayer owes household employment taxes for a household worker such as a nanny.
- If the taxpayer must recapture an education credit, investment credit, or other credit.

# Basic Tax Forms for Individuals: A Summary

## Form 1040EZ

Of the tax return forms, Form 1040EZ is the simplest. The one-page form is designed for single and joint filers with *no dependents*. It shows the taxpayer's filing status, income, adjusted gross income, standard deduction, taxable income, tax, Earned Income Credit, amount owed or refund, and signature. A taxpayer may use the 1040EZ if:

- Taxable income is below $100,000
- The filing status is single or married filing jointly
- The taxpayer is under age 65 and not blind
- The taxpayer is not claiming any dependents
- Interest income is $1,500 or less
- The taxpayer claims no adjustments to income or credits other than the Earned Income Credit.

## Form 1040A

Form 1040A is a two-page form. Page one shows the filing status, exemptions, income, and adjusted gross income. Page two shows standard deduction, exemption amount, taxable income, tax, credits, payments, amount owed or refund, and signature.

Taxable income must be less than $100,000, and there can be no self-employment income. A taxpayer may not itemize deductions when using Form 1040A, and is limited to certain adjustments to income and credits.

## Form 1040

This form is also called the "long form." It is a two-page form that contains all specialized entries for additional types of income, itemized deductions, and other taxes. If a taxpayer cannot use Form 1040EZ or Form 1040A, he must use Form 1040. Form 1040 is designed to report all types of income, deductions, and credits.

Among the most common reasons why taxpayers must use Form 1040 are:

- Their taxable income exceeds $100,000.
- They want to itemize their deductions. [14]
- They are reporting self-employment income.
- They are reporting income from the sale of property (such as the sale of stock or rental property).

## Form 1040NR

This is the form used by nonresident aliens to report their U.S. source income. It is used by investors overseas, as well as nonresident taxpayers who earn money while in the U.S. The 1040NR is not used by U.S. citizens or U.S. residents.

| **Example:** Cisco Ramos is a boxing champion, and a legal citizen and resident of Mexico. Cisco receives a non-immigrant visa in order to attend and participate in a boxing match in the United States, where he earns $500,000 for his appearance. After his appearance, he returns to Mexico. Cisco is not eligible for an SSN and must request an ITIN in order to report his U.S. income. Without the ITIN, Cisco would be subject to automatic backup withholding[15] on his U.S. earnings. Cisco's income is subject to a special treaty provision and his tax accountant reports his income and his tax on Form 1040NR. |
|---|
| **Example:** Yao Lee is a Chinese citizen. He has never been to the United States. Yao owns various U.S. investments, on which he earns dividends and capital gains income. He is not eligible for an SSN. In order to prevent backup withholding on his earnings, Yao requests an ITIN. His tax preparer files Form 1040NR every year to report Yao's U.S.-source income. |

---

[14] Remember that when a married couple chooses to file separately, if one spouse itemizes deductions, the other must do so as well, meaning they both must use Forms 1040.

[15] Backup withholding is when an entity is required to withhold certain amounts from a payment and remit the amounts to the IRS.

# Nonresidents

A tax preparer is required to determine a taxpayer's residency in order to determine whether or not the taxpayer is considered a *resident* or *nonresident*.

For tax purposes, an alien is an individual who is not a U.S. citizen. Aliens are further classified as nonresident aliens and resident aliens. Tax preparers must determine a taxpayer's correct status because the two groups are taxed in different ways:

- Resident aliens are generally taxed on their worldwide income, the same as U.S. citizens.
- Nonresident aliens are taxed only on their income from sources within the United States and on certain income connected with the conduct of a trade or business in the U.S.

Residency for IRS purposes is not the same as legal immigration status. An individual may still be considered a U.S. resident for tax purposes based upon the *physical* time he spends in the United States, regardless of immigration status.

A nonresident can be someone who lives outside the U.S. and simply invests in U.S. property or stocks, and is therefore required to file a tax return in order to correctly report his earnings.

Each year, thousands of nonresident aliens are gainfully employed in the United States. Thousands more own rental property or earn interest or dividends from U.S. investments, and are therefore required to file U.S. tax returns.

## How to Determine Alien Tax Status

If the taxpayer is an alien, he is considered a *nonresident* for tax purposes *unless* he meets at least ONE of two tests:

**1. The Green Card Test, or**

**2. The Substantial Presence Test.**

**The Green Card Test:** A taxpayer is considered a U.S. resident if he is a "lawful permanent resident" of the United States at any time during calendar year 2012. A taxpayer generally has this status if he is a lawful immigrant and has been issued an alien registration card, also known as a green card. An alien who has been present in the United States at *any time* during a calendar year as a lawful permanent resident may choose to be treated as a resident alien for the entire calendar year.[16]

**The Substantial Presence Test:** The substantial presence test is based on a calendar year. A taxpayer will be considered a U.S. resident for tax purposes only if he meets the substantial presence test for the calendar year.

---

[16] In some cases, an alien taxpayer can choose to be treated as both a nonresident alien and a resident alien during the same tax year. This usually occurs in the year the person arrives or departs from the United States. If so, some taxpayers may elect to be treated as a dual-status alien for this taxable year and a resident alien for the next taxable year if they meet certain tests.

To meet this test, the taxpayer must be physically present in the United States on at least:

- 31 days during the current year (2012), and
- 183 days during the three-year period that includes the current year (2012) and the two years immediately before that, counting:

All the days he was present in the current year (2012), and

- 1/3 of the days he was present in the first year before the current year (2011), and
- 1/6 of the days he was present in the second year before the current year (2010).

> **Note:** An individual who meets the requirements of the "substantial presence" test is, for tax purposes, a resident alien of the United States. This status applies even though the person may be an undocumented alien. Remember: Filing a tax return as a resident does **not affect** or alter immigration status.

There are numerous exceptions to the substantial presence test. Days in the United States are not counted if the alien taxpayer:

- Regularly commutes to work in the U.S. from a residence in Canada or Mexico.
- Is in the U.S. as a crew member of a foreign vessel.
- Is unable to leave the U.S. because of a medical condition that arose while in the United States.
- Is an exempt individual. Exempt individuals include aliens who are:
  - Foreign government-related individuals who are in the U.S. temporarily, such as diplomats.
  - A teacher or trainee on a temporary visa.
  - A student on a temporary visa who does not intend to reside permanently in the U.S.
  - A professional athlete in the U.S. to compete in a charitable sports event. These athletes exclude only the days in which they actually competed in the sports event, but do not exclude practice, travel, or promotional events.[17]

If the taxpayer does *not* meet either the green card test or the substantial presence test, then the taxpayer is considered a nonresident for tax purposes. Unlike U.S. citizens and U.S. residents, nonresident aliens are subject to U.S. income tax *only* on their U.S. source income.

---

[17] These exceptions may seem minor, but they have appeared on EA exams in the past.

**Example:** Juliana is a Brazilian citizen who was physically present in the United States for 15 days in each of the years 2010, 2011, and 2012. She is not a green card holder. Juliana earned $32,000 in 2012 as a Portuguese translator for the U.S. government. Since the total days she was present in the U.S. for the three-year period does not meet the substantial presence test, Juliana is not considered a resident for tax purposes for 2012 and her earnings are taxed as a nonresident. Juliana is required to file a nonresident tax return in 2012 (Form 1040NR, *U.S. Nonresident Alien Income Tax Return*). If she does not file a U.S. tax return, then income tax will be withheld at the highest rate. This is called backup withholding.[18]

**\*Special rule for nonresident spouses:** Nonresident alien individuals who are *married* to U.S. citizens or green card holders may choose to be treated as resident aliens for income tax purposes.

**Example:** Lola and Bruno are married and both are nonresident aliens at the beginning of the year. In February, Bruno becomes a legal U.S. resident alien and obtains a green card and a Social Security Number. Lola and Bruno may both choose to be treated as resident aliens for tax purposes by attaching a statement to their joint return. Lola is not eligible for a Social Security Number, so she must apply for an Individual Tax Identification Number (ITIN). Lola and Bruno must file a joint return for the year they make the election, but they can file either joint or separate returns for later years.

## *Due Dates for Nonresident Aliens*

Nonresident aliens who have income that is not subject to U.S. withholding are required to file a tax return by June 15, two months *after* the regular filing deadline for individuals.

However, nonresident employees (such as a nonresident alien who earns money while living or visiting the U.S.) who received wages that are subject to U.S. income tax withholding must file Form 1040NR by the due date.

---

[18] In most cases, a foreign person is subject to tax on his U.S. source income. Most types of U.S. source income received by a foreign person are subject to U.S. tax of 30%. A reduced rate, including exemption, may apply if there is a tax treaty between the foreign person's country of residence and the United States. Nonresidents who do not provide a TIN (either an SSN or ITIN) are generally subject to automatic backup withholding on their U.S. source income.

# Unit 1: Questions

1. Generally, every taxpayer that files a tax return must use an identifying number. All of the following are Taxpayer Identification Numbers for IRS purposes except_____:

A. Social Security Number (SSN).
B. Adoption Taxpayer Identification Number (ATIN).
C. Individual Tax Identification Number (ITIN).
D. Preparer Tax Identification Number (PTIN).

**The answer is D.** A Preparer Tax Identification Number (PTIN) is used by preparers to identify themselves on a taxpayer's return. It is not an identifying number for taxpayer use. ###

2. Which of the following taxpayers is required to have an Individual Taxpayer Identification Number (ITIN)?

A. A nonresident alien with an SSN who moves outside the U.S.
B. A nonresident alien who must file a return and is not eligible for a valid SSN.
C. Anyone who does not have a Social Security Number.
D. All nonresident and resident aliens.

**The answer is B.** If a taxpayer must file a U.S. tax return or is listed on a tax return as a spouse or dependent and is not eligible for an SSN, he must apply for an ITIN. ###

3. Ray and Maggie are married, but he and his wife are filing MFS. Their combined income was $100,000. Ray earned $60,000 in wage income and plans to itemize his deductions. Maggie has $40,000 in self-employment income and has nothing to itemize. Which is the simplest form that Maggie can use for her tax return?

A. Form 1040.
B. Form 1040A.
C. Form 1040EZ.
D. Either Form 1040 or Form 1040A.

**The answer is A.** Maggie will be forced to file Form 1040 for two reasons: she had self-employment income and because Ray plans to itemize deductions. When a married couple files separate returns and one spouse chooses to itemize deductions, the other spouse cannot claim the standard deduction and therefore must itemize. If Maggie has no itemized deductions, then her deduction would be zero. ###

4. The issuance of an ITIN does not:

A. Entitle the recipient to Social Security benefits or the Earned Income Credit.
B. Create a presumption regarding the individual's immigration status.
C. Give the individual the right to work in the United States.
D. All of the above.

**The answer is D.** An ITIN is for reporting purposes only and does not entitle the taxpayer to the EIC or to Social Security benefits. An ITIN also does not create a presumption about the taxpayer's immigration or work status. ###

5. All of the following statements regarding the ATIN are correct except_____:

A. An ATIN may be used to claim the Earned Income Credit.
B. The ATIN may not be used to claim the Earned Income Credit.
C. An ATIN may be requested by a taxpayer who is unable to secure a Social Security Number for a child until his adoption is final.
D. An ATIN can be obtained even if an adoption has not been finalized.

**The answer is A.** An ATIN may not be used to claim the Earned Income Credit. If the taxpayer is unable to secure a Social Security Number for a child until the adoption is final, he may request an ATIN. ###

6. Steven and Rochelle had a child on December 2, 2012. The child only lived for an hour and died before midnight. Which of the following statements is true?

A. They may not claim the child as a dependent on their tax return, because the child did not live with them for the entire tax year.
B. They may not claim the child as a dependent on their tax return unless they obtain a Social Security Number for the child.
C. They may claim the child as a dependent on their tax return, even if they are unable to get a Social Security Number.
D. They may not claim the child as a dependent on their tax return for 2012, but they may do so for tax year 2013.

**The answer is C.** If a child is born and died in the same tax year, an SSN is not required in order to take the dependency exemption in that tax year. The tax return must be filed on paper, and the taxpayer must enter the word "DIED" in the space normally reserved for the SSN. ###

7. Helen, age 65, and Edward, age 72, were married in 2012. They have no dependents. Helen had gross income of $2,000 and Edward had gross income of $28,000 for the year. Edward wants to file jointly, but Helen wants to file separately. Which of the following statements is true?

A. Edward is required to file a tax return, using the MFS status. Helen is not required to file a return.
B. Edward may still file jointly with Helen and sign on her behalf, so long as he notifies her in writing.
C. Edward and Helen are both required to file tax returns, and they must both file MFS.
D. Edward and Helen may both file single.

**The answer is A**. Since Edward and Helen are married, they must either file jointly or separately. Since Helen does not agree to file jointly with Edward, Edward is forced to file MFS. Helen is not required to file a tax return because her gross income in 2012 was $2,000. The filing requirement threshold for married filing separately is $3,800 for any age. ###

8. Janet and Harry are married and file jointly. During the tax year, Janet turned 67 and Harry turned 66. Janet's gross income was $19,000, and Harry's gross income from self-employment was $620. Harry had no other income. Based on this information, which of the following statements is true?

A. Janet and Harry are not required to file a tax return.
B. Janet and Harry are required to file a tax return.
C. Only Janet is required to file a tax return.
D. Only Harry is required to file a tax return.

**The answer is B.** Janet and Harry must both file a tax return. Normally, Janet and Harry would not be required to file because their combined gross income was less than $21,800 in 2012, and they are both over 65 (this threshold applies to taxpayers who are 65 or over, both spouses). However, they are required to file a tax return because they file jointly, and Harry's self-employment income exceeds $400. ###

9. Trinity, age 22, is single and a full-time college student who is claimed as a dependent on her father's tax return. In 2012, Trinity earned $5,975 in wages from her part-time job as an administrative assistant. She has no other income. Is she required to file a tax return?

A. Yes, she is required to file a tax return.
B. No, she is not required to file a tax return.
C. Trinity is only required to file a tax return if she is a full-time student.
D. Trinity should file a return because she will receive a refund, but she is not required to file.

**The answer is A.** A single dependent whose earned income was more than $5,950 in 2012 must file a return. ###

10. What is the minimum amount of time taxpayers should normally keep the supporting documents for their tax returns?

A. Five years.
B. Three years.
C. Two years.
D. One year.

**The answer is B.** Taxpayers should keep the supporting documentation for their tax returns for at least three years from the date the return was filed, or two years from the date the tax was paid, whichever is later. This includes applicable worksheets and forms. ###

11. Clark and Christy are both age 34 and will be filing jointly. They have no dependents. Their combined income was $31,000, which included $35 in interest income. The remainder of their income was from wages. They want to take the standard deduction. Which is the simplest form that Clark and Christy can use for their tax return?

A. Form 1040.
B. Form 1040A.
C. Form 1040EZ.
D. Form 1040NR.

**The answer is C.** Clark and Christy have no dependents, their combined income was less than $100,000, and they do not plan to itemize. Their interest income was also less than $1,500, so they may use Form 1040EZ to file their tax return. ###

12. Cynthia is divorced and files as head of household. She has two children she will claim as dependents. She works as a secretary and earned $35,000 in wages for the tax year. She plans to itemize her deductions. Which tax form should Cynthia use?

A. Form 1040.
B. Form 1040A.
C. Form 1040EZ.
D. Form 1040NR.

**The answer is A.** Since Cynthia plans to itemize her deductions, she must file Form 1040. ###

13. A taxpayer who claims a dependent can use any form except _____.

A. Form 1040.
B. Form 1040A.
C. Form 1040EZ.
D. None of the above. A taxpayer who is claiming a dependent can use any of these forms.

**The answer is C.** A taxpayer who is claiming a dependent cannot use Form 1040EZ. ###

14. Munir is a citizen of Pakistan who is granted a green card and comes to the U.S. to work as an engineer. Munir arrives in the U.S. on November 1, 2012. He earns $26,000 in U.S. wages in November and December. Which of the following is true?

A. Munir is not required to file a U.S. tax return.
B. Munir is required to file a U.S. tax return, and he must file using Form 1040NR.
C. Munir is required to file a U.S. tax return, and he may file using Form 1040.
D. Munir is not required to file a U.S. tax return in 2012, but he will be required to file a return in 2013.

**The answer is C.** Munir is required to file a U.S. tax return in 2012, and he may file using Form 1040. Munir is a green card holder, and therefore he may choose to be treated as a U.S. resident for tax purposes, regardless of how much time he has been present in the United States. An alien who has been present in the United States at any time during a calendar year as a "lawful permanent resident" may choose to be treated as a resident alien for the entire calendar year. As a resident alien, Munir will be taxed on income from worldwide sources, including any income he earned while he was in Pakistan. ###

15. A person who is not required to file a tax return should still file a return for any of the following reasons except to _____.

A. Report self-employment net earnings of $400 or more.
B. Claim a refund of withheld taxes.
C. Claim the Earned Income Credit.
D. Claim the Additional Child Tax Credit.

**The answer is A.** Even if the thresholds indicate that a return does not have to be filed, individuals who want to claim tax refunds, the EIC, or Additional Child Tax Credits should still file a return. A taxpayer with self-employment earnings of $400 or more is required to file a tax return. ###

16. Angela's husband, Enzo, has neither a green card nor a visa, and he does not have a tax home in another country. He was physically present in the United States for 150 days in each of the years 2010, 2011, and 2012. Is Enzo a resident alien under the substantial presence test?

A. Yes, he is a resident for tax purposes.
B. No, he is a nonresident for tax purposes.
C. Enzo is a nonresident for tax purposes, but he may elect to file as a resident with his spouse.
D. None of the above is correct.

**The answer is A.** Enzo is a resident for tax purposes. He was present in the United States a total of 225 days. He meets the substantial presence test and is considered a resident alien for tax purposes. The full 150 days are counted for 2012; 50 days for 2011 (1/3 of 150); and 25 days for 2010 (1/6 of 150). ###

17. In order to prepare an accurate return, a tax preparer needs all of the following biographical information about a client except _____:

A. Date of birth.
B. National status.
C. SSN or other TIN.
D. Occupation.

**The answer is D.** To prepare an accurate return, a tax preparer must gather biographical information including a client's legal name, date of birth, marital status, nationality, dependents, and SSN or other TIN. A preparer does not need to know a client's occupation. ###

18. Kerstin is a professional tennis player from Germany who travels around the world to play in tournaments. In 2012, she comes to the United States on the following dates:

May 3: Travel from Frankfurt to New York.
May 4-5: Practice for the tournament.
May 6: Promotional event for the tournament.
May 7-9: Play in the tournament that benefits the American Cancer Society.
May 10-11: Vacation in New York.
May 12: Travel from New York to Frankfurt.
Sept. 5: Travel from Frankfurt to Atlanta.
Sept. 6-7: Practice for the tournament.
Sept. 8: Play in the tournament that benefits the Arthritis Foundation.
Sept. 9-10: Fly to Miami and vacation.
Sept. 11: Fly from Miami to Frankfurt.

Kerstin receives no compensation from playing in either tournament. How many days must she count toward the substantial presence test in 2012?

A. 4.
B. 8.
C. 13.
D. 17.

**The answer is C**. Kerstin is an exempt individual under the substantial presence rules. However, she may only exclude the days she is actually playing in a charitable sports events, which means days devoted to traveling, practice, promotion, or leisure do not count. She is in the United States a total of 17 days, but only plays in charity tournaments for four days, meaning she must count 13 days toward the substantial presence test. ###

19. Malik and his wife, Stacey, are married and file jointly. In 2012, she earned $4,600 in wages before she became pregnant and had to quit her job due to complications. Malik worked as a bartender and earned $11,000 in wages for the year. He owes Social Security and Medicare tax on $2,500 in tip income he did not report to his employer. Do Malik and Stacey have to file a tax return?

A. No, because their gross income is below the threshold for MFJ.
B. Yes, because their gross income is above the threshold for MFJ.
C. Yes, because Malik owes Social Security and Medicare tax on his unreported tip income.
D. Stacey is not required to file, if Malik files separately and chooses not to report the tip income.

**The answer is C.** Even though their gross income is below the MFJ filing threshold of $19,500 for 2012, the couple must file a tax return because Malik owes Social Security and Medicare tax on his unreported tip income. (A taxpayer who fails to disclose tip income to his employer as required is also subject to IRS penalties.) ###

20. All of the following are required to file an income tax return except:

A. A taxpayer who owes household employment tax for a nanny.
B. A church employee who is exempt from payroll taxes and who earned $106 in wages in 2012.
C. A 74-year-old qualifying widower who earned $17,000 in 2012.
D. A single taxpayer who earned $6,500 in 2012 and who owes tax on a Health Savings Account.

**The answer is B.** Church employees who are exempt from Social Security and Medicare taxes and have wages of $108.28 or more for the year are required to file a tax return. In Answer "B," the church employee's wages were below that threshold. In all of the other answers, the taxpayer would be required to file a return. ###

21. Kylie is an 18-year-old senior in high school. She works as a grocery store bagger on weekends and earned $1,400 in 2012. She also received $1,000 for a winning scratch-off lottery ticket. Her parents claim her as a dependent on their tax return. Does Kylie have to file her own return?

A. Yes, because of the amount of her unearned income.
B. Yes, because of the amount of her unearned and earned income combined.
C. No, because her earned income is below the threshold for a dependent.
D. No, because it is illegal for a high school student to play the lottery.

**The answer is A.** Kylie has to file a tax return because of the amount of her unearned income: the $1,000 lottery prize. A dependent with unearned income of more than $950 is required to file a tax return. Her earned income—$1,400—was not high enough to trigger a filing requirement. In 2012, dependents with earned income of more than $5,950 are required to file.

# Unit 2: Tax Rates, Estimates, and Due Dates

> **More Reading:**
> Publication 505, *Tax Withholding and Estimated Tax*
> Tax Topic 556, *Alternative Minimum Tax*
> Publication 594, *Understanding the Collection Process*
> Publication 3, *Armed Forces' Tax Guide*

## Tax Rates

An individual's income is taxed at progressive rates in the United States. The more taxable income a taxpayer has, the higher the percentage of that income he pays in taxes. The IRS groups individuals by their taxable income levels and places them into different tax rates, or "brackets." Each tax rate applies to a specific range of taxable income, which is income after various deductions have been subtracted.

In 2012, there are six tax brackets for individuals: 10%, 15%, 25%, 28%, 33%, and 35%. Each year, the IRS adjusts these income ranges for inflation and issues tax tables that show how much tax is owed for specific income levels depending upon a taxpayer's filing status.

For example, in 2012 a single taxpayer with $8,000 in taxable income would be in the 10% tax bracket. If he had $50,000 in taxable income, he would be in the 25% tax bracket, while a taxpayer with $400,000 in taxable income would be in the highest tax bracket of 35%.

However, this does not mean that taxpayers in the highest income ranges owe a full 35% of tax on all their taxable income. The *marginal tax rate* applies tax to any additional dollars of taxable income earned. The tax rate does not increase for a taxpayer's entire income, merely dollar for dollar for taxable income over a certain threshold.

> **Example:** Jamie is single and has $35,500 in taxable income for 2012. For the first $8,700 she is taxed at a 10% rate. From $8,701 to $35,350 she is taxed at a 15% rate. It is only for the remaining $149 in income (on $35,351 to $35,500) that she is taxed at a 25% rate.

### Alternative Minimum Tax

Federal tax law gives special treatment to certain types of income and allows deductions and credits for certain types of expenses. Taxpayers who benefit from this special treatment may have to pay at least a minimum amount of tax through an additional alternative minimum tax (AMT). First enacted in 1969, the AMT was adopted by Congress in an attempt to ensure that individuals and corporations pay at least a minimum amount of tax.[19]

The AMT is the excess of the tentative minimum tax over the regular tax. Thus, the AMT is owed only if the tentative minimum tax is greater than the regular tax. The tentative minimum tax is calculated separately from the regular tax. In general, the tentative minimum tax is computed by:

1. Starting with AGI less itemized deductions, or with AGI for taxpayers who are not claiming itemized deductions, for regular tax purposes,
2. Eliminating or reducing certain exclusions, deductions, and credits that are allowed in computing the regular tax, to derive alternative minimum taxable income (AMTI),
3. Subtracting the AMT exemption amount,
4. Multiplying the amount computed in (3) by the AMT rate, and
5. Subtracting the AMT Foreign Tax Credit.

When calculating the AMT using this formula, the following "tax preference items" must be included, many of which apply more to business taxpayers than to individuals: depletion, excess intangible drilling costs, interest on private activity bonds, accelerated depreciation on property placed in service before 1987, and exclusion of gain on qualified small business stock.

When figuring the AMT, an individual taxpayer cannot claim deductions for miscellaneous expenses; certain mortgages used to refinance other mortgages; for tax payments to state, local, or foreign governments; and for medical expenses except to the extent they exceed 10% of AGI (as opposed to the 7.5% floor under the regular income tax). Also, deductions for expenses are limited to net investment income.

For 2012, the AMT exemption amounts are as follows, and they are phased out at a rate of 25% when the alternative minimum tax income is within the indicated ranges:

| Filing Status | AMT Exemption | Exemption Phase-out Range |
| --- | --- | --- |
| MFJ or QW | $78,750 | $150,000 to $465,000 |
| MFS | $39,375 | $75,000 to $232,500 |
| Single or HOH | $50,600 | $112,500 to $314,900 |

A credit may be available for alternative minimum tax paid in prior years that relates to certain of the items above that create special treatment for regular tax purposes. In general, a portion of the AMT paid in a given year and credit carried

---

[19] The American Taxpayer Relief Act retroactively increased the AMT exemption amounts for 2012. Lawmakers also created a permanent fix to the AMT, which has been modified 19 times since 1969. Going forward, the AMT will be indexed to inflation, meaning the income threshold for being subject to the AMT will rise automatically each year.

forward from earlier years can be used in the following year to the extent that the taxpayer's regular tax is greater than his tentative minimum tax. For example, if a taxpayer paid AMT in 2011, in 2012 he may be able to calculate a credit on Form 8801, *Credit for Prior Year Minimum Tax*, which can be used on Form 1040.

## Due Dates and Extensions

The regular due date for individual tax returns is usually April 15; if April 15 falls on a Saturday, Sunday, or legal holiday, the due date will be delayed until the next business day. This year's due date is Monday, April 15, 2013.

If a taxpayer cannot file his tax return by the due date, he may request an extension by filing IRS Form 4868, *Application for Automatic Extension of Time to File*, which may be filed electronically. Extended individual tax returns are due by October 15, 2013.

An extension will grant a taxpayer an additional six months to file his individual tax return. An extension will give a taxpayer extra time to file his return, but it does not extend the time to pay any tax due.

A taxpayer will owe interest on any unpaid amount that is not paid by the filing deadline, plus a late payment penalty if he has not paid at least 90% of his total tax due by that date. Taxpayers are expected to estimate and pay the amount of tax due by the filing deadline.

The IRS will accept a postmark as proof of a timely-filed return. For example, if the tax return is postmarked on April 14 but does not arrive at the IRS Service Center until April 18, the IRS will accept the tax return as having been filed on time.

E-filed tax returns are also given an "electronic postmark" to indicate the day that they are transmitted. You should memorize the due dates for tax returns and extensions for the EA exam.

# IRS Penalties in General

If a taxpayer does not file on time, he will face a *failure-to-file* penalty.

If a taxpayer does not pay on time, he will face a *failure-to-pay* penalty.

## Penalties and Interest on Late Filing

An extension only grants a taxpayer additional time to file, not additional time to pay. Interest and penalties will continue to accrue on any unpaid balance until the taxpayer finally files his tax return and pays any amounts that are owed. There are two separate penalties:

- Failure-to-file penalty (the failure to file on time)
- Failure-to-pay penalty (the failure to pay on time)

Taxpayers may also be assessed interest on the delinquent amount due.

**\*Note:** Penalties are tested on all three parts of the EA exam. Be sure you memorize the most common types of taxpayer and preparer penalties.

## Failure to File

The failure-to-file penalty is much greater than the failure-to-pay penalty. The IRS recommends that even if a taxpayer cannot pay all the taxes he owes, he should still file his tax return on time. The penalty for late filing is usually 5% of the unpaid taxes for each month (or part of a month) that a return is late. This penalty will not exceed 25% of the unpaid tax on the return.

The failure-to-file penalty is calculated based on the time from the due date of the return to the date the taxpayer actually files. This penalty is calculated on the amount due on the return, so if the taxpayer is due a refund or has no tax liability, then this penalty will not be assessed.[20]

However, if a taxpayer files his return more than 60 days after the due date (or extended due date), the *minimum* penalty is the smaller of:

- $135, or
- 100% of the unpaid tax.

## Failure to Pay

If the taxpayer does not pay his taxes by the due date, he will have to pay a failure-to-pay penalty. This is 0.5% (½ of 1 percent) of the unpaid tax for each month after the due date that the taxes are not paid. This penalty will not exceed 25% of the unpaid tax.

If a taxpayer files a request for an extension of time to file and pays *at least* 90% of the actual tax liability by the original due date, he will not be faced with a failure-to-pay penalty if the remaining balance is paid by the *extended* due date.

If both of these penalties apply in any month, the 5% failure-to-file penalty is reduced by the failure-to-pay penalty.

A taxpayer will not be assessed either penalty if he can show that he failed to file or pay on time because of reasonable cause and not because of willful neglect.[21]

Interest is charged on any unpaid tax from the due date of the return until the date of payment. The interest rate is determined quarterly and is the federal short-term rate plus 3%, compounded daily.

---

[20] We are only talking about penalties for individual taxpayers at this point. The penalties for entities are different and will be covered in Part 2: Businesses.

[21] There are exceptions to the general deadlines for filing a return and paying tax. One exception is for armed forces personnel serving in a combat zone. The second is for citizens or resident aliens working abroad.

| Penalty | Dollar Amount |
|---|---|
| Failure to file | • 5% of unpaid balance per month, up to a maximum of 25%.<br>• More than 60 days late, the smaller of $135 or 100% of the tax due on the return.<br>• No penalty if the taxpayer is due a refund.<br>• The failure-to-file penalty is reduced by the failure-to-pay penalty if both apply to the same tax return. |
| Failure to pay | • 0.5% of unpaid balance per month, up to a maximum of 25%.<br>• 0.25% of the unpaid balance while an installment agreement is in place. |

# Estimated Tax Payments

The federal income tax is a "pay-as-you-go" tax. A taxpayer must pay taxes as he earns or receives income throughout the year. If a taxpayer earns income that is not subject to withholding, such as self-employment income, rents, and alimony), he will often be required to make estimated tax payments each quarter of the tax year. Estimated tax is used to pay not only income tax, but self-employment tax and alternative minimum tax as well. Taxes are generally not withheld from payments that are made to independent contractors (1099 income). Taxes are withheld from wages, salaries, and pensions. Taxpayers can avoid making estimated tax payments by ensuring they have enough tax withheld from their income. A taxpayer must make estimated tax payments if:

• He expects to owe at least $1,000 in tax (after subtracting withholding and tax credits)
• He expects the total amount of withholding and tax credits to be less than the smaller of:
   o 100% of the tax shown on the taxpayer's prior year return
   o 90% of the tax shown on the taxpayer's current year return

A U.S. citizen or U.S. resident is not required to make estimated tax payments if he had zero tax liability in the prior year.[22]

**Example**: Cassius, who is single and 25 years old, was unemployed for most of 2011. He earned $2,700 in wages before he was laid off, and he received $1,500 in unemployment compensation afterward. He had no other income. Even though he had gross income of $4,200, he did not have to pay income tax because his gross income was less than the filing requirement. In 2012, Cassius began working as a carpenter, but made no estimated tax payments during the year. Even though he owed $3,000 in tax at the end of the year, Cassius does not owe the underpayment penalty for 2012 because he had zero tax liability in the prior year.

---

[22] This rule only applies to U.S. citizens or residents; it does not apply to nonresident aliens.

A taxpayer will not face an underpayment penalty if the total tax shown on his return (minus the amount paid through withholding) is less than $1,000. This safe harbor only applies to individual taxpayers and not to entities.

> **Example:** Dominique has a full-time job as a secretary. She also earns money part-time as a self-employed manicurist. In 2012, she did not make estimated payments. However, Dominique made sure to increase her withholding at her job in order to cover any amounts that she would have to pay on her self-employment earnings. When she files her tax return, she discovers that she owes $750. She will not owe an underpayment penalty, because the total tax shown on her return was less than $1,000.

## Safe Harbor Rule for Estimated Payments

The majority of taxpayers who pay estimated tax rely on the "safe harbor rule" in order to avoid any potential penalties.

There will be no underpayment penalty if the taxpayer pays at least 90% of whatever the current year's tax bill turns out to be. Since it is often difficult to guess what a person or business will earn during the year, most taxpayers find it easier to use the safe harbor rule.

The first safe harbor applies to taxpayers whose adjusted gross income is $150,000 or less. The taxpayer will not be assessed penalties in 2012 if the taxpayer pays *at least* the amount of the tax liability on his previous year's tax return (the amount on line 60 of Form 1040 reduced by any tax credits).

> **Example:** Gerald earned $95,000 in 2011. His overall tax liability for the tax year was $8,200, after taking into account his deductions and credits. Although Gerald expects his income to increase in 2012, he will not be assessed a penalty for underpayment of estimated taxes so long as he pays at least $8,200 in estimated tax during the year.

> **\*Note:** For high income taxpayers with adjusted gross income of over $150,000 ($75,000 if MFS), the safe harbor amount is 110% of the previous year's tax liability.

## Estimated Payment Due Dates (Quarterly Payments)

The year is divided into four payment periods for estimated taxes, each with a specific payment due date. Taxpayers generally must have made their first estimated tax payment for the year by April 15.

If the due date falls on a Saturday, Sunday, or legal holiday, the due date is the next business day. If a payment is mailed, the date of the U.S. postmark is considered the date of payment.

> **First Payment Due: April 15**
> **Second Payment Due: June 15**
> **Third Payment Due: September 15**
> **Fourth Payment Due: January 15 (of the following year)**

# *Special Exception for Farmers and Fishermen*

Farmers and fishermen are not required to pay estimated taxes throughout the year. Unlike other taxpayers, farmers and fishermen may choose to pay all their estimated tax in one installment.

Qualified farmers and fishermen only have one due date for estimated taxes (if they choose). They have two choices:

- They may pay all of their 2012 estimated taxes by January 15, 2013, or
- If they are able to file their 2012 tax return by March 1, 2013 and pay all the tax they owe, they do not need to make an estimated tax payment. They may file and pay their tax along with the return.[23]

**Example #1:** Jay is the self-employed owner of a commercial fishing vessel. One hundred percent of his income is from commercial fishing, so Jay is not required to pay quarterly estimated taxes. Jay's records are incomplete, so he asks his tax accountant to file an extension on his behalf. Since Jay is unable to file his tax return by March 1, 2013, his enrolled agent notifies Jay that he is required to pay his estimated taxes in a lump sum by January 15, 2013.

**Example #2:** Karla earns 100 percent of her income from growing organic strawberries. She is not required to pay quarterly estimated taxes. Karla filed her tax return on February 20, 2013 and enclosed a check for her entire balance due, which was $4,900. Since she filed before the March 1 deadline, she will not be subject to any penalty.

In order to qualify for this special treatment, the farmer or fisherman must have at least two-thirds of his total gross income from farming or fishing. For purposes of this rule, qualified "farming" income includes:
- Gross farming income from Schedule F, *Profit or Loss From Farming*
- Gross farming rental income
- Gains from the sale of livestock used for draft, breeding, sport, or dairy purposes
- Crop shares for the use of a farmer's land

Qualifying gross income from farming does not include:
- Gains from sales of farmland and/or depreciable farm equipment
- Income received from contract harvesting and hauling with workers and machines furnished by the taxpayer

---

[23] For the 2012 tax year, the IRS is waiving estimated tax penalties for farmers and fishermen who file by April 15. Since Congress did not finalize the tax rules for 2012 until early 2013, the IRS could not guarantee that common IRS forms that farmers use would be ready by March 1, so it extended the due date for avoiding the penalty.

*Note: Income from wages received as a farm employee is not considered farm income for purposes of this special estimated tax treatment.

---

**Example:** Dennis owns a dairy farm and files a Schedule F showing 2012 farm income of $95,000. He also had $3,500 in interest income and $41,500 in rental income from an unrelated business. Dennis's total gross income for the year was $140,000 ($3,500 + $41,500 + $95,000). Dennis qualifies to use the special estimated tax rules for qualified farmers, since 67.9% (at least two-thirds) of his gross income is from farming ($95,000 ÷ $140,000 = .679).

---

## Backup Withholding

Sometimes individuals will be subject to backup withholding. This is when an entity is required to withhold certain amounts from a payment and remit the amounts to the IRS. Most U.S. taxpayers are exempt from backup withholding. However, the IRS requires backup withholding if a taxpayer's name and Social Security Number on Form W-9, *Request for Taxpayer Identification Number and Certification*, does not match its records.

---

**Example:** Heath owns a number of investments through the Top Finances Corporation. In 2012, the IRS notifies Top Finances that Heath's Social Security Number is incorrect. Top Finances notifies Heath by mail that the company needs his correct Social Security Number, or it will have to start automatic backup withholding on his investment income. Heath ignores the notice and never updates his SSN. Top Finances is forced to begin backup withholding on Heath's investment income.

---

The IRS will sometimes require mandatory backup withholding if a taxpayer has a delinquent tax debt, or if he fails to report all his interest, dividends, and other income.

Payments that may be subject to backup withholding include interest, dividends, rents, and royalties, payments to independent contractors for services, and broker payments. The current backup withholding rate is 28% for all U.S. citizens and legal U.S. residents. Under the backup withholding rules, the business or bank must withhold on a payment if:

- The individual did not provide the payer with a valid Taxpayer Identification Number or Social Security Number.
- The IRS notified the payer that the TIN or SSN is incorrect.
- The IRS has notified the payer to start withholding on interest and dividends because the payee failed to report income in prior years.
- The payee failed to certify that it was not subject to backup withholding for underreporting of interest and dividends.

If a taxpayer wishes to change his withholding amounts from his wages, he must use Form W-4, *Employee's Withholding Allowance Certificate* and submit it to his employer, not to the IRS.

## *Oddball Situations: Exceptions to the Normal Deadlines*

There are special rules that are favorable for taxpayers who live outside the United States. A taxpayer will be granted an automatic two-month extension to file **and pay any tax due** if the taxpayer is a U.S. citizen or legal U.S. resident, and

- The taxpayer is living outside the United States and his main place of business is outside the United States; or
- The taxpayer is on active military service duty outside the U.S.

### Taxpayers Serving in a Combat Zone

Additionally, the deadline for filing a tax return, claim for refund, and deadline for tax owed will be automatically extended for any service member, Red Cross personnel, accredited correspondents, or contracted civilians serving in a combat zone. In fact, taxpayers serving in a combat zone have all of their tax deadlines suspended until they leave the combat zone.

> **Example:** Philip is a Marine who has been serving in a combat zone since March 1. He is entitled to an extension of time for filing and paying his federal income taxes. In addition, IRS deadlines for assessment and collections are suspended while Philip is serving in the combat zone, plus another 180 days after his last day in the combat zone. During this period, Philip will not be charged interest or penalties attributable to the extension period.

The deadline extensions also apply to spouses of armed services members serving in combat zones.

## Statute of Limitations

Generally, the taxpayer must file a claim for a credit or refund within three years from the date the original return was filed or two years from the date the taxpayer paid the tax, whichever is later.[24]

There is no penalty for failure to file if the taxpayer is due a refund. However, the taxpayer may have many legal deductions that the IRS does not know about. In order to claim a refund and avoid possible collection action, a tax return must be filed. If the taxpayer does not file a claim for a refund within this three-year period, he usually will not be entitled to the refund.

> **Example:** Juan has not filed a tax return for a long time, and now he wants to file six years of delinquent tax returns: 2007 through 2012. Juan files the returns and realizes that he had refunds for each year. If Juan files all the back tax returns by April 15, 2013, he will receive the refunds for his 2009, 2010, 2011, and 2012 tax returns. His refunds for 2007 and 2008, however, have expired.

---

[24] Section 6511 (3-year refund statute).

The same statute of limitations applies on refunds being claimed on amended returns. In general, if a refund is expected on an amended return, taxpayers must file the return within three years from the due date of the original return, or within two years after the date they paid the tax, whichever is later.

> **Example:** David made estimated tax payments of $1,000 and filed an extension to file his 2009 income tax return. When he filed his return on August 15, 2010, he paid an additional $200 tax due. He later finds an error on the return and files an amendment. Three years later, on August 15, 2013, David files an amended return and claims a refund of $700.

> **Example:** Aisha's 2009 tax return was due April 15, 2010. She filed it on March 20, 2010. In 2012, Aisha discovered that she missed a big deduction on her 2009 return. Now she wants to amend that return, expecting the correction to result in a large refund. If she gets it postmarked on or before April 15, 2013, it will be within the three-year limit and the return will be accepted. But if the IRS receives the amended 2009 return after that date, it will fall outside the three-year period and Aisha will not receive the refund.

## *Special Cases (Extended Statute for Claiming Refunds)*

In some cases, a request for a tax refund will be honored past the normal three-year deadline. These special cases are:

- A bad debt from a worthless security (up to **seven years** prior)
- A payment or accrual of foreign tax
- A net operating loss carryback
- A carryback of certain tax credits
- Exceptions for military personnel
- For taxpayers in presidentially declared disaster areas
- For taxpayers who have been affected by a "terroristic or military action"

Time periods for claiming a refund are also extended when a taxpayer is "financially disabled." This usually requires that the taxpayer be mentally or physically disabled to the point that he is unable to manage his financial affairs. If the taxpayer qualifies, he may file a refund after the three-year period of limitations.

## Statute of Limitations for IRS Assessment

The IRS is required to assess tax or audit a taxpayer's return within three years after the return is filed.[25] If a taxpayer files his tax return late, then the IRS has the later of three years from:

- The due date of the return, or
- The date the return was actually filed.

---

[25] Internal Revenue Code, section 6501 (3-year audit statute).

If a taxpayer never files a return, the statute remains open. If a taxpayer files his return prior to the return deadline, the time is measured from the April 15 deadline.

The IRS has additional time—six years—to assess tax on a return if a "substantial understatement" is identified. A substantial understatement is defined as 25% or more of the income shown on the return.

There is an exception for outright fraud: If the taxpayer files a fraudulent tax return, the statute for IRS audit never expires. However, the burden of proof switches to the IRS in cases where the statute has expired.

> **Example:** Caroline filed her 2009 tax return on February 27, 2010. The three-year statute period for an audit began April 15, 2010 (the filing deadline) and will stop on April 15, 2013. After that date, the IRS must be able to prove fraud or a substantial understatement of income in order to audit the tax return.

## Statute of Limitations for IRS Collections

The statute of limitations for IRS collection is ten years.[26] However, the clock only starts ticking when the tax return is filed. The statute of limitations on a tax assessment begins on the day *after* the taxpayer files his tax return. So, if a taxpayer never files a return, the IRS can attempt to collect indefinitely. In other words, there is no statute of limitations for assessing and collecting tax if no return has been filed.

| Statute of Limitations: Snapshot | |
|---|---|
| **Claims for a refund** | Three years from the time the original return was filed, or two years from the time the tax was paid, whichever is later. |
| **IRS assessment** | Three years after the return is considered filed. Exceptions apply in cases of fraud, failure to file, and substantial understatement. |
| **Substantial understatement** | If a substantial understatement is discovered (25% or more income is omitted on the return), the statute for IRS assessment is six years. |
| **Fraud** | No limit. |
| **Unfiled returns** | No limit. |
| **Collections** | The statute of limitations for IRS collections is 10 years from the day after a tax return is filed. |

---

[26]Section 6502 (10-year debt collection statute).

# Unit 2: Questions

1. Theo forgot to file his tax return, and mailed his return more than 60 days late. He did not file an extension. Theo owed $120 with his return. What is his minimum penalty for late filing?

A. $0.
B. $120.
C. $135.
D. $220.

**The answer is B.** If a return is filed more than 60 days late, the minimum penalty for late filing is the smaller of $135 or 100% of the tax owed. Since he owed $120 with the return, his penalty is 100% of the amount due. ###

2. All of the statements about estimated tax payments are correct except_____:

A. An individual whose only income is from self-employment will have to pay estimated payments.
B. If insufficient tax is paid through withholding, estimated payments may still be necessary.
C. Estimated tax payments are required when the withholding taxes are greater than the overall tax liability.
D. Estimated tax is used to pay not only income tax, but self-employment tax and alternative minimum tax as well.

**The answer is C.** If a taxpayer's withholding exceeds his tax liability, no estimated payments would be required. The taxpayer would receive a refund of the overpaid tax when he files his tax return. ###

3. Which of the following is not an acceptable reason for extending the statute of limitations for a refund past the normal deadline?

A. A bad debt from a worthless security.
B. Living in a presidentially declared federal disaster area.
C. Exceptions for military personnel.
D. Living outside the country for three years.

**The answer is D.** Living outside the country is not a valid excuse for extending the statute of limitations for claiming a refund. In some cases, a request for a tax refund will be honored past the normal three-year deadline. Exceptions include those for military personnel, individuals who are "financially disabled," taxpayers who live in presidentially declared disaster areas, and taxpayers who have bad debts from worthless securities. ###

4. Dottie is a U.S. resident who paid estimated tax in 2012 totaling $2,500. In 2013, Dottie quit her business as a self-employed contractor and is now unemployed. She expects to have zero tax liability in 2013. Which of the following statements is true?

A. Dottie is still required to make estimated tax payments in 2013.
B. Dottie is not required to make estimated tax payments in 2013.
C. Dottie must pay a minimum of $2,500 in estimated tax in 2013, or she will be subject to a failure-to-pay penalty.
D. Dottie must make a minimum of $2,250 (90% X $2,500) in estimated tax payments in 2013, or she will be subject to an underpayment penalty.

**The answer is B.** A taxpayer is not required to pay estimated tax if she expects to have zero tax liability. ###

5. Charles had a $4,500 tax liability in 2012. In 2013, Charles expects to owe approximately $3,200 in federal taxes. He has $1,200 in income tax withheld from his paycheck. Which of the following statements is true?

A. Charles is required to make estimated tax payments in 2013.
B. Charles is not required to pay estimated taxes in 2013.
C. Charles is required to adjust his withholding. He cannot make estimated tax payments because he is an employee.
D. None of the above.

**The answer is A.** Charles is required to make estimated tax payments because his expected tax liability for 2013 exceeds $1,000. His withholding is insufficient to cover his tax liability. Charles could elect to adjust his withholding with his employer so the taxes are taken out of his pay automatically. If Charles does not adjust his withholding, he will be required to make estimated tax payments. If he does not make estimated tax payments, then he will be subject to a penalty. ###

6. Which of the following statements is true regarding the filing of Form 4868, *Application for an Automatic Extension of Time to File U.S. Individual Income Tax Return?*

A. Form 4868 provides the taxpayer with an automatic six-month extension to file and pay.
B. Even though a taxpayer files Form 4868, he will owe interest and may be charged a late payment penalty on the amount owed if the tax is not paid by the due date.
C. Interest is not assessed on any income tax due if Form 4868 is filed.
D. A U.S. citizen, who is out of the country on vacation on the due date, will be allowed an additional twelve months to file so long as "Out of the Country" is written across the top of Form 1040.

**The answer is B.** Even though a taxpayer files Form 4868, he will owe interest and a late payment penalty on the amount owed if he does not pay the tax due by the regular due date. ###

7. What is the statute of limitations for IRS assessment on a tax return in which more than 25% of the taxpayer's income was omitted?

A. There is no statute of limitations on a return where income was omitted.
B. Three years from the date the return was filed.
C. Six years from the date the return was filed.
D. Ten years from the date the return was filed.

**The answer is C.** If a taxpayer omitted 25% of his income or more, the IRS has up to six years to assess a deficiency. ###

8. Todd is a self-employed architect and must make estimated tax payments. What is the due date for his third estimated tax payment for tax year 2012?

A. June 15, 2012.
B. August 15, 2012.
C. September 15, 2012.
D. October 15, 2012.

**The answer is C.** The third-quarter payment for estimated tax is due September 15, 2012. For estimated tax payments, a year is divided into four quarterly payment periods. Each period has a due date. The payments are due as follows:

| Periods | Due Date |
|---|---|
| Jan. 1-March 31 | April 15 |
| April 1-May 31 | June 15 |
| June 1-Aug. 31 | September 15 |
| Sept. 1-Dec. 31 | January 15 (following year) |

###

9. Logan had the following gross income amounts in 2012:

1. Taxable interest: $3,000
2. Dividends: $42,000
3. Farm income (Schedule F): $80,000

Is Logan allowed to use the special estimated tax rules for farmers and fishermen?

A. Unable to determine based on the information given.
B. Logan is a farm employee.
C. Yes, Logan is a qualified farmer.
D. No, Logan is not a qualified farmer, and he must make quarterly estimated tax payments.

**The answer is D.** Based on his income, Logan does not qualify to use the special estimated tax rules for qualified farmers. At least two-thirds of his gross income (66.6%) must be from farming in order to qualify. Logan's gross farm income is 64% of his total gross income ($80,000 ÷ $125,000 = 0.64). Therefore, Logan is not a qualified farmer. ###

10. Which of the following best describes AMT?

A. The excess of regular tax over tentative minimum tax.
B. The tax calculated by applying the regular tax rate to alternative minimum tax income.
C. An additional tax payable to the extent that calculated minimum tax exceeds the regular tax.
D. The excess of regular tax over the AMT exemption amount.

**The answer is C.** The AMT is the excess of the tentative minimum tax over the regular tax. Thus, the AMT is owed only if the tentative minimum tax is greater than the regular tax. The tentative minimum tax is calculated separately from the regular tax. Congress passed the AMT in an attempt to ensure that individuals and corporations that benefit from certain exclusions, deductions, or credits pay at least a minimum amount of tax. ###

11. In which year(s) could a taxpayer who paid AMT during 2011 potentially take a credit on Form 8801, *Credit for Prior Year Minimum Tax?*

A. 2010.
B. 2013.
C. 2012.
D. 2012 or 2013.

**The answer is D.** A portion of the AMT paid in a given year and credit carried forward from earlier years can be used in the following year to the extent that the taxpayer's regular tax is greater than his tentative minimum tax. The credit can be carried forward indefinitely, but cannot be carried back. ###

# Unit 3: Filing Status

**More Reading:**
**Publication 501, *Exemptions, Standard Deduction, and Filing Information***

In order to file a tax return, a tax preparer must identify the taxpayer's filing status. There are five filing statuses, and for the EA exam you must clearly understand the rules governing each. There are also special rules for annulled marriages and widows/widowers.

In general, a taxpayer's status depends on whether he is married or unmarried. For federal tax purposes, a marriage means only a legal union between a man and a woman as husband and wife. The word "spouse" means a person of the opposite sex who is a husband or a wife.[27]

## 1. Single or "Considered Unmarried"

A taxpayer is considered single for the *entire tax year* if, on the last day of the tax year, he or she was:

- Unmarried
- Legally separated or divorced, or
- Widowed (and not remarried during the year).

**Example:** Kenneth and Jennifer legally divorced on December 31, 2012. They do not have any dependents. They may not file a joint return for tax year 2012, but instead must each file SINGLE.

**\*Special Note: Annulled Marriages (Single):** If a marriage is annulled, then it is considered *never to have existed*. Annulment is a legal procedure for declaring a marriage null and void. Unlike divorce, an annulment is retroactive. If a taxpayer obtains a court degree of annulment that holds no valid marriage ever existed, the couple is considered unmarried even if they filed joint returns for earlier years.

Taxpayers who have annulled their marriage must file amended returns (Form 1040X) claiming single (or head of household status, if applicable) for all the tax years affected by the annulment that are not closed by the statute of limitations. The statute of limitations for filing generally does not expire until *three years* after an original return was filed or the date the return was due, whichever is later.

---

[27] This is true even in states where marriage is legal between same-sex couples. However, the Supreme Court is going to weigh in on the issue, so the current law may change. In the spring of 2013, the court will hear arguments on whether a same-sex partner can claim the estate tax marital deduction. The decision, which is expected by late June 2013, also should settle whether same sex-sex couples may file jointly. Regardless of how justices rule, it will not affect tax law for 2012, the basis of the EA exam.

**Example:** Sarah and Robert were granted an annulment on October 31, 2012. They were married for two years. They do not have any dependents. They must each file single for 2012, and the prior two years' tax returns must be amended to reflect single as their filing status.

## 2. Married Filing Jointly (MFJ)

Taxpayers may use the MFJ status if they are married and:

- Live together as husband and wife
- Live together in a common law marriage recognized in the state where they now reside or in the state where the common law marriage began
- Live apart but are not legally separated or divorced
- Are separated under an interlocutory (not final) divorce decree
- The taxpayer's spouse died during the year and the taxpayer has not re-married

A U.S. resident or U.S. citizen who is married to a nonresident alien can elect to file a joint return as long as both spouses agree to be taxed on their worldwide income.

On a joint return, spouses report all of their combined income, allowable expenses, exemptions, and deductions. Spouses can file a joint return even if only one spouse had income. Both husband and wife must agree to sign the return and are responsible for any tax owed, even if all the income was earned by only one spouse.

A subsequent divorce usually does not relieve either spouse of the liability associated with the original joint return.

**Note:** In certain situations, one spouse may be relieved of joint responsibility for tax on a joint return for items that the other spouse incorrectly reported. There are three types of relief: innocent spouse relief; separation of liability (available only to joint filers who are divorced, widowed, legally separated, or who have not lived together for 12 months ending on the date the relief request is filed); and equitable relief.[28]

## 3. Married Filing Separately (MFS)

The MFS status is for taxpayers who are married and either:

- Choose to file separate returns, or
- Do not agree to file a joint return.

If one spouse chooses to file MFS, the other is forced to do the same, since a joint return must be signed by both spouses.

---

[28] This type of relief from liability is covered extensively in Part 3 of the PassKey EA Review. For Part 1 of the EA exam, you should be familiar with the terms and know that this type of relief exists in certain cases.

> **Example:** Jerry and Danielle usually file jointly. However, Danielle has chosen to separate her finances from her husband. Jerry wishes to file jointly with Danielle, but she has refused. Danielle files using married filing separately as her filing status; therefore, Jerry is forced to file MFS as well.

The MFS filing status means the husband and wife report their own incomes, exemptions, credits, and deductions on separate returns, even if one spouse had no income. This filing status may benefit a taxpayer who wants to be responsible only for his own tax, or if it results in less tax than filing a joint return. Typically, however, a spouse will pay more when filing MFS than he would by filing MFJ.

Special rules apply to the MFS filing status, including:

- The tax rate is generally higher than on a joint return.
- The exemption amount for figuring the alternative minimum tax is half that allowed on a joint return.
- Various credits, including the Earned Income Credit and ones for child care expenses, education, adoption, and retirement savings, are generally not allowed or are much more limited than on a joint return.
- The capital loss deduction is limited to $1,500, half that allowed on a joint return.
- The standard deduction is half the amount allowed on a joint return, and cannot be claimed if the taxpayer's spouse itemizes deductions.

> **Example:** Tom and Judith keep their finances separate and choose to file MFS. Tom plans to itemize his casualty losses, so then Judith is forced to either itemize her deductions or claim a zero standard deduction.

One common reason taxpayers choose the MFS filing status is to avoid an offset of their refund against their current spouse's outstanding prior debt. This includes past due child support, past due student loans, or a tax liability a spouse incurred before the marriage.

> **Example:** Dinesh and Maya were married in 2012. Dinesh owes past due taxes from a prior year. Maya chooses to file separately from Dinesh, so her refund will not be offset by his overdue tax debt. If they were to file jointly, their refund would be retained in order to pay the debt.

There are rules for when married taxpayers are allowed to change their filing status. To change from a separate return to a joint return, a taxpayer must:

- File an amended return using Form 1040X.

- Make the change any time within three years from the due date of the separate[29] returns.

A taxpayer cannot change from a joint return to a separate return after the due date of the return.

So, for example, if a married couple filed their joint 2012 tax return on March 13, 2013 and one of the spouses decides to file MFS, then they only have until April 15, 2013 to elect (or amend to) MFS filing status.

---

**\*Exception:** A personal representative for a decedent (deceased taxpayer) can change from a joint return elected by the surviving spouse to a separate return for the decedent, up to a year *after* the filing deadline.

---

**Example:** Kurt and his wife Susan have always filed jointly. Susan dies suddenly in 2012, and her will names Harriet, her daughter from a previous marriage, as the executor for her estate and all her legal affairs. Kurt files a joint return with Susan in 2012, but Harriet, as the executor, decides that it would be better for Susan's estate if her tax return was filed MFS. Harriet files an amended return claiming MFS status for Susan, and signs the return as the executor.

---

# 4. Head of Household (HOH)

The HOH status is available to taxpayers who meet all three of the following requirements:

- The taxpayer must be single, divorced, or legally separated on the last day of the year, or meet the tests for married persons living apart with dependent children.
- The taxpayer must have paid more than half the cost of keeping up a home for the year. head
- The taxpayer must have had a qualifying person living in his home for *more* than half the year. (Exceptions exist for temporary absences, such as school, and for a qualifying parent, who does not have to live with the taxpayer.)

Taxpayers who qualify to file as head of household will usually have a lower tax rate than the rates for single or MFS, and will receive a higher standard deduction.

For the HOH status, a taxpayer must either be unmarried or "considered unmarried" on the last tax day of the year. To be "considered unmarried," a taxpayer must meet the following conditions:

- File a separate return.
- Pay more than half the cost of keeping up the home for the tax year.
- Not live with his spouse in the home during the last six months of the tax year.

---

[29] Besides MFS returns, a "separate" return also refers to returns with the single and head of household filing status.

- The home must be the main residence of the qualifying child, stepchild, or foster child for more than half the year.
- Be able to claim an exemption for the child.

Valid household expenses used to calculate whether a taxpayer is paying more than half the cost of maintaining a home include:
- Rent, mortgage interest, property taxes
- Home insurance, repairs, utilities
- Food eaten in the home

Costs do not include clothing, education, medical treatment, vacations, life insurance, or transportation. Welfare payments are not considered amounts that the taxpayer provides to maintain a home.

**Special Rule for Dependent Parents:** If a taxpayer's qualifying person is a dependent *parent*, the taxpayer may still file HOH even if the parent *does not live* with the taxpayer. The taxpayer must pay more than half the cost of keeping up a home that was the parent's main home for the entire year. This rule also applies to a parent in a rest home.

| |
|---|
| **Example:** Sharon is 54 years old and single. She pays the monthly bill for Shady Pines Nursing Home, where her 75-year-old mother lives. Sharon's mother has lived at Shady Pines for two years and has no income. Since Sharon pays more than half of the cost of her mother's living expenses, Sharon qualifies to use the head of household filing status. |
| **Example:** Tina is single and financially supports her mother, Rue, who lives in her own apartment. Rue dies suddenly on September 15, 2012. Tina may still claim her mother as a dependent and file HOH in 2012. |

This rule also applies to parents, stepparents, grandparents, etc. who are related to the taxpayer by blood, marriage, or adoption (other examples include a stepmother or father-in-law).

**Special Rule for a Death or Birth during the Year:** A taxpayer may still file as HOH if the qualifying individual is born or dies during the year. The taxpayer must have provided more than half of the cost of keeping up a home that was the individual's main home while the person was alive.

| |
|---|
| **Example:** Tony and Velma have a child in September 2012 who dies after a few weeks. Tony and Velma may still claim the child on their tax return as a qualifying child. That is because a dependent can still be claimed, even though the child only lived a short while. |

For purposes of the HOH status, a "qualifying person" is defined as:

- A qualifying child,
- A married child who can be claimed as a dependent, or
- A dependent parent.

The taxpayer's qualifying child includes the taxpayer's child or stepchild (whether by blood or adoption); foster child, sibling, or stepsibling; or a descendant of any of these. For example, a niece or nephew, stepbrother, foster child, or a grandchild may all be eligible as "qualifying persons" for the HOH filing status.

> **Example:** Lewis's unmarried son, Lincoln, lived with him all year. Lincoln turned 18 at the end of the year. Lincoln does not have a job, did not provide any of his own support, and cannot be claimed as a dependent of anyone else. As a result, Lincoln is Lewis's qualifying child. Lewis may claim the HOH filing status.

The qualifying person for HOH filing status must always be related to the taxpayer either by blood or marriage (with the exception of a foster child, who also qualifies if the child was legally placed in the home by a government agency or entity).

> **Example:** Jeffrey has lived with his girlfriend, Patricia, and her son, Nolan, for five years. Jeffrey pays all of the costs of keeping up their home. Patricia is unemployed and does not contribute to the household costs. Jeffrey is not related to Nolan and cannot claim him as a dependent. No one else lives in the household. Jeffrey cannot file as HOH because neither Patricia nor Nolan is a qualifying person for Jeffrey.

An unrelated individual may still be considered a "qualifying relative" for a dependency exemption[30], but will not be a qualifying person for the HOH filing status.

> **Example:** Since her husband died five years ago, Joan has lived with her friend, Wilson. Joan is a U.S. citizen, is single, and lived with Wilson all year. Joan had no income and received all of her financial support from Wilson. Joan falls under the definition of a qualifying relative, and Wilson can claim Joan as a dependent on his return. However, Joan does not qualify Wilson to file as head of household.

## Special Rule for Divorced or Noncustodial Parents

In order for a taxpayer to file as HOH, a qualifying child does not have to be a dependent of the taxpayer (unless the qualifying person is married).

That means a taxpayer may still file as HOH and not claim the qualifying person as his dependent. This happens most often with divorced parents.

---

[30] The rules regarding dependency exemptions are covered in detail in Unit 4, *Exemptions and Dependents.*

> **Example:** George and Elizabeth Garcia have been divorced for five years. They have one child, a 12-year-old daughter named Rebecca, who lives with her mother and only sees her father on weekends. Therefore, Elizabeth is the custodial parent. They agree, however, to allow George to claim the dependency exemption for Rebecca on his tax return. In 2012, George correctly files single and claims Rebecca as his dependent. Elizabeth may still file as HOH, as shown in the following example.

The "considered unmarried" rules apply in determining who may claim a child for dependency and HOH purposes. Couples, even if not formally separated or divorced, must live apart for more than half the year in order to claim HOH status.

> **Example:** Luke and Pauline separated in February 2012 and lived apart for the rest of the year. They do not have a written separation agreement and are not yet divorced. Their six-year-old daughter, Kennedy, lived with Luke all year, and he paid more than half the cost of keeping up the home. Luke files a separate tax return and claims Kennedy as a dependent because he is the custodial parent. Luke can also claim HOH status for 2012. Although Luke is still legally married, he can file as HOH because he meets all the requirements to be "considered unmarried."

> **Example:** Janine and Richard separated on July 10, but were not yet divorced at the end of the year. They have one minor child, Madeline, age 8. Even though Janine lived with Madeline and supported her for the remainder of the year, Janine does not qualify for HOH filing status because she and Richard **did not live apart** for the last six months of the year.

**\*Special Rule for Nonresident Alien Spouses:** A taxpayer who is married to a *nonresident alien* spouse may elect to file as HOH even if both spouses lived together throughout the year.

> **Example:** In 2011, Tim Bianchi met and married Aom Mookja, a nonresident alien. Aom is a citizen and resident of Thailand. The couple lived together in Thailand while Tim was on sabbatical from his university teaching position. They have a son who was born in 2012. Tim may still file as HOH, even though Tim and Aom lived together all year, because Aom is a nonresident alien.

## 5. Qualifying Widow(er) With a Dependent Child

"Qualifying widow(er)" is the least common filing status. However, because of its complexity, it is still often tested on the EA exam.

This filing status yields a tax rate *equal to* MFJ. What this means is that surviving spouses receive the same standard deduction and tax rates as taxpayers who are married filing jointly.

In the year of the spouse's death, a taxpayer can file a joint return. For the following two years after death, the surviving spouse can use the qualifying widow(er) filing status as long as he or she has a qualifying dependent. After two years, the taxpayer's filing status converts to single or HOH, whichever applies.

For example, if the taxpayer's spouse died in 2011 and the surviving spouse did not remarry, he or she can use the "qualifying widow(er)" filing status for 2012 and 2013.

---

**Example:** Barbara's husband dies on December 3, 2012. She has one dependent child, a 15-year-old daughter. Barbara does not remarry. Therefore, Barbara's filing status for 2012 is MFJ (the last year her husband was alive). She can file as a qualifying widow in 2013 and 2014, which is a more favorable filing status than single or HOH.

---

However, if a surviving spouse *remarries* before the end of the year, MFS must be used for the decedent's final return.

---

**Example:** Shelly and her husband, Rodney, have an infant son. Rodney dies of cancer in January 2012. Shelly remarries in December 2012. Since she remarried in the same year her former husband died, she no longer qualifies for the joint return filing status with her deceased husband. Shelly does qualify for MFJ with her *new* spouse. It also means that Rodney's filing status for 2012 would be considered MFS.

---

To qualify for the qualifying widow(er) filing status, the taxpayer must:
- Not have remarried before the end of the tax year.
- Have been eligible to file a joint return for the year the spouse died; it does not matter if a joint return was actually filed.
- Have a qualifying child for the year.
- Have furnished over half the cost of keeping up the child's home for the entire year.

---

**Example:** Hazel's husband, Randy, died on July 20, 2010. Hazel has a dependent daughter who is three. Hazel files a joint return with Randy in 2010, and in 2011 she correctly files as a qualifying widow with dependent child. In 2012, however, Hazel remarries, so she no longer qualifies for the qualifying widow filing status. She must now file jointly with her new husband, or file MFS.

---

## After a Spouse's Death

The chart shows which filing status to use for a widowed taxpayer who does not remarry and has a qualifying dependent.

| Tax Year | Filing Status | Exemption for Deceased Spouse? |
|---|---|---|
| The year of death | Married filing jointly or married filing separately | Yes |
| First year after death | Qualifying widow(er) | No |
| Second year after death | Qualifying widow(er) | No |
| After second year of death | Head of household | No |

# Filing Status: Summary

Take a moment to review the information from this unit. The five filing statuses are:

- Single
- Married filing jointly (MFJ)
- Married filing separately (MFS)
- Head of household (HOH)
- Qualifying widow(er) with dependent child

Filing status is used to determine a taxpayer's filing requirements, standard deduction, eligibility for certain credits and deductions, and the correct tax.

If a taxpayer qualifies for more than one filing status, he may choose the one that produces a lower tax. If married taxpayers choose to file separately (MFS), they must show their spouse's name and Social Security Number on the return.

1. A person's marital status on the *last day of the year* determines the marital status for the entire year.
2. Single filing status generally applies to anyone who is unmarried, divorced, or legally separated.
3. A married couple may elect to file a joint return together. Both spouses must agree to file a joint return.
4. If one spouse died during the year, the taxpayer may file a joint return in the year of death.
5. Head of household usually applies to taxpayers who are unmarried. A taxpayer must have paid more than half the cost of maintaining a home for a qualifying person in order to qualify for HOH.
6. A widow or widower with one or more dependent children may be able to use the qualifying widow(er) with dependent child filing status, which is only available for two years following the year of the spouse's death.

# Unit 3: Questions

1. Which of the following statements is true regarding the head of household filing status?

A. The taxpayer must be single on the first day of the year in order to qualify for head of household filing status.
B. The taxpayer's spouse must live in the home during the tax year.
C. The taxpayer's dependent parent does not have to live with the taxpayer in order to qualify for head of household.
D. The taxpayer must have paid less than half of the cost of keeping up the house for the entire year.

**The answer is C.** Parents do not have to live with a taxpayer in order for the taxpayer to elect the head of household filing status. This is a special rule for dependent parents. This rule also applies to parents or grandparents who are related to the taxpayer by blood, marriage, or adoption. A taxpayer must pay more than half of the household costs in order to qualify for this filing status. ###

2. The person who qualifies a taxpayer as head of household must be _____.

A. A minor child.
B. A blood relative.
C. The taxpayer's dependent or the taxpayer's qualifying child.
D. A minor child or a full-time student.

**The answer is C.** The taxpayer must claim the person as a dependent unless the noncustodial parent claims the child as a dependent. Answer A is incorrect, because a qualifying dependent does not have to be a minor in many cases. Answer B is incorrect because a qualifying dependent may be related by blood, marriage, or adoption. Answer D is incorrect because a dependent parent may also qualify a taxpayer for HOH status. ###

3. Clarence takes care of his 10-year-old grandson. How long must his grandson live in Clarence's home in order for Clarence to qualify for head of household status?

A. At least three months.
B. More than half the year.
C. The entire year.
D. More than 12 months.

**The answer is B.** The relative must have lived with the taxpayer more than half the year (over six months) and be the taxpayer's dependent. The exception is that a taxpayer's dependent parent does not have to live with the taxpayer. ###

4. Dana's husband died on January 24, 2012. She has one dependent son who is eight years old. What is Dana's best filing status for tax year 2012?

A. Married filing jointly.
B. Single.
C. Qualifying widow.
D. Head of household.

**The answer is A.** If a taxpayer's spouse died during the year, the taxpayer is considered married for the whole year and may file as "MFJ." So Dana may file a joint return with her husband in 2012, which is the year he died. ###

5. When may a taxpayer amend a joint tax return from "married filing jointly" to "married filing separately" after the filing deadline?

A. Never.
B. Only within the statute of limitations for filing amended returns.
C. Only in the case of annulled marriages.
D. Only when an estate's personal representative changes a joint return elected by the surviving spouse to a separate return for the decedent.

**The answer is D.** This is the only exception to the rule that prevents a taxpayer from amending his MFJ return to a MFS return. ###

6. Victor is 39 years old and has been legally separated from his wife, Eleanor, since February 1, 2012. Their divorce was not yet final at the end of 2012. They have two minor children. Since they separated, one child has lived with Victor and the other with Eleanor. Victor provides all of the support for the minor child living with him. Eleanor refuses to file jointly with Victor this year. Therefore, the most beneficial filing status that Victor qualifies for is:

A. Married filing separately.
B. Single.
C. Head of household.
D. Qualifying widower with a dependent child.

**The answer is C.** Victor qualifies for head of household filing status. His child lived with him for more than six months, and he did not live with his spouse the last half of the year. Victor may file as HOH because he is "considered unmarried" for tax purposes, and he paid more than half the cost of keeping up a home for the year for a qualifying child. Victor cannot file jointly with Eleanor, if she does not agree. ###

7. Lisa married Stuart in 2009. Stuart died in 2011. Lisa never remarried and has one dependent child. Which filing status should Lisa use for her 2012 tax return?

A. Single.
B. Married filing jointly.
C. Head of household.
D. Qualifying widow with dependent child.

**The answer is D.** In 2012, Lisa is eligible for qualifying widow with dependent child filing status. Lisa and Stuart qualified to file MFJ in 2011, the year he died, with Lisa signing the tax return as a surviving spouse. The year of death is the last year for which a taxpayer can file jointly with a deceased spouse. Then, in 2012, Lisa would be eligible to file as a qualifying widow with dependent child. ###

8. Sean is single. His mother, Clara, lives in an assisted living facility. Sean provides all of Clara's support. Clara died on June 1, 2012. Clara had no income. Which of the following is true?

A. Sean may file as head of household and may also claim his mother as a dependent on his 2012 tax return.
B. Sean must file single in 2012, and he cannot claim his mother as a dependent on his tax return.
C. Sean may claim his mother as a dependent on his tax return, but he cannot claim head of household status for 2012.
D. Sean may claim head of household status for 2012, but he cannot claim his mother as a dependent.

**The answer is A.** Because Sean paid more than half the cost of his mother's care in a care facility from the beginning of the year until her death, then he is entitled to claim an exemption for her, and he can also file as head of household. ###

9. Mary and Troy are married and live together. Mary earned $7,000 in 2012, and Troy earned $42,000. Mary wants to file a joint return, but Troy refuses to file with Mary and instead files a separate return. Which of the following statements is true?

A. Mary may file a joint amended tax return and sign Troy's name.
B. Mary and Troy must both file separate returns.
C. Mary may file as single because Troy refuses to sign a joint return.
D. Mary does not have a filing requirement.

**The answer is B.** In this case, both spouses are required to file a tax return because both are above the earnings threshold for MFS. Married couples must agree to file jointly. If one spouse does not agree to file jointly, they must file separately. ###

10. Kathy's marriage was annulled on February 25, 2013. She was married to her husband in 2010 and filed jointly with him in 2010 and 2011. She has not yet filed her 2012 return. Kathy has no dependents. Which of the following statements is true?

A. Kathy must file amended returns, claiming single filing status for all open years affected by the annulment.
B. Kathy is not required to file amended returns, and she may file jointly with her husband in 2012.
C. Kathy is not required to file amended returns, and she must file married filing separately on her 2012 tax return.
D. Kathy is not required to file amended returns, and she should file as single on her 2012 tax return.

**The answer is A.** Kathy must file amended tax returns for 2010 and 2011. She cannot file jointly with her husband in 2012. If a couple obtains a court decree of annulment, the taxpayer must file amended returns (Form 1040X) claiming single or head of household status for all tax years affected by the annulment that are not closed by the statute of limitations for filing a tax return. ###

11. The two filing statuses that generally result in the lowest tax amounts are married filing jointly and _____.

A. Married filing separately.
B. Head of household.
C. Qualifying widow(er) with dependent child.
D. Single.

**The answer is C.** The qualifying widow(er) with dependent child filing status generally yields the same tax amount as married filing jointly. ###

12. Dwight and Angela are married, but they choose to file separate tax returns for tax year 2012, because Dwight is being investigated by the IRS for a previous tax issue. Dwight and Angela file their separate tax returns on time. A few months later, after the investigation is over and Dwight is cleared of all wrongdoing, he wishes to file amended returns and file jointly with his wife in order to claim the Earned Income Credit. Which of the following is true?

A. Dwight is prohibited from changing his filing status in order to claim this credit.
B. Dwight and Angela may amend their MFS tax returns to MFJ in order to claim the credit.
C. Dwight may amend his tax return to MFJ filing status, but he may not claim the credit.
D. Angela may not file jointly with Dwight after she has already filed a separate tax return.

**The answer is B.** Dwight and Angela are allowed to amend their separate returns to a joint return in order to claim the credit. If a taxpayer files a separate return, the taxpayer may elect to amend the filing status to married filing jointly at any time within three years from the due date of the original return. This does not include any extensions. However, the same does not hold true in reverse. Once a taxpayer files a joint return, the taxpayer cannot choose to file a separate return for that year after the due date of the return (with a rare exception for deceased taxpayers). ###

13. Which of the following is not a valid filing status?

A. Married filing jointly.
B. Qualifying widow(er) with dependent child.
C. Head of household.
D. Annulled.

**The answer is D.** There is no such thing as an "annulled" filing status. There are five filing statuses: married filing jointly, qualifying widow(er) with dependent child, head of household, single, and married filing separately.###

14. Carol and Raul were married four years ago and have no children. They split up in 2011, but did not file for divorce. Although they lived apart during all of 2012, they are neither divorced nor legally separated. Which of the following filing statuses can they use?

A. Single or married filing separately.
B. Married filing jointly or married filing separately.
C. Married filing separately or head of household.
D. Single or qualifying widow(er).

**The answer is B.** As long as they are married and are neither divorced nor legally separated, Carol and Raul can file a joint return, or they can choose to file separately. They cannot file single. ###

15. Which dependent relative may qualify a taxpayer for head of household filing status?

A. An adult stepdaughter supported by the taxpayer who lives across town.
B. A family friend who lives with the taxpayer all year.
C. A parent who lives in his own home and not with the taxpayer.
D. A child who lived with the taxpayer for three months of the tax year.

**The answer is C.** A parent is the only dependent relative who does not have to live with the taxpayer in order for the taxpayer to claim head of household status. ###

16. Samantha is divorced and provided over half the cost of keeping up a home. Her five-year-old daughter, Mollie, lived with her for seven months last year. Samantha allows her ex-husband, Jim, to claim Mollie as a dependent. Which of the following statements is true?

A. Jim may take Mollie as his dependent and also file as head of household.
B. Jim may take Mollie as his dependent, and Samantha may still file as head of household.
C. Neither parent qualifies for head of household filing status because Mollie did not live with either parent for the entire year.
D. Samantha cannot release the dependency exemption to Jim, because their daughter did not live with Jim for over six months.

**The answer is B.** Samantha may use head of household status because she is not married and she provided over half the cost of keeping up the main home of her dependent child for more than six months. However, because Samantha's ex-husband claims Mollie as his dependent, the preparer must write Mollie's name on line 4 of the filing status section of Form 1040 or Form 1040A. ###

17. Madison and Todd are not married and do not live together, but they have a two-year-old daughter named Amanda. Madison and her daughter lived together all year while Todd lived alone in his own apartment. Madison earned $13,000 working as a clothing store clerk. Todd earned $48,000 managing a hardware store. He paid over half the cost of Madison's apartment for rent and utilities. He also gave Madison extra money for groceries. Todd does not pay any expenses or support for any other family member. Which of the following is true?

A. Todd may file as head of household.
B. Madison may file as head of household.
C. Todd and Madison may file jointly.
D. Neither may claim head of household filing status.

**The answer is D.** Todd provided over half the cost of maintaining a home for Madison and Amanda, but he cannot file head of household since Amanda did not live with him for more than half the year. Madison cannot file HOH either, because she did not provide more than one-half the cost of keeping up the home for her daughter. However, either Todd or Madison may still claim Amanda as their dependent. ###

18. Louisa legally separated from her husband during 2012. They have a 10-year-old son. Which of the following would prevent Louisa from filing as head of household?

A. Louisa has maintained a separate residence from her husband since November 2011.
B. Her son's principal home is with Louisa.
C. Louisa's parents assisted with 40% of the household costs.
D. Her son lived with Louisa from July 3, 2012 to December 31, 2012.

**The answer is D.** For Louisa to file as head of household, her home must have been the main home of her qualifying child for *more than half* the tax year. Since her son started living with her in July, he would not have been in the household sufficient time to qualify for this filing status. ###

19. Alexandra's younger brother, Sebastian, is seventeen years old. Sebastian lived with friends in January and February of 2012. From March through July of 2012, he lived with Alexandra. On August 1, Sebastian moved back in with his friends and stayed with them the rest of the year. Since Sebastian did not have a job, Alexandra gave him money every month. Alexandra had no other dependents. Which of the following statements is true?

A. Alexandra may file as head of household for 2012.
B. Alexandra may file jointly with Sebastian in 2012.
C. Alexandra cannot file as head of household in 2012.
D. Sebastian may file as head of household in 2012.

**The answer is C.** Alexandra cannot claim head of household status because Sebastian lived with her for only five months, which is less than half the year. ###

20. Taxpayers are considered to be married for the entire year if:

A. One spouse dies during the year and the surviving spouse does not remarry.
B. The spouses are legally separated under a separate maintenance decree.
C. The spouses are divorced on December 31 of the tax year.
D. The spouses had their marriage annulled December 31 of the tax year.

**The answer is A.** Taxpayers are considered "married" for the entire year if:
- They were married on the last day of the tax year, or
- The spouse died during the year and the surviving spouse has not remarried. ###

21. A U.S. resident or citizen who is married to a nonresident alien can file a joint return so long as both spouses _____.

A. Sign the return and agree to be taxed on their worldwide income.
B. Are living overseas.
C. Have valid Social Security Numbers
D. Are physically present in the United States.

**The answer is A.** A U.S. resident or citizen who is married to a nonresident alien can elect to file a joint return so long as both spouses agree to sign the return and be taxed on their worldwide income. A Social Security Number is not required, because a nonresident spouse that is ineligible for a Social Security Number may request an ITIN. ###

22. The married filing separately (MFS) status is for taxpayers who:

A. Are legally divorced on the last day of the year.
B. Are married and choose to file separate returns.
C. Are unmarried, but engaged to be married.
D. Are unmarried, but have a dependent child.

**The answer is B.** The married filing separately (MFS) status is for taxpayers who are married and either:
- Choose to file separate returns, or
- Cannot agree to file a joint return. ###

23. The MFS filing status typically results in a higher tax. However, in which of the following instances may it be beneficial for spouses to file separately?

A. When the taxpayer has significant capital losses to deduct.
B. When the taxpayer is claiming the Earned Income Credit.
C. When the taxpayer is claiming the standard deduction.
D. When the taxpayer's spouse has a past due student loan that was incurred prior to the marriage.

**The answer is D.** The MFS filing status generally has a tax rate that is higher than that of MFJ, and has many restrictions, including which credits a taxpayer may claim. However, when a taxpayer's spouse has an outstanding tax liability such as past due student loans, the other spouse might benefit from the MFS status. If filing jointly, the couple would have the prior debt offset against their refund. By filing separately, a spouse could protect his or her share of the refund. ###

# Unit 4: Exemptions and Dependents

> **More Reading:**
> Publication 501, *Exemptions, Standard Deduction, and Filing Information*

Taxpayers are allowed to take an exemption for themselves and also for their dependents. The 2012 exemption amount is $3,800 per person. The personal exemption is just like a tax deduction. It can reduce a person's taxable income to zero.

Taxpayers may qualify to claim two kinds of exemptions:

- Personal exemptions, which taxpayers claim for themselves
- Dependency exemptions, which taxpayers claim for their dependents

On a joint tax return, a married couple is allowed *two* personal exemptions, one for each spouse. A spouse is never considered the "dependent" of the other spouse. However, taxpayers may claim a personal exemption for their spouse simply because they are married, regardless of whether only one spouse had income during the year. If a taxpayer's spouse dies during the year and the surviving spouse files a joint return, the surviving spouse can claim an exemption for the deceased spouse.

Only one exemption is allowed per person. So, for example, a married couple with one child would claim three exemptions on a jointly filed return.

**Example:** Jenny married Rick in April of 2012. Neither Jenny nor Rick can be claimed as a dependent on another taxpayer's return. Jenny and Rick may claim two personal exemptions on their jointly filed return.

**Example:** Hao and Bình are married and have four dependent children. On their jointly filed return, they may claim a total of six exemptions: four dependency exemptions for their children and two personal exemptions for themselves.

## Basic Rules for Dependents

A taxpayer can claim one dependency exemption for each qualified dependent, thereby reducing his taxable income. Some examples of dependents include a child, stepchild, brother, sister, or parent.

If a taxpayer can claim another person as a dependent—even if the taxpayer does not actually do so—the dependent *cannot* take a personal exemption on his own tax return. The dependent is only entitled to one personal exemption, whether he files his own return or is listed as a dependent on someone else's return.

A dependent may still be required to file a tax return. This happens most often with teenagers who have jobs. They are usually claimed as dependents on their parents' tax return, but they also file their own return to report their wage income and receive a refund of income tax withheld.

**Example:** Cole is a 16-year-old high school student who also works part-time for his city's recreation department. In 2012, he earned $4,210 from his part-time job. Cole still lives with his parents, who file jointly and claim him as a dependent on their return. Although his income is below the 2012 filing requirement, Cole files his own tax return in order to obtain a refund of the income taxes that were withheld at his job. He does not claim a personal exemption for himself because his parents already claimed his exemption on their joint return. However, Cole is still entitled to the standard deduction for single taxpayers. This wipes out all of his taxable income, and he receives a refund of the income tax that was withheld on his Form W-2.

Whether or not a dependent is required to file is determined by the amount of the dependent's earned income, unearned income, and gross income. Even though a dependent child may lose a personal exemption, most dependent children usually owe little or no tax on their individual returns because they can still offset a small amount of income with the standard deduction. In actual practice, it is rare to see a dependent who owes a large amount of tax.

There are certain rules that must be followed in order to claim a dependent on a tax return. Dependency rules are extremely complex and frequently tested on the EA exam. A dependent is always defined as either a:

- Qualifying child, or a
- Qualifying relative

The following sections discuss these rules in detail.

# The Primary Tests for Dependency

In order to determine if a taxpayer may claim a dependency exemption for another person, it must first be determined if the dependent can legally be claimed on the taxpayer's return. There are four main tests to determine this:

- **Citizenship or Residency Test**
- **Joint Return Test**
- **Qualifying Child of More Than One Person Test**
- **Dependent Taxpayer Test**

## 1. Citizenship or Residency Test

In order for a taxpayer to claim a dependency exemption for someone, the "citizen, national, or resident test" must be met. To qualify the dependent must be a citizen of the United States, a resident of the United States, or a citizen or resident of Canada or Mexico. There is also an exception for foreign-born adopted children.

> **Example:** Horatio is an American citizen. He provides all of the financial support for his mother, who is a resident of Canada. Horatio may claim his mother as a dependent. (**\*Note:** She does not have to live with him, since she is a dependent parent). Horatio may need to request an ITIN number for his mother if she does not have a valid Social Security Number.

## 2. Joint Return Test

A dependent cannot file a joint return with his spouse. In other words, once an individual files a joint return, that individual cannot be taken as a dependent by another taxpayer.

> **Example:** Ellen is 18 years old and had no income in 2012. She got married on November 1, 2012. Ellen's new husband had $26,700 income and they file jointly, claiming two personal exemptions on their tax return. Ellen's father supported her throughout the year and even paid for their wedding. However, her father cannot claim Ellen as his dependent because she already filed a joint return with her new husband.

However, the Joint Return Test does *not apply* if the joint return is filed by the dependent only to claim a refund and no tax liability exists for either spouse, even if they filed separate returns.

> **Example:** Greg and Taylor are both 18 and married. They live with Taylor's mother, Michelle. In 2012, Greg had $1,800 of wage income from a part-time job and no other income. Neither Greg nor Taylor is required to file a tax return. Taxes were taken out of Greg's wages due to regular withholding, so they file a joint return only to obtain a refund of the withheld taxes. The exception to the Joint Return Test applies, so Michelle may claim exemptions for both Greg and Taylor on her tax return, as long as all the other tests for dependency are met.

## 3. Qualifying Child of More Than One Person Test

Sometimes a child meets the rules to be a qualifying child of more than one person. However, only one person can claim that dependent on his tax return.

> **Example:** Dan and Linda live together with their daughter, Savannah. They are not married. Savannah is a qualifying child for both Dan and Linda, but only one of them can claim her as a dependent on their tax return.

## 4. Dependent Taxpayer Test

If a person can be claimed as a dependent by another taxpayer, that person cannot claim *anyone else* as a dependent. A person who is claimed as a dependent on *someone else's* return cannot claim a dependency exemption on *his own* return.

> **Example:** Eva is a 17-year-old single mother who has an infant son. Eva is claimed as a dependent by her parents. Therefore, since Eva is a dependent of her parents, she is prohibited from claiming her infant son as a dependent on her own tax return.

# Qualifying Child or Qualifying Relative?

Once the preparer determines that a dependent may be claimed on a taxpayer's return, then he must decide the type of dependency relationship the dependent has with the taxpayer.

There are only two types of dependents, a *qualifying child* and a *qualifying relative*, with very specific tests for identifying the difference between the two.

# Tests for a Qualifying Child

The tests for a qualifying child are more stringent than the tests for a qualifying relative. A qualifying child entitles a taxpayer to numerous tax credits, including the Earned Income Credit and the Child Tax Credit. A qualifying relative, on the other hand, does not qualify a taxpayer for the EIC.

There are five tests for a qualifying child:

- **Relationship Test**
- **Age Test**
- **Residency Test**
- **Support Test**
- **Tie-breaker Test (for a qualifying child of more than one person)**

## 1. Relationship Test

The qualifying child must be related to the taxpayer by blood, marriage, or legal adoption. Qualifying children include:

- A child or stepchild
- An adopted child
- A sibling or stepsibling
- A descendant of one of the above (such as a grandchild, niece, or nephew)
- An eligible foster child

## 2. Age Test

In order to be a qualifying child, the dependent must be:

- Under the age of 19 at the end of the tax year, or
- Under the age of 24 *and* a full-time student, or
- Permanently and totally disabled at any time during the year (of any age).

A child is considered a full-time student if he attends a qualified educational institution full-time at least five months out of the year.

**Example:** Andrew is 45 years old and totally disabled. Karen, his 37-year-old sister, provides all of Andrew's support and cares for him in her home, where he lives with her full-time. Although Andrew does not meet the age test, since he is **completely disabled,** he is still considered a *qualifying child* and a dependent for tax purposes. Karen may claim Andrew as her qualifying child, and also file as head of household.

Also, a child who is claimed as a dependent must be *younger than* the taxpayer who is claiming him, except in the case of dependents who are disabled. For taxpayers filing jointly, the child must be *younger* than *one spouse* listed on the return, but does not have to be younger than both spouses.

**Example #1:** Owen and Sydney are both 22 years old and file jointly. Sydney's 23-year-old brother, Parker, is a full-time student, unmarried, and lives with Owen and Sydney. Parker is not disabled. Owen and Sydney are both younger than Parker. Therefore, Parker is not their qualifying child, even though he is a full-time student.

**Example #2:** Lucius, age 34, and Paige, age 20, are married and file jointly. Paige's 23-year-old nephew, Jason, is a full-time student, unmarried, and lives with Lucius and Paige. Lucius and Paige provide all of Jason's support. In this case, Lucius and Paige may claim Jason as a qualifying child on their joint tax return because he is *younger than* Lucius. Jason is a full-time student, so he is a qualifying child for tax purposes.

# 3. Support Test

A qualifying child cannot provide more than one-half of his own support. A full-time student does not take scholarships (whether taxable or nontaxable) into account when calculating the support test.

**Example #1**: Samuel has an 18-year-old daughter named Tiffany. Samuel provided $4,000 toward his teenage daughter's support for the year. Tiffany also has a part-time job and provided $13,000 of her own support. Therefore, Tiffany provided over half of *her own support* for the year. Tiffany does not pass the support test, and consequently, she is not Samuel's qualifying child. Tiffany can file a tax return as "single" and claim her own exemption.

**Example #2:** Penelope is 15 years old and had a small role in a television series. She earned $40,000 as a child actor, but her parents put all the money in a trust fund to pay for college. She lived at home all year. Penelope meets the support test since her earnings were not used for her own support. Since she meets the tests for a qualifying child, Penelope can be claimed as a dependent by her parents.

## Foster Care Payments

Payments received for the support of a foster child from a child placement agency are considered support provided by the agency (not support provided by the child).

> **Example:** Gina is a foster parent who provided $3,000 toward her 10-year-old foster child's support for the year. The state government provided $4,000, which was considered support provided by the state, not by the child. Gina's foster child did not provide more than half of her own support for the year. Therefore, the child may be claimed as a qualifying child by Gina if all the other tests are met.

# 4. Residence Test

A qualifying child must live with the taxpayer for more than half the tax year (over six months). Exceptions apply for children of divorced parents, kidnapped children, temporary absences, and for children who were born or died during the year.[31]

A *temporary absence* includes illness, college, vacation, military service, and incarceration in a juvenile facility. It must be reasonable to assume that the absent child will return to the home after the temporary absence.

The taxpayer must continue to maintain the home during the absence.

> **Example:** Douglas and Andrea file jointly. They have one daughter named Isabella who is 29 years old. In March of 2012, Isabella lost her job and moved back in with her parents. Isabella earned $4,000 at the beginning of 2012 before she was laid off. Douglas and Andrea therefore provided the majority of Isabella's support for the rest of the year. Isabella got a new job in December and moved out. Isabella is not a qualifying child for federal tax purposes. Although Isabella meets the relationship, residence, and support test, she *does not* meet the age test.

> **Example**: Scott is unmarried and lives with his 10-year-old son, Elijah. Scott provides all of Elijah's support. In 2012, Elijah became very ill and was hospitalized for seven months. Elijah is still considered Scott's qualifying child, because the illness and hospitalization count as a temporary absence from home. Scott may claim Elijah as his qualifying child and also file for head of household status.

## *Special rules: Kidnapped child

A taxpayer can treat a kidnapped child as meeting the residency test, but both of the following must be true:

- The child is presumed to have been kidnapped by someone who is not a family member.
- In the year the kidnapping occurred, the child lived with the taxpayer for more than half of the year before the kidnapping.

This special tax treatment applies for all years until the child is returned. However, the last year this treatment can apply is the earlier of:

- The year there is a determination that the child is dead, or
- The year the child would have reached age 18.

---

[31] A taxpayer cannot claim an exemption for a stillborn child. The child must be born alive, even if it lives only for a short time.

# 5. The Tie-Breaker Test

Only one person can claim the same qualifying child, even if the child would qualify more than one person. If two taxpayers disagree on who gets to claim a child as their qualifying child and more than one person attempts to claim the same child, then the tie-breaker rules apply.

Under the tie-breaker rule, the child is treated as a qualifying child only by:

- The parents, if they file a joint return.
- The parent, if only one of the persons is the child's parent.
- The parent with whom the child lived the longest during the year.
- The parent with the highest AGI if the child lived with each parent for the same amount of time during the tax year and they do not file a joint return together.
- The person with the highest AGI, if no parent can claim the child as a qualifying child.
- A person with the higher AGI than any parent who can also claim the child as a qualifying child but does not.

**Example:** Sophia, who is single, has a three-year-old son named Orlando. They live with Sophia's father, Theodore (the child's grandfather). Sophia claims Orlando as her qualifying child, which means the child may not be treated as a qualifying child of the grandfather, Theodore.

**Example:** Penny and her sister, Rosa, live together. They also live and take care of their seven-year-old niece, Brianna, who lived with her aunts all year because Brianna's mother is incarcerated. Penny's AGI is $12,600. Rosa's AGI is $19,000. Brianna is a qualifying child of both Penny and Rosa because she meets the relationship, age, residency, and joint return tests for both aunts. However, Rosa has the primary right to claim Brianna as her qualifying child because her AGI is higher than Penny's.

# Tests for Qualifying Relatives

A person who is not a qualifying child may still qualify as a dependent under the rules for qualifying relatives.

There is a six-part test for qualifying relatives. Under these tests, even an individual who is not a family member can still be a qualifying relative. Unlike a qualifying child, a qualifying relative can be any age.

**\*Note:** There is no age test for a qualifying relative, and the support test and relationship test have different criteria.

In order to be claimed as a qualifying relative, the dependent must meet all of the following criteria:

- **Relationship (or Member of Household) Test**
- **Gross Income Test**
- **Total Support Test**
- **Joint Return Test**
- **Citizenship or Residency Test**

# 1. Relationship Test (or Member of Household)

The dependent must be related to the taxpayer in certain ways. A family member who is related to the taxpayer in any of the following ways **does not** have to live with the taxpayer to meet this test:

- A child, stepchild, foster child, or a descendant of any of them (for example, a grandchild).
- A sibling, stepsibling, or a half sibling.
- A parent, grandparent, stepparent, or other direct ancestor (but this does not include foster parents).
- A niece or nephew, a son-in-law, daughter-in-law, father-in-law, mother-in-law, brother-in-law, or sister-in-law[32].
- *Or the dependent **must have lived with** the taxpayer the entire tax year.

This means that an unrelated person who lived with the taxpayer for the entire year can also meet the member of household or relationship test.

---

*Note: If a relationship violates local laws, this test is not met. For example, if a taxpayer's state prohibits cohabitation, then that person cannot be claimed as a dependent, even if all other criteria are met.

---

Example: Isaac's 12-year-old grandson, Josh, lived with him for three months in 2012. For the rest of the year, Josh lived with his mother, Natalie, in another state. Natalie is Isaac's 32-year-old daughter. Even though Josh and Natalie lived in another state, Isaac still provided all of their financial support. Josh is not Isaac's *qualifying child* because he does not meet the residency test (Josh did not live with Isaac for more than half the year). However, Josh is Isaac's *qualifying relative*.

---

*Note: Any of these relationships that are established by marriage are *not ended* by death or divorce. So, for example, if a taxpayer supports his mother-in-law, he can

---

[32] *Note: The listing of family members for the relationship test does not include cousins. A cousin must live with the taxpayer for the entire year and also meet the gross income test in order to qualify as a dependent. In that respect, the IRS treats a cousin just like an unrelated person.

continue to claim her as a dependent even if he and his ex-spouse are divorced or if he becomes widowed.

---

**Example #1**: Mia and Caleb have always financially supported Mia's elderly mother, Gertrude, and claim her as their dependent on their jointly filed returns. However, in 2010, Mia dies and Caleb becomes a widower. Caleb remarries in 2012, but continues to support his former mother-in-law. Caleb can continue to claim Gertrude on his tax returns, even though he has remarried. This is because of the special rule that dependency relationships established by marriage do not end by death or divorce.

---

**Example #2:** Todd has lived all year with his girlfriend, Ava, and her two children in his home. Their cohabitation does not violate local laws. Ava does not work and is not required to file a 2012 tax return. Ava and her two children pass the "not a qualifying child test" to be Todd's qualifying relatives. Todd can claim them as dependents if he meets all the other tests.

---

## 2. Gross Income Test

A *qualifying relative* cannot earn more than the personal exemption amount. In 2012, the personal exemption amount is $3,800. For purposes of this test, gross income includes:

- All taxable income in the form of money, property, or services
- Gross receipts from rental property
- A partner's share of gross partnership income (not net)
- Unemployment compensation
- Taxable scholarships and grants

For purposes of this test, gross income does not include:

- Tax-exempt income
- Income earned by a disabled person at a sheltered workshop

## 3. Total Support Test

In order to claim an individual as a qualifying relative, the taxpayer must provide over half of the dependent's total support during the year. "Support" includes amounts from Social Security and welfare payments, even if that support is nontaxable. "Support" does not include amounts received from nontaxable scholarships. Support can include the fair market value of lodging.

---

**Example #1:** Ella is 78 and lives in her own apartment. She received $7,000 in Social Security benefits in 2012, which she used to pay for her apartment. Ella's daughter, Laurie, provided $2,200 in support to her mother by paying her utility bills and buying her groceries. Even though Ella's Social Security benefits are not taxable and she does not have a filing requirement, Laurie cannot claim her mother as a dependent because Ella provided over one-half of her own support.

---

**Example #2**: Nicholas lives with Gavin, who is an old army buddy of his. Nicholas provided all of the support for Gavin, who lived with Nicholas all year in his home. Gavin has no income and does not file a 2012 tax return. Nicholas can claim Gavin as his qualifying relative if all of the other tests are met.

**Example #3:** Morgan provided $4,000 toward her father's support during the year. In 2012, Morgan's father earned income of $600, had nontaxable Social Security benefits of $4,800, and tax-exempt interest of $200. He uses all these for his support. Morgan cannot claim an exemption for her father because the $4,000 she provides is not more than half of her father's total support of $9,600 ($4,000 + $600 + $4,800 + $200).

**Multiple Support Agreements:** There are special rules for claiming a dependency exemption for a qualifying relative when a taxpayer has a *multiple support agreement*. A multiple support agreement is when two or more people agree to join together to provide a person's support. This happens commonly with adult children who are taking care of their parents.

In order for the dependency exemption to apply under a multiple support agreement, family members together must pay more than half of the person's total support, but no one member individually may pay more than half. In addition, the taxpayer who claims the dependent must provide *more than 10%* of the person's support. Only one of the family members can claim the dependency exemption. A different qualifying family member can claim the dependency exemption each year.

**Example:** Benjamin, Matthew, and Pamela are siblings who support their disabled mother, Abigail. Abigail is 83 and lives with Benjamin. In 2012, Abigail receives 20% of her financial support from Social Security, 40% from Matthew, 30% from Benjamin, and 10% from Pamela. Under IRS rules for multiple support agreements, either Matthew or Benjamin can take the exemption for their mother if the other signs a statement agreeing not to do so. Pamela may not claim the dependency exemption because she does not provide *more than* 10% of the support for her mother.

**Example:** Graciela and Pilar are sisters who help support their 64-year-old father, Alonso. Each provides 20% of his care. The remaining 60% is provided equally by two persons not related to Alonso. He does not live with them. Because more than half of his support is provided by persons who cannot claim an exemption for him, no one can take the exemption.

# 4. Joint Return Test

If the dependent is married, he cannot file a joint return with his spouse, unless the return is filed solely to obtain a refund of withheld income taxes. (With the Joint Return Test, the same exceptions apply for a qualifying relative as for qualifying children.)

# 5. Citizenship or Residency Test

A qualifying relative must be either a citizen or resident alien of:

- The United States,
- Canada, or
- Mexico.

This means that a child who lives in Canada or Mexico may still be a *qualifying relative* of a U.S. taxpayer.

Even If the child does not live with the taxpayer at all during the tax year, the child may still be eligible to be claimed as a *qualifying relative*.

> **Example:** Manuel provides all the financial support of his children, ages 6 and 12, who live in Mexico with Manuel's mother, their grandmother. Manuel is unmarried and lives in the United States. He is a legal U.S. resident alien and has a valid Social Security Number. Manuel's children are citizens of Mexico and do not have SSNs. Regardless, both his children are still qualifying relatives for tax purposes. Manuel may claim them as dependents if all the tests are met. He may also be able to claim his mother as a dependent if all the tests are met.

## Special Rules for Children of Divorced or Separated Parents

Generally, to claim a child as a dependent, the child must live with the taxpayer for over half the year (over six months). There is an exception to this rule for divorced/separated parents.

If the child did not live with the taxpayer, the custodial parent may still allow the noncustodial parent to claim the dependency exemption. The noncustodial parent must attach IRS Form 8332 in order to claim the dependency exemption.

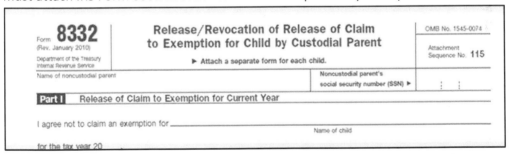

If a divorce decree does not specify which parent is the custodial parent or which parent receives the dependency exemption, the exemption will automatically go to the parent who has physical custody for the majority of the year.

> **Example**: Alexis and Nathan are divorced. They have one child named Dylan. In 2012, Dylan lived with Alexis for 300 nights and with Nathan for 65 nights. Therefore, Alexis is the custodial parent. Alexis has the right to claim Dylan on her tax return as her qualifying child. However, Alexis may choose to release the exemption to Nathan by signing Form 8332.

**\*Note:** Even if the custodial parent releases the dependency exemption to the noncustodial parent, the custodial parent still has the right to claim head of household status, the Earned Income Credit, and dependent care credit.

> **Example:** Gary and Frieda are divorced, and have one minor child named Sunny. Frieda is the custodial parent, but she agrees to release the dependency exemption for their child over to Gary by signing Form 8332. Gary will file as single and claim Sunny as his dependent. Frieda may still file as head of household even though she does not claim the dependency exemption for Sunny. That is because Frieda is the parent who lived with Sunny and maintained the home in which her child lived for most of the year.

# The "Nanny" Tax (Household Employees)

A taxpayer *may not* claim a dependency exemption for a household employee such as a nanny, even if the employee lived with the taxpayer.

However, a taxpayer who has household employees may need to pay employment taxes, commonly referred to as the "nanny tax." The tax applies to any taxpayer who pays wages of $1,800 or more in 2012 to any one household employee. The worker is the taxpayer's employee if the taxpayer can control not only what work is done but how it is done, regardless of whether the work is full-time or part-time; the employee is paid on an hourly, daily, weekly, or per job basis; or the employee is hired through an agency. Examples of household employees include babysitters, housekeepers, private nurses, yard workers, and drivers. A self-employed worker, such as a daycare provider who cares for several children from different families in her own home, is not a taxpayer's household employee.

If a taxpayer pays a household employee $1,800 or more in 2012, he must withhold and pay Social Security and Medicare taxes. The employer's share of the tax is 7.65% and the employee's is 5.65% in 2012.

If a taxpayer pays wages of $1,000 or more to a household employee in any one quarter in 2012, he must also pay federal unemployment tax. The tax is 6% of cash wages. Wages over $7,000 a year per employee are not taxed.

Wages paid to a taxpayer's spouse, parent, or child under the age of 21 are exempt from the nanny tax rules.

Taxpayers who pay household income taxes must file a Schedule H along with their Form 1040.

# The Kiddie Tax

The "kiddie tax" deals with the taxation of unearned income of children. Years ago, wealthy families would transfer investments to their minor children and save thousands of dollars in investment income because the money would be taxed at a lower rate. This was completely legal until Congress closed this tax loophole, and now investment income earned by dependent children is taxed at the parents' marginal rate.

This law became known as the "kiddie tax." The kiddie tax does not apply to wages or self-employment income—it applies to *investment income* only. Examples of unearned income include bank interest, dividends, and capital gains distributions.

Part of a children's investment income may be taxed at the parent's tax rate if:

- The child's investment income was more than $1,900 in 2012.
- The child is under the age of 19 or a full-time college student under the age of 24.
- The child is required to file a tax return for the end of the tax year.
- The child does not file a joint return for the tax year.

For 2012, the first $950 of unearned income a child or college student earns is offset by the $950 standard deduction for dependents (assuming the child has no earned income), and the next $950 is taxed at the child's rate. All of the child's unearned income in excess of $1,900 is taxed at the parent's rate.

**Example:** Bill and Donna have one 14-year-old son named Jack. In 2012, Jack has $2,900 of interest income from a CD that his grandfather gave him. He does not have any other income. The first $950 of investment income is not taxable, because the standard deduction for dependents is $950. The next $950 is taxed at the 10% income tax rate. The remainder, $1,000, is taxed at the parents' tax rate.

Parents can avoid paying the kiddie tax only if the child has enough *earned* income to provide greater than half of his own support. In that case, the child's unearned income would be based on the child's tax rates, and not the parents.

# Dependency Tests (Snapshot)

## Tests for a Qualifying Child

| |
|---|
| The child must be a son, daughter, stepchild, foster child, brother, sister, half-brother, half-sister, stepbrother, stepsister, or a descendant of any of these. |
| The child must be: <br> • Under age 19 at the end of the year and younger than the taxpayer (or his spouse, if filing jointly), <br> • Under age 24 at the end of the year, a full-time student, and younger than the taxpayer (or his spouse, if filing jointly), or <br> • Any age if disabled. |
| The child must have lived with the taxpayer for more than half of the year (over six months). Exceptions exist for temporary absences, kidnapped children, and dependents that died/were born during the year. |
| The child must not have provided more than half of his own support for the year. |
| The child cannot file a joint return for the year (unless that joint return is filed only as a claim for refund). |
| If the child meets the rules to be a qualifying child of more than one person, only one taxpayer can claim the child. |

## Tests for a Qualifying Relative

| |
|---|
| The person cannot be the qualifying child of anyone else. |
| The person either (a) must be related to the taxpayer in certain ways or (b) must live with the taxpayer all year as a member of the household. There is no age test for a qualifying relative. |
| The person's gross income for the year must be less than $3,800 in 2012. |
| The taxpayer must provide more than half of the person's total support for the year. |

# Unit 4: Questions

1. Dan is unmarried and lives alone. His mother received $5,600 in Social Security benefits and $100 in taxable interest income in 2012. She paid $4,000 for living expenses and $400 for recreation. She also put $1,300 in a savings account. Dan also spent $4,800 of his own money on his mother's support in 2012, which paid her rent for the entire year. Dan and his mother did not live together. Which of the following is true?

A. Dan may claim his mother as a dependent, and also file as head of household.
B. Dan may not claim his mother as a dependent, but he may file as head of household.
C. Dan may claim his mother as a dependent, but he may not file as head of household.
D. Dan may not claim his mother as a dependent, and he cannot file as head of household.

**The answer is A.** Dan may claim his mother as a dependent, and also file as head of household. Even though Dan's mother received a total of $5,700 ($5,600 + $100), she spent only $4,400 ($4,000 + $400) for her own support. Since Dan spent more than $4,400 for her support and no other support was received, Dan has provided more than half of her support. Also, Dan paid for all her rental expenses, so he paid more than half the cost of keeping up a home that was the main home for the entire year for his parent. Therefore, Dan is also eligible to file as head of household. ###

2. Roy is a client who tells you that his wife died in February 2012. Based on this information, Roy can claim _____.

A. Only the personal exemption for himself.
B. Only the personal exemption for his wife.
C. Personal exemptions for both himself and for his wife.
D. A personal exemption for himself and a partial exemption for his wife.

**The answer is C.** In 2012, Roy can claim a personal exemption for his deceased wife, along with a personal exemption for himself. A taxpayer whose spouse dies during the year may file jointly in the year of death. ###

3. Alyssa is 18 years old and a full-time student. She comes into your office with some questions about her tax return. She says that she is claimed as a dependent on her parents' tax return. Over the summer, she worked in a clothing boutique and earned $7,000. Alyssa wants to file a tax return to report her wage income and get a refund. How many exemptions may she claim on her tax return?

A. Zero.
B. One.
C. Two.
D. Three.

**The answer is A.** Since Alyssa is claimed as a dependent on her parents' tax return, she cannot claim an exemption for herself. Therefore, her total number of exemptions is zero. She can still file a tax return in order to claim a refund of taxes withheld. ###

4. John is the sole support of his mother. To claim her as a dependent on his Form 1040, John's mother must be a resident or citizen of which of the following countries?

A. United States.
B. Mexico.
C. Canada.
D. Any of the above.

**The answer is D.** To qualify as a dependent, the dependent must be a citizen or resident alien of the United States, Canada, or Mexico. ###

5. In a multiple support agreement, what is the minimum amount of support that a taxpayer can provide and still claim the dependent?

A. 11% support.
B. 15% support.
C. 50% support.
D. 75% support.

**The answer is A.** The law provides for multiple support agreements, which usually exist when family members collectively support a relative, often a parent. The taxpayer can claim the dependent as a qualifying relative if he paid *more than* 10% of the support. The taxpayer would not be entitled to the exemption if someone else provided more than 50% of support of the family member. ###

6. Joseph, 52, is a single father who lives with an adopted son named Wyatt who has Down syndrome. Wyatt is 32 years old and permanently disabled. Wyatt had $800 in interest income and $5,000 in wages from a part-time job in 2012. Which of the following statements is true?

A. Joseph can file as head of household, with Wyatt as his qualifying child.
B. Joseph does not qualify for head of household, but he could still claim Wyatt as his qualifying relative, because Wyatt does not meet the age test for a qualifying child.
C. Joseph can file as head of household, with Wyatt as his qualifying relative.
D. Joseph must file single and he cannot claim Wyatt, because Wyatt earned more than the standard deduction amount.

**The answer is A.** Even though Wyatt is over the normal age threshold for a qualifying child, he is still considered a qualifying child for tax purposes. This is because Wyatt is permanently disabled and Joseph provides his financial support and care. Since Wyatt is disabled, he is therefore also a "qualifying child" for purposes of head of household filing status. ###

7. Clifford and Lily divorced in 2011 and they have one child together. Clifford's child lived with him for ten months of the year in 2012. The child lived with Lily for the other two months. The divorce decree states that Lily is supposed to be the custodial parent, not Clifford. Who is considered the custodial parent for IRS purposes?

A. Clifford.
B. Lily.
C. Neither.
D. Both.

**The answer is A.** For IRS purposes, the "custodial parent" is the parent with whom the child lived for the greater part of the year. The other parent is the noncustodial parent. If the parents divorced or separated during the year and the child lived with both parents before the separation, the custodial parent is the one with whom the child lived for the greater part of the rest of the year. ###

8. Haley is 23 and a full-time college student. During the year, Haley lived at home with her parents for four months and lived in the dorm for the remainder of the year. During the tax year, Haley worked part-time and earned $6,000, but that income did not amount to half of her total support. Can Haley's parents still claim her as a dependent?

A. No, because Haley earned more than the personal exemption amount.
B. No, because Haley did not live with her parents for more than half the year, and she does not meet the age test.
C. Yes, Haley's parents can claim her as a qualifying child.
D. Yes, Haley's parents can claim her as a dependent, but only as a qualifying relative, not as a qualifying child.

**The answer is C.** Haley meets all the qualifying child tests: the relationship test; the age test (because she is under 24 and was a full-time student); the residence test (because the time spent at college is a legitimate temporary absence); and the support test (because she did not provide over half of her own support). ###

9. Carson has a 12-year-old daughter named Emma. In 2012, Emma had $925 in interest income from a bank account. Which of the following statements regarding Emma's unearned income is correct?

A. Tax will be assessed to Carson and is calculated using Emma's tax rate.
B. Emma is not required to file a return, and Carson is not required to report his daughter's income on his own tax return.
C. Emma is required to file a tax return, and income tax will be assessed at a flat rate of 10%.
D. Carson may elect to report Emma's interest income on his own tax return. Her income will be taxed at the parent's highest marginal rate.

**The answer is B.** Emma is not required to file a tax return, because her unearned income is less than the standard deduction amount for dependents. The first $950 of investment income (which is equal to the dependent´s standard deduction) escapes income tax. Emma has no filing requirement, and her father is not required to report the income on his own return. ###

10. Cheryl is 46 and unmarried. Her nephew, Bradley, lived with her all year and was 18 years old at the end of the year. Bradley did not provide more than half of his own support. He had $4,200 in income from wages and $1,000 in investment income. Which of the following is true?
A. Bradley qualifies as Cheryl's qualifying child for tax purposes.
B. Bradley is not a qualifying child; however, he can be claimed by Cheryl as a qualifying relative.
C. Bradley is not a qualifying child or qualifying relative, because he had income that exceeded the personal exemption amount.
D. Cheryl can claim Bradley only if he is a full-time student, since he is no longer a minor child.

**The answer is A.** Bradley is Cheryl's qualifying child because he meets the age test, support test, and relationship test. Also, because Bradley is single, he is a qualifying person for Cheryl to claim head of household filing status. Bradley is not required to be a full-time student, because the IRS says that any child under the age of 19 at the end of the tax year will be treated as a qualifying child if all the other tests are met. Bradley is only 18 years old, and therefore he passes the age test. ###

11. There are many tests that must be met for a taxpayer to claim an exemption for a dependent as a qualifying relative. Which of the following is not a requirement?
A. Citizen or resident test.
B. Member of household or relationship test.
C. Disability test.
D. Joint return test.

**The answer is C.** There is no such thing as a "disability test" for a qualifying relative. ###

12. Tony and Isabelle are the sole support of all the following individuals. (All are U.S. citizens but none lives with them, files a tax return, or has any income.)

1. Jennie, Tony's grandmother.
2. Julie, Isabelle's stepmother.
3. Jonathan, father of Tony's first wife.
4. Timothy, Isabelle's cousin.

How many exemptions may Tony and Isabelle claim on their joint return?

A. 3.
B. 4.
C. 5.
D. 6.

**The answer is C.** They may take three dependency exemptions on their tax return, and two personal exemptions for themselves. Tony and Isabelle may take dependency exemptions for all the dependents listed, except for Timothy, since he is Isabelle's cousin. Timothy would have to live with Tony and Isabelle all year in order for them to claim him as their dependent. Parents (or grandparents, in-laws, stepparents, etc.) do not have to live with a taxpayer in order to qualify as dependents. Tony can claim Jonathan, because Jonathan was once his father-in-law. ###

13. Ted and Sharon are married and are the sole support of their 23-year-old son, Ashton, who lives with them. Ashton is not a student and not disabled. He was unable to find steady work in 2012, but received $4,900 from a charitable foundation for painting a mural. Which of the following statements is true?

A. Ted and Sharon may claim Ashton as a qualifying child on their federal income tax return.
B. Ted and Sharon may claim Ashton as a qualifying relative on their federal income tax return.
C. Ted and Sharon may only claim Ashton if they file MFS.
D. Ted and Sharon may not claim Ashton as a dependent.

**The answer is D.** Ashton is not a minor, not a student, and not disabled and therefore does not qualify as a qualifying child. He does not qualify as a qualifying relative, either, because he fails the gross income test. A qualifying relative cannot earn more than the personal exemption amount. In 2012, the personal exemption amount is $3,800. Since Ashton earned $4,900 in 2012, he cannot be claimed as a dependent. ###

14. Peter filed for divorce in 2012, and he and his wife moved into separate residences on April 20. Peter's 10-year-old daughter lived with him for the entire year. Peter owns the home and pays all the costs of upkeep for it. Which of the following is true?

A. Peter must file jointly with his wife in 2012, since they are still legally married. They may claim their daughter as a dependent on their jointly filed return.
B. Peter must file single in 2012.
C. Peter must file MFS in 2012.
D. Peter qualifies for HOH filing status.

**The answer is D.** Peter qualifies for head of household filing status. Since Peter and his wife lived in separate residences for the last six months of the year and Peter had a qualifying child, he may file as head of household. ###

15. Tyler is single and 17 years old. He works a part-time job at night and goes to school full-time. His total income for 2012 was $10,500. Tyler lives with his parents, who provided the majority of Tyler's support. Tyler's parents are claiming him as a dependent on their 2012 tax return. Which of the following statements is true?

A. Tyler is required to file his own return, and he may also take an exemption for himself.
B. Tyler is not required to file his own return.
C. Tyler's parents may not claim him as a dependent because Tyler earned more than the standard deduction amount for 2012.
D. His parents may claim Tyler as their qualifying child. Tyler is required to file a tax return, but he cannot claim a personal exemption for himself. He is still entitled to the standard deduction for single filers.

**The answer is D.** Tyler's parents may claim him as their qualifying child because he is under the age of 19 and does not provide more than half of his own support. Tyler is required to file a tax return but cannot claim an exemption for himself. ###

16. A child has investment income. What is the income limit threshold for when the kiddie tax kicks in?

A. $0.
B. $950.
C. $1,900.
D. $3,700.

**The answer is C.** In 2012, a child's unearned income in excess of $1,900 is subject to the kiddie tax rules. ###

17. Frank provided $4,000 toward his 17-year-old son's support for the year. Frank's son has a part-time job and provided $16,000 to his own support. Which of the following is true?

A. Frank may claim his son as a qualifying child on his return.
B. Frank may claim his son as his business partner on his return.
C. Frank may not claim his son as a dependent on his return.
D. None of the above is correct.

**The answer is C.** Frank's son provided more than half of his *own support* for the year. Therefore, he is not Frank's qualifying child. ###

18. Persons who can be claimed as a dependent may file a tax return, but they cannot:

A. Claim any deductions.
B. Claim any exemptions.
C. File a claim for a refund.
D. File an amended return.

**The answer is B.** Persons who can be claimed as a dependent may file a tax return, but they cannot claim any exemptions. If a taxpayer can claim another person as a dependent—even if the taxpayer does not actually do so—the dependent cannot take a personal exemption on *his* tax return. ###

19. Mateo is a U.S. resident. He has a 10-year-old child named Rey, who is a legal resident of Mexico. Rey does not have an SSN. Mateo would like to claim Rey as a dependent on his tax return. Rey lived with Mateo for eight months and with his grandmother in Mexico for the remaining part of the year. Does Rey meet the requirements of the citizen or resident test?

A. No, because Rey does not have a valid SSN.
B. No, because Rey is a resident of Mexico.
C. Yes, Rey meets the requirements of the citizen or resident test.
D. None of the above.

**The answer is C.** Rey meets the requirements of the citizen or resident test. In order to meet this test, a person must be a U.S. citizen or resident, or a resident of Canada or Mexico for at least some part of the year. ###

20. Donna Wiley has three children: Luther, Tim, and Mary. Each child contributes toward Mrs. Wiley's support. Luther and Tim each provide 45%, and Mary provides 10%. Which of Mrs. Wiley's children would be eligible to claim a dependency exemption for her in 2012 under a multiple support agreement?

A. Luther or Tim.
B. Both Luther and Tim.
C. Luther, Tim, or Mary.
D. None of the three are eligible to claim the dependency exemption because no one child provided more than half of his or her mother's support.

**The answer is A.** Only Luther or Tim would be eligible to claim the exemption under a multiple support agreement in 2012. Answer "B" is incorrect because only a single taxpayer may claim the exemption in a tax year. Mary is not eligible in either case because she does not provide more than 10% of her mother's support. ###

21. In 2012, when does an employer have to withhold and pay Social Security and Medicare taxes for a household employee?

A. Whenever the taxpayer pays any employee for household services.
B. When the taxpayer pays a household employee $1,000 or more in wages a year.
C. When the taxpayer pays a household employee $1,800 or more in wages a year.
D. When the taxpayer pays his 20-year-old daughter to care for her younger siblings.

**The answer is C.** In 2012, the "nanny tax" kicks in when a taxpayer pays a household employee $1,800 or more in wages a year.

# Unit 5: Taxable and Nontaxable Income

> **More Reading:**
> Publication 525, *Taxable and Nontaxable Income*
> Publication 504, *Divorced or Separated Individuals*
> Publication 4681, *Canceled Debts, Foreclosures, Repossessions, and Abandonments*
> Publication 544, *Sales and Other Dispositions of Assets*
> Publication 550, *Investment Income and Expenses*

For a taxpayer to determine how much tax he owes, he first needs to figure out his gross income. Gross income includes all money, goods, property, and services that are not exempt from tax. In addition to wages, salaries, commissions, fees, and tips, this includes other forms of compensation such as fringe benefits and stock options.

The IRS's position is that all income is taxable unless it is specifically excluded. An exclusion is not the same as a deduction, and it is important to understand the distinction because many deductions are phased out as a taxpayer's gross income increases. Excluded income, on the other hand, retains its character as excluded income no matter what the taxpayer's gross income is.

Most of the time, excluded income does not have to be reported on a tax return. There are other instances where excluded income must be reported, but it is still not taxable to the recipient.

> **Example:** Brock is a popular recording artist and makes more than $600,000 in wages per year. Because of his high income, Brock is phased out for many deductions. However, in 2012 Brock is involved in an auto accident where he sustains major injuries. Brock sues the other driver and receives a settlement of $80,000 from the insurance company. The insurance settlement is excluded income because compensation for physical injuries is not taxable to the recipient.

## Sources of All Income

When taxpayers prepare a federal income tax return such as IRS Form 1040, they must calculate three levels of income:

1. **Gross Income:** This is the sum of all sources of taxable income that the taxpayer receives during the year.
2. **Adjusted Gross Income (AGI):** AGI is total income minus certain allowable deductions. These deductions include, but are not limited to, IRA contributions, qualified student loan interest, certain expenses for self-employed individuals, alimony payments, and moving expenses.
3. **Taxable Income:** This is the amount of income on which a taxpayer owes income taxes. It is calculated by subtracting any deductions and exemptions from AGI.

> ## How to Calculate Gross Individual Income (Tax Formula)
> Start with GROSS INCOME
> MINUS- Adjustments to Income ("Above the Line" Deductions)
> = ADJUSTED GROSS INCOME
> MINUS- Greater of Itemized Deductions or Standard Deduction
> MINUS- Personal Exemptions
> = TAXABLE INCOME
> X Tax Rate
> = GROSS TAX Liability
> MINUS- Credits
> **= NET TAX Liability or Refund Receivable**

The Internal Revenue Code (IRC) describes types of income that are taxable and nontaxable. In this unit, we will cover the most common types of both.

# *Earned Income vs. Unearned Income*

*Earned* income is received for services performed, such as wages, salaries, tips, or professional fees. *Unearned* income is also called "passive income," or investment income. Earned income (such as wages) is treated differently from passive income (such as dividends).

Earned income is generally subject to Social Security tax and Medicare tax (also called the FICA tax). Investment income and other passive income are generally not subject to FICA tax.

Some income is variable, which means it is considered earned income for some taxpayers and unearned income for others.

## The Doctrine of Constructive Receipt

The doctrine of constructive receipt is premised on the IRS position that taxpayers should be taxed on their income when it becomes available, regardless of whether it is actually in their physical possession.

For example, a check that a taxpayer receives before the end of the tax year is considered income constructively received in that year, even if the taxpayer does not deposit the check into his bank account until the next year. Taxpayers must include in income any amounts that are constructively received during the tax year.

> **Example:** Jerrald is on vacation in Las Vegas. On December 30, 2012, the postal service delivers a check for $500 to his home mailbox in Boise, Idaho. Even though he did not have the check in his physical possession, he is still considered to have constructive receipt of it. Jerrald must include the $500 in gross income on his 2012 tax return.

If there are significant restrictions on the income or if the income is not accessible to the taxpayer, it is not considered to have been constructively received. If a taxpayer refuses income, such as a prize or an award, then the income also is not considered to have been constructively received.

> **Example:** Opal won a big prize for concert tickets from a local radio station. The front-row concert tickets were valued at $1,200. This was a taxable award for Opal, and she is required to pay taxes on the fair market value of the tickets. However, on the day of the concert, the radio station does not receive the tickets in time from the promoter. Opal is not able to attend the concert. Since she never actually received the proceeds, the prize is not taxable to her. She never had constructive receipt of her prize.

## Claim of Right Doctrine

Under the claim of right doctrine, income received without restriction—income the taxpayer has complete control over—must be reported in the year received, even if there is a possibility it may have to be repaid in a later year.

If there is a dispute and income is later repaid, the repayment is deductible in the year repaid. As a result, taxpayers are not required to amend their federal gross income for an earlier year based on a subsequent repayment of amounts held under a claim of right by filing an amended return.

> **Example:** In 2012, a gallery owner named Courtney receives $25,000 from the sale of a painting. She properly includes $25,000 in her gross income and pays taxes on the income for the 2012 tax year. On March 1, 2013, the customer discovers that the painting is a forgery and returns it for a full refund of $25,000. Since Courtney pays back the $25,000 in tax year 2013, she is entitled to deduct the amount from her gross income in 2013. No further claim of right deduction is allowed.

However, this does not include income that has substantial restrictions applied to it. The issue usually lies with control over the income. Income received by an agent for a taxpayer is income constructively received in the year the agent received it.

If a taxpayer agrees by contract that a third party is to receive income for him, he must include the amount in his own income when the third party receives it.

> **Example:** Holden's employer garnishes part of his salary for back child support. Since the amount would have normally been included in Holden's paycheck, he must still recognize the income as if he had received it himself. Holden must include that amount in his gross income, even though he never actually received it.

## Prizes and Awards

Prizes and awards are usually taxable. If the prize or award is in a form other than cash, the FMV of the property is treated as the taxable amount. The winner may avoid taxation of the award by rejecting the prize. The taxpayer may also choose to transfer the prize to a charity or other nonprofit.

**Example:** Jerry is a college instructor. He is chosen as teacher of the year by a national education association. He is awarded $3,000, but he does not accept the prize. Instead, Jerry directs the association to transfer his winnings to a college scholarship fund. Jerry never receives a check or has control over the funds. Therefore, the award is not taxable to Jerry.

Some prizes and awards are excludable from income. An award recipient may exclude the FMV of the prize from gross income if:

- The amount received is in recognition of religious, scientific, charitable, or similar meritorious achievement (**Example**: a nonprofit charity awards a Christmas gift to a needy individual);
- The recipient is selected without action on his part;
- The receipt of the award is not conditioned on substantial future services; and
- The amount is paid by the organization making the award to a tax-exempt organization (including a governmental unit) designated by the recipient.

## *Employee Awards (Exclusion from Income)*

There is also an exclusion for awards given to employees. Certain employee awards may qualify for exclusion from the employee's gross income as a nontaxable fringe benefit. A prize may also qualify for exclusion from income if it is a scholarship.

Amounts paid for employee awards are still deductible to the employer and not taxable to the employee if certain rules are followed.[33] A cash award is always taxable to the employee. An achievement award in the form of property, if given to the employee for length of service or as a safety achievement, is not taxable to the employee and is still deductible by the employer.

Employers can exclude from wages the value of achievement awards given to an employee from the employee's wages if the cost is not more than the amount the employer can deduct as a business expense for the year. The excludable annual amount is $1,600 for qualified plan awards per employee.

There is a $400 annual limit for nonqualified awards that are given to highly compensated executives, but not to rank-and-file employees.

**Example:** Space Corporation awards a set of golf clubs to an employee as a nonqualified plan employee achievement award. The FMV of the golf clubs is $750. The amount included in taxable wages to the employee is $350 ($750 − $400). If the award had been a qualified plan award, the employee would not have been taxed on the FMV of the award.

---

[33] Employee awards and fringe benefits are covered in more detail in Part 2. For Part 1 of the EA exam, you must understand the tax implications of how an employee award would be reported by an individual who receives the award (the employee). For Part 2 of the exam, you would need to understand the tax implications of employee awards from the perspective of the employer that offers the benefit.

> **Example:** Rowan received three employee achievement awards during the year: a watch valued at $250, a stereo valued at $1,000, and a set of golf clubs valued at $500. She received each of the awards for length of service and exceptional safety achievement. They are all qualified plan awards and would normally be excluded from her income, assuming that the other requirements for qualified plan awards are satisfied. However, because the $1,750 total value of the awards is more than $1,600, Rowan must include $150 ($1,750 – $1,600) in her income.

The employer must make the award as part of a meaningful presentation, and it cannot simply be disguised pay.

# Income from Canceled Debt

Generally, if a taxpayer's debt is canceled or forgiven, the taxpayer must include the canceled debt in his gross income. There is no income from a canceled debt if it is intended as a gift (for example, if a taxpayer owes his parents money but the parents choose to forgive the debt.)

Cancellation of debt can involve auto loans, credit card debt, medical care, professional services, installment purchases of furniture or other personal property, mortgages, and home equity loans. A debt includes any indebtedness for which a taxpayer is liable or which attaches to the taxpayer's property.

Taxpayers often question the taxability of canceled debt because they did not receive any actual money. In situations where property is surrendered or repossessed such as a foreclosure, taxpayers may feel that by giving up the property, they should be relieved from any further obligation. However, canceled debt is taxable because the benefit to the taxpayer is the relief from personal liability to pay the debt.

If the debt is a *nonbusiness* debt, the canceled debt amount should be reported as "other income" on line 21 of a taxpayer's Form 1040. If it is a business debt, it is reported on Schedule C of Form 1040.

When an entity cancels a debt of $600 or more, the taxpayer should receive a Form 1099-C, *Cancellation of Debt.*

> **Example:** Phoebe borrows $10,000 to take a vacation and defaults on the loan after paying back only $2,000. She spends all the money and is unwilling to make payments on the loan. The lender is unable to collect the remaining amount of the loan. Phoebe is not insolvent. Therefore, there is a cancellation of debt of $8,000, which is taxable income to Phoebe. She must include it on her tax return as "other income."

If a financial institution offers a discount for the early payment of a mortgage loan, the amount of the discount is taxable as canceled debt. This occurs when a lender discounts or reduces the principal balance of a loan to reward an early payoff.

# Recourse and Nonrecourse Debt

Knowing whether a loan is recourse or nonrecourse will often determine the taxability of a canceled debt.

Recourse debt holds the borrower personally liable for any amount not satisfied by the surrender of secured property. If a lender forecloses on property subject to a recourse debt and cancels the portion of the debt in excess of the FMV of the property, the canceled portion is treated as ordinary income. This amount must be included in gross income unless it qualifies for an exception or exclusion.

In a recourse loan, the taxpayer must generally report two transactions:

1.  The cancellation of debt income
2.  Gain or loss on the sale or repossession

In addition to this cancellation of indebtedness income, the taxpayer may realize a gain or loss on the disposition of the property; this amount is generally the difference between the FMV of the property at the time of the foreclosure and the taxpayer's adjusted basis in the property.

**\*Note:** If a personal vehicle is repossessed, then the repossession is treated as a sale, and the gain or loss must be computed. The loss would be nondeductible for personal vehicles.

---

**Example:** Zach lost his yacht because he could no longer make his payments. At the time of repossession, he owed a balance of $170,000 to the lender, and the FMV of the yacht was $140,000. Zach is personally liable for the debt (recourse loan), so the abandonment is treated as a sale. The "selling price" from the repossession is $140,000, and Zach must recognize $30,000 in debt forgiveness income.

---

**Example:** Doreen bought a new car for $15,000. She made a $2,000 down payment and borrowed the remaining $13,000 from her bank. Doreen is personally liable for the car loan (recourse debt). The bank repossessed her car because she stopped making payments. The balance due on the loan at the time of the repossession was $10,000. The FMV of the car when repossessed was only $9,000. Since a repossession is treated as a sale, the gain or loss must be computed. Doreen compares the amount realized ($9,000) with her adjusted basis ($15,000) to determine that she has a $6,000 nondeductible loss. She also has ordinary income from cancellation of debt. That income is $1,000 ($10,000 canceled debt – $9,000 FMV). Doreen must report the canceled debt as income on line 21 of her Form 1040.

---

A nonrecourse debt is a type of loan that is secured by collateral in which the borrower does not have liability for the loan. Many mortgages are nonrecourse. This means that if the borrower defaults, the lender can seize the home, but cannot seek out the borrower for any further compensation, even if the FMV of the home does not cover the full value of the loan amount.

If the taxpayer abandons property that secures debt for which the taxpayer is not personally liable (a nonrecourse loan), the abandonment is treated as a sale or exchange. If a loan is nonrecourse and the borrower does not retain the asset, then the borrower does not have to recognize cancellation of debt income.

# Qualified Principal Residence Indebtedness (QPRI)

The *Mortgage Debt Relief Act of 2007* allows taxpayers to exclude income from the discharge of debt on their principal residence, which is defined as the home where the taxpayer ordinarily lives most of the time. This exception does not apply to second homes or vacation homes.

The provision applies to debt forgiven in 2007 through 2012, and has been extended through 2013 by the 2012 American Taxpayer Relief Act. Up to $2 million of forgiven debt is eligible for this exclusion ($1 million if MFS). The exclusion does not apply unless it is directly related to a decline in the home's value or the taxpayer's financial condition.

Normally, when a bank forecloses on a home and sells it for less than the borrower's outstanding mortgage, it forgives the unpaid mortgage debt. That canceled debt then becomes taxable income to the homeowner. The Mortgage Debt Relief Act, however, allows an exclusion of income realized as a result of loan modification or foreclosure of a taxpayer's principal residence. The taxpayer must report the amount of debt forgiven on his return by completing Form 982, *Reduction of Tax Attributes Due to Discharge of Indebtedness.*

"Qualified principal residence indebtedness" (QPRI) is a mortgage secured by a taxpayer's principal residence that was taken out to buy, build, or substantially improve that residence. QPRI cannot be more than the cost of the home plus improvements. QPRI also may include debt from refinancing.

**\*Note:** A loss on the sale of a personal residence is not deductible.

**Example:** Adam's home is subject to a $320,000 mortgage debt. Adam's creditor forecloses in April 2012. Due to declining real estate values, the residence is sold for $280,000 in December 2012. Adam has $40,000 of income from discharge of indebtedness and may claim the exclusion by filing Form 982 with his 2012 tax return.

## "Ordering Rule" for Principal Residence Indebtedness

If only a part of a loan is qualified principal residence indebtedness, the exclusion from income for QPRI applies only to the extent the amount canceled exceeds the amount of the loan that is not QPRI. However, the remaining part of the loan may qualify for a different exclusion (such as the exclusion for insolvency).

> **Example:** Ken incurred debt of $800,000 when he purchased his home for $880,000. He made a down payment of $80,000 and financed the rest. When the FMV of the property was $1 million, Ken refinanced the debt for $850,000. At the time of the refinancing, the balance of the original loan was $740,000. Ken used the $110,000 he obtained from the refinancing ($850,000 minus $740,000) to buy a luxury car and take a vacation to the Bahamas. Two years after the refinancing, Ken lost his job. Ken's home declined in value to $750,000. Based on Ken's circumstances, the lender agreed to a short sale of the property for $735,000 and to cancel the remaining $115,000 of the $850,000 debt. Under the "ordering rule," Ken can exclude only $5,000 of the canceled debt from his income using the exclusion for canceled QPRI ($115,000 canceled debt minus the $110,000 amount of the debt that was not QPRI—basically the money he spent on personal purchases). Ken must include the remaining $110,000 of canceled debt in income.

## HAMP Loan Modifications

The Home Affordable Modification Program (HAMP) attempts to help financially distressed homeowners lower their monthly mortgage payments. If a borrower continues to make timely payments on the loan for three years, he can have his mortgage reduced by a predetermined amount (known as the PRA Forbearance Amount). The loan holder is then reimbursed through incentive payments by the HAMP program administrator. To the extent the mortgage reduction exceeds the incentive payments, the borrower may be required to include the excess amount in gross income as a discharge of indebtedness. However, the borrower may be eligible to exclude the discharge of indebtedness income from gross income if:

- The mortgage loan is qualified principal residence indebtedness and the loan is modified before January 1, 2014, or

- The discharge of indebtedness occurs when the borrower is insolvent.

Any portion of the discharge of indebtedness that is excluded from income must also be reflected as a reduction in basis.

## Canceled Debt that is Otherwise Deductible

If a taxpayer uses the cash method of accounting, he should not recognize canceled debt income if payment of the debt would have otherwise been a deductible expense.

> **Example:** Jiao is a self-employed interior designer. She receives $2,200 in accounting services for her business on credit. Later, Jiao loses a major account and has trouble paying her debts, so her accountant forgives the amount she owes. Jiao does not include the canceled debt in her gross income because payment of the debt would have been deductible as a business expense anyway.

# Nontaxable Canceled Debt

Besides the QPRI and HAMP rules already discussed, there are other types of canceled debt that qualify for exclusion from gross income. Among the most common are:

- Debt canceled in a Title 11 bankruptcy case
- Debt canceled during insolvency
- Cancellation of qualified farm indebtedness

## Bankruptcy

Debts discharged through bankruptcy court in a Title 11 bankruptcy case are not considered taxable income. The taxpayer must attach Form 982 to his federal income tax return to report debt that is canceled in bankruptcy.

## Insolvency

If a taxpayer is insolvent when the debt is canceled, the canceled debt is not taxable. A taxpayer is "insolvent" when total debts are more than the FMV of his total assets. For purposes of determining insolvency, assets include the value of everything the taxpayer owns, including the value of pensions and retirement accounts.

> **Example:** In 2012, Darla had $5,000 in credit card debt, which she did not pay. She received a Form 1099-C from her credit card company showing canceled debt of $5,000. Darla's total liabilities immediately before the cancellation were $15,000, and the FMV of her total assets immediately before the cancellation was $7,000. This means that at the time the debt was canceled, Darla was insolvent to the extent of $8,000 ($15,000 total liabilities minus $7,000 FMV of her total assets). Therefore, Darla can exclude the entire $5,000 canceled debt from income.

## Qualifying Farm Debts

If a taxpayer incurred the canceled debt in farming, it is generally not considered taxable income.

## Certain Canceled Student Loans are Not Taxable

Certain student loans contain a provision that all or part of the debt incurred to attend a qualified educational institution will be canceled if the student later works for a specified period of time in certain professions. The canceled debt does not have to be recognized as income on a taxpayer's return.

> **Example:** Tatum is a medical student completing her residency. She agrees to work as a doctor in a state program in Minnesota serving rural and poor communities. Tatum agreed to take a job as a pediatrician in the state's rural towns for four years in return for the forgiveness of her student loans. The canceled debt qualifies for nonrecognition treatment, and the canceled debt does not have to be recognized as income.

# 529 Plans

529 plans (also known as "prepaid" qualified tuition programs) are operated by a state or an educational institution to provide tax advantages that make it easier for taxpayers to save for college for their designated beneficiaries. Earnings are not subject to federal income tax, though contributions to a 529 plan are not deductible.

Under a 529 plan, a taxpayer purchases tuition credits or waivers on behalf of a designated beneficiary that entitle the beneficiary to the waiver or payment of qualified higher education expenses. Expenses include tuition, fees, books, computer equipment and software, and room and board for any time the beneficiary is enrolled in college. A beneficiary may be whomever the taxpayer chooses: himself, a child, a grandchild, or an unrelated person.

Contributions cannot exceed the amount necessary to provide for the qualified education expenses of the beneficiary. There may also be gift tax considerations for the taxpayer, depending on how much he contributes to a 529 plan in a given year.

# Gambling Winnings

Gambling winnings are fully taxable and must be reported on a taxpayer's return. Gambling winnings are reported on IRS Form W-2G, and will be sent if a taxpayer wins:

- $600 or more in winnings from gambling
- $1,200 or more in winnings from bingo or slot machines
- $1,500 or more in proceeds from keno
- Or any gambling winnings subject to federal income tax withholding

A taxpayer must report and pay tax on all gambling winnings, regardless of whether he receives a Form W-2G. Gambling income includes winnings from lotteries, raffles, horse races, and casinos. It also includes cash winnings and the fair market value of prizes such as cars and trips.

Gambling losses are deductible, but only on Schedule A as an itemized deduction. The amount of the deduction is limited to the amount of gambling winnings.

---

**Example:** Yolanda had $1,000 in gambling winnings for the year. She had $3,000 in gambling losses. Her deduction for gambling losses cannot exceed $1,000, the amount of her gambling winnings. Yolanda must itemize and list her gambling losses on Schedule A (Form 1040.)

---

An accurate diary or similar record of gambling winnings and losses must be kept along with tickets, receipts, canceled checks, and other documentation. These supporting records need not be sent in with the tax return, but should be retained in case of an audit.

Gambling winnings are reported as "other income" on line 21 of Form 1040.

# Self-Employment Income and SE Tax

Self-employment income is earned by taxpayers who work for themselves. Generally, these are small business owners. Any taxpayer who has self-employment income of $400 or more in a year must file a tax return and report the earnings to the IRS.

Most self-employed people report their income and loss on Schedule C, Form 1040. Self-employed farmers or fishermen report their earnings on Schedule F, Form 1040. Self-employment income also includes:

- Income of ministers, priests, and rabbis for the performance of services such as baptisms and marriages
- The distributive share of partnership income allocated to general partners or managers of a limited liability company, with the income reported to the partner on IRS Form K-1.

Self-employment tax (SE tax) is a tax consisting of Social Security and Medicare taxes primarily for self-employed individuals. It is similar to the Social Security and Medicare taxes withheld from the pay of most wage earners. If an employee is working for an employer, the employer pays half of these taxes and the employee pays the other half. But self-employed people are responsible for paying the entire amount of Social Security and Medicare taxes.

The SE tax rate for 2012 is 13.3% on self-employment income up to $110,100 of a taxpayer's combined wages, tips, and net earnings. If net earnings exceed $110,100, the taxpayer will continue to pay only the Medicare portion of the SE tax, which is 2.9%, on the rest of their earnings.

This SE tax rate for 2012 includes a temporary decrease in the employee's share of payroll tax, with Social Security taxed at a rate of 4.2% rather than the normal 6.2%, up to the Social Security wage limit of $110,100.[34] There is no cap on the 2.9% Medicare tax, which is imposed on all net earnings no matter how high the income (true for both wage earners and self-employed individuals.) If a taxpayer has wages in addition to self-employment earnings, the Social Security tax on the wages is paid first.

---

**Example:** In 2012, Devon has a full-time job and also makes money on weekends as a self-employed musician. In 2012, his wages from his job are $79,000. He also has $35,000 in net earnings from his music business for total income of $115,000. Devon does not pay dual Social Security taxes on his earnings that exceed $110,100. His employer withholds 5.65% in Social Security and Medicare taxes on his $79,000 in wages. That means Devon must pay 13.3% in Social Security and Medicare taxes on his first $31,100 in self-employment earnings and 2.9% in Medicare tax on the remaining $3,900 in earnings.

---

[34] Congress has chosen not to extend this "payroll tax" holiday. That means in tax year 2013 the Social Security tax rate for employees and self-employed individuals rose 2 percentage points to 6.2%. The self-employment tax rate increased from 13.3% to 15.3%, up to the $110,100 income threshold.

There are two income tax deductions related to the self-employment tax that reduce overall taxes on a taxpayer with self-employment income.

- First, net earnings from self-employment are reduced by 7.65% of the total Social Security tax. This is similar to the way employees are treated under the tax laws, because the employer's share of the Social Security tax is not considered wages to the employee.
- Second, the taxpayer can deduct half of the Social Security tax on IRS Form 1040 as an adjustment to gross income.

Self-employment tax is calculated on IRS Schedule SE. If a taxpayer operates more than one business, he may combine the net incomes and use only one Schedule SE.

## *More than One Business*

If a taxpayer runs more than one business, then he will net the profit (or loss) from each to determine the total earnings subject to SE tax. Taxpayers cannot combine a spouse's income (or loss) to determine their individual earnings subject to SE tax. However, a single person with two sole proprietorships may combine income and losses from both businesses to figure self-employment tax.

**Example:** Tanner is a sole proprietor who owns a barbershop. He has $19,000 in net income for 2012. His wife, Erin, has a candle-making business, which has a loss of $12,000 in 2012. Tanner must pay self-employment tax on $19,000, regardless of how he and Erin choose to file. That is because married couples cannot offset each other's self-employment tax. The income of each business is allocated to the individual—not the gross amount shown on a joint tax return.

**Example:** Darren is a single taxpayer who is a sole proprietor with two small businesses, a computer repair shop and a car wash business. The computer business has net income of $45,000 in 2012, while the car wash has a net loss of $23,000 in 2012. Darren only has to pay self-employment tax on $22,000 ($45,000-$23,000) of income, because he may net the income and losses from both his businesses.

## Employee Fringe Benefits (Taxable and Nontaxable)

Fringe benefits are offered to employees by employers as a condition of their employment. Some fringe benefits are taxable and some are not. This next section will cover each type of fringe benefit, both from the perspective of the individual (the employee receiving the benefits) and the business owner (the entity providing the benefits.) Common fringe benefits include health benefits, vacation pay, and parking passes. Although most employee fringe benefits are nontaxable, some benefits must be included in an employee's taxable income and are usually reported on the taxpayer's Form W-2. Examples of *taxable* fringe benefits include:

- Off-site athletic facilities and health club memberships.
- The value of employer-provided life insurance over $50,000.

- Any cash benefit or benefit in the form of a credit card or gift card.
- Season tickets to sporting events, although single tickets can be excluded in certain cases.
- Transportation benefits, if the value of a benefit for any month is more than the nontaxable limit. Employers cannot exclude the excess from the employee's wages as a *de minimis* transportation benefit.
- Employer-provided vehicles, if they are used for personal purposes.

**Example:** Tanning Town Inc. owns a tropical resort employees may use free of charge. Sam visits the resort with his family for two weeks. The fair market value of the stay is $5,000, which will be included in his taxable wages.

# Nontaxable Employee Fringe Benefits

Most fringe benefits are not taxable and may be excluded from an employee's income. The following are some common types of nontaxable employee fringe benefits.

## Cafeteria Plans

A *cafeteria plan* provides employees an opportunity to receive certain benefits on a pretax basis. An employer may choose to make benefits available to employees, their spouses, and dependents. Generally, qualified benefits under a cafeteria plan are not subject to FICA, FUTA, Medicare tax, or income tax withholding.

Employee contributions to the cafeteria plan are usually made via salary reduction agreements taken directly out of the employee's paycheck. The employee usually agrees to contribute a portion of his salary on a pretax basis to pay for a portion of the qualified benefits.

Participants in a cafeteria plan must be permitted to choose among at least one taxable benefit (such as cash) and one qualified benefit. A qualified benefit is a benefit that is nontaxable. Qualified benefits include:

- Accident, dental, vision, and medical benefits (but not Archer medical savings accounts or long-term care insurance)
- Adoption assistance
- Dependent care assistance
- Group-term life insurance coverage (up to $50,000 of life insurance coverage may be provided as a nontaxable benefit to an employee.)
- Health savings accounts

**\*Note:** If an employer pays the cost of an accident insurance plan for an employee, then the amounts received under the plan are taxable to the employee. If a taxpayer pays the cost of an accident insurance plan for himself, then the benefits received under the plan are not taxable.

# Flexible Spending Arrangement (FSA)

An FSA is a form of cafeteria plan benefit, funded by salary reduction, which reimburses employees for expenses incurred for certain qualified benefits. An FSA may be offered for dependent care assistance, adoption assistance, and medical care reimbursements. The benefits are subject to an annual maximum and an annual "use-or-lose" rule. An FSA cannot provide a cumulative benefit to the employee beyond the plan year. The employee must substantiate his expenses, and then the distributions to the employee are tax-free.

## Dependent Care Assistance

An employee can generally exclude from gross income up to $5,000 in 2012 ($2,500 if MFS) of benefits received under a dependent care assistance program each year. Amounts paid directly to the taxpayer or to a daycare provider qualify for exclusion. The amount that qualifies for exclusion is limited to:

- The total amount of the dependent care benefits received
- The employee's earned income
- The spouse's earned income
- $5,000 ($2,500 if married filing separately)

**Example:** John's employer offers a cafeteria plan that allows for dependent care assistance. John files jointly with his wife, Cindy. John makes $50,000 in 2012. Cindy earns $4,500 as a part-time bookkeeper. They have $5,500 in daycare costs for 2012. The maximum amount that can be excluded in 2012 is $4,500, the amount of Cindy's earned income.

**Example:** Tina's employer provides a dependent care assistance flexible spending plan to its employees through a cafeteria plan. In addition, it provides occasional onsite dependent care to its employees at no cost. Tina had $4,500 deducted from her pay for the dependent care flexible spending arrangement. She also used the on-site dependent care several times. The FMV of the on-site care was $700. Tina's Form W-2 will report $5,200 of dependent care assistance ($4,500 flexible spending + $700 FMV of on-site dependent care.) Since the IRS only allows an exclusion of $5,000 in dependent care assistance per year, Boxes 1, 3, and 5 of her Form W-2 should include $200 (the amount in excess of the nontaxable assistance), and applicable taxes should be withheld on that amount.

## De Minimis Employee Benefits

Some employee benefits are so small that it would be impractical for the employer to account for them. These are called *de minimis* benefits. The exclusion applies, for example, to the following items:

- Coffee, doughnuts, or soft drinks provided to employees
- Occasional meals while employees work overtime (100% of the cost)

118

- Occasional company picnics for employees
- Occasional use of the employer's copy machine
- Holiday gifts, other than cash, such as a Thanksgiving turkey
- An employer-provided cell phone

**De Minimis Meals:** Meals that are provided to an employee at his place of work and that are for the employer's convenience are not taxable to the employee. They are also 100% deductible by the employer and not subject to the normal 50% limit.[35] Meals that employers furnish to a restaurant employee during, immediately before, or after the employee's working hours are considered furnished for the employer's convenience.

---

**Example:** Ellen is a registered nurse who is not allowed to leave the hospital premises during her long shifts. She works in the emergency room and must be available to help patients immediately, so the hospital provides meals and a place for her to sleep during her shift. Ellen does not have to recognize the value of the meals as income. The hospital also does not have to add the FMV of Ellen's meals to her wages. In addition, the meals are 100% deductible by the hospital, not subject to the 50% limit, because they are provided as a condition of her employment and are for the convenience of her employer.

---

**Example:** A commuter ferry breaks down unexpectedly, and the engineers are required to work overtime to make repairs. After working eight hours, the engineers break for dinner because they will be working overtime until the engine is repaired. The supervisor gives each employee $10 for a meal. The meal is not taxable to the engineers because it was provided to permit them to work overtime in a situation that is not routine.

---

# Employer-Provided Cell Phones

The value of the business use of an employer-provided cell phone is excludable from an employee's income to the extent that, if the employee paid for its use, the payment would be deductible. The IRS has ruled that there must be substantial "noncompensatory" reasons for use of a phone that relate to the employer's business.

Legitimate reasons include the employer's need to contact the employee at all times for work-related emergencies and the employee's need to be available to speak with clients away from the office. However, a cell phone provided simply to promote an employee's morale or to attract a prospective employee is not noncompensatory. In those cases, the value of a cell phone would no longer be a de minimis benefit and must be added to an employee's wages.

---

[35] Meals are generally 50% deductible. This means when a business pays for a meal, only 50% of its cost is normally deductible by the employer, except in certain situations such as those described above.

If an employer provides an employee with a cell phone primarily for noncompensatory business purposes, then personal use of the phone also is excludable from an employee's income as a *de minimis* fringe benefit.[36]

**\*NOTE:** Most *cash* benefits or their equivalent (such as gift cards or credit cards) cannot be excluded as de *minimis* fringe benefits, except in certain cases of minimal amounts given for meals or transportation.

## No-Additional-Cost Services

Nontaxable fringe benefits include services provided to employees that do not impose any substantial additional cost because the employer already offers those services in the ordinary course of doing business. Employees do not need to include these no-additional-cost services in their income.

An employer can offer discounts, as well as on-site benefits, such as an on-site gym.

If an employee is provided with the free or low cost use of a health club on the employer's premises, the value is not included in the employee's compensation. The gym must be used primarily by employees, their spouses, and their dependent children. If the employer pays for a fitness program provided to the employee at an off-site resort hotel, country club, or athletic club, the value of the program is included in the employee's compensation.

| |
|---|
| **Example:** Trey works for a local fitness club. He is allowed to work out for free as a condition of his employment. This is because this fringe benefit is a no-additional-cost service to his employer. Trey is also allowed a 10% discount on vitamins that the gym sells to patrons, so long as the vitamins are for his own use (Publication 15-B). |

Typically, no-additional-cost services are excess capacity services, such as airline, bus, or train tickets; hotel rooms; or telephone services provided free or at a reduced rate to employees working in those lines of business.

| |
|---|
| **Example:** Henrietta is a flight attendant with Jet Way Airlines. She is allowed to fly for free on stand-by flights when there is an extra seat. This is an example of a fringe benefit that is allowed for no additional cost to the employer and is therefore nontaxable to the employee. |

# Employer-Provided Educational Assistance

An employer-provided educational assistance program can be excluded up to a certain amount. The amounts must be for tuition, books, required fees, and supplies. Room and board do not qualify as educational expenses for purposes of an employer-sponsored educational assistance plan.

---

[36] IRS Notice 2011-72.

The maximum excluded educational benefit is $5,250 in 2012. If an employee receives these employer-provided benefits, he cannot use any of the tax-free education expenses as the basis for any other education-related deduction or credit.

# Transportation Fringe Benefits

Employers may provide transportation benefits to their employees up to certain amounts without having to include the benefit in the employee's income. Qualified transportation benefits include transit passes, paid parking, a ride in a commuter highway vehicle between the employee's home and workplace, and qualified bicycle commuting reimbursement.

In 2012, employees may exclude:

- $240 per month in combined commuter highway vehicle transportation and transit passes,[37] and
- $240 per month in parking benefits.

This nontaxable benefit is a combined maximum of $480 per month in 2012. Employees may receive transit passes and benefits for parking during the same month; they are not mutually exclusive.

An employer may also reimburse an employee for a bicycle that is used for commuting purposes. A qualified bicycle commuting reimbursement is a reimbursement of up to $20 per month for reasonable expenses incurred by the employee in conjunction with his commute to work by bike.

However, the use of a company car for commuting purposes is a taxable benefit. So, if an employer allows an employee to use a company vehicle for commuting, then the value of the vehicle's use is taxable to the employee.

Personal use of an employer's vehicle is also considered taxable wages to the employee.

> **Example:** Joe, an employee of Carsonville Lumber Company, uses an employer-provided pickup truck. He uses the truck on job sites, to haul equipment, and to deliver lumber to customers. In 2012, Joe drives the truck 20,000 miles, of which 4,000 were personal miles or 20% (4,000/20,000 = 20%). The truck has an annual lease value of $4,100. Personal use is therefore valued at $820 and is included in Joe's wages.

---

[37] Congress's fiscal cliff legislation of January 1, 2013 retroactively reinstated parity between the benefits for parking and transit benefits for 2012. The parity had expired at the end of 2011, so that for all of 2012 employers had expected the amount excluded for commuter highway vehicles or transit passes to be $125 a month, not $240. The IRS has issued guidance on FICA tax refunds and W-2 adjustments for businesses that gave transit benefits of more than $125 a month in 2012. Employers that treated the excess as wages can make adjustments, but they will have to reimburse their employees for the over-collected FICA tax before doing so.

# Accountable Plans

An accountable plan is a plan in which an employer reimburses employees for business-related expenses such as mileage, meals, and travel expenses. For expenses to qualify under an accountable plan, employees must meet all of the following requirements:

- Have incurred the expenses while performing services as employees
- Adequately account for the expenses within a reasonable period of time
- Adequately account for their travel, meals, and entertainment expenses
- Provide evidence of their employee business expenses, such as receipts or other records
- Return any excess reimbursement or allowance within a reasonable period of time

Under an accountable plan, a business may advance money to employees; however, certain conditions must be met. The cash advance must be reasonably calculated to equal the anticipated expenses. The business owner must make the advance within a reasonable period of time. If any expenses reimbursed under this arrangement are not substantiated, a business is not allowed to deduct them under an accountable plan.

Instead, the reimbursed expenses are considered a nonaccountable plan and become taxable to the employee.

**Example:** Donna is an EA who runs a tax preparation business. She advances $250 to her employee, Mel, so that he can become a notary. Mel spends $90 on a notary course and then another $100 to take the notary exam, which he passes. Mel returns the unused funds ($60) as well as copies of his receipts to Donna, his boss. The expenses are qualified expenses under an accountable plan. Donna may deduct the $190 ($90 + $100) as a business expense, and the amounts are not taxable to Mel.

Cash reimbursements are excludable if an employer establishes a bona fide reimbursement plan. This means there must be reasonable procedures to verify reimbursements and employees must substantiate the expenses using receipts or other substantiation.

**Example:** Mai Ling buys a parking permit for $240 each month in 2012. At the end of each month, she presents her used parking pass to her employer and certifies that she purchased and used it during the month. The employer reimburses her $240 in cash. The employer has established a bona fide reimbursement arrangement for purposes of excluding the $240 reimbursement from the employee's gross income in 2012. The reimbursement is not taxable to Mai Ling, and it is deductible by the employer.

# Accountable Plans: Travel Reimbursements

Qualifying expenses for travel are excludable from an employee's income if they are incurred for *temporary* travel on business away from the area of the employee's tax home. Travel expenses paid in connection with an indefinite work assignment are not excludable. Any work assignment in excess of one year is considered "indefinite." Travel expense reimbursements include:

- Costs to travel to and from the business destination (flights, mileage reimbursements)
- Transportation costs while at the business destination (taxi fare, shuttles)
- Lodging, meals, and incidental expenses
- Cleaning, laundry, and other miscellaneous expenses

**Example:** Woody works for a travel agency in Detroit. He flies to Seattle to conduct business for an entire week. His employer pays the cost of transportation to and from Seattle, as well as lodging and meals while there. The reimbursements for substantiated travel expenses are excludable from Woody's income, and the reimbursements are deductible by his employer.

## Employer-Provided Life Insurance as a Fringe Benefit

Employers may deduct the cost of life insurance premiums provided to employees. Employer-provided life insurance is a nontaxable fringe benefit only up to $50,000. Coverage amounts over $50,000 are taxable to the employee. The employer must calculate the taxable portion of the premiums for coverage that exceeds $50,000.

**Example:** Carol, a 47-year-old employee, receives $40,000 of life insurance coverage per year under a policy carried by her employer. Her employer agrees to pay the premiums on the first $40,000 of coverage as part of Carol's cafeteria plan. She may also elect another $100,000 of additional life insurance coverage. This optional coverage is also carried by her employer. The cost of $10,000 of this additional amount is excludable; the cost of the remaining $90,000 of coverage is included in income. Since only $50,000 of life insurance coverage can be nontaxable to the employee, Carol will be taxed on the difference between the premiums.

# Employer-Provided Retirement Plan Contributions

Many employers contribute to their employees' retirement plans. This contribution is not taxable to the employee when it is made. The contribution only becomes taxable when the employee finally withdraws the funds from his retirement account.[38]

This rule also applies to elected deferrals. Employees may elect to have part of their pretax compensation contributed to a retirement fund. An elective deferral is

---

[38] The IRS has very detailed rules for retirement plans, and they are often tested on the EA exam. Retirement plans are covered extensively in Unit 14, *Individual Retirement Arrangements*.

excluded from wages, but is still subject to Social Security and Medicare tax. Elective deferrals include contributions into the following retirement plans:

- 401(k) plans, 403(B) plans, section 457 plans
- SIMPLE plans
- Thrift Savings Plans for federal employees

Elective deferrals to a Roth retirement plan are taxable to the employee. That is because a Roth plan is always funded with post-tax income. Roth IRAs are tax-free when they are withdrawn.

## Special Rules for Highly Compensated Employees (HCEs)

If a benefit plan favors highly compensated employees, the value of their benefits become taxable. There cannot be special rules that favor eligibility for HCEs to participate, contribute, or benefit from a cafeteria plan. This is to discourage companies from offering spectacular tax-free benefits to their highly compensated executives, while ignoring the needs of lower-paid employees.

An HCE is any of the following:

- an officer
- a shareholder who owns more than 5% of the voting power or value of all classes of the employer's stock
- an employee who is highly compensated based on the facts and circumstances; or
- a spouse or dependent of a person described above.

Employer-provided benefits also cannot favor "key employees," defined as:

- An officer with annual pay of more than $165,000 in 2012, or
- An employee who is either a 5% owner of the business or a 1% owner of the business whose annual pay was more than $150,000 in 2012.

The law for highly compensated employees includes a "look-back provision," so employees who were previously considered HCEs are generally still considered HCEs for 2012 plan year testing (Publication 15-B).

---

**Example:** Fengrew Inc. is a C Corporation with 300 employees, 45 of whom are considered "highly compensated employees." Fengrew's cafeteria plan is available to all the employees; therefore, the discrimination rules do not apply, and the employees' benefits are not taxable.

---

If a plan favors HCE or key employees, the employer is required to include the value of the benefits they could have selected in their wages. A plan is considered to have "favored" HCEs if over 25% of all the benefits are given to HCEs.

A benefit plan that covers union employees under a collective bargaining agreement is not included in this rule.

# Interest Income

Interest is a passive form of income received from bank accounts and other sources.

Interest income is reported to the taxpayer on IRS Form 1099-INT. If interest income exceeds $1,500, the taxpayer must report the interest on Schedule B (Form 1040). A taxpayer cannot file Form 1040EZ if his interest income exceeds $1,500.

Tax-exempt interest is reported on page one of IRS Form 1040.

The following are some other sources of taxable interest:

- Credit unions (which uses the term "dividends," but the IRS has ruled it should actually be considered interest)
- Domestic building and loan associations
- Domestic savings and loan associations
- Federal savings and loan associations
- Mutual savings banks
- Certificates of deposits (CDs) and other deferred interest accounts

## Gift for Opening a Bank Account

If a taxpayer receives noncash gifts or services for making deposits or for opening an account in a savings institution, the value of the gift may have to be reported as interest. For deposits of less than $5,000, gifts or services valued at more than $10 must be reported as interest. For deposits of $5,000 or more, gifts or services valued at more than $20 must be reported as interest. The value of the gift is determined by the financial institution.

A cash bonus for opening a new checking or credit card account is also taxable interest. However, the IRS has ruled that cash back and reward points earned on credit and debit card purchases are not taxable interest income.

### Interest on Insurance Dividends

Interest on insurance dividends left on deposit with an insurance company that can be withdrawn annually is taxable in the year it is credited to the taxpayer's account. However, if the taxpayer cannot withdraw the income except on a certain date (the anniversary date of the policy or other specified date), the income is considered restricted and not taxable when it is earned. The interest is taxable in the year that the withdrawal is allowed.

### Interest Earned on U.S. Treasury Bills, Notes, and Bonds

Interest on U.S. obligations, such as U.S. Treasury bills, notes, and bonds issued by any agency of the United States, is taxable for federal income tax purposes.

**\*Special note:** The interest a taxpayer pays on loans borrowed from a bank to meet the minimum deposit required for a CD and the interest a taxpayer earns on the

CD are two separate things. The taxpayer must include the total interest earned on the CD in income. If the taxpayer itemizes deductions, he can deduct the interest paid as investment interest paid, up to the amount of net investment income.

**Example:** Sienna wanted to invest in a $10,000 six-month CD. She deposited $5,000 in a CD with a credit union and borrowed $5,000 from another bank to make up the $10,000 minimum deposit required to buy the six-month CD. The certificate earned $575 at maturity in 2012, but Sienna actually received net $265 in interest income that year. This represented the $575 Sienna earned on the CD, minus $310 interest charged on the $5,000 loan. The credit union gives Sienna a Form 1099-INT for 2012 showing the $575 interest she earned. The other bank also gives Sienna a statement showing that she paid $310 interest for 2012. Sienna must include the total interest amount earned, $575, in her interest income for 2012. Only if Sienna itemizes can she deduct the interest expense of $310.

# Wages and Employee Compensation

Wages, salaries, bonuses, and commissions are compensation received by employees for services performed. All income from wages, salaries, and tips is taxable to the employee and deductible by the employer. Employers are generally required to issue Form W-2s by January 31, which show the amount of wages paid to employees for the previous year. Wages are reported by the employee as taxable income on Form 1040.

Employers are required by law to withhold Social Security and Medicare taxes. If the employer fails to withhold Social Security and Medicare, the employee is required to file IRS Form 8919, *Uncollected Social Security and Medicare Tax on Wages.*

Advance commissions and other advance earnings are all taxable in the year they are received, whether or not the employee has earned the income. If the employee receives wages in advance, he must recognize the income in the year it is constructively received.

This is true even if the employee is forced to pay back some of the money at a later date. If the employee later pays back a portion of the earnings, that sum would be deducted from wages at that time.

**Example:** Maddox requests a salary advance of $1,000 on December 18, 2012 in order to go on a two-week vacation. Maddox must recognize the income on his 2012 tax return, even though he will not actually earn the money until 2013, when he returns from his vacation.

"Supplemental wages" is compensation that is paid to an employee in addition to his regular pay. These amounts are listed on the employee's Form W-2 and are taxable just like regular wages, even if the pay is not actually for work performed. Vacation pay is an example of supplemental wages that is taxable just like any other wage income, even though the employee has not technically "worked" for the income. Supplemental wages include:

- Bonuses, commissions, prizes
- Severance pay, back pay, and holiday pay
- Accumulated vacation pay and sick leave
- Payment for nondeductible moving expenses

Severance pay is taxable as ordinary income, just like wages. Even though severance pay is usually issued to employees who are being terminated and is not actually for work performed, it is still taxable to the employee and still subject to Social Security and Medicare tax. Unemployment benefits are taxable income. However, all forms of welfare benefits, such as food stamps and heating assistance programs, are exempt from federal taxation. Non-federal assistance benefits from a state or local agencies are also exempt.

## Reporting Tip Income

Tips received by food servers, baggage handlers, hairdressers, and others for performing services are taxable as ordinary income. Individuals who receive $20 or more per month in tips must report their tip income to their employer. Employers must withhold Social Security, Medicare, and income taxes due on reported tips. The employer withholds FICA taxes due on tips from the employee's wages and pays both employer and employee portions of the tax in the same manner as the tax on the employee's regular wages.

Taxpayers who do not report all of their tips to their employer must report the Social Security and Medicare taxes on their Form 1040. Employees use Form 4137, *Social Security and Medicare Tax on Unreported Tip Income,* to compute and report the additional tax.

Taxpayers who are *self-employed* and receive tips must include their tips in gross receipts on Schedule C. Examples of this type of taxpayer include self-employed hair stylists and manicurists.

---

**Example:** Lydia works two jobs. She is an administrative assistant during the week and a bartender on the weekends. She reports all of her tip income ($3,000) to her employer. Her Forms W-2 show wage income of $21,000 (assistant) and $8,250 (bartender). Lydia must report $29,250 on her Form 1040, which is the total amount earned at both jobs. Lydia reported the tip income to her employer, so her bartending tips are already included on her Form W-2 for that job, so the amount she reports is $21,000 + $8,250.

---

Individuals who receive *less than* $20 per month in tips while working one job do not have to report their tip income to their employer. While all tips are subject to income tax, tips of less than $20 per month are:

- Exempt from Social Security and Medicare taxes

- Still subject to federal income tax and must be reported on Form 1040

Noncash tips (for example, concert tickets or other items) do not have to be reported to the employer, but they must be reported and included in the taxpayer's income at their fair market value.

## Garnished Wages

An employee may have his wages garnished for many different reasons. Sometimes the employee owes child support, back taxes due, or other debts. Regardless of how much is actually garnished from the employee's paycheck, the full amount (the gross wages) is taxable to the employee and must be included in the employee's wages at year end.

## Disability Retirement Benefits

Disability retirement benefits are taxable as wages if a taxpayer retired on disability before reaching the minimum retirement age. Once the taxpayer reaches retirement age, the payments are no longer taxable as wages. They are then taxable as pension income.

## Disability Payments from an Insurance Policy

Disability income benefits from an insurance policy are excluded from income if the taxpayer pays the premiums for the policy. For health insurance paid for by the employer, the employer deducts the cost and the employee pays no tax on the premiums paid by the employer. The employee also does not pay any tax on the benefits received.

Sick pay is not the same thing as "disability pay." Sick pay is always taxable as wages, just like vacation pay.

## Property In Lieu Of Wages

An employee who receives property instead of wages for services performed must generally recognize the FMV of the property when it is received. However, if an employee receives stock or other property that is restricted, the property is not included in income until it is available without restriction to the employee.

---

**Example:** As part of his promotion, Barry's company gives him $5,000 worth of stock, a total of 500 shares. However, he cannot sell or exercise the shares for five years. If Barry quits his job, he forfeits the shares. He does not have to recognize this restricted stock as income in the year he received it. This is because the stock is subject to multiple restrictions. This stock will be taxable when Barry chooses to sell it or otherwise gains complete control over it.

---

# Military Pay Exclusion-Combat Zone Wages

Wages earned by military personnel are generally taxable. However, there are special rules for military personnel regarding taxable income, including many exclusions for those on active duty.

Combat zone wages and hazardous duty pay are excludable for certain military personnel. Enlisted persons who serve in a combat zone for any part of a month may exclude their pay from tax. For officers, pay is excluded up to a certain amount, depending on the branch of service.

> **Example:** Lee is a Navy pilot who served in a combat zone from January 1, 2012 to November 3, 2012. He will only be required to report his income for December 2012, because all of the other income is excluded from taxation as combat zone pay. Even though Lee only served three days in November in a combat zone, his income for the entire month of November is excluded.

## Substitute W-2 Form

If for some reason an employee does not receive his Form W-2 (perhaps the employer went out of business), the employee may file his tax return on paper using IRS Form 4852, *Substitute for Form W-2, Wage and Tax Statement*. An earnings statement or similar document may be used to re-create the data required in order to complete and file the taxpayer's return.

> **Example:** Manny worked for a plumbing company in 2012. In December 2012, the owner died, and final payroll returns were not filed. The business was closed and Manny never received a Form W-2 for the wages he earned in 2012. Manny may file a Form 4852 instead, explaining the circumstances why he could not obtain a W-2. Then Manny may use his earnings statement or other records to attempt to re-create his taxable income and withholding.

## Barter Exchanges and Barter Income

Bartering is an exchange of property or services, usually without an exchange of cash. Barter may take place on an informal, one-on-one basis between individuals and businesses, or it may occur on a third party basis through a barter exchange company.

While our ancestors may have exchanged eggs for corn, today a person can barter a variety of services: computer tune-ups for auto repair, or dental work for carpet cleaning, for example. The FMV must be reported as income by both parties in the year the goods were exchanged or services sold.

If two people have agreed ahead of time as to the value of the services, the agreed-upon value will be accepted as the fair market value.

> **Example:** Brayden builds custom kitchen cabinets. Annemarie is a veterinarian. In 2012, Brayden builds new cabinets for Annemarie's kitchen, and she performs hip dysplasia surgery on Brayden's German shepherd. They agree in advance that the cost for the kitchen cabinets and the surgery is $2,500. They each must report $2,500 in income on their 2012 tax returns.

# Alimony (as Income to the Recipient)

The concept of alimony needs to be understood in two ways: from the perspective of the payer and the payee. In this section, we will cover the concept of alimony as income to the recipient.

Alimony is *taxable income* to the recipient and *deductible* by the payer.

**Example:** Mark and Sibba are divorced. Their divorce decree calls for Mark to pay Sibba $200 a month as child support and $150 a month as alimony. Mark makes all of his child support and alimony payments on time. Therefore, in 2012, Mark may deduct $1,800 ($150 X 12 months) as alimony paid and Sibba must report $1,800 as alimony received. The amount paid as child support, $2,400 ($200 X 12), is not deductible by Mark and is not reported as income by Sibba.

Alimony paid is an adjustment to income for the payer, and is taxable to the receiving spouse as ordinary income. Spouses do not have to itemize in order to deduct their alimony payments. The alimony paid is listed on the first page of Form 1040; Form 1040A or Form 1040EZ cannot be used.

If a divorce agreement specifies payments of both alimony and child support and only partial payments are made by the payer, then the partial payments are considered to be child support until this obligation is fully paid. Any excess is then treated as alimony. Child support is not taxable income to the receiver and not deductible by the payer.

**Example:** Sandra and Jessie are divorced. Their divorce decree calls for Jessie to pay Sandra $2,000 a month ($24,000 [$2,000 x 12] a year) as child support and $1,500 a month ($18,000 [$1,500 x 12] a year) as alimony. Jessie falls behind on his payments and only manages to pay $36,000. In this case, $24,000 is considered child support and only the remaining amount is considered alimony. Jessie can deduct only $12,000 ($36,000 - $24,000) as alimony paid. Sandra would report $12,000 as alimony income received.

If the payment amount is to be reduced based on a contingency *relating to a child* (e.g., attaining a certain age, marrying), the amount of the reduction will be treated as child support.

It is important to remember that child support is not alimony, as the IRS treats the two very differently. Child support is never deductible because it is viewed as a payment that a parent is making simply for the support of his child.

Also, any alimony payments that continue after the receiving spouse has died will automatically be considered child support, not alimony.

> **Example:** Under Cary's divorce decree, he must pay his ex-wife, Eugenia, $30,000 per year. The payments will stop after 15 years or upon Eugenia's death. The divorce decree provided that if Eugenia dies before the end of the 15-year period, Cary must still pay Eugenia's estate the difference between $450,000 ($30,000 annually × 15 years) and the total amount paid up to that time. Eugenia dies at the end of the tenth year, and Cary must pay her estate $150,000 ($450,000 − $300,000). Since the payment is required even after Eugenia's death, none of the annual payments are considered alimony for tax purposes. The payments are actually "disguised child support" and cannot be deducted by Cary as alimony.

Alimony payments made under a divorce agreement are deductible by the payer if all of the following requirements are met:

- The spouses may not file joint returns with each other.
- Payments are made in cash or a cash equivalent (such as checks or money orders). Payments made to a third party can be considered alimony. For example, if one spouse pays the medical bills of his ex-wife, the cash payment to the hospital can count as alimony.

> **Example:** Ben is required to pay $1,000 per month in alimony to Karen, his former spouse. Karen has a medical bill of $1,500 that Ben agrees to pay in lieu of the regular alimony payment. The $1,500 would qualify as alimony payment to a third party, since it was made on Karen's behalf to her creditor.

In order for a payment to qualify as alimony:

- The divorce agreement may not include a clause indicating that the payment is something else (such as child support or repayment of a loan, etc.)
- If the spouses are legally separated, the spouses cannot live together when the payments are made.
- The payer must have no liability to make any payment (in cash or property) after the death of the former spouse.

Alimony does not include:

- Child support
- Payments that are community income
- Payments to keep up the payer's property
- Free use of the payer's property
- Noncash property settlements

Property settlements, which are simply a division of property, are not treated as alimony. Property transferred to a former spouse incident to a divorce is treated as a gift. "Incident to a divorce" means a transfer of property within one year after the date of the divorce, or a transfer of property related to the cessation of the marriage, as determined by the courts.

# Securities Income (Dividends from Stocks & Bonds)

Investors typically buy and sell securities and then report income from dividends, interest, or capital appreciation. The income that is earned on these investments is reported on Schedule B. A taxpayer must file Schedule B, *Interest and Ordinary Dividends*, when any of the following apply:

- The taxpayer had over $1,500 of taxable interest or ordinary dividends.
- The taxpayer is claiming the education exclusion of interest from series EE savings bonds.
- The taxpayer received ordinary dividends as a nominee. "Nominee interest" occurs when a taxpayer receives a 1099-INT form, but the interest really belongs to another party. This is very common when taxpayers set up accounts for family members and minor children.
- The taxpayer had foreign accounts or received a distribution from a foreign trust.
- The taxpayer received interest as part of a seller-financed mortgage.

## A. Ordinary Dividends

A "dividend" is a distribution of income made by a corporation to its shareholders, out of net earnings and profits. Ordinary dividends are corporate distributions in cash (as opposed to property or stock shares). Amounts received as dividends are taxed as ordinary income. Dividends are passive income, so they are not subject to self-employment tax.

Any distribution *in excess* of earnings and profits (both current and accumulated) is considered a recovery of capital and is therefore not taxable. Distributions in excess of earnings and profits reduce the taxpayer's basis. Once basis is reduced to zero, any additional distributions are capital gain and are taxed as such.

Ordinary dividends are reported to the taxpayer on Form 1099-DIV on Schedule B. If the total dividend income is $1,500 or less, all of the income can be reported directly on page one of IRS Form 1040.

## B. Qualified Dividends

Qualified dividends are given preferred tax treatment. They must meet specific criteria in order to receive the lower maximum tax rate that applies to capital gains. Qualified dividends are reported to the taxpayer on Form 1099-DIV. Qualified dividends are subject to a 15% tax rate if the taxpayer's regular tax rate is 25% or higher. If the taxpayer's regular tax rate is under 25%, the qualified dividends are subject to a zero percent rate, which means they are essentially nontaxable. In order for the dividends to qualify for the lower rate, all of the following requirements must be met:

- The dividends must have been paid by a U.S. corporation or a qualified foreign corporation.

- The taxpayer must meet the holding period. The taxpayer must have held the stock for more than 60 days during the 121-day period that begins 60 days before the ex-dividend date. The ex-dividend date is the date *following* the dec-declaration of a dividend.

When trying to figure the holding period for qualified dividends, the taxpayer may count the number of days he held the stock and include the day he disposed of the stock. The date the taxpayer *acquires* the stock is not included in the holding period.

---

**Example:** Israel bought 5,000 shares of Sundowner Corp. stock on July 9, 2012. Sundowner Corp. paid a cash dividend of 10 cents per share. The ex-dividend date was July 17, 2012. Israel's Form 1099-DIV from Sundowner Corp. shows $500 in dividends. However, Israel sold the 5,000 shares on August 12, 2012. Israel held his shares of Sundowner Corp. for only 34 days of the 121-day required holding period. The 121-day period began on May 18, 2012 (60 days before the ex-dividend date) and ended on September 15, 2012. Israel has no qualified dividends from Sundowner Corp. because he held the Sundowner stock for less than the required 61 days. He does not qualify for the preferred tax treatment that is given to qualified dividends.

---

## C. Mutual Fund Distributions/Capital Gain Distributions

Taxpayers who receive mutual fund distributions during the year will also receive IRS Form 1099-DIV identifying the type of distribution received. A distribution may be an ordinary dividend, a qualified dividend, a capital gain distribution, an exempt-interest dividend, or a nondividend distribution. Mutual fund distributions can be reported on Form 1040 or Form 1040A, but not on Form 1040EZ.

Mutual fund distributions are reported depending upon the character of the income source. Capital gain distributions from a mutual fund are *always* treated as long-term *regardless* of the actual period the mutual fund investment is held.

Distributions from a mutual fund investing in tax-exempt securities will be tax-exempt interest. In some cases, a mutual fund may pay tax-exempt interest dividends, paid from tax-exempt interest earned by the fund. Since the exempt-interest dividends keep their tax-exempt character, they are not taxable. Even so, the taxpayer must report them on his tax return. This is an information reporting requirement only, and does not convert tax-exempt interest to taxable interest. However, this income is generally a "tax preference item" and may be subject to the alternative minimum tax.

The mutual fund will supply the taxpayer with a Form 1099-INT showing the tax-exempt interest dividends.

If a mutual fund or Real Estate Investment Trust (REIT) declares a dividend in October, November, or December payable to shareholders but actually pays the dividend during January of the following year, the shareholder is still considered to have received the dividend on December 31 of the prior tax year. The taxpayer must report the dividend in the year it was declared.

## D. Stock Dividends

A stock dividend is simply a distribution of stock by a corporation to its own shareholders. This happens when a corporation chooses to distribute stock rather than money. A stock dividend is also called a "stock grant" or a "stock distribution."

Generally, a stock dividend is not a taxable event. This is because the receiver of the stock (a shareholder) is not actually receiving any money. A nontaxable stock dividend does not affect a taxpayer's income in the year of distribution. A stock dividend will affect a shareholder's basis in his existing stock. The basis of the stockholder's existing shares is divided to include the new stock. So a stock dividend will essentially reduce basis.

---

**Example:** Razor Ball Corporation agrees to a year-end stock dividend. Scarlett is a shareholder in Razor Ball. She currently owns 100 shares, and her basis in the shares is $50 each, for a total of $5,000. Scarlett is granted a stock dividend of 100 shares. After the dividend, Scarlett owns 200 shares. Her new basis in each individual share is $25 per share. However, her overall basis in the shares does not change (it is still $5,000). Scarlett would recognize income when she decided to sell the shares.

---

**\*Exception:** If the taxpayer (shareholder) has the option to receive *cash instead of stock*, then the stock dividend becomes taxable. The recipient of the stock must include the FMV of the stock in his gross income. That amount then becomes the basis of the new shares received.

---

**Example:** The Jausta Corporation agrees to issue a year-end stock dividend. Dale owns 1,000 shares in Jausta, and his current basis in the shares is $10 each, for a total of $10,000. In 2012, Dale is granted a stock dividend of 100 shares, but Jausta gives all the shareholders the option of receiving cash instead of stock. Therefore, the stock dividend becomes a taxable event. Dale decides to take the stock instead of the cash. The FMV of the stock at the time of the distribution is $15 per share. Dale must recognize $1,500 in income ($15 FMV X 100 shares=$1,500). After the dividend, Dale owns 1,100 shares and his basis in the new shares is $15 per share. Dale's basis in the old shares remains the same.

---

## Social Security Benefits

Usually, if the taxpayer *only* has Social Security income, the income is not taxable, and a taxpayer is not required to file a tax return.

Social Security benefits *become* taxable once the taxpayer starts to receive other types of income, such as wages or interest income. The taxable portion of Social Security benefits is never more than 85%. In most cases, the taxable portion is less than 50%.[39]

---

[39] Social Security income is not the same as Supplemental Security Income (SSI). SSI is a federal income supplement program for the poor and the disabled, and is not taxable.

To better understand the thresholds, if a taxpayer is filing single or HOH and combined income* is:

- Between $25,000 and $34,000 the taxpayer may have to pay income tax on up to 50% of Social Security benefits.
- More than $34,000, up to 85% of Social Security benefits may be taxable.

If a taxpayer filed jointly and combined income* is

- Between $32,000 and $44,000, the taxpayer may have to pay income tax on up to 50% of Social Security benefits.
- More than $44,000, up to 85% of Social Security benefits may be taxable.

If a taxpayer is filing MFS, he will probably pay taxes on his Social Security benefits.

| *Formula: The taxpayer's adjusted gross income |
| :---: |
| + Nontaxable interest |
| + ½ of Social Security benefits |
| = "combined income" |

If the taxpayer also received other income in addition to Social Security, such as income from a job, the benefits will not be taxed unless modified adjusted gross income (MAGI) is more than the base amount for the taxpayer's filing status.

To figure the taxable portion of Social Security, first compare the BASE AMOUNT (shown below) for the taxpayer's filing status with the total of:

- One-half of the Social Security benefits, plus
- All other income, including tax-exempt interest.

When making this comparison, do not reduce other income by any exclusions for:

- Interest from qualified U.S. savings bonds,
- Employer-provided adoption benefits,
- Foreign earned income or foreign housing, or
- Income earned by bona fide residents of American Samoa or Puerto Rico.

| BASE AMOUNTS: SOCIAL SECURITY |
| :---: |
| A taxpayer's BASE AMOUNT for figuring the taxability of Social Security is: |
| $25,000 for single, head of household, or qualifying widow(er), |
| $32,000 for married filing jointly, or |
| $25,000 for married filing separately (and lived *apart* from his spouse all year) |
| $-0- if the taxpayer is MFS (if lived with spouse at any time during the tax year) |

## How to Figure the Taxability of Social Security

To figure out what percentages of a taxpayer's Social Security benefits are taxable, the taxpayer must first determine the sum of modified AGI (MAGI) and add one-half of the Social Security benefits. After doing this calculation on a worksheet, if the amount is less than the base amount, then none of the Social Security is taxable.

> **Example:** Bo and Yvonne are both over 65. They file jointly and they both received Social Security benefits during the year. At the end of the year, Bo received a Form SSA-1099 showing net benefits of $7,500. Yvonne received a Form SSA-1099 showing net benefits of $3,500. Bo also received wages of $20,000 and interest income of $500. He did not have any tax-exempt interest.
>
> | | |
> |---|---|
> | 1. Total Social Security benefits: | $11,000 |
> | 2. Enter one-half of SS | $5,500 |
> | 3. Enter taxable interest and wages | $20,500 |
> | 4. Add ($5,500 + $20,500) | $26,000 |
>
> Bo and Yvonne's benefits are not taxable for 2012 because their income is not more than the base amount ($32,000) for married filing jointly.

## Taxable State Income Tax Refunds

State income tax refunds are reportable as taxable income in the year received only if the taxpayer itemized deductions in the prior year. The state should send Form 1099-G, *Certain Government Payments*, by January 31. The IRS also will receive a copy of the Form 1099-G.

> **Example:** Wally claimed the standard deduction on last year's tax return and received a state tax refund of $600. The state tax refund is not taxable. Only taxpayers who itemize deductions and receive a state or local refund in the prior year are required to include the state tax refund in their taxable income.

## Rents and Royalties

Income from rents and royalties must be included in gross income. Rental income is income from the use or occupation of property, such as a rental home. Income from royalties includes income from copyrights, trademarks, and franchises. Rental and royalty income is reported on **Schedule E**, and will be covered at length in Unit 13.

# Nontaxable Income

Some types of income are nontaxable, some of which must be reported to the IRS, and others do not.

## A. Veterans' Benefits

Veterans' benefits are nontaxable. Amounts paid by the Department of Veterans Affairs to a veteran or his family are nontaxable if they are for education, training, disability compensation, work therapy, dependent care assistance, or other benefits or pension payments given to the veteran because of disability.

## B. Workers' Compensation

Workers' compensation is not taxable income if it is received because of an occupational injury. However, disability benefits paid by an employer (also called "sick pay") are taxable to the employee. Long-term disability income payments are included in gross income and are taxable to the employee.

## C. Life Insurance Proceeds

Proceeds from life insurance are not taxable to the recipient. Consequently, life insurance premiums are not deductible by the payer, but an employer may choose to provide employees with life insurance as a fringe benefit and deduct the cost. However, a private individual, such as a sole proprietor purchasing life insurance for himself, may not deduct the premiums.

Sometimes, a taxpayer will choose to receive life insurance in installments, rather than a lump sum. In this case, part of the installment usually includes interest income. If a taxpayer receives life insurance proceeds in installments, he can exclude part of each installment from his income. To determine the excluded part, divide the amount held by the insurance company (generally the total lump sum payable at the death of the insured person) by the number of installments to be paid. Include anything over this excluded part as interest income.

**Example:** Libby's brother died in 2012, and she is the beneficiary of his life insurance. The face amount of the policy is $75,000 and, as beneficiary, Libby chooses to receive 120 monthly installments of $1,000 each. The excluded part of each installment is $625 ($75,000 ÷ 120), or $7,500 for an entire year. The rest of each payment, $375 a month (or $4,500 for an entire year), is interest income to Libby.

## D. Compensatory Damages and Court Settlements

Compensatory damages for personal physical injury or physical sickness are not taxable income, whether they are from a settlement or from an actual court award.

**Example:** Felix was injured in a car accident in 2012. His legs were broken and he suffered other serious physical injuries. He received a settlement from the insurance company for his injuries totaling $950,000. This is nontaxable income, because it is payment for a physical injury.

Compensatory damages for "emotional distress" are usually taxable. Emotional distress itself is not a physical injury. If the emotional distress is due to unlawful discrimination or injury to reputation, the taxpayer must include the damages in taxable income, except for any damages received for medical care due to that emotional distress.

**Example:** Kristina recently won a court award for emotional distress due to unlawful discrimination. The emotional distress resulted in a nervous breakdown and her hospitalization. The court awarded her damages of $100,000, including $20,000 to refund the cost of her medical care due to the nervous breakdown. In this case, $80,000 ($100,000 - $20,000) would be considered a taxable court award. The $20,000 of damages for her medical care would be nontaxable.

Punitive damages are taxable income. It does not matter if they relate to a physical injury or physical sickness.

Court awards for lost wages are always taxable as ordinary income.

# Nontaxable Types of Interest Income

There are numerous examples of interest income that are not taxable to the recipient.

## A. Municipal Bonds

A taxpayer may exclude interest income on municipal or "muni" bonds, which are debt obligations by state and local governments. Taxpayers must still report the interest on their income tax returns, but it is not taxable. Although a muni bond is generally exempt from federal income tax, it is often still taxable at the state level.

## B. Frozen Deposits

A taxpayer may exclude interest income on frozen deposits. A deposit is considered frozen if, at the end of the year, the taxpayer cannot withdraw any part of the deposit because:

- The financial institution is bankrupt or insolvent, or
- The state where the institution is located has placed limits on withdrawals because other financial institutions in the state are bankrupt or insolvent.

---

**Example:** Creed earned $2,500 in interest from his bank in 2012, but it became insolvent at the end of the year and all of Creed's money was frozen. He was unable to access any of his accounts until the following year. Creed does not have to recognize the income as taxable in 2012 because the interest qualified as a frozen deposit. He would recognize the income in 2013 when the funds finally became available for him to withdraw and use. Creed must still report the income on his 2012 tax return, but he may mark it as a "frozen deposit" and therefore not subject to income tax in the current tax year.

---

## C. Mutual Funds Investing in Tax-Exempt Securities

Distributions from a fund investing in tax-exempt securities are tax-exempt interest. For 2012, tax-exempt interest paid by mutual funds is now shown on Form 1099-DIV, not Form 1099-INT as before.

## D. Education Savings Bond Interest Exclusion

Taxpayers may choose to purchase and then eventually redeem Series EE bonds on a tax-free basis to pay college expenses. The expenses must be for the taxpayer, the taxpayer's spouse, or the taxpayer's dependents.

For 2012, the amount of the interest exclusion is phased out for married filing jointly taxpayers or qualifying widow(er)taxpayers whose modified AGI is between $109,250 and $139,250. If the modified AGI is $139,250 or more, no exclusion is allowed.

> **Caution:** Married taxpayers who file separately do not qualify for the educational savings bond interest exclusion.

For single and head of household filing statuses, the interest exclusion is phased out for taxpayers whose modified AGI is between $72,850 and $87,850. If the modified AGI is $87,850 or more, no exclusion is allowed.

The exclusion is calculated and reported on IRS Form 8815, *Exclusion of Interest from Series EE and I U.S. Savings Bonds*. There are certain rules that must be followed in order for the educational exclusion to qualify:

- The bonds must be purchased by the owner. They cannot be a gift.
- The money received on redemption must be used for tuition and fees. The taxpayer cannot use tax-exempt bond proceeds for tuition and also attempt to take educational credits (such as the Lifetime Learning Credit) for the same amount. No "double dipping" is allowed.
- The total interest received may *only* be excluded if the combined amounts of the principal and the interest received *do not exceed* the taxpayer's qualified educational expenses.

> **Example:** In February 2012, Daniel and Blythe, a married couple, cash a qualified Series EE savings bond they bought ten years ago. They receive proceeds of $8,124, representing principal of $5,000 and interest of $3,124. In 2012, they paid $4,000 of their daughter's college tuition. They are not claiming an education credit for that amount, and their daughter does not have any tax-free educational assistance (scholarships or grants). Daniel and Blythe can exclude $1,538 ($3,124 × [$4,000 ÷ $8,124]) of interest in 2012. They must pay tax on the remaining $1,586 ($3,124 − $1,538) interest, since not all the interest was used for qualified tuition costs.

> **Example:** In 2012, Denise redeems her Series EE Bonds and receives a total of $4,000. Of that amount, $1,000 is interest income and the remainder is the return of principal ($3,000). Denise's qualified educational expenses (tuition and fees) are $5,800. Therefore, all of the interest earned on her Series EE Bonds qualifies for tax-exempt treatment.

If the taxpayer does not use the bonds for educational expenses, the interest income is taxable. Most taxpayers report the total interest when they cash the bonds. Some taxpayers choose instead to report savings bond interest as it accrues. Either method is acceptable.

# Foreign Earned Income Exclusion

Generally, the income of U.S. citizens is taxed even if the income is earned outside the United States. Foreign earned income is income received for services performed in a foreign country while the taxpayer's tax home is also in a foreign country. The taxpayer must pass one of two tests in order to claim the foreign earned income exclusion. If eligible for this option, the taxpayer's income up to a certain threshold is not taxed.

- Test #1: "Bona Fide Residence Test," or
- Test #2: The "Physical Presence" Test

**Bona Fide Residence Test:** A U.S. citizen or U.S. resident alien who is a bona fide resident of a foreign country for an uninterrupted period that includes an entire tax year.

**The Physical Presence Test:** A U.S. citizen or U.S. resident alien who is physically present in a foreign country or countries for at least 330 full days during 12 consecutive months. A taxpayer may qualify under the physical presence test, and the income may span over a period of multiple tax years. If so, the taxpayer must prorate the foreign earned income exclusion based on the number of days spent in the foreign country.

For 2012, the maximum foreign earned income exclusion is $95,100. If the taxpayer is married filing jointly and both individuals live and work abroad, both taxpayers can choose to claim the foreign earned income exclusion.

---

**Example:** Brenda earned $80,000 while employed in Peru, and she qualifies for the foreign earned income exclusion. Brenda also has $6,000 in work-related expenses. She cannot deduct any of her expenses, because she is already excluding all of her income from taxation by taking the foreign earned income exclusion.

**Example:** Leila was a bona fide resident of China for all of 2012. She was paid $105,000 for her work in China. She can exclude $95,100 of the amount she was paid.

---

It does not matter whether the income is paid by a U.S. employer or a foreign employer.

The foreign earned income exclusion is figured using Form 2555, *Foreign Earned Income,* which must be attached to Form 1040. Once the choice is made to exclude foreign earned income, that choice remains in effect for the year the election is made and all later years, unless revoked.

Nonresident aliens do not qualify for the foreign earned income exclusion. A taxpayer must be either a U.S. citizen or a legal resident alien of the United States who lives and works abroad and who meets certain other qualifications to exclude a specific amount of his foreign earned income.

The exclusion does not apply to the wages and salaries of members of the Armed Forces and civilian employees of the U.S. government.

**Foreign Tax Credit:** The Foreign Tax Credit can be used by U.S. taxpayers to avoid or reduce double taxation. A taxpayer cannot take the Foreign Tax Credit on income that has already been excluded from taxation by the foreign earned income exclusion. This credit is covered in detail in Unit 9, *Tax Credits.*

# Clergy: Special Rules

There are special rules regarding the taxation of clergy members. "Ministers" or "clergy" are individuals who are ordained, commissioned, or licensed by a religious body or church denomination. They are given the authority to conduct religious worship, perform religious functions, and administer ordinances or sacraments according to the prescribed tenets and practices of that church.

Clergy members must include offerings and fees received for marriages, baptisms, and funerals as part of their income. A clergy member's salary is reported on IRS Form W-2. Additional payments for services are reported on the clergy member's Schedule C.

## Minister's Housing Allowance

A minister's housing allowance (sometimes called a parsonage allowance) is excludable from gross income for income tax purposes, but not for self-employment tax purposes. A minister who receives a housing allowance may exclude the allowance from gross income to the extent it is used to pay expenses in providing a home.

The exclusion for minister's housing is limited to:

- The lesser of the fair market rental value (including utilities, etc.), or
- The actual amount used to provide a home.

The housing allowance cannot exceed reasonable pay and must be used for housing in the year they are received by the minister.

**Example:** William is an ordained minister who receives $32,000 in salary in 2012. He also receives an additional $4,000 for performing marriages and baptisms. His housing allowance was $500 per month, for a total of $6,000 per year. William must report the $32,000 as wages, $4,000 as self-employment income, and $6,000 as the housing allowance subject only to self-employment tax, not income tax.

Both salary and housing allowances must be included in income for purposes of determining self-employment tax.

**Example:** Abby is a full-time ordained minister at Waterfront Presbyterian Church. The church allows her to use a cottage that has a rental value of $5,000. The church also pays Abby a salary of $12,000. Her income for self-employment tax purposes is $17,000 ($5,000 + $12,000 salary). Ministers must include the FMV of a home on Schedule SE.

**Example:** Father Benicio is an ordained priest at the local Catholic Church. His annual salary is $26,000, and he also receives a $10,000 housing allowance. His housing costs for the year are $14,000. Therefore, Benicio's self-employment income is $36,000 ($26,000 salary + $10,000 housing allowance). But only his base salary ($26,000) is subject to income tax, because his actual housing expenses are more than his housing allowance.

## Vow of Poverty

If a minister or other individual (nun, monk, etc.) is a member of a religious order who has taken a vow of poverty, the individual is exempt from paying SE tax on his earnings for qualified services. For income tax purposes, the earnings are tax-free, because the earnings are considered the income of the religious order, rather than of the individual.

## Exemption from Social Security

A minister can request an exemption from self–employment tax if he is "conscientiously opposed" to public insurance for religious reasons.

# Summary: Taxable vs. Nontaxable Income

| TAXABLE INCOME | NONTAXABLE INCOME |
|---|---|
| Wages, salaries, tips, bonuses, vacation pay, severance pay, commissions | Gifts and inheritances |
| Interest | Life insurance proceeds |
| Unemployment compensation | Child support |
| Dividends | Certain veterans' benefits |
| Strike benefits | Interest on muni bonds (state and local bonds) |
| Bank "gifts" and cash bonuses for opening accounts | Employer-provided fringe benefits such as health insurance |
| Cancellation of debt (unless excludable) | Welfare payments, food stamps, other forms of public assistance |
| Alimony | Compensation or court awards for physical injury or illness |
| Gains from sales of property, stocks and bonds, stock options, etc. | Workers' compensation |
| Social Security benefits (above the base amount) | Combat pay |
| Most court awards or damages | Scholarships, employer-provided educational assistance, |
| Barter income | Canceled debt from a primary residence, bankruptcy, or insolvency |
| Prizes, awards, gambling winnings | Foreign earned income (if qualifying for the exclusion) |

| Earned Income | Unearned Income | Can be variable |
|---|---|---|
| Salaries | Dividends | Business profits |
| Wages | Interest | Partnership income |
| Commissions | Capital gains | Royalties |
| Bonuses | Gambling winnings | Rents |
| Professional fees | Annuities | Scholarships |
| Vacation pay | Alimony | Fellowships |
| Tips | Social Security | Fringe benefits |
| Self-employment income | Pensions | Court/lawsuit proceeds |

# Unit 5: Questions

1. Hank received Social Security in 2012 totaling $11,724. Also in 2012, Hank sold all of his stock and moved into senior housing. He received $31,896 of taxable income from the sale of the stock. What is the maximum taxable amount of Hank's Social Security benefits?

A. $31,896.
B. $20,172.
C. $9,965.
D. Not enough information provided.

**The answer is C.** The maximum amount that can ever be taxable on net Social Security benefits is 85%, which in Hank's case is $9,965. ###

2. Bruce and Ann are married and file jointly. They have three Forms 1099-INT:

1.  Epping National Bank, $62 (Bruce)
2.  Epping Credit Union, $178 (Ann)
3.  Breton Savings and Loan, $760 (Ann)

How much interest income should they report on Schedule B (Form 1040)?

A. None.
B. $760.
C. $240.
D. $1,000.

**The answer is A.** Schedule B is not used to report regular interest totaling $1,500 or less. Instead, these amounts can be reported directly on the taxpayer's Form 1040. ###

3. Which of the following types of income are exempt from federal tax?

A. Interest income.
B. Canceled debt.
C. Tips.
D. Inheritances.

**The answer is D.** Of the types of income listed here, only inheritances are exempt from federal taxes. ###

4. Under what circumstances must a person report taxable income?
A. Always.
B. Always, unless the income is only from interest.
C. Always, unless the income is so small that reporting it is not required by law.
D. Always, unless the person is identified as a dependent on someone else's tax return.

**The answer is C.** All taxable income must be reported on a tax return, unless the amount is so small that the individual is not legally required to file a return. Filing thresholds depend on a taxpayer's marital status, age, and dependency status. ###

5. Which of the following types of income are taxable?

A. Credit union dividends.
B. Veterans' life insurance dividends.
C. Workers' compensation.
D. Child support.

**The answer is A.** Credit union dividends are considered interest income and are subject to federal income tax. ###

6. Toni owns a savings bond, which she purchased as an investment to help pay for her daughter's education. She redeems the bond in 2012 and immediately uses all the funds to pay for her daughter Tyler's college tuition. The bond's interest is reported on _____.

A. Toni's tax return and is 100% taxable.
B. Tyler's tax return and is 100% taxable.
C. Toni's tax return and is 100% exempt from taxes.
D. Nothing. It is not taxable and not required to be reported, so long as Toni uses all the funds to pay for qualified higher education costs.

**The answer is C.** As the buyer and owner of the bond, Toni reports the interest on her tax return, but excludes the interest from her income because she paid for qualified higher education expenses the same year.###

7. Joyce and Craig, a married couple, received $200 in interest from bonds issued by the state of Virginia. How should they report this on their Form 1040?

A. It must be reported as interest income, and it is 100% taxable.
B. It must be reported, but it is not taxable income on their Form 1040.
C. They do not have to report it.
D. None of the above.

**The answer is B.** The interest is tax-exempt municipal bond interest (state and local bonds). Although it is not taxable at the federal level, it must be reported on the taxpayer's return. ###

8. Leona received the following income: wages, interest, child support, alimony, inheritance, workers' compensation, and lottery winnings. Determine what amount of her income is taxable.

**Leona's Income:**

| SOURCE | Amounts |
|---|---|
| Wages | $13,000 |
| Interest | $15 |
| Child support | $6,000 |
| Alimony | $2,000 |
| Inheritance | $10,000 |
| Workers' compensation | $1,000 |
| Lottery winnings | $5,000 |

A. $13,015.
B. $16,015.
C. $20,015.
D. $30,015.

**The answer is C.** The wages, interest, alimony, and lottery winnings are taxable income and will appear on Leona's tax return ($13,000 + $15 + $2,000 + $5,000 = $20,015). Child support, inheritances, and workers' compensation are nontaxable income and will not appear on her tax return. ###

9. Which of the following tip income is exempt from federal income tax?

A. Tips of less than $20 per month.
B. Noncash tips.
C. Tips not reported to the employer.
D. All tips are taxable.

**The answer is D.** All tip income is subject to federal income tax, whether it is cash or noncash. Individuals who receive less than $20 per month in tips while working one job do not have to report their tip income to their employer, but the income is still subject to federal income tax and must be reported on the taxpayer's Form 1040. ###

10. Salvador is in the U.S. Army and served in a combat zone from January 1 to September 2 of 2012. He returned to the United States and received his regular duty pay for the remainder of the year. How many months of income are taxable?

A. Zero. All the income is tax-free.
B. Three months are subject to tax.
C. Four months are subject to tax.
D. All twelve months are subject to income tax.

**The answer is B.** Since Salvador served for a few days in September, all the income in September is excluded as combat pay. If a taxpayer serves in a combat zone as an enlisted person for any part of a month, all of his pay received for military service that month is excluded from gross income. ###

11. A customer at a casino left a $10 poker chip as a tip for Steve, who is a hotel employee. Steve did not have any other tip income for the month. What is Steve's reporting requirement for this tip?

A. The poker chip is not legal tender, and is therefore not taxable.
B. Steve should report this tip income to his employer, and it will be taxed as wages on his Form W-2.
C. Steve must report the tip income on his return at its fair market value, which would be $10.
D. The tip is a gift, and therefore not taxable income.

**The answer is C.** Although this is not actual money, it is still taxable at its fair market value, which would be $10. The tip is not reportable to Steve's employer, since he earned less than $20 of tip income during the month. He should report the tip income on his return, subject to regular income tax. ###

12. Sven and Samantha file jointly in 2012 and received the following income for 2012. How much income should be reported on their 2012 joint tax return?

1. W-2 income for Samantha for wages of $40,000.
2. W-2 for Samantha for $2,000, the value of a trip she won to the Bahamas. She never went on the trip. But she is planning to take the trip in 2012.
3. Court settlement of $10,000 paid to Sven from a car accident for serious injuries he suffered.
4. $4,000 child support for Samantha's son from a previous marriage.

A. $40,000.
B. $42,000.
C. $46,000.
D. $52,000.

**The answer is B.** The wages earned and prize won by Samantha should be included on the joint return, and the accident settlement should be excluded from income. Samantha must recognize the prize, because even though she did not take the trip, she had constructive receipt of the winnings. Child support is not taxable. The answer is $42,000 ($40,000 wages + $2,000 prize). ###

13. Sandy received the following income in 2012:

1. Wages: $70,000.
2. Gambling winnings: $500 (Gambling losses, $1,000).
3. Dependent care benefits through her employer: $5,000.
4. Employer-provided parking pass: $240 per month.

Sandy had only $4,000 in qualified daycare expenses. How much gross income must she report on her tax return?

A. $70,500.
B. $71,500.
C. $71,740.
D. $73,400.

**The answer is B**. Dependent care assistance programs are not taxable, but only up to the amount of qualified expenses. Since Sandy received $5,000 but only had $4,000 in actual day care expenses, $1,000 is taxable to Sandy. The parking pass is an excluded benefit. Both the wages and gambling winnings must be included in the gross income total of $71,500 ($70,000 + $500 + $1,000). The gambling losses are not deductible from the net. Gambling losses are only allowable up to gambling winnings, and even then, only as an itemized deduction on Schedule A. ###

14. Ginny had the following income in 2012:

Social Security income: $14,000
Interest income: $125
Gambling winnings: $1,000
Gambling losses: $2,000
Settlement for a bodily injury: $20,000
Child support payments: $13,000
Food stamp benefits: $5,000

How much income must Ginny report on her tax return?

A. $14,000.
B. $14,125.
C. $15,125.
D. $30,000.
E. $48,000.

**The answer is C**. The Social Security income, gambling income, and interest income must all be reported. The accident settlement and the child support are not taxable. Food stamps and welfare payments also are not taxable income. The gambling losses do not affect the reporting of the gambling income. Gambling losses are a deduction on Schedule A, should Ginny choose to itemize. If Ginny does not itemize, the gambling losses are not deductible. ###

15. Brendan, a flight attendant, received wages of $30,000 in 2012. The airline provided transportation on a standby basis, at no charge, from his home in Little Rock to the airline's hub in Charlotte. The fair market value of the commuting flights was $5,000. Also in 2012, Brendan received reimbursements under an accountable plan of $10,000 for overnight travel, but only spent $6,000. He returned the excess to his employer. Brendan became injured on the job in November of 2012 and received workers' compensation of $4,000. What amount must he include in gross income on his 2012 tax return?

A. $30,000.
B. $34,000.
C. $35,000.
D. $37,000.

**The answer is A.** Brendan only has to include his wages in his 2012 return. The free flights offered on standby to airline personnel are considered a nontaxable fringe benefit. Reimbursements under an accountable plan and amounts paid for workers' compensation are nontaxable. Since Brendan returned the unspent amounts to his employer, the travel reimbursements qualify under an accountable plan, and the amounts spent are not taxable to him. ###

16. Debby broke her leg in a car accident in 2012 and was unable to work for three months. She received an accident settlement of $13,000 from the car insurance company. During this time she also received $7,500 in sick pay from her employer. In addition, she received $5,000 from her personally purchased accident policy. How much of this income is taxable income to Debby?

A. $5,000.
B. $7,500.
C. $12,500.
D. $18,000.

**The answer is B.** Only Debby's sick pay is taxable as wages. Sick pay from an employer is taxable like wages (similar to vacation pay), and is therefore includable in Debby's gross income. If a taxpayer pays the full cost of an accident insurance plan, the benefits for personal injury or illness are not includable in income. If the employer pays the cost of an accident insurance plan, then the amounts are taxable to an employee. ###

17. Income was "constructively received" in 2012 in each of the following situations except:

A. Wages were deposited in the taxpayer's bank account on December 26, 2012, but were not withdrawn by the taxpayer until January 3, 2013.
B. A taxpayer was informed his check for services rendered was available on December 15, 2012. The taxpayer did not pick up the check until January 30, 2013.
C. A taxpayer received a check by mail on December 31, 2012, but could not deposit the check until January 5, 2013.
D. A taxpayer's home was sold on December 28, 2012. The payment was not received by the taxpayer until January 2, 2013 when the escrow company completed the transaction and released the funds.

**The answer is D.** Constructive receipt does not require the taxpayer to have physical possession of the income. However, income is not considered constructively received if the taxpayer cannot access the funds because of restrictions. Since the taxpayer's control of the receipt of the funds in the escrow account was substantially limited until the transaction had closed, the taxpayer did not constructively receive the income until the closing of the transaction in the following year. ###

18. Jon and Li-hua filed a joint return for 2012. Jon received $10,000 in Social Security benefits and Li-hua received $16,000. They received no other income. What part of their Social Security benefits will be taxable for 2012?

A. $0.
B. $6,000.
C. $24,000.
D. $12,000.

**The answer is A.** If the only income received by the taxpayer is Social Security, the benefits generally are not taxable and the taxpayer probably does not have to file a return. If the taxpayer has additional income, he may have to file a return even if none of the Social Security benefits are taxable. ###

19. James is a self-employed attorney who performs legal services for a client, a small corporation. The corporation gives James 100 shares of its stock as payment for his services. The stock is valued at $2,000. Which of the following statements is true?

A. James does not have to include this transaction on his tax return.
B. James should report the income when he sells the stock.
C. The stock is taxable to James at its fair market value.
D. None of the above.

**The answer is C.** James must include the FMV of the shares in his gross income on Schedule C (Form 1040) in the year he receives them. The income would be considered payment for services he provided to his client, the corporation. ###

20. Rob owns a business that has a $10,000 profit in 2012. His wife, Cecilia, has a business loss of $12,000 for 2012. They both file Schedule C to report their self-employment income. Which of the following statements is true?

A. On their joint return, they will not have to pay self-employment tax because the losses from Cecilia's business offset Rob's income.
B. The spouses can file MFS and offset each other's self-employment tax.
C. Rob must pay self-employment tax on $10,000, regardless of his wife's losses.
D. If they choose to file separate returns, they may split the profits and losses equally between their two businesses.

**The answer is C.** Rob must pay self-employment tax on $10,000, regardless of how he and Cecilia choose to file. Taxpayers cannot combine a spouse's income or loss to determine their individual earnings subject to SE tax. However, if a taxpayer has more than one business, then he must combine the net profit or loss from each to determine the total earnings subject to SE tax. ###

21. Brent, a plastic surgeon, agreed to exchange services with a handyman. Brent removed a mole and the handyman fixed Brent's running toilet in his doctor's office. Mole removal is generally charged at $200, and the handyman generally charges $150 to fix a toilet. They agreed in advance that the fee would be $150. Neither exchanged actual cash. How much income must Brent recognize for this barter transaction?

A. $50.
B. $150.
C. $200.
D. $250.

**The answer is B.** Brent must include $150 in income. He may also deduct the cost of the repair ($150) if it qualifies as a business expense. If a taxpayer exchanges services with another person and both have agreed ahead of time on the value of those services, that value will be accepted as fair market value unless the value can be shown to be otherwise. ###

22. Ed received $32,000 in wages from his employer in 2012. He also won a prize from his employer because he helped develop a handbook for new employees. The prize was free lawn care service for a year, valued at $600. Ed also received $7,000 in child support and $2,000 in alimony from his ex-wife. Ed has full custody of his children. What is Ed's taxable income (before deductions and adjustments) for tax year 2012?

A. $32,000.
B. $32,600.
C. $34,600.
D. $39,600.

**The answer is C.** The wages and prize are both taxable income. Child support is not taxable to the receiver, nor deductible by the payer. The alimony is taxable to Ed and deductible by his ex-wife. The answer is figured as follows: ($32,000 + $600 + $2,000) = $34,600. ###

23. Scott opened a savings account at his local bank and deposited $800. The account earns $20 interest in 2012. Scott also received a $15 calculator as a gift for opening the account. On his credit card account, Scott received $100 worth of "reward points" for charging $10,000 in purchases, which he used to pay a portion of his credit card bill. How much interest income must Scott report on his IRS Form 1040?

A. $15.
B. $20.
C. $35.
D. $800.

**The answer is C.** If no other interest is credited to Scott during the year, the Form 1099-INT he receives will show $35 interest for the year. Scott must report the fair market value of the calculator on his return as interest income. A gift for opening a bank account is taxed as interest income. The IRS does not count reward points or cash back from a credit card as taxable interest income, so Scott neither has to report the $100 nor does he have to pay tax on it. ###

24. During the current year, Andrew received interest income of $300 from municipal bonds and $200 in interest from a certificate of deposit (CD). Which of the following statements is true?

A. Andrew is required to report the $500 in interest income on his income tax return, but none of the interest is taxable.
B. Andrew is not required to report any of the income on his tax return.
C. Andrew is required to report the $500 in interest income on his income tax return. The CD interest is taxable, but the muni bond interest is not.
D. Andrew is required to report only $200 of CD interest on his income tax return.

**The answer is C.** Under present federal income tax law, the interest income received from investing in municipal bonds is free from federal income taxes. However, the taxpayer is required to show any tax-exempt interest received on his tax return. This is an informational reporting requirement only. It does not change tax-exempt interest to taxable interest. The $200 interest from the CD is taxable and must be reported as interest income. ###

25. Kent invested in a mutual fund in 2012. The fund declared a dividend, and Kent earned $19. He did not get a Form 1099-DIV for the amount, and he did not withdraw the money from his mutual fund. Kent pulled the money out of his mutual fund on January 2, 2013. Which of the following statements is true?

A. The dividend is not reportable in 2012 because Kent did not receive the money yet.
B. The dividend is not reportable in 2012 because Kent did not receive a 1099-DIV.
C. The dividend must be reported in 2012.
D. The dividend is taxable and reportable in 2013.

**The answer is C.** Kent earned the money in 2012, and whether or not he received a 1099 for the income is irrelevant. Mutual fund dividends are taxable in the year declared regardless of whether the taxpayer withdraws the money or reinvests it. The money was constructively earned and available for withdrawal in 2012, so Kent must report the earnings in 2012. ###

26. Fran's bank became insolvent in 2012. One hundred dollars in interest was credited to her frozen bank account during the year. Fran withdrew $80, but could not withdraw any more as of the end of the year. Her 1099-INT showed $100 in interest income. Which of the following is true?

A. Fran's tax return must reflect the full amount of the interest.
B. Fran must include the $20 in her income for the year she is able to withdraw it.
C. None of the interest is taxable on a frozen deposit.
D. There is no such thing as a "frozen deposit."

**The answer is B.** Fran must include $80 in her income for 2012 but may exclude $20. She must include the $20 in her income in the year she is able to withdraw it. A deposit is considered frozen if, at the end of the year, the taxpayer cannot withdraw the deposit because the financial institution is bankrupt or insolvent. ###

27. Verla wanted to start investing. She deposited $4,000 of her own funds with a bank and also borrowed another $12,000 from the bank to make up the $16,000 minimum deposit required to buy a six-month certificate of deposit. The certificate earned $375 at maturity in 2012, but Verla only received $175 in interest income, which represented the $375 she earned minus $200 in interest charged on the $12,000 loan. The bank gives Verla a Form 1099-INT showing the $375 interest she earned. The bank also gives her a statement showing that she paid $200 in interest. How should Verla report all the interest amounts on her tax return?

A. Verla can choose to report only $175 of income.
B. Verla must report the $375 interest income. The $200 interest she paid to the bank is not deductible.
C. Verla must include the $375 in her income. Verla may deduct $200 on her Schedule A, subject to the net investment income limit.
D. Verla does not have to report any income from this transaction.

**The answer is C.** Verla must include the total amount of interest—$375—in her income. If she itemizes deductions on Schedule A (Form 1040), she can deduct $200 in interest expense, subject to the net investment income limit. To deduct investment expenses, the taxpayer must itemize. She may not "net" the investment income and expenses. ###

28. What is the maximum percentage of taxable Social Security benefits for a beneficiary?

A. 0%.
B. 50%.
C. 85%.
D. 100%.

**The answer is C.** Up to 85% of Social Security benefits may be taxable. No one pays federal income tax on more than 85% of his Social Security benefits. ###

29. Sheila and Ralph are married and both have life insurance. In December 2011, Ralph dies and Sheila, as the beneficiary, is awarded the life insurance. The face amount of the policy is $270,000. Instead of a lump sum, Sheila chooses to receive 180 monthly installments of $1,800 each over 15 years, starting January 1, 2012. How should Sheila treat these installments on her 2012 tax return?

A. All of the payments are excluded from income.
B. $18,000 is excluded from income per year, and $3,600 must be recognized as interest income.
C. $21,600 must be included in Sheila's income.
D. $18,000 will be excluded from income, and the remainder is taxed as a capital gain.

**The answer is B.** Life insurance proceeds are not taxable. However, the *interest* or investment gains earned on a life insurance installment contract are taxable. The face amount of the policy is $270,000. Therefore, the excluded part of each installment is $1,500 ($270,000 ÷ 180 months), or $18,000 for an entire year. The rest of each payment, $300 a month (or $3,600 for an entire year), is interest income to Sheila. ###

30. Randall is an ordained minister in the Evangelical Church of Chicago. He owns his own home and his monthly house payment is $900. His monthly utilities total $150. Fair rental value in his neighborhood is $1,000. Randall receives a housing allowance from his church in the amount of $950 per month. How much income must Randall include from his housing allowance amount?

A. $0.
B. $50 per month.
C. $150 per month.
D. $950 per month.

**The answer is A.** Ministers may exclude from gross income the rental value of a home or a rental allowance to the extent the allowance is used to provide a home, even if deductions are taken for home expenses paid with the allowance. A minister's housing allowance is excludable from gross income for income tax purposes, but not for self-employment tax purposes. ###

31. Alexander, age 64, is single and retired. He earned the following income in 2012. To determine if any of his Social Security is taxable, Alexander should compare how much of his income to the $25,000 base amount?

| Part-time job | $8,000 |
|---|---|
| Bank interest | $5,000 |
| Social Security | $11,000 |
| Taxable pension | $6,000 |
| **Total** | **$30,000** |

A. $30,000.
B. $11,000.
C. $24,500.
D. $25,000.

**The answer is C.** In order to figure out the taxable portion of Social Security, the taxpayer's modified adjusted gross income must be compared to the base amount.

Modified adjusted gross income equals adjusted gross income plus tax-exempt interest. To figure the amount of income that should be compared to the $25,000 base amount:

| Part-time job | $8,000 |
|---|---|
| Interest | $5,000 |
| ½ of Social Security | $5,500 |
| Taxable pension | $6,000 |
| **Total** | **$24,500** |

Alexander does not have to pay tax on his Social Security. His provisional income plus Social Security is less than the base amount ($25,000). However, he is still required to file a tax return, because his overall income exceeds the minimum filing requirement. ###

32. Robert receives supplemental wages and a holiday bonus in 2012. Which items listed below are not considered taxable income to Robert?

A. Holiday bonus.
B. Overtime pay.
C. Vacation pay.
D. Travel reimbursements.

**The answer is D.** Travel reimbursements are considered part of an accountable plan and are not included in an employee's wages. ###

33. Tim is a priest at a Catholic church. He receives an annual salary of $18,000 and a housing allowance of $2,000 to pay for utilities. Tim lives rent-free in a small studio owned by the church. The fair rental value of the studio is $300 per month. Only the $18,000 salary was reported on the W-2. How much of Tim's income is subject to income tax?

A. $0.
B. $18,000.
C. $20,000.
D. $21,600.

**The answer is B.** Only $18,000, Tim's wages, is subject to income tax. The other amounts for the housing allowance and use of the studio are not subject to income tax, but they are subject to self-employment tax. ###

34. Jacob's personal car is repossessed. His auto loan was a recourse loan. He later receives a Form 1099-C, showing $3,000 in cancellation of debt income. How must this transaction be reported by Jacob?

A. The repossession is treated as a sale. Jacob must report the cancellation of debt income and any gain on the sale or repossession.
B. No reporting is required, because the loan was a recourse loan.
C. The amount must be reported as taxable interest income.
D. Not enough information to answer.

**The answer is A.** If a personal vehicle is repossessed, the repossession is treated as a sale, and the gain or loss must be computed. If the taxpayer is personally liable for a loan (a recourse loan), the canceled debt is taxable unless an exception applies. If a loan is "recourse," then the taxpayer must generally report two transactions: the cancellation of debt income and the gain or loss on the repossession. Since this was Jacob's personal car, any loss is not deductible.

35. Polly receives the following income and fringe benefits in 2012:

1. $30,000 in wages.
2. $2,000 Christmas bonus.
3. Parking pass at $90 per month.
4. Employer contributions to Polly's 401K plan in the amount of $900 for the year.
5. Free use of an indoor gym on the employer's premises, FMV valued at $500.

How much income must Polly report on her 2012 tax return?

A. $30,000.
B. $32,000.
C. $32,900.
D. $33,980.

**The answer is B.** Only the wages and the bonus are taxable. The parking pass is considered a nontaxable transportation benefit, and the employer contributions are not taxable until Polly withdraws the money from her retirement account. Polly does not have to report the use of the gym, because it is on the employer's premises and therefore not taxable. ###

36. Which of the following fringe benefits is taxable (or partially taxable) to the employee?

A. Health insurance covered 100% by the employer.
B. Employer-provided parking at $275 per month.
C. Group-term life insurance coverage of $50,000.
D. Employer contributions to an employee's 401K plan.

**The answer is B.** Employer-provided parking is an excludable benefit, but only up to $240 per month for qualified parking. Therefore, the amount above $240 ($275 - $240 = $35) becomes taxable to the employee. ###

37. Max owns a restaurant. He furnishes one of the waitresses, Caroline, two meals during each workday. Max encourages (but does not require) Caroline to have her breakfast on the business premises before starting work so she can help him answer phones. She is required to have her lunch on the premises. How should Max treat this fringe benefit to Caroline?

A. Caroline's meals are not taxable.
B. Caroline's meals are all taxable.
C. Caroline's lunch is not taxable, but her breakfast is.
D. Caroline's meals are taxed at a flat rate of 15%.

**The answer is A.** Meals furnished to Caroline are not taxable because they are for the convenience of the employer. Meals that employers furnish to a restaurant employee during, immediately before, or after the employee's working hours are considered furnished for the employer's convenience. Since Caroline is a waitress who works during the normal breakfast and lunch periods, Max can exclude from her wages the value of those meals. If Max were to allow Caroline to have meals without charge on her days off, the value of those meals would have to be included in her wages. ###

38. Sheng spends two years working overseas in Australia as a computer programmer for a private company. He has qualified foreign earned income, and makes $120,000 in 2012. What is the maximum amount Sheng can exclude from his income?

A. $0.
B. $92,400.
C. $95,100.
D. Sheng may exclude the full amount of his salary, with no income threshold.

**The answer is C.** For 2012, the maximum exclusion for the foreign earned income exclusion is $95,100. ###

39. Elaine is a cash-basis taxpayer and sells cosmetics on commission. She sells $200,000 in 2012, and her commission is 5% of sales. Elaine receives $10,000 in income from commissions, plus an advance of $1,000 in December 2012 for future commissions in 2013. She also receives $200 in expense reimbursements from her employer after turning in her receipts as part of an accountable plan. How much income should Elaine report on her 2012 tax return?

A. $0.
B. $11,000.
C. $11,200.
D. $10,200.

**The answer is B**. Elaine's commissions must be included in gross income, as well as advance payments in anticipation of future services, if the taxpayer is on a cash basis. The expense reimbursements from her employer would not be included in gross income. ###

40. Antonio is employed as an accountant by the Dawson and Enriquez firm. When Antonio travels for his audit work, he submits his travel receipts for reimbursement by his firm, which has an accountable plan for its employees. Which of the following statements is true?

A. Under an accountable plan, the reimbursed amounts are not taxable to Antonio.
B. Under an accountable plan, Antonio may still deduct his travel expenses on his tax return.
C. Under an accountable plan, Antonio's employer, Dawson and Enriquez, may not deduct the travel expenses, even though Antonio was reimbursed in full.
D. Under an accountable plan, reimbursed expenses are taxable to the employee, and the employer may also deduct the expenses as they would any other current expense.

**The answer is A.** Under an accountable plan, employee reimbursements are not included in the employee's income. The employer can deduct the expenses as current expenses on their tax return. The employee is not required to be taxed on any amounts received under a qualified accountable plan. ###

41. Bart had a $15,000 loan from his local credit union. He lost his job and was unable to make the payments on this loan. The credit union determined that the legal fees to collect might be higher than the amount Bart owed, so it canceled the $5,000 remaining amount due on the loan. Bart did not file bankruptcy nor is he insolvent. How much must he include in his income as a result of this occurrence?

A. $0.
B. $5,000.
C. $10,000.
D. $15,000.

**The answer is B.** Since Bart's inability to pay his debt is not a result of bankruptcy nor insolvency, the amount of the canceled debt ($5,000) should be included in gross income. ###

42. Which of the following fringe benefits provided by the employer will result in taxable income to the employee?

A. A cell phone used by a pharmaceutical salesperson who uses it to talk to clients while on the road.
B. Reimbursements paid by the employers for qualified business travel expenses.
C. Use of a company van for commuting.
D. Occasional coffee, doughnuts, and soft drinks.

**The answer is C.** Use of a company vehicle for commuting is not a qualified fringe benefit. Commuting expenses are not deductible. Use of a company van after normal working hours is a personal use and not a business use. This would result in taxable income to the employee. The parking permit, reimbursements for business travel, and the occasional coffee and doughnuts are considered noncash fringe benefits that are not taxable. ###

43. Carly was released from her obligation to pay a large credit card debt. She owed $10,000 to her credit card company, which agreed to accept $2,500 as payment in full. Carly was not insolvent and not in bankruptcy when the debt was canceled. What amount would be reported on Carly's Form 1040, line 21 (other income)?

A. $0.
B. $10,000.
C. $2,500.
D. $7,500.

**The answer is D.** Carly would report $7,500 on line 21 of her Form 1040 as cancellation of debt income. ###

44. Jan owns and operates a store in the downtown shopping mall. She reports her income and expenses as a sole proprietor on Schedule C. Jan is having financial difficulties and cannot pay all of her debts. In 2012, one of the banks that she borrowed money from in order to start her business cancels her debt. Jan is not insolvent. She had a loan balance of $5,000 when the debt was canceled. Which of the following statements is true?

A. Jan does not have to report the forgiveness of the debt as income.
B. Jan must report the $5,000 debt cancellation on Schedule A.
C. Jan must report the $5,000 debt cancellation as business income on Schedule C.
D. Jan must report the $5,000 debt cancellation as a long-term gain on Schedule D.

**The answer is C**. Canceled debt that is related to business income must be included on a taxpayer's Schedule C as business income. ###

45. During 2012 Lily received payments of $20,000 for alimony and $15,000 for child support. Based upon the terms of her divorce settlement, her ex-spouse was also required to pay $14,000 in mortgage payments for the house they owned jointly.

What portion of the amounts above must Lily include in income?

A. $49,000.
B. $27,000.
C. $35,000.
D. $34,000.

**The answer is B.** Lily must report the cash alimony payments and one-half of the mortgage payments as taxable alimony. The child support payments are not taxable. ###

46. Gene, a married taxpayer who files separately from his wife, bought his house in Florida in 2004 for $4.5 million, and financed the purchase with a mortgage loan of the same amount that required payments of interest only for the first five years. In 2006, the house appraised for $5.5 million, and he refinanced, this time with an interest-only mortgage loan of $5 million.

In 2012, the mortgage lender agrees to a short sale of the house for $3.2 million, and cancels the remaining $1.8 million (the amount in which the balance of the mortgage exceeded the sale proceeds.)

Based upon the information provided, what portion of the amount forgiven can Gene exclude from income?

A. $1.8 million.
B. $1.3 million.
C. $1 million.
D. Zero.

**The answer is C.** Absent an additional exclusion based upon insolvency, the excludable amount is $1 million. The additional amount of $500,000 that was borrowed when the property was refinanced in 2006 exceeds the purchase cost and therefore was not qualified personal residence indebtedness eligible for exclusion. The remaining portion of the debt forgiveness ($1.3 million) exceeds the limitation of $1 million for a MFS taxpayer.

Supporting calculations:

| | |
|---|---|
| Balance of mortgage | $5,000,000 |
| Proceeds of short sale | (3,200,000) |
| Amount of debt canceled | $1,800,000 |

| | |
|---|---|
| Balance of mortgage | $5,000,000 |
| Amount of QPRI | ($4,500,000) |
| Portion that is not QPRI | $500,000 |

| | |
|---|---|
| Amount of debt canceled | $1,800,000 |
| Less portion that is not QPRI | ($500,000) |
| **Subtotal** | **$1,300,000** |
| Less limit for MFS | ($1,000,000) |
| Portion of QPRI not eligible for exclusion | $300,000 |

###

47. In 2012 Mina was discharged from her liability to repay $10,000 of credit card debt. The lender reported the discharged debt on Form 1099-C. Immediately prior to the debt cancellation, Mina had liabilities of $15,000 and the fair market value of her assets was $2,000.

What portion of the canceled debt must Mina include in income?

A. $10,000.
B. $3,000.
C. $5,000.
D. $0.

**The answer is D.** The amount of Mina's insolvency immediately prior to the debt cancellation exceeded the amount of debt that was discharged. Therefore, the entire amount of the debt cancellation can be excluded from income.

Supporting calculations:

| Liabilities | $15,000 |
|---|---|
| Fair market value of assets | ($2,000) |
| **Amount of insolvency** | **$13,000** |

| Amount of debt cancellation | $10,000 |
|---|---|
| **Excess** | **$3,000** |

###

# Unit 6: Adjustments to Gross Income

**More Reading:**
**Publication 590**, *Individual Retirement Arrangements*
**Publication 521**, *Moving Expenses*
**Publication 970**, *Tax Benefits for Education*

An *adjustment to income* directly reduces a taxpayer's income and thus the amount of tax he owes. Adjustments are deducted from gross income to arrive at adjusted gross income (AGI). An adjustment is not the same as a tax deduction. Rather, an adjustment is the best type of deduction—it occurs "above-the-line" on the tax form for adjusted gross income. Adjustments appear as direct subtractions from gross income in order to arrive at AGI. It is easier to visualize if you look at the front of IRS Form 1040.

**Adjustments to income**

This is "*the line*" where AGI is calculated.

# Common Adjustments to Gross Income

There are many types of adjustments to gross income. Some are obscure, and some are very common. We will cover the most common ones in this unit, which are also the most common adjustments tested on the EA exam. These are the adjustments, listed in order, found on the 2012 Form 1040.

1. Educator expenses
2. Certain business expenses of reservists, performing artists, and fee-basis government officials
3. Health savings account deduction
4. Moving expenses
5. Deductible part of self-employment tax
6. Self-employed SEP, SIMPLE, and qualified plans
7. Self-employed health insurance deduction
8. Penalty for early withdrawal of savings
9. Alimony paid
10. IRA deduction
11. Student loan interest deduction
12. Tuition and fees
13. Domestic production activities deduction
14. Other adjustments (Line 36)
    o Archer MSA deduction
    o Jury duty pay remitted to an employer
    o Repayment of unemployment benefits
    o Other adjustments

## Line 23: Educator Expense Deduction

Teachers are allowed to deduct up to $250 of unreimbursed expenses that they pay for books, supplies, computer equipment (including related software and services), other equipment, and supplementary materials used in the classroom.

Since they are an adjustment to income, teachers can deduct these expenses even if they do not itemize deductions.[40]

For courses in health and physical education, expenses are deductible only if they are related to athletics. Nonathletic supplies for physical education and expenses related to health courses do not qualify. Materials used for home schooling also cannot be deducted.

---

[40] This adjustment was scheduled to expire in 2012, but was retroactively reinstated for 2012 and extended through 2013 as part of the fiscal cliff legislation.

Only certain teachers qualify. An eligible educator must work at least 900 hours a school year in a school that provides elementary or secondary education (K-12). College instructors do not qualify. The term "educator" includes:

- Teacher or instructor
- Counselor
- Principal
- Teacher's aide

> **Example:** Devina is a third grade teacher who works full-time in a year-round school. She had 1,600 hours of employment during the tax year. She spent $262 on supplies for her students. Of that amount, $212 was for educational software. The other $50 was for supplies for a unit she teaches on health. Only the $212 is a qualified expense that she can deduct.

On a joint tax return, if both taxpayers are teachers, they both may take the credit, up to a maximum of $500. Any expenses that exceed the adjustment to income may still be deducted as "unreimbursed employee expenses" on Schedule A, subject to the 2% AGI limit.

## Line 24: Certain Business Expenses of Reservists, Performing Artists, and Fee-Basis Government Officials

Certain employees are allowed to take their work-related expenses as an adjustment to income, rather than a deduction on Schedule A. The following individuals qualify for this tax treatment:

- **Reservist:** Members of the reserve component of the Armed Forces of the United States, National Guard, or the Reserve Corps of the Public Health Service. The adjustment is allowed for work-related expenses incurred while traveling more than 100 miles away from the taxpayer's home. The expense is limited to the regular federal per diem rate.
- **Qualified Performing Artist:** To qualify, the taxpayer must meet the following requirements for 2012:
  - Worked in the performing arts as an employee for at least two employers
  - Received at least $200 each from any two of these employers
  - Have related performing-arts business expenses that are more than 10% of gross income from the performance of those services
  - Have AGI of $16,000 *or less* before deducting expenses as a performing artist
- **Fee-Based Government Official:** A state or local government official who is compensated on a fee basis may deduct his employee business expenses whether or not he itemizes other deductions on Schedule A.

In the case of these special occupations, the workers' business expenses are deductible whether or not the taxpayer itemizes deductions.

# Line 25: Health Savings Accounts

A health savings account (HSA) allows taxpayers to save and pay for health care expenses on a tax-preferred basis. The taxpayer can then take withdrawals from the HSA based on the amount of his qualifying medical expenses.

HSA contributions are 100% tax deductible from gross income. The amounts deposited in an HSA become an above-the-line deduction on Form 1040, and itemization of other deductions is not required.

An HSA must be set up exclusively for paying medical expenses for the taxpayer, his spouse, and his dependents. HSA accounts are usually set up with a bank, an insurance company, or by an employer.

To qualify, the taxpayer:

- Must not be enrolled in Medicare
- May not be claimed as a dependent on anyone else's 2012 tax return
- Must be covered under a high deductible health plan and have no other health coverage, other than that for a specific disease or illness; a fixed amount for a certain time period of hospitalization; or liabilities incurred under workers' compensation laws or tort liabilities.

Any eligible individual can contribute to an HSA. For example, an employee and his employer are both allowed to contribute to the employee's HSA in the same year. If an employer makes an HSA contribution on behalf of an employee, it is excluded from the employee's income and not subject to income tax or payroll tax.

In 2012, HSAs allow a taxpayer to avoid federal income tax on up to $3,100 for singles or $6,250 for joint filers. Taxpayers who are 55 and over may contribute an extra $1,000 to their HSAs.

## 2012 Health Savings Account Contribution Limits (HSA)

| Taxpayer | Minimum Deductible | Maximum Out-of-Pocket | Contribution Limit | 55 and Over |
|----------|--------------------|-----------------------|--------------------|-------------|
| Single | $1,200 | $6,050 | $3,100 | +$1,000 |
| Family | $2,400 | $12,100 | $6,250 | +$1,000 |

Excess contributions over these limits are subject to a 6% penalty.

Allowable medical expenses are those that would generally qualify for the medical and dental deduction. Qualified expenses include breast pumps, childbirth classes, dental treatment, hearing aids, Lasik eye surgery, long-term care premiums, weight loss and stop smoking programs, and nursing home care. As of 2011, over-the-counter medicines (other than insulin), unless prescribed by a doctor, are not considered qualified medical expenses.

A taxpayer generally pays medical expenses during the year without being reimbursed by his high deductible health plan, until he reaches the annual deductible for the plan. Withdrawals for nonmedical expenses from an HSA are allowed, but are subject to a 20% penalty, except in the following instances:

- When a taxpayer turns age 65 or older
- When a taxpayer becomes disabled
- When a taxpayer dies

Taxpayers will receive Form 5498-SA from the HSA trustee showing the amount of their contributions for the year. The deduction for an HSA is reported on Form 8889, *Health Savings Accounts*.

To claim the HSA deduction for a particular year, the HSA contributions must be made on or before that year's tax filing date. For 2012, HSA contributions must be made on or before the filing deadline, which is April 15, 2013.

# Line 26: Moving Expenses

If a taxpayer moves due to a change in job or business location, he may deduct moving expenses that his employer has not reimbursed him for. The move must be work-related in order to qualify for this deduction.

A taxpayer who starts a first job or returns to full-time work after a long absence can also qualify for the deduction. Moving expenses incurred within one year from the date the taxpayer first reported to work at the new location can generally be deducted. Although the move must be work-related, there is no requirement that the job be in the same field or similar employment.

If a taxpayer does not move within one year of the date he begins the new job, the moving expenses are not deductible unless he can prove that circumstances existed that prevented the move within that time. Simply failing to sell one's former home, for example, would not be an adequate excuse.

Moving expenses are figured on Form 3903, *Moving Expenses*. The amount is then transferred to Form 1040 as an adjustment to income. To qualify for the moving expense deduction, the taxpayer must satisfy these tests:

- The move must be related to work or business, and
- The taxpayer must meet the **"Distance Test"** and the **"Time Test."**

## *The Time Test*

The *time test* is different for employees than for people who are self-employed. For employees, moving costs are deductible only if the taxpayer works full-time at the new work location for at least 39 weeks in the first 12 months. For joint filers, only one spouse has to qualify for the time test in order to deduct moving expenses.

Self-employed taxpayers must work full-time 39 weeks in the first 12 months at the new location, and then at least 78 weeks within the first 24 months (two years) at the new location. For this test, any combination of full-time work as an employee or as a self-employed person qualifies.

If the taxpayer fails to meet the time test, the taxpayer must report the moving expenses as "other income" on a later tax year, or amend the tax return on which the moving expenses was claimed.

> **Example:** Randy quit his job and moved from California to Oregon to begin a full-time job as a mechanic for Motorcycle Customs, Inc. He worked at the motorcycle shop 40 hours each week. Shortly after his move, Randy also began operating a part-time motorcycle repair business from his home garage for several hours each afternoon and on weekends. Because Randy's principal place of business is Motorcycle Customs, he can satisfy the time test by meeting the 39-week test. However, if Randy is unable to satisfy the requirements of the 39-week test during the 12-month period, he can satisfy the 78-week test because he also works as a self-employed person.

## Exceptions to the Time Test

There are certain times the time test does not need to be met, and the moving expenses will be deductible regardless.

A taxpayer does not have to meet the time test if any of the following applies:

- The taxpayer is in the armed forces and moved because of a permanent change of station.
- The taxpayer's main job location was outside the United States and he moved back to the United States because he retired from his position.
- A taxpayer is the surviving widow(er) of a person whose main job location at the time of death was outside the United States.
- The taxpayer's job at the new location ends because of death or disability.
- The taxpayer is transferred or laid off for a reason other than willful misconduct.

> **Example:** Darrell's company transfers him from New York to Tennessee. He correctly deducts his moving expenses. Darrell expects to continue his full-time employment in Tennessee for many years and does not expect it to be a temporary move. A few months later, his employer is forced into bankruptcy and closes the entire Tennessee division. Darrell is laid off. He does not have to satisfy the time test.

> **Example:** Shelby moves from Michigan to Ohio for a new job as a building manager. Six months after she starts the job, she dies. On Shelby's final tax return, her executor will be able to deduct Shelby's moving expenses, since her job ended at the new location due to death.

# The Distance Test

Under the distance test, the new job must be at least 50 miles farther from the taxpayer's old home than the old job location was from the taxpayer's old home. If the taxpayer had no previous workplace, the new job must be at least 50 miles from the old home (see the diagram for clarification).

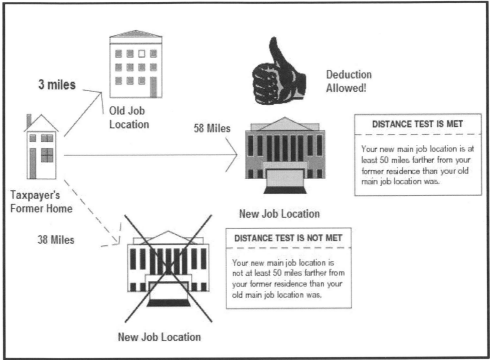

This means that if a taxpayer starts a job for the first time, the place of work must be at least 50 miles from his former home to meet the distance test.

**Example:** Abe moved to a new city and took a job as an attorney in a different law firm. His old job was three miles from his former home. Therefore, in order to deduct his moving expenses, his new job location must be at least 53 miles from that former home. The distance test considers only the location of the former home, not the location of the former job.

For the EA exam, remember that members of the armed forces moving because of a permanent change of station or a military order are not required to meet the distance test or the time test.

**Example:** Matt is enlisted in the Air Force, and has been transferred to another base 32 miles from his former home. Matt may still deduct his moving expenses without meeting the distance test or the time test, since he is a member of the armed forces and his move was due to a military order.

## *Qualifying Moving Expenses*

Only certain expenses qualify for the moving expense deduction. Deductible moving expenses include:

- The cost of packing and moving household effects and family members.
- Storage costs (only while in transit and up to 30 days after the day of the move).
- Travel expenses (including lodging but not meals) for one trip per person. However, family members are not required to travel together. The taxpayer may choose to deduct actual costs or mileage.
- Any costs of connecting or disconnecting utilities required because a taxpayer is moving his household goods, appliances, or personal effects.
- The cost of shipping a car or pet to a new home.

Actual car expenses such as gas and oil are tax deductible if accurate records are kept, or a taxpayer can use the standard mileage rate instead. Parking fees and tolls are also tax deductible, but general car repairs, maintenance, insurance, or depreciation of a taxpayer's car are not tax deductible.

> **Example:** In February 2012, Ethan and Jackie moved from Minnesota to Washington, D.C. where Ethan was starting a new job. He drove the family car to Washington, D.C., a trip of 1,100 miles. His actual expenses were $281.50 for gas, plus $40 for tolls and $150 for lodging, for a total of $471.50. One week later, Jackie flew from Minnesota to Washington, D.C. Her only expense was a $400 plane ticket. The couple's moving expense deduction is $771.50 (Ethan's $471.50 + Jackie's $400).

For purposes of this rule, a taxpayer's home means his main residence. It does not include other homes owned by the taxpayer, such as vacation homes.

# Nondeductible Moving Expenses

Moving expenses that cannot be deducted for income tax purposes include:

- Pre-move house-hunting expenses
- Temporary living expenses
- Meals while traveling
- Expenses of buying or selling a home, home improvements to help sell a home, or loss on a home sale
- Real estate taxes
- Car tags, driver's license renewal fees
- Storage charges except those incurred in transit or for a foreign move

**Extended Example: Nondeductible Moving Expenses**

Ross and Claudia Kim are married and have two children. They owned a home in Charleston, South Carolina where Ross worked. On February 8, 2012, Ross's employer told him that he would be transferred to Albuquerque as of April 10, 2012. Claudia flew to Albuquerque on March 1 to look for a new home. She put a down payment of $25,000 on a house being built and returned to Charleston on March 4, 2012. The Kims sold their Charleston home for $1,500 less than they paid for it. They contracted to have their personal belongings moved to Albuquerque on April 3, 2012. The family drove to Albuquerque where they found that their new home was not finished. They stayed in a nearby motel until the house was ready on May 1. On April 10, 2012, Ross went to work at his new job in Albuquerque.

| | |
|---|---|
| Pre-move house-hunting expenses | $524 |
| Down payment on the Albuquerque home | $25,000 |
| Real estate commission on the sale of the Charleston home | $3,500 |
| Loss of on the sale of the Charleston home | $1,500 |
| Meal expenses for the drive to Albuquerque | $320 |
| Motel expenses while waiting for their home to be finished | $3,730 |
| Moving truck expense | $8,000 |
| Gas and hotel expenses while driving to Albuquerque | $980 |
| **Total expenses** | **$43,554** |

Out of all the expenses that the Kims incurred, only the cost of the moving truck and the actual trip to Albuquerque (the gas and hotel expense) can be deducted ($8,000 + $908 = $8,908). The rest of the expenses cannot be deducted. Meals are not deductible as moving expenses. Losses on the sale of a primary residence and pre-move house-hunting expenses are not deductible.

## Employer-Reimbursed Moving Expenses

When an employer reimburses a taxpayer for moving expenses, the reimbursement is excluded from taxable income

However, if an employer reimburses an employee for "nondeductible" expenses (such as the expense incurred from breaking a lease), this reimbursement is taxable as wages. It must be treated as paid under a nonaccountable plan and be included as income on the employee's Form W-2.

Expenses of buying or selling a home or breaking a lease (including closing costs, mortgage fees, and points) are never deductible as moving expenses.

> **Example:** Xavier is an engineer who has been offered a job at XelCorp Engineering. He only agrees to accept the offer if XelCorp pays all his moving expenses. The cost of his professional movers was $9,600, which the company agrees to pay. This amount is deductible by XelCorp as a business expense and not taxable to Xavier, since it is a legitimate moving expense and allowable by the IRS. However, in order to entice him to move out of state, XelCorp also reimburses Xavier for a $7,500 loss on the sale of his home. Because this is a reimbursement of a nondeductible expense, it is treated as taxable to the employee and must be included in Xavier's Form W-2. Xavier has $7,500 added to his wages. The $7,500 is also deductible to XelCorp, but it is categorized as a wage expense and subject to payroll tax.

## Seasonal Work and Temporary Absences: Exceptions

For purposes of the moving expense deduction, if a taxpayer's trade or business is seasonal, the off-season weeks when no work is available may still be counted as weeks during which he worked full time. In order to qualify, the off-season must be less than six months and the taxpayer must work full-time before *and* after the off-season.

Temporary absences from work are allowed. A taxpayer is still considered to be employed on a full-time basis during any week he is temporarily absent from work because of illness, labor strikes, natural disasters, or similar causes.

> **Example:** Marcus moves from Colorado to Jackson Hole, Wyoming to take a job as a manager of a ski resort. He works full-time during the ski season, and he is off for five months during the summer. Marcus may still count this time as full-time work, since his regular employment is expected to be seasonal.

> **Example:** Marlene moves to Florida from Missouri to take a job with a new employer. After working 25 weeks, her union votes to go on strike. She is off work for five weeks until the issue is resolved. Those five weeks count as a temporary absence and still may be counted as full-time work for purposes of satisfying the time test. Marlene still qualifies for the moving expenses deduction, because the time she spent on strike is considered a "temporary absence" for purposes of this test.

## Line 27: One-Half of Self-Employment Tax

As detailed in Unit 5, self-employed taxpayers can subtract half of their self-employment tax from their income. This is equal to the amount of Social Security tax and Medicare tax that an employer normally pays for an employee, which is excluded from an employee's income.

SE tax must be paid if either of the following applies:
- The taxpayer had income as a church employee of $108.28 or more, or
- The taxpayer had self-employment income of $400 or more.

## Line 28: Self-Employed SEP, SIMPLE, and Qualified Plans

Self-employed individuals are allowed to take a deduction for contributions to certain types of retirement plans. Line 28 of Form 1040 is used to report contributions to the following types of plans:

- Self-employed SEP (Simplified Employee Pension)
- Self-employed SIMPLE (Savings Incentive Match Plan for Employees)
- Self-employed qualified plans

Generally under these plans, contributions that are set aside for retirement may be currently deductible by the taxpayer, but are not taxable until later. Therefore, the contribution grows tax-free until the monies are distributed.

A taxpayer must have self-employment income in order to contribute to his own plan. However, a self-employed person with employees may still contribute to his employee's retirement plans, even if his business shows a loss for the year.

## Line 29: Self-Employed Health Insurance Deduction

A self-employed taxpayer may also deduct 100% of his health insurance premiums as an adjustment to income. Premiums paid by the taxpayer for his spouse and dependents are also deductible as an adjustment to income. For the first time, health insurance premiums paid for coverage of an adult child under age 27 at the end of the year also qualify for this deduction, even if the child is not the taxpayer's dependent.

In addition, long-term care insurance is considered health insurance for purposes of this deduction. The policy can be in the name of the business or in the name of the business owner.

A self-employed taxpayer must have a net profit for the year in order to take this deduction. So if the taxpayer is showing a loss on his Schedule C, he is not allowed to take this deduction.

A self-employed taxpayer also may not take the deduction if either he or his spouse (if MFJ) is eligible to participate in an employer-sponsored and subsidized health insurance plan. This is true even if they decline coverage.

## Line 30: Penalty on Early Withdrawal of Savings

If a taxpayer withdraws money from a certificate of deposit (CD) or other time-deposit savings account prior to maturing, he usually incurs a penalty for early withdrawal. This penalty is charged by the bank and withheld directly from a taxpayer's proceeds from the certificate.

Taxpayers can take an adjustment to income for early withdrawal penalties. The penalties are reported on a taxpayer's Form 1099-INT, *Interest Income*, or Form 1099-OID, *Original Issue Discount*. These forms will list the interest income, as well as the penalty amount.

> **Example:** Earlier in 2012, Gloria invested in a certificate of deposit. However, in November, she had an unexpected medical expense and had to withdraw all the money early. Gloria made an early withdrawal of $15,000 from a one-year, deferred-interest CD in the current tax year. She had to pay a penalty of three months' interest, which totaled $150. Gloria can claim the penalty ($150) as an adjustment to income.

**\*Note:** The penalty for early withdrawal of an IRA (retirement plan) is not tax-deductible.

## Line 31: Alimony Paid as an Adjustment to Income

In Unit 5, we covered alimony as taxable income. Alimony is also a deductible expense by the individual who pays the alimony. Taxpayers may claim the deduction for "alimony paid" on Page 1 of Form 1040. They cannot use Form 1040A or Form 1040EZ.

By definition, alimony is a payment to a former spouse under a divorce or separation instrument. The payments do not have to be made directly to the ex-spouse. For example, payments made on behalf of the ex-spouse for expenses such as medical bills, housing costs, and other expenses can also qualify as alimony.

> **Example:** Victoria divorced two years ago. Her divorce settlement agreement states that she must pay her ex-husband $16,000 a year. She is also required, per the divorce agreement, to pay his ongoing medical expenses. In 2012, the medical expenses were $9,500. She can deduct the full amount ($25,500) because it is all required by her divorce agreement.

Alimony does not include child support, which is never deductible. Alimony will be disallowed and reclassified as child support if the divorce decree states that the "alimony" will discontinue based on a contingency relating to the child.

> **Example:** Neil pays child support and alimony to his ex-wife. They have one child together. The divorce decree states that he must pay $400 per month in child support and $500 per month in alimony. However, Neil's divorce agreement states that all payments will discontinue if the child gets married. This means that for tax purposes, all the payments must be treated as child support.

### Requirements for Payments to Qualify as Alimony

Noncash property settlements, whether in a lump sum or installments, are not considered alimony. Voluntary payments (i.e., payments not required by a divorce decree or separation instrument) do not qualify as alimony. To qualify as alimony, all of these requirements must be met:

- The payments must be in cash or cash equivalents (checks or money orders).
- Payments must be required by the divorce decree.
- If only legally separated, spouses may not live in the same household.
- The payment may not be child support.

- The payer's liability for the alimony payments must stop upon the death of the recipient spouse.
- The parties may not file jointly.

**Payments after Death and Voluntary Payments are not Alimony**

If any alimony payments must continue after the ex-spouse's death, those payments are not considered alimony for tax purposes, even if they are made before death. These payments would normally be reclassified as child support, and therefore are not taxable to the recipient and nondeductible to the payer. Voluntary payments *outside* the divorce agreement do not count as alimony.

The person paying alimony can subtract it as an adjustment to income; the person receiving alimony claims it as taxable income.

> **Example:** Anthony has been divorced for three years. Under his divorce decree, he paid his ex-wife $12,600 in 2012. As a favor, he also made $2,400 in payments to cover part of her vehicle lease so she could keep steady employment. Anthony can take the $12,600 as an adjustment to income. He cannot count the lease payments because they were not required by the divorce agreement.

If a taxpayer's decree of divorce or separate maintenance provides for alimony and child support and the payer pays *less* than the total amount required, the payments apply first to child support. Any remaining amount is considered alimony.

> **Example:** Jeff must pay alimony and child support to his ex-wife, Liz. His monthly payment for alimony is $200, and his monthly payment for child support is $800. Jeff falls behind on his payments and is only able to pay $500 per month in 2012. The amount is calculated as follows: $200 x 12 = $2,400 (alimony due), $800 x 12 = $9,600 (child support due). Jeff can only pay $500 x 12 = $6,000; therefore he is short by $6,000 ($2,400 + $9,600 = $12,000 − $6,000). Since the amount he can pay falls short of the required child support payment by itself, all of his $6,000 will be reclassified as child support. Therefore, Jeff can deduct none of his payments as alimony. Also, Jeff's ex-wife does not have to claim any of the payments as alimony income. Child support is not taxable and not deductible by either party.

# Line 32: Deduction for Traditional IRA Contributions

An IRA (Individual Retirement Arrangement) is a personal savings plan that offers tax advantages for setting aside money for retirement. Generally, amounts in an IRA, including earnings and gains, are not taxed until they are distributed.

The complex rules regarding contributions, withdrawals, and rollovers to IRAs will be covered extensively in Unit 14. Here, we will only discuss the adjustment to income that is allowed on Page 1 of Form 1040.

Only traditional IRAs qualify for tax-deductible contributions. Amounts that do not qualify for a deduction include:

- Roth IRA contributions

179

- Contributions that apply to the previous tax year
- Rollovers
- Nondeductible contributions due to the taxpayer's active participation in an employer-sponsored plan

To contribute to a traditional IRA, the taxpayer must:

- Be *under* the age of 70½ at the end of the tax year
- Have taxable compensation, such as wages income from self-employment (Taxable alimony and nontaxable combat pay are treated as compensation for IRA purposes)

For purposes of a contribution to a traditional IRA, compensation does not include passive income such as:

- Pension income
- Rental income
- Interest and dividend income

Contributions can be made to a traditional IRA at any time during the year or by the *due date* for filing the return, not including extensions.

> **Example:** Daniel wants to make a contribution to his traditional IRA for 2012, but he is unsure how much he should contribute. He sees his accountant on April 1, 2013, and Daniel decides that he wants to contribute the maximum amount. Daniel files his tax return on April 1 and takes the deduction for his contribution. Daniel now has until April 15, 2013 to make a tax deductible contribution to his traditional IRA for the 2012 tax year.

For 2012, the most a taxpayer can contribute to his traditional IRA generally is the *smaller* of the following amounts:

- 5,000 ($6,000 if age 50 or older), or
- The amount of taxable compensation.

> **Example:** Wes is 52 and self-employed. Normally, he would be able to contribute $6,000 to a traditional IRA. However, in 2012, he has $3,700 in self-employment income, and $23,000 in dividend income. Since only his self-employment income counts as "compensation" for purposes of an IRA contribution, the maximum he can contribute for the 2012 tax year is $3,700.

## Line 33: Student Loan Interest Deduction

Generally, personal interest (other than mortgage interest) is not deductible on a tax return. However, there is a special deduction for interest paid on a student loan used for higher education.

Only student loan interest paid to an accredited college or university is eligible for this deduction. A "qualified student loan" is used solely to pay qualified education expenses for the taxpayer, his spouse, or dependents.

A taxpayer can claim the deduction if:

- He paid interest on a qualified loan in 2012
- He is legally obligated to pay interest on a qualified student loan
- His filing status is not married filing separately
- He (or his spouse if filing jointly) cannot be claimed as dependents on someone else's return

The maximum deduction for student loan interest in 2012 is $2,500. The loan begins to phase out for married taxpayers filing a joint return at $125,000 and phases out completely at $155,000. For single taxpayers the phase-out range is from $60,000 to $75,000.

**Example:** Veronica and her husband file jointly. Their modified adjusted gross income (MAGI) is $162,000. She completed her doctoral degree in 2012 and paid $3,400 in student loan interest in 2012. Due to their high MAGI, they may not deduct any of their student loan interest as an adjustment to income.

In order for the student loan interest to qualify, the student must have been enrolled at least half-time in a higher education program leading to a degree, certificate, or other recognized educational credential. A student who is taking classes for his own recreation does not qualify.

**Example:** Peter attends a local technical college where he is enrolled full-time in a certificate program for automotive repair. Peter may take the student loan interest deduction.

Qualified expenditures are the total cost of attending an eligible educational institution, including graduate school. Qualified expenses include:

- Tuition and fees
- Room and board
- Books, supplies, and equipment
- Other necessary school-related expenses, such as transportation

Before calculating "qualified expenses" on a tax return, the following tax-free income amounts must be subtracted:

1. Employer-provided educational assistance benefits
2. Tax-free withdrawals from a Coverdell Education Savings Account
3. U.S. savings bond interest already excluded from income
4. Tax-free scholarships and fellowships
5. Veterans' educational assistance benefits
6. Any other nontaxable payments (except gifts, bequests, or inheritances) received for educational expenses

> **Example**: In 2012, Katelyn's educational expenses are $7,200. She also receives a gift of $1,000 from her aunt and $1,000 in veterans' educational assistance. Therefore, in 2012 Katelyn's qualified higher education expenses for purposes of the student loan interest deduction are $6,200. This is because veterans' assistance benefits must be subtracted from a taxpayer's educational expenses. The gift from her aunt does not have to be subtracted.

Under the terms of this deduction, a loan is not eligible if it was granted by a family member. This includes a spouse, brothers and sisters, half-brothers and half-sisters, ancestors (parents, grandparents, etc.), and lineal descendants (children, grandchildren, etc.). Loans from an employer plan also do not qualify.

The student loan interest deduction is "per return" not "per student." So, for example, if a taxpayer has three children in college and pays over $2,000 in student loan interest for each of them, the maximum deduction is still only $2,500.

## Student Loan Interest Deduction: A Summary

| Rules | Description |
|---|---|
| **Maximum benefit** | $2,500 per tax return, per year |
| **Loan qualifications** | The student loan: |
| | • Must have been taken out solely to pay qualified education expenses, and <br> • Cannot be from a related person or made under a qualified employer plan. |
| **Student qualifications** | The student must be: |
| | • The taxpayer, a spouse, or a dependent, and <br> • Enrolled at least half-time in a degree program. |
| **Time limit** | The taxpayer can deduct interest paid during the remaining period of the student loan. |
| **Phase-out ranges** | In 2012, the phase-out range is $60,000 to $75,000 of MAGI for single filers and $125,000 to $155,000 for MFJ. MFS filers do not qualify. |

# Line 34: Tuition and Fees Deduction

The tuition and fees deduction allows taxpayers to deduct qualified tuition and related expenses as an adjustment to income. The deduction is allowed for qualified higher education expenses paid for academic periods beginning in 2012 and the first three months of 2013.

In 2012, the maximum deduction is either $2,000 or $4,000, depending on MAGI. The deduction is calculated as follows:

- $4,000 if MAGI is $65,000 or less ($130,000 if MFJ)
- $2,000 if MAGI is $80,000 or less ($160,000 if MFJ)

The deduction is eliminated completely once a taxpayer's MAGI exceeds $80,000 for single filers and $160,000 if filing jointly.

A qualified student is:

- The taxpayer
- The taxpayer's spouse (if filing jointly)
- The taxpayer's dependent

## Qualifying Educational Expenses: Tuition and Fees Deduction

The expenses that qualify for the tuition and fees deduction are very different than the expenses that qualify for the student loan interest deduction.

Generally, for the tuition and fees deduction, qualified education expenses are amounts paid for tuition expenses only at an eligible college or vocational institution. It does not matter whether the expenses are paid in cash, by check, by credit card, or with student loans. Qualified education expenses do not include amounts paid for:

- Room and board, medical expenses (including student health fees), transportation, or other personal expenses
- Course-related books, supplies, equipment, and nonacademic activities, unless they are required as a condition of enrollment
- Any course or other education involving sports, games, or hobbies, or any noncredit course

A taxpayer cannot claim the tuition and fees deduction based on expenses that have already been paid with a tax-free scholarship, fellowship, grant, or education savings account funds such as a Coverdell education savings account, tax-free savings bond interest, or employer-provided education assistance.

### Tuition Received as a Gift (Special Rule)

Another individual may make a payment directly to an eligible educational institution to pay for a student's education expenses. In this case, the student is treated as receiving the payment as a gift from the other person and, in turn, paying the institution. In order for the taxpayer to claim the deduction for tuition received as a gift, the taxpayer may not be claimed on anyone else's tax return. If someone else can claim an exemption for the student, no one will be allowed a deduction for the tuition payment. In this case, there is also a special exemption in the law; the giver does not have to file a gift tax return.

Specifically, any tuition payments made by a grandparent (or anyone else) directly to a college to cover a student's tuition expenses are exempt from federal gift tax. The money will not qualify for a gift tax exemption if it is first given to the student, with instructions to pay the college.

### Reporting Refunded Tuition After Claiming the Deduction

Sometimes a student will have his tuition refunded. If, after a tax return, a student receives a refund of amounts that were previously used to figure the tuition and fees deduction, the taxpayer must report the refund as income in the following year. The refunded amount is added to income by entering it on the "Other Income" line of Form 1040 in the following year—the year the refund of tuition is received. The taxpayer's current year tax return does not need to be amended.

---

**Example:** Keith has one daughter named Robin. He paid $8,000 in tuition and fees for Robin's college education in December 2012, and she began college in January 2013. Keith filed his 2012 tax return on March 1, 2013 and properly claimed a tuition and fees deduction of $4,000. After Keith filed his return, Robin dropped three classes and Keith received a refund of $5,600. Keith must refigure his tuition and fees deduction using $2,400 of qualified expenses instead of $8,000 ($8,000 - $5,600). He must include the difference of $1,600 ($4,000 - $2,400) on his 2013 Form 1040.

---

**\*Study Tip:** On the EA exam, be prepared to understand the difference between the tuition and fees deduction and the student loan interest deduction; qualifying expenses, AGI limits, and deduction amounts are all different. A common "trick question" might be to verify a type of qualifying expense. Remember that in the case of the student loan interest deduction, qualifying expenses include housing, but they are not for the tuition and fees deduction.

A taxpayer filing MFS cannot take the tuition and fees deduction. Nonresident aliens also do not qualify for this deduction.

To prevent double-dipping, a taxpayer cannot claim the tuition and fees deduction and an education credit for the *same student*. A taxpayer who is eligible to claim the American Opportunity Credit or Lifetime Learning Credit[41] is allowed to figure his return both ways and choose the deduction that results in the lowest tax.

A taxpayer does not have to itemize in order to take the tuition and fees deduction.

# Line 35: Domestic Production Activities Deduction

The Domestic Production Activities Deduction (DPAD) is a tax deduction that is given to businesses that have employees and also do manufacturing and other qualifying activities in the United States. The aim of this deduction is to stimulate domestic production.

This deduction is covered primarily in Part 2 of the exam, because it applies mainly to businesses. However, it is possible for a sole proprietor to qualify for this deduction, so long as the taxpayer has employees and pays wages to those employees.

# Line 36: Other Adjustments

Line 36 of Form 1040 is reserved for more obscure deductions. There is a dotted line on the form that allows the taxpayer to indicate what type of adjustment is being taken, and most software programs will fill this in automatically. These are some of the miscellaneous adjustments that are entered on line 36:

---

[41] These education credits are discussed in Unit 9, Tax Credits.

1. **Archer MSA:** An Archer MSA[42] is a tax-exempt account that is set up with a U.S. financial institution in which a taxpayer can save money exclusively for future medical expenses. It is similar to a health savings account.

2. **Jury duty pay remitted to an employer:** Jury duty pay is reported as taxable income on Form 1040. However, some employees continue to receive their regular wages when they serve on jury duty even though they are not at work, and their jury pay is turned over to their employers. In that case, the amount is reported as a write-in adjustment.

3. **Repayment of unemployment benefits:** A taxpayer who repaid unemployment benefits may take the repaid amounts as an adjustment to income in the year the amount is repaid.[43]

---

[42] Although Archer MSAs still exist, they were superseded by HSAs, which were created in 2003 and are more widely available.

[43] Sometimes, a person will be forced to repay unemployment benefits back to the state. This happens most often when an individual continues to draw unemployment after he has started working again.

# Unit 6: Questions

1. Jermaine and Anna have a MAGI of $45,000. They are married and file a joint return. Two years ago, they took out a loan so their daughter, Miranda, could earn her degree. Miranda is their dependent. In 2012, they paid $3,000 in student loan interest. How much student loan interest can Jermaine and Anna deduct on their tax return?

A. $0.
B. $1,000.
C. $2,500.
D. $3,000.

**The answer is C.** The maximum deduction for student loan interest is $2,500. The deduction is limited to the lesser of $2,500 or the amount of interest actually paid. ###

2. Contributions to a traditional IRA can be made:

A. Any time during the year or by the due date of the return, not including extensions.
B. Any time during the year or by the due date of the return, including extensions.
C. By December 31 (the end of the tax year).
D. Any time during the year, but only while the taxpayer is gainfully employed.

**The answer is A.** IRA contributions for tax year 2012 must be made by April 15, 2013. A taxpayer cannot make a contribution to an IRA after the due date of his tax return, even if he files for an extension. ###

3. All of the following statements are correct except:

A. A school counselor may qualify for the educator expense deduction.
B. A part-time teacher may qualify for the educator expense deduction.
C. A school principal may qualify for the educator expense deduction.
D. A college instructor may qualify for the educator expense deduction.

**The answer is D.** College instructors do not qualify. An eligible educator must work 900 hours a year in a school that provides elementary or secondary education (K-12). Part-time teachers qualify, so long as they meet the yearly requirement for hours worked. The term educator includes teachers, instructors, counselors, principals, and aides. ###

4. What is the maximum educator's expense deduction for two teachers who are married and file jointly?

A. $100.
B. $250.
C. $500.
D. $750.

**The answer is C.** On a jointly filed tax return, if both taxpayers are teachers, they both may take the deduction, up to a maximum of $500 ($250 each). ###

5. Which of the following statements is true?

A. Credit card interest can be deductible as student loan interest if qualifying educational expenses are paid.
B. On a married filing jointly return, a taxpayer may deduct student loan interest paid on behalf of his spouse.
C. The maximum deduction for student loan interest is $5,000 per student.
D. Taxpayers may deduct student loan interest even if they are not liable for the loan.

**The answer is B.** On a MFJ return, a taxpayer may deduct student loan interest paid on behalf of his spouse or dependents. This deduction is a maximum of $2,500 in 2012. Credit card interest does not qualify, and taxpayers must be liable for the loan in order to deduct the interest expense. ###

6. Drew borrowed $15,000 from his sister to pay for college. He signed a notarized loan statement and is paying regular payments of $500 per month at 10% interest. In 2012, he paid $3,200 in student loan interest. Which of the following is true?

A. Drew can deduct all the interest as qualified student loan interest.
B. Drew can deduct $2,500 of the interest as qualified student loan interest.
C. Drew cannot deduct the interest.
D. Drew can deduct $6,000 ($500 X 12 months).

**The answer is C.** Interest paid to a family member is not qualified interest for purposes of the student loan interest deduction. Related persons include a spouse, brothers and sisters, half-brothers and half-sisters, ancestors (parents, grandparents, etc.), and lineal descendants (children, grandchildren, etc.). ###

7. Years ago, Sammy took out a student loan for $90,000 to help pay the tuition at a university in the Ivy League. He graduated and began making payments on his student loan in 2012. Sammy made twelve payments in 2012, and he paid $1,600 in required interest on the loan. He also paid an additional $1,000 in principal payment voluntarily, attempting to get the debt paid off faster. How much is Sammy's student loan interest deduction?

A. $1,600.
B. $2,500.
C. $2,600.
D. $90,000

**The answer is A.** Only the interest is deductible. A payment toward the principal on the loan is not a deductible expense. Student loan interest is interest a taxpayer paid during the year on a qualified student loan. It includes both required and voluntary interest payments. ###

8. Which of the following expenses does not qualify for the student loan interest deduction?

A. Dorm housing.
B. Required books.
C. Required equipment.
D. Tuition for a non-degree candidate.

**The answer is D.** The student must be enrolled at least half-time in a program leading to a degree, certificate, or other recognized educational credential in order to qualify for the student loan interest deduction. Tuition for a non-degree candidate or someone who is taking classes just for fun or for general improvement does not qualify. ###

9. Which of the following qualifies as a deductible education expense for the tuition and fees deduction?

A. College club dues.
B. Student health fees.
C. Room and board.
D. Student activity fees required as a condition for enrollment.

**The answer is D.** Only the student activity fees qualify for the tuition and fees deduction. Deductions are not allowed for room and board and other basic expenses of going to college, other than required tuition and fees. Student activity fees, course-related books, supplies, and equipment may be deductible only if they are required by the institution as a condition of enrollment. ###

10. Addie paid $2,000 tuition and fees in December 2012, and she began college in January 2013. She filed her 2012 tax return on February 1, 2013, and correctly claimed a tuition and fees deduction of $2,000. But after Addie filed her return, she became ill and dropped two courses. She received a refund of tuition in the amount of $1,100 in April 2013. How must Addie report the refund of fees?

A. Addie may use the refund to pay qualified tuition in 2013 and not report the refund.
B. Addie may report the refund on her next year's tax return as "Other Income."
C. Addie is not required to report the refund.
D. Addie is required to amend her 2012 return and remove the deduction for tuition and fees.

**The answer is B.** Addie may include the difference of $1,100 on the "Other Income" line of her Form 1040 in 2013. Her 2012 return does not have to be amended. ###

11. Alimony does not include:
A. Noncash property settlements.
B. Payments to a third-party on behalf of an ex-spouse.
C. Medical expenses paid on behalf of an ex-spouse.
D. Cash alimony payments.

**The answer is A.** Noncash property settlements do not qualify as alimony. Alimony does not include child support, noncash property settlements, payments to keep up the payer's property, or use of the payer's property. Payments made to a third party or medical expenses paid on behalf of a former spouse may qualify as alimony. ###

12. In 2012, Patricia was offered a new job in a different state. She had the following moving expenses:
- $1,200 for transporting her household goods
- $550 in lodging for travel between her old home and her new home
- $250 in meals during the trip
- $250 to break the lease on her old home

Patricia moved to start a new job and met the distance and time tests. What are the total moving expenses that can be deducted on her tax return?

A. $2,150.
B. $1,900.
C. $1,750.
D. $2,000.

**The answer is C.** The answer is figured as follows:

| Cost of moving goods: | $1,200 |
|---|---|
| Lodging | $550 |
| Deductible expenses | $1,750 |

A taxpayer cannot deduct any moving expenses for meals. The cost of breaking a lease to move to a new location is also not a deductible expense. ###

13. Dave and Bea file jointly. In March 2012, they move from Arizona to Connecticut, where Dave is starting a new job. Dave drives the car to Hartford. His expenses are $400 for gas, $40 for tolls, $150 for lodging, and $70 for meals. One week later, Bea drives to Hartford. Her expenses are $500 for gas, $40 for tolls, $35 for parking, $100 for lodging, and $25 for meals. A week later, they pay $600 to ship their pet, a miniature horse, to Connecticut. How much is their deduction for moving expenses?

A. $590.
B. $1,265.
C. $1,300.
D. $1,865.

**The answer is D.** The cost of meals is not deductible. The costs of travel, transportation, and lodging are all deductible. The costs of moving personal items and pets are deductible. The answer is figured as follows:

Dave's expenses $400 + $40 + $150 = $590
Bea's expenses $500+ $40 +$35 + $100 = $675
Cost of shipping horse = $600
Total deductible expenses: $590 + $675 + $600 = $1,865

If a married couple files jointly, *either* spouse can qualify for the full-time work test. Family members are not required to travel together. ###

14. Lynn was offered a position in another city. Her new employer reimburses her for the $9,500 loss on the sale of her home because of the move. How should this reimbursement be treated?

A. The employer can reimburse Lynn and make the payment nontaxable through an accountable plan, if properly documented.
B. Because this is a reimbursement of a nondeductible expense, it is treated as wages and must be included as pay on Lynn's Form W-2.
C. The reimbursement is tax-exempt because it is a qualified moving expense.
D. The expense is nontaxable so long as Lynn's employer makes the payment directly to her mortgage lender.

**The answer is B.** Because this is a reimbursement of a nondeductible expense, it is treated as paid under a nonaccountable plan and must be included as pay on Lynn's Form W-2. Expenses of buying or selling a home (including closing costs, mortgage fees, and points) are never deductible as moving expenses. If an employer offers to pay these expenses as a condition of employment, then the amounts are treated like taxable compensation and must be reported and treated as such. ###

15. Ian and Pam are divorced. Pam has an auto accident and dies. Under their divorce decree, Ian must continue to pay his former spouse's estate $30,000 annually. The divorce decree states that upon Pam's death, the continued payments will be put into trust for their daughter, who is 12 years old. What is true about the $30,000 annual payment?

A. For tax purposes, it is alimony.
B. For tax purposes, it is child support.
C. For tax purposes, it is a gift.
D. Once Pam dies, the payments are taxable to the daughter.

**The answer is B.** The trust is to be used for the child's benefit and must continue after Pam's death. Therefore, the $30,000 annual payment is not alimony and is instead classified as child support for tax purposes. Any payment that is specifically designated as child support or treated as specifically designated as child support under a divorce agreement is not alimony. ###

16. Under his divorce decree, Rick must pay the medical expenses of his former spouse, Linda. In January 2012, Rick sends a check totaling $4,000 directly to General Medical Hospital in order to pay for Linda's emergency surgery. Which of the following statements is true?

A. This payment qualifies as alimony, and Linda must include the $4,000 as income on her return.
B. This payment does not qualify as alimony, but Rick can claim a deduction for the medical expenses on his return.
C. Linda must include the $4,000 as income on her return, but Rick cannot deduct the expense as alimony because it was paid to a third party.
D. None of the above.

**The answer is A.** The payment may be treated as alimony for tax purposes, because the medical payments are a condition of the divorce agreement. Payments to a third party on behalf of an ex-spouse under the terms of a divorce instrument can be alimony, if they qualify. These include payments for a spouse's medical expenses, housing costs (rent and utilities), taxes, and tuition. The payments are treated as received by the ex-spouse and included as income. ###

17. George paid $14,000 in alimony to his wife during the year. Which of the following is true?

A. George can only deduct alimony if he itemizes deductions on his tax return.
B. The deduction for alimony is entered on Schedule A as an itemized deduction.
C. George can deduct alimony paid, even if he does not itemize.
D. George can deduct alimony paid on Form 1040A.

**The answer is C.** George can deduct alimony paid, even if he does not itemize. He must file Form 1040 and enter the amount of alimony paid as an adjustment to income. An adjustment for alimony cannot be claimed on Form 1040EZ or Form 1040A. ###

18. Under the terms of a divorce decree, Blake transfers appreciated property to his ex-wife, Ming. The property has a fair market value of $75,000 and an adjusted basis of $50,000 to Blake. This transaction creates taxable alimony of _____ to Ming.

A. $0.
B. $25,000.
C. $75,000.
D. $50,000.

**The answer is A.** Transfers of property in the fulfillment of a divorce decree are not taxable events. Property settlements due to a divorce decree are not alimony; they are simply a division of assets and are treated as such. ###

19. If a taxpayer's decree of divorce provides for alimony and child support, and the payer pays less than the total amount required, the payments apply first to _____.

A. Alimony.
B. Child support.
C. Separate maintenance.
D. Tax delinquencies.

**The answer is B.** If a taxpayer's decree of divorce or separate maintenance provides for alimony and child support, and the payer pays less than the total amount required, the payments apply first to child support. Any remaining amount is considered alimony. ###

20. Kyle has an HSA, and he becomes permanently disabled in 2012. Which of the following statements is true?

A. Kyle may withdraw money from his HSA for nonmedical expenses, but the withdrawals will be subject to income tax and also an additional penalty.
B. Kyle may withdraw money from his HSA for nonmedical expenses. The withdrawals will be subject to income tax, but will not be subject to penalty.
C. Kyle may not take nonmedical distributions from his account.
D. Kyle must be at least 65 to take nonmedical distributions from an HSA.

**The answer is B.** Kyle is disabled, so his withdrawals are not subject to penalty. Withdrawals for nonmedical expenses from an HSA are allowed, but nonmedical distributions are subject to an additional penalty tax, except when the taxpayer turns 65, becomes disabled, or dies. ###

21. Seth makes an excess contribution to his HSA, by accidentally contributing over the maximum allowable amount. What is the penalty on excess contributions if Seth does not correct the problem?

A. No penalty.
B. 6% penalty.
C. 10% penalty.
D. 20% penalty.

**The answer is B.** The 6% penalty applies to excess contributions. Excess contributions made by an employer must be included in an employee's gross income. Excess contributions to an HSA are not deductible. ###

22. Emilio is a sophomore at California State University's degree program in Anthropology. This year, he paid $3,000 in tuition and $10,000 to live in optional on-campus housing. In addition to tuition, he is required to pay a fee of $300 to the university for the rental of the equipment he will use in this program. How much of these expenses qualify for the tuition and fees deduction?

A. $3,000.
B. $3,300.
C. $13,000.
D. $13,300.

**The answer is B.** The rental fee and the tuition costs qualify for the tuition and fees deduction, and Emilio may deduct the cost on his tax return. Because the equipment rental fee must be paid to the university and is a requirement for enrollment and attendance, it is a qualified expense. Student activity fees and expenses for course-related books, supplies, and equipment can be included in qualified educational expenses if the fees and expenses paid to the institution are required. The housing is not a qualified educational expense. ###

23. In 2012, Caylie had an HSA account set up with her employer. At the end of the year, she had $3,000 in the account. Then she quit her job and withdrew all the funds from her HSA. She did not use the $3,000 for qualifying medical expenses. What is the consequence of this action?

A. Nothing; taxpayers are allowed to withdraw from their HSA accounts at any time.
B. Nonmedical withdrawals from an HSA are prohibited and will result in a forfeiture of the funds.
C. Withdrawals from an HSA for non-eligible expenses are subject to a 20% penalty.
D. Withdrawals from an HSA for non-eligible expenses are subject to a 6% penalty.

**The answer is C.** Withdrawals from an HSA for non-eligible expenses are allowed, but the withdrawal will be subject to a 20% penalty, in addition to regular income tax. ###

24. During 2012, Deborah was self-employed. She had self-employment tax of $4,896. Which of the following statements is true?

A. Deborah may deduct 100% of the self-employment tax she paid on Schedule C.
B. Deborah may deduct 50% of the self-employment tax she paid on Schedule C.
C. Deborah may deduct 50% of the self-employment tax she paid as an adjustment to income on Form 1040.
D. Deborah may not deduct self-employment tax.

**The answer is C.** Deborah may deduct 50% of the self-employment tax she paid as an adjustment to income on page 1 of her Form 1040. A taxpayer can deduct one-half (not 100%) of self-employment tax paid as an adjustment on Form 1040. ###

25. Marshall lost his job last year and withdrew money from a number of accounts. He paid the following penalties:

1. $100 penalty for early withdrawal from a certificate of deposit (CD).
2. $200 penalty from early withdrawal from a traditional IRA.
3. $50 late penalty for not paying his rent on time.

How much of these listed amounts can Marshall deduct as an adjustment to income on his Form 1040?

A. $0.
B. $100.
C. $200.
D. $250.

**The answer is B.** Early withdrawal penalties are tax-deductible if made from a time deposit account, such as a certificate of deposit. Taxpayers deduct any penalties on Form 1040 as an adjustment to income. ###

26. Jasmine is a part-time art teacher at an elementary school. She spends $185 on qualified expenses for her art students and $75 on materials for a health course that she also teaches. She has 440 hours of documented employment as an educator during the tax year. How much can she deduct as a qualified educator expense as an adjustment to income?

A. $0.
B. $185.
C. $250.
D. $260.

**The answer is A.** Because she has only 440 hours of documented employment as an educator during the tax year, she cannot deduct her educator expenses as an adjustment to income. An educator must have at least 900 hours of qualified employment during the school year in order to take this deduction as an adjustment to income. ###

27. Chuck and Mallory are married and file jointly. Chuck is self-employed and his profit was $50,000 in 2012. They pay $500 per month for health insurance coverage. Mallory was a homemaker until March 1, 2012, when she got a job working for a local construction company. Mallory was eligible to participate in an employer health plan, but she and Chuck did not want to switch doctors, so she declined the coverage. Which of the following statements is true?

A. No deduction is allowed in 2012 for self-employed health insurance.
B. Chuck and Mallory may only deduct $1,000 in self-employed health insurance, which is for January and February, the two months they were not eligible to participate in an employer plan.
C. Chuck and Mallory may deduct 100% of their insurance premiums because they declined the employer coverage.
D. Chuck and Mallory may deduct 50% of their health insurance premiums on Chuck's Schedule C.

**The answer is B.** Chuck and Mallory may only deduct $1,000 in self-employed health insurance for the two months that they were ineligible to participate in an employer plan. No deduction is allowed for self-employed health insurance for any month that the taxpayer has the option to participate in an employer-sponsored and subsidized plan. This is true even if the taxpayer declines the coverage. Self-employed taxpayers may deduct 100% of health insurance premiums as an adjustment to income but only if neither they nor their spouses were able to participate in an employer health plan. ###

28. An adjustment to income is considered the most beneficial type of deduction because_____:

A. It favors taxpayers who choose to itemize their deductions.
B. It is simpler to figure out qualifying expenses for adjustments to income than it is other deductions.
C. It lowers a taxpayer's adjusted gross income, and thus his overall tax liability.
D. There is no significant difference between an adjustment to income and a regular tax deduction.

**The answer is C.** An adjustment to income directly reduces a taxpayer's income, and thus the amount of tax he owes. Adjustments are deducted from gross income to arrive at adjusted gross income. They are often referred to as "above-the-line" deductions.

29. Chase is moving for a new job. He has the following expenses:

| | |
|---|---|
| cost of moving truck rental | $500 |
| cost of moving family and pets | $300 |
| cost for a storage unit while moving | $200 |
| cost of breaking his existing apartment lease | $400 |
| pre-move house-hunting. | $500 |

Assuming that Chase passes all the required tests, what is his moving expense deduction?

A. $500.
B. $800.
C. $1,000.
D. $1,900.

**The answer is C.** The cost of breaking a lease is not a deductible moving expense. House-hunting before a move is also not deductible. The cost of a storage unit while moving is deductible. Therefore, Chase may deduct the following: ($500 + $300 + $200 = $1,000). ###

30. Marina is a software specialist who works and lives in Boston. A company offers her a new job in Raleigh, North Carolina, more than 700 miles away. As part of the offer, she negotiates a deal to work part-time for the first six months. Marina's husband is a stay-at-home father to the couple's two young children. The family makes the move from Boston to Raleigh, and Marina begins work at her new job. Does she meet both the time and distance tests in order to deduct her moving expenses as an adjustment to income?

A. No, she does not meet the distance test.
B. No, she does not meet the time test or distance test.
C. She meets the distance test, but not the time test.
D. Marina meets both tests, and is able to deduct her moving expenses.

**The answer is C.** Marina is not able to deduct her moving expenses. She meets the distance test because her old home in Boston is more than 50 miles from her new office in Raleigh. However, to meet the time test, she must work full-time for a period of at least 39 weeks in the first 12 months. Since she is only working part-time for six months, this does not fulfill the requirements of the time test. A spouse does not to be employed for a MFJ couple to deduct moving expenses.

# Unit 7: The Standard Deduction and Itemized Deductions

| More Reading: |
|---|
| Publication 502, *Medical and Dental Expenses*<br>Publication 600, *State and Local General Sales Taxes*<br>Publication 936, *Home Mortgage Interest Deduction*<br>Publication 526, *Charitable Contributions* |

Taxpayers may choose to take the standard deduction or itemize their deductions on their tax returns. If a taxpayer chooses to itemize, then he must file a Schedule A along with his Form 1040. Taxpayers should elect the type of deduction that results in the lower tax.

The standard deduction eliminates the need for taxpayers to itemize actual deductions, such as medical expenses, charitable contributions, and state and local taxes. It is available to U.S. citizens and resident aliens who are individuals, married persons, and heads of household. The standard deduction is adjusted every year for inflation. In some cases, the standard deduction can consist of two parts: the *basic* standard deduction and an *additional* standard deduction amount for age, blindness, or both.

The additional amount for blindness will be allowed if the taxpayer is blind on the last day of the tax year, even if he did not qualify as "blind" the rest of the year. A taxpayer must obtain a statement from an eye doctor that states:

- The taxpayer cannot see better than 20/200 even while corrected with eyeglasses, or
- The taxpayer's field of vision is not more than 20 degrees (the taxpayer has disabled peripheral vision).

The additional amount for age will be allowed if the taxpayer is at least age 65 at the end of the tax year.

# 2012 Standard Deduction Amounts

The standard deduction is a dollar amount that reduces the amount of income that is taxed. The amount is based on the taxpayer's filing status.

| Standard Deduction Amounts ||
|---|---|
| **Filing status** | **2012** |
| Single or MFS | $5,950 |
| Married filing jointly | $11,900 |
| Head of household | $8,700 |
| Qualifying widow(er) | $11,900 |

An *increased* standard deduction is available to taxpayers who are:

- 65 or older and/or
- Blind or partially blind

> **\*Note**: The "additional" standard deduction is not a credit or an itemized deduction. It is simply an increase over the regular standard deduction amount that Congress has decided to give taxpayers who are over 65 and/or blind.

The increased standard deduction amount in these cases is $1,150 per taxpayer for married filers and $1,450 for single and head of household.

> **Example:** Joel, 46, and Christine, 33, are filing a joint return for 2012. Neither is blind. They decide not to itemize their deductions. Their standard deduction in 2012 is $11,900.

> **Example:** Gilbert, 66, and Lisa, 59, are filing a joint return for 2012 and do not itemize deductions. Lisa is blind. Because they are married filing jointly, their base standard deduction is $11,900. Since Gilbert is over age 65, he can claim an additional standard deduction of $1,150. Since Lisa is blind, she can also claim an additional $1,150. Therefore, their total standard deduction is $14,200 ($11,900 + $1,150 +$1,150).

The standard deduction for a deceased taxpayer is the same as if the taxpayer had lived the entire year, with one exception: if the taxpayer died *before* his 65th birthday, the higher standard deduction for being 65 does not apply.

> **Example:** Richard is single and died on November 1, 2012. He would have been 65 if he had reached his birthday on December 12, 2012. He does not qualify for a higher standard deduction for being 65, because he died before his 65th birthday. His standard deduction would be $5,950 on his final tax return, which should be filed by his executor.

## Standard Deduction for Dependents (who file a return)

A dependent is also allowed a standard deduction. If a dependent is claimed on another person's return, his standard deduction amount is the greater of:

- $950, or
- The dependent's *earned* income (such as wages) plus $300, but not more than the regular standard deduction amount. For a single person, this is $5,950 in 2012.

> **Example:** Georgia is single, 22, and a full-time student who has a part-time job on campus. Her parents supported her, so they claimed her as a dependent on their 2012 tax return. Georgia will also file a return, and she will take the standard deduction. In 2012, Georgia has interest income of $120, taxes withheld from her wages totaling $35, and total wages of $780 from her part-time job. Her standard deduction is $1,080 ($780 wages + $300).

The standard deduction will be higher if the dependent is 65 or older and/or blind.

> **Example:** Amy is 19, single, and legally blind. She is claimed on her parents' 2012 return. Amy has interest income of $1,300 and wages from a part-time job of $2,900. She has no itemized deductions. Her base amount for the standard deduction is $3,200 ($2,900 + $300, which equals her wages plus $300). Because Amy is also blind, she is allowed an *additional* standard deduction amount of $1,450. So her standard deduction is figured as follows: ($2,900 + $300 + $1,450) = $4,650.

# Itemized Deductions

Itemized deductions allow taxpayers to reduce their taxable income based on specific personal expenses. Itemized deductions are taken *instead* of the standard deduction. If the total itemized deductions are greater than the standard deduction, they will result in a lower taxable income and lower tax.

In general, taxpayers benefit from itemizing deductions if they have mortgage interest, significant unreimbursed medical expenses, or other expenses such as large charitable contributions. In most cases, the taxpayer may choose whether to take itemized deductions or the standard deduction, and may take whichever is more beneficial. However, taxpayers are *forced* to itemize in the following cases:

- Married filing separately when one spouse itemizes: the other spouse is also forced to itemize.
- A nonresident or dual-status alien during the year (who is not married to a U.S. citizen or resident).
- A taxpayer with a short year return.

Itemized deductions are claimed on Schedule A and include amounts paid for:

- Qualified medical and dental expenses
- Certain taxes (property tax and state income tax are the most common)
- Mortgage interest
- Gifts to charity
- Casualty and theft losses
- Certain miscellaneous deductions

We will review the specific requirements for these various itemized deductions over the course of the next two units.

## Medical and Dental Expenses (Subject to the 7.5% Limit)

Medical and dental expenses are deductible only if taxpayers itemize their deductions. Further, taxpayers can deduct only the amount of unreimbursed medical expenses that exceeds 7.5% of their adjusted gross income (AGI).

Qualified medical expenses include expenses paid for:

- The taxpayer
- The taxpayer's spouse
- Dependents (the individual must have been a dependent at the time the medical services were provided or at the time the expenses were paid)

*Exceptions: If a child of divorced or separated parents is claimed as a dependent on *either* parent's return, each parent may deduct the medical expenses he or she individually paid for the child. There is also an exception for medical expenses paid on behalf of former spouses pursuant to a divorce decree. In addition, a taxpayer may deduct medical expenses that were paid on behalf of an adopted child, even before the adoption is final. The child must qualify as a dependent and must be a member of the taxpayer's household during the year the medical expenses were paid.

Example: Raymond and Carmen are divorced. Their son, Colby, lives with Carmen, who claims him as a dependent. Carmen deducts Colby's annual medical and dental bills, including orthodontia expenses for his braces. However, in April, Colby falls on the playground and fractures his leg and arm. The out-of-pocket expenses are $5,500. Colby's father, Raymond, pays for the emergency room visit and the expenses related to the injury, and may deduct them even though he does not claim his son as a dependent on his return. This is based on the exception for divorced/separated parents.

A taxpayer can deduct medical expenses paid for a dependent parent. All the standard rules for a dependency exemption apply, so a dependent parent would not have to live with the taxpayer in order to qualify.

Example: Julie pays all the medical expenses for her mother, who is her dependent but does not live with Julie. The medical expenses are still deductible on Julie's tax return as an itemized deduction if the 7.5% limit is reached.

In this section, the term *7.5% limit* is used to refer to 7.5% of adjusted gross income. A taxpayer must subtract 7.5% (.075) of his AGI from gross medical and dental expenses to figure the medical expense deduction.

Example: Tracy's AGI is $40,000. She had actual medical expenses totaling $2,500. Tracy cannot deduct any of her medical expenses because they are not more than 7.5% of her AGI (7.5% of which is $3,000).

Example: Olivia's AGI is $100,000. In 2012, she paid for a knee operation. She had $10,000 of out-of-pocket medical expenses related to the surgery. In this case, $2,500 would be allowed as an itemized deduction, the amount in excess of the $7,500 base ($100,000 X .075 = $7,500).

# Qualifying Medical Expenses

Qualifying medical expenses include the costs of diagnosis, cure, mitigation, treatment, or prevention of disease, and the costs for medical (not cosmetic) treatments. They include the costs of:

- Medically necessary equipment, supplies, and diagnostic devices
- Dental and vision care expenses, such as prescription eyeglasses and contact lenses
- Transportation costs to obtain medical care
- Qualified long-term care insurance

Deductible medical expenses may include but are not limited to:

- Fees paid to doctors, dentists, surgeons, chiropractors, psychiatrists, psychologists, and nontraditional medical practitioners
- In-patient hospital care or nursing home services, *including* the cost of meals and lodging charged by the hospital or nursing home
- Payments for acupuncture treatments
- Lactation supplies
- Treatment at a center for alcohol or drug addiction, for participation in a smoking-cessation program, and for prescription drugs to alleviate nicotine withdrawal
- A weight-loss program prescribed by a physician (but not payments for diet food items)
- Payments for insulin and payments for drugs that require a prescription
- Payments for admission and transportation to a medical conference relating to a chronic disease (but not the costs for meals and lodging while attending the conference)

Other examples of deductible medical expenses include the cost of false teeth, laser eye surgery, orthodontia, hearing aids, crutches, and wheelchairs. Even veterinary care can be deducted as a medical expense when it relates to the care of animals trained to assist persons who are visually-impaired, disabled, or hearing-impaired.

Medical expenses must be primarily to alleviate or prevent a physical or mental defect or illness. Medical expenses do not include expenses that are merely beneficial to general health, such as vitamins, spa treatments, gym memberships, or vacations. In addition, over-the-counter medications cannot be deducted.

## Medical insurance and long-term care premiums

Qualifying medical expenses include medical insurance premiums that the taxpayer has paid with after-tax dollars. A taxpayer may not deduct insurance premiums paid by an employer-sponsored plan unless the premiums are included in Box 1 of his Form W-2.[44]

A taxpayer may only include the medical expenses paid during the year, regardless of when the services were provided. Along with regular medical insurance, a taxpayer may also deduct the costs of qualified long-term care insurance premiums as a medical expense, assuming the 7.5% limit is met.

If a taxpayer or a dependent is in a nursing home and the primary reason for being there is medically related, the entire cost, including meals and lodging, is a medical expense.

## Medically related legal fees

A taxpayer can deduct legal fees that are necessary to authorize treatment for a mental illness. However, legal fees for the management of a guardianship estate or legal fees for conducting the affairs of a person being treated are not deductible as medical expenses.

## Medical expenses of deceased taxpayers

An election can be made to deduct medical expenses paid by a deceased taxpayer. This is legal for one year *after* the date of the taxpayer's death. The expenses may be treated as if paid when the medical services were provided (even if the medical expenses are not actually paid until after the taxpayer's death). In some cases the taxpayer's Form 1040 must be amended by filing a Form 1040X. The medical expenses of a deceased taxpayer are still subject to the 7.5% floor.

> **Example:** Anne had heart surgery in November 2012 and incurred $20,000 in medical bills. She died on January 2, 2013. The 2012 medical bills were still unpaid at the time of her death. The executor of Anne's estate may elect to deduct her medical expenses in 2012, even though the medical expenses are paid at a later date.

## Cosmetic surgery

Cosmetic surgery is only deductible if it is used to correct a defect or disease. A cosmetic procedure simply for the enhancement of someone's physical appearance is not a deductible medical expense.

> **Example:** Adrienne undergoes surgery to remove a breast as part of treatment for cancer. She pays a surgeon to reconstruct her breast to correct a deformity that is directly related to the disease. The cost of the surgery is includable in her medical expenses.

---

[44] New for 2012, the value of a taxpayer's annual health care coverage is now reported in Box 12 on Form W-2. The amount reported in the box should include both the portions paid by an employer and by the employee. It is a provision of the Affordable Health Care Act to try to show taxpayers the true cost of health care. However, while this amount is reported on a W-2, it does *not* mean the amount is taxable; it is for informational purposes only.

> **Example:** Miles, age one, was born with a cleft palate. His parents pay for cosmetic surgery to correct the deformity. The surgery is deductible as a medical expense because it corrects a defect.

## Medically related meals, lodging, and transportation

Vehicle mileage may be deducted if the transportation is for medical reasons, such as trips to and from doctors' appointments. A taxpayer can choose to deduct the actual costs for taxis, buses, trains, planes, or ambulances, as well as tolls and parking fees.

If a taxpayer uses his own car for medical transportation, he can deduct actual out-of-pocket expenses for gas and other expenses, or he can deduct the standard mileage rate for medical expenses, which is 23 cents per mile in 2012.

A taxpayer can deduct the cost of meals and lodging at a hospital or similar institution if the principal reason for being there is to receive medical care. The care must be provided by a doctor, hospital, or a medical care facility, and there must not be any significant element of personal pleasure or recreation.

The IRS imposes a $50 limit, per person, per night, for lodging for medically-related issues. There is no deduction for meals.

# Capital Improvements for Medical Reasons

Capital improvements such as home improvements are usually not deductible by the taxpayer. However, a home improvement may qualify as a deductible expense if its main purpose is to provide a medical benefit to the taxpayer or to dependent family members.

The deduction for capital improvements is limited to the excess of the actual cost of the improvements over the increase in the fair market value of the home. Home improvements that qualify as deductible medical expenses include:

- Wheelchair ramps
- Lowering of kitchen cabinets
- Railings and support bars
- Elevators

Tenants may deduct the entire cost of disability-related improvements, since they are not the owners of the property.

> **Example:** Lonnie has a heart condition. He cannot easily climb stairs or get into a bathtub. On his doctor's advice, he installs a special sit-in bathtub and a stair lift on the first floor of his rented house. The landlord did not pay any of the cost of buying and installing the special equipment and did not lower the rent. Lonnie can deduct the entire amount as a medical expense, assuming he meets the 7.5% limit.

### Medical Expenses: A Summary

1. In order to claim medical expenses, the taxpayer must itemize on Schedule A.

2. The deduction is limited. A taxpayer can only claim medical expenses that exceed 7.5% of adjusted gross income for the year.

3. The medical expenses must have been paid during the year, *regardless* of when the services were provided.

4. Taxpayers cannot deduct any reimbursed expenses. Therefore, total medical expenses for the year must be reduced by any insurance reimbursement.

5. A taxpayer may include qualified medical expenses paid for themselves, a spouse, and any dependents. Special rules apply to divorced or separated parents.

6. Medical expenses must be primarily to alleviate or prevent a physical or mental defect or illness. Taxpayers may deduct premiums for Medicare B; self-employed taxpayers may deduct premiums for health care coverage, if they had a net profit for the year and were not eligible to be covered by an employer-sponsored plan, including that of their spouses.[45] For drugs, taxpayers can only deduct prescription medication and insulin.

7. Medical-related transportation costs can be deducted.

8. Distributions from health savings accounts and withdrawals from flexible spending arrangements are generally tax free if used to pay qualified medical expenses.

9. Expenses that are not deductible as medical expenses include funeral or burial expenses, nonprescription medicines, toiletries, cosmetics, any program for the general improvement of health, maternity clothes, and cosmetic surgery unless it is to correct a defect.

# Deductible Taxes

Taxpayers can deduct certain taxes if they itemize their deductions. To be deductible, the tax must have been imposed on the taxpayer and paid by the taxpayer during the tax year. Taxes that are deductible include:

- State, local, and foreign income taxes
- Real estate taxes
- Personal property taxes (such as DMV fees)
- State and local sales taxes

---

[45] An employee may not deduct health insurance premiums paid by an employer-sponsored health insurance plan unless the premiums are included in Box 1 of the employee's Form W-2.

## State and local taxes

Taxpayers are allowed to deduct state and local sales taxes in lieu of deducting state and local income taxes.[46] The taxpayer may choose whichever method gives them the larger deduction. Taxpayers can choose one of the following taxes, but not both:

- **Income taxes:** This includes withheld taxes, estimated tax payments, or other tax payments such as a prior year refund of a state or local income tax that taxpayers applied to their estimated state or local income taxes.
- **Sales taxes:** Taxpayers may deduct state and local sales taxes paid.

## Personal property taxes (DMV fees)

Personal property taxes are deductible if they are:

- Charged on personal property
- Based on the value of the property, and
- Charged on a yearly basis, even if collected more or less than once a year.

The most common type of personal property tax is a DMV fee. In order to be deductible, the tax must be based on the value of a property, such as a car or boat.

## Foreign income taxes

Under the foreign earned income exclusion or the foreign housing exclusion, these taxes can be deducted on income that is not exempt from U.S. tax. Generally, income taxes paid to a foreign country can be deducted as:

- An itemized deduction on Schedule A, or
- A credit against U.S. income tax.

A taxpayer can choose between claiming the Foreign Tax Credit and claiming any foreign tax paid on Schedule A as an itemized deduction. The taxpayer may use whichever method results in the lowest tax.

# Real estate taxes

State, local, or foreign real estate taxes that are based on the assessed value of the taxpayer's real property (such as a house or land) are deductible. Real estate taxes are reported to the taxpayer on Form 1098, *Mortgage Interest Statement*. A taxpayer may deduct real estate taxes on any real estate property he owns, including foreign property.

If a portion of a taxpayer's monthly mortgage payment goes into an escrow account, the taxpayer can only deduct the amount *actually paid* out of the escrow account during the year to the taxing authority. Some real estate taxes are not deduct-

---

[46] This deduction expired at the end of 2011. However, on January 1, 2013 Congress reinstated the deduction retroactively for 2012 and extended its provisions through 2013 as part of the American Taxpayer Relief Act of 2012, more commonly known as the "fiscal cliff" legislation.

ible, including taxes imposed for local benefits for improvements to property, such as assessments for streets, sidewalks, and sewer lines. In addition, itemized charges for services and homeowners' association fees are not deductible.

---

**Example:** Genevieve makes the following tax payments: state income tax, $2,000; real estate taxes, $900; local benefit tax for improving the sewer system, $75; homeowners' association fee, $250. Genevieve's total tax deduction is $2,900 ($2,000 + $900 = $2,900). The $75 local benefit tax and the $250 homeowners' association fee are not deductible.

---

If a property is sold, the real estate taxes must be prorated between the buyer and the seller according to the number of days that each owned the property. It does not matter who actually paid the real estate taxes. If, for example, the buyer paid all the taxes including delinquent taxes on a property, the amounts paid while the buyer was not the legal owner must be added to the property's basis[47], rather than deducted on the taxpayer's current year return.

---

**Example:** Mandy bought her home on September 1. The property tax was already overdue on the property when she decided to purchase it. The real estate taxes on the home were $1,275 for the year and were paid by Mandy as a condition of the sale. Since Mandy did not own the home during the time the property tax was due, then the amount paid must be added to the basis of the residence. Mandy cannot deduct the $1,275 on her Schedule A as an itemized deduction.

---

# Mortgage Interest and Other Deductible Interest

Certain types of interest are deductible as itemized deductions on Form 1040, Schedule A:

- Home mortgage interest (including certain points and mortgage insurance premiums) [48]
- Mortgage interest on a second home or vacation home, with a maximum of two homes
- Investment interest

## Qualifying Home Mortgage Interest

Home mortgage interest is interest paid on a loan secured by a taxpayer's home. The loan may be a mortgage, a second mortgage, a home equity loan, or a line of credit. A taxpayer is allowed to deduct the interest on a primary residence and one second home. In order to qualify, the "home" can be a house, condominium, mobile

---

[47] A full discussion of how to calculate basis can be found in Unit 10, *Basis of Property*.

[48] Because of uncertainty about whether Congress would restore this deduction in 2012, the IRS eliminated the box for this item on Form 1098. Some mortgage companies have said they will not put the premiums paid on the 1098s. In that case, taxpayers will have to check their mortgage statements to figure what they paid. Since the write-off also applies for tax year 2013, the IRS will restore the box for mortgage interest premiums paid on 1098 forms for 2013.

home, house trailer, or houseboat. So long as a residence has sleeping, cooking, and toilet facilities, it may qualify for this deduction.

A second home can include any other residence a taxpayer owns and treats as a second home. A taxpayer does not have to actually use the home during the year in order to get a deduction of the mortgage interest paid on a second home. Home mortgage interest and points are reported to a taxpayer on Form 1098, *Mortgage Interest Statement,* by the financial institution to which the taxpayer made the payments.

Home mortgage interest is only deductible if the mortgage is secured debt, meaning the taxpayer must be legally liable for the debt.

An empty lot (bare land) does not qualify for the mortgage interest deduction. In order to be deductible as home mortgage interest, the loan must be secured by an actual home. If a taxpayer is planning to build a house, he can start deducting mortgage interest once construction begins.

**Note:** Although a taxpayer may deduct real estate taxes on *more than* two properties, a taxpayer may not deduct mortgage interest on more than two homes.

A taxpayer may deduct late charges on the loan as mortgage interest.

**Example:** Reese owns his home and pays his mortgage on a monthly basis. During the year, he falls behind on his mortgage payments and sends in his payment late on two occasions. The mortgage company charges Reese a $35 late fee for each late payment. The late fees are deductible as mortgage interest.

## Limits on the Mortgage Interest Deduction

If all of the taxpayer's mortgages fit into one or more of the following three categories, he can deduct the interest:

- Any mortgage the taxpayer obtained on or before 1987 (grandfathered debt.)
- Any mortgage obtained after 1987 to buy or improve a home, but only if the mortgage debt totaled $1 million or less ($500,000 if MFS).
- A home equity mortgage, even if used for expenses other than to improve the home, but only if the home equity line is $100,000 or less. ($50,000 if MFS).

**Example:** Shirley borrowed $800,000 against her primary residence and $500,000 against her secondary residence. Both loans were used solely to acquire the residences. The loan amounts add up to $1.3 million. Since the total loan amount exceeds the $1 million limit for home acquisition debt, Shirley's mortgage interest deduction is limited.

## Qualified Mortgage Insurance Premiums (PMI)

Taxpayers can deduct private mortgage insurance (PMI)[49] premiums paid during the tax year on Schedule A, though the deduction is phased out at higher income levels. The deduction is phased-out ratably by 10% for each $1,000 by which the taxpayer's AGI exceeds $100,000. The deduction was scheduled to expire in 2012, but the fiscal cliff legislation extended it for tax years 2012 and 2013.

## Home Mortgage Points

Points are the charges paid by a borrower to secure a loan. They are actually prepaid interest that a buyer pays at closing in order to secure a lower interest rate. They are also called:

- Loan origination fees (including VA and FHA fees)
- Maximum loan charges
- Premium charges
- Loan discount points
- Prepaid interest

Only points paid as a form of interest can be deducted. Points paid to refinance a mortgage are generally not deductible in full the year the taxpayer paid them, unless the points are paid in connection with the improvement of a main home.

Loan fees paid for specific services, such as home appraisal fees, document preparation fees, VA funding fees, or notary fees are not interest and are not deductible.

In order to deduct points in the year paid, the taxpayer must meet these requirements:

- The mortgage must be secured by the taxpayer's main home, and the mortgage must have been used to buy or build the home.
- The points must not be an excessive or unusual amount for the local area.
- The total points paid must not be more than the total amount of unborrowed funds.
- The points must be computed as a percentage of the loan principal, and they must be listed on the settlement statement.

Despite these restrictions, most homebuyers still qualify to take the deduction for points on the purchase of their primary residence.

# Interest Paid on Home Equity Debt

The interest paid on a home equity line of credit is deductible by the taxpayer if certain rules are met. There is a $100,000 limit on the amount of debt that can be treated as home equity debt, and it is not deductible if it exceeds the property's fair market value.

---

[49] Lenders charge private mortgage insurance to protect themselves if a borrower defaults. It allows homebuyers to make smaller down payments than are ordinarily allowed.

> **Example:** Carla bought her home for cash ten years ago. Its fair market value is now $80,000. She did not have a mortgage on her home until last year when she took out a $45,000 loan, secured by her home, to pay for her daughter's college tuition. This loan is home equity debt. Since the $45,000 loan is secured by her home and the loan amount is less than $100,000 in equity debt, the mortgage interest on the equity line is deductible.

The interest on home equity indebtedness is deductible by the taxpayer no matter how the proceeds are used.

> **Example:** Jeremy and Ashley obtained two home equity loans totaling $90,000. They used the loans to pay off gambling debts, overdue credit card payments, and some nondeductible medical expenses. The couple can deduct the interest on their home equity loans because the total does not exceed $100,000.

> **Example:** Chad bought his home five years ago. Its FMV now is $110,000, and the current balance on Chad's original mortgage is $95,000. His bank offers Chad a home mortgage loan of 125% of the FMV of the home. To consolidate some of his other debts, Chad agrees to take out a $42,500 home mortgage loan [(125% × $110,000) – $95,000] with his bank. Chad's home equity line exceeds the fair market value of the home. Therefore, his mortgage interest deduction relating to his equity line is limited. For tax purposes, Chad's qualified home equity debt is limited to $15,000. This is the amount that the FMV of $110,000 exceeds the amount of home acquisition debt of $95,000.

## Deductible Investment Interest

If a taxpayer borrows money to buy property held for investment, the interest paid is investment interest. The deduction for investment interest expense is limited to the amount of net investment income. A taxpayer cannot deduct interest incurred to produce tax-exempt income, such as the purchase of municipal bonds. Investment interest expense is calculated on IRS Form 4952, *Investment Interest Expense Deduction.*

> **Example:** Mariko borrows money from a bank in order to buy $3,000 worth of short-term bonds. The bonds mature during the year and Mariko makes $400 in investment interest income. She also has $210 in investment interest expense, which she paid on the loan originally taken out to buy the bonds. Mariko must report the full amount of $400 as investment interest income. The $210 in investment interest expense is a deduction on Schedule A.

A taxpayer can carry over to the next tax year the amount of investment interest that he could not deduct because of the passive activity rules. The interest carried over is treated as investment interest paid or accrued in that next year.

**Example:** Jackson borrows money from a bank in order to buy $10,000 worth of U.S. gold coins. During the year, the coins lose value and he has no investment income. Jackson has $326 in investment interest expense, which he paid on the loan originally taken out to buy the coins. Jackson may not take a deduction for the investment interest expense, because he has no investment income to offset it. Jackson must carry over to the next tax year the amount of investment interest that he could not deduct because of this limit.

Investment income is any income that is produced by property that is held for investment. A taxpayer must first determine net investment income by subtracting his investment expenses (other than interest expense) from the investment income.

## Nondeductible Interest and Investment Expenses

The following expenses cannot be deducted:

- Interest on personal car loans or other personal loans
- Annual fees for credit cards and finance charges for nonbusiness credit card purchases
- Loan fees for services needed to get a loan
- Interest on a debt the taxpayer is not legally obligated to pay
- Service charges
- Interest to purchase or carry tax-exempt securities
- Late payment charges paid to a public utility
- Expenses relating to stockholders' meetings or investment-related seminars
- Interest expenses from single-premium life insurance, endowment, and annuity contracts
- Interest incurred from borrowing on insurance
- Expenses incurred to produce tax-exempt income (this includes expenses incurred for both tax-exempt and taxable income that cannot be properly allocated)
- Short-sale expenses

A taxpayer cannot deduct fines and penalties paid to any government entity for violations of the law, regardless of their nature.

**Example:** José and Blanca file a joint return. During the year, they paid:

1. $3,180 of home mortgage interest reported to them on Form 1098
2. $400 in credit card interest
2. $1,500 paid to a lender for an appraisal fee
3. $2,000 in interest on a car loan

José and Blanca may report only their home mortgage interest ($3,180) as deductible interest. None of the other charges are deductible.

# Charitable Contributions

Charities need funds to operate their tax-exempt programs, and most of the time these contributions come from taxpayers. A "charitable contribution" is a donation to a qualified organization. Taxpayers must itemize deductions to be able to deduct a charitable contribution.

Taxpayers can deduct contributions to qualifying organizations that:

- Operate exclusively for religious, charitable, educational, scientific, or literary purposes, or
- Work to prevent cruelty to children or animals, or
- Foster national or international amateur sports competition.

Other qualifying organizations include:

- War veterans' organizations, and
- Certain nonprofit cemetery companies or corporations.

Qualified donations also include donations for public purposes to the federal government of the United States, to any state, or to an Indian tribal government (example: a donation to the state capital's yearly toy drive).

To be deductible, contributions must be made to a qualifying organization, not to an individual. Taxpayers *must keep records* to prove the amounts of cash and noncash contributions they make during the year. Taxpayers can only deduct a contribution in the year it is actually made.

## Nonqualifying Organizations

Even if an organization is a nonprofit, that does not automatically mean that it is a "charity" and contributions are deductible by donors.

There are some organizations that still qualify as nonprofit groups for tax purposes, but they do not qualify as charitable organizations for purposes of deductible contributions. The following are examples of donations that do not qualify:

- Gifts to civic leagues, social and sports clubs, labor unions, and Chambers of Commerce
- Gifts to groups run for personal profit
- Gifts to political groups, candidates, or political organizations
- Gifts to homeowners' associations
- Direct donations to needy individuals
- The cost of raffle, bingo, or lottery tickets, even if the raffle is part of a qualified organization's fundraiser
- Dues paid to country clubs or similar groups

> **Example:** Renee ran a 10K race organized by the Chamber of Commerce, with the Chamber to donate proceeds to a cancer charity. She paid the race organizers a $30 entry fee and received a "free" T-shirt and pancake breakfast after the race. Renee did not make a contribution directly to the qualifying organization, the cancer charity. She paid the Chamber of Commerce, which is not a qualifying charitable organization. Therefore, none of her entry fee is tax deductible as a charitable expense. If the race had been organized by the qualifying organization itself, part of her entry fee may have been deductible.

## Charitable Contributions: Substantiation Requirements

There are strict recordkeeping requirements for taxpayers who make charitable contributions. The IRS has different substantiation requirements for different types and amounts of contributions:

- Cash contributions of $250 or less
- Cash contributions of $250 or more
- Noncash contributions less than $500
- Noncash contributions more than $500
- Special rule for donated vehicles
- Volunteering expenses

### Cash Donations of $250 or Less

Cash contributions include those paid by cash, check, debit card, credit card, or payroll deduction. For a contribution by cash or check, the taxpayer must maintain a record of the contribution. It must be either a bank record or a written receipt from the organization. If the value of the individual donation is *less than* $250, the taxpayer must keep at least a canceled check or credit card slip, a receipt, or some other reliable written record or evidence.

A taxpayer cannot deduct a cash contribution, regardless of the amount, unless he keeps one of the following:

- A bank record that shows the name of the qualified organization, the date of the contribution, and the amount of the contribution. Bank records may include:
  - o A canceled check,
  - o A bank or credit union statement, or
  - o A credit card statement.
- A receipt (or a letter or other written communication) from the qualified organization showing the name of the organization, the date of the contribution, and the amount of the contribution.

- For payroll deductions, a pay stub or Form W-2, plus a pledge card or other document showing the name of the qualified organization.
- For text donations, a telephone bill, so long as it shows the name of the qualified organization, the date of the contribution, and the amount given.

> **Example:** Gary donates $10 per week to the Humane Society. He always pays by check, and he keeps the canceled check as a record of his contribution. This is a valid method of recordkeeping for small donations under $250.

## Cash Donations over $250

For cash donations over $250 dollars, the taxpayer must have a receipt or written acknowledgement from the organization that meets certain tests. It must include:

- The amount of cash the taxpayer contributed.
- The date of the contribution.
- Whether the qualified organization gave any goods or services as a result of the contribution (other than certain token items and membership benefits.) The absence of this simple statement by a charity has led to recent court cases in which major cash contributions have been challenged.
- A description and good faith estimate of the value of any goods or services provided in return by the organization (if applicable.)

The taxpayer must obtain the receipt on or before:

- The date the taxpayer files his tax return for the year he makes the contribution, or
- The due date, including extensions, for filing the return.

If the donation is via payroll deduction, any amount that exceeds $250 must be substantiated with a pay stub, W-2, and a statement about whether goods or services were given by the qualified organization.

# Noncash Contributions: Substantiation Rules

In order to claim a deduction for noncash donations, the donated items must be in good condition. The taxpayer must get a receipt from the receiving organization and keep a list of the items donated. In most cases, the taxpayer will be able to claim a deduction for the fair market value of the contribution (generally what someone would be willing to pay at a garage sale or thrift store).

No deduction is allowed for items that are in poor or unusable condition. Deductible items include:

- Fair market value of used clothing and furniture in good condition.
- Unreimbursed expenses that relate directly to the services the taxpayer provided for the organization. The value of time or services donated cannot be deducted.

- Part of a contribution above the fair market value for items received such as merchandise and tickets to charity balls or sporting events.
- Transportation expenses, including bus fare, parking fees, tolls, and either the actual cost of gas and oil or a standard mileage deduction of 14 cents per mile in 2012.

> **Example:** Emily is an attorney who donates her time to her local church for their legal needs. In 2012, she spent 10 hours drafting documents for the church, which is a qualified organization. She also has $200 in out-of-pocket expenses because she purchased a new printer and office supplies for the church. The printer and office supplies were delivered directly to the church rectory for its use. Emily can take a charitable deduction for $200, the amount she spent on behalf of her church. She cannot take a deduction for the "value" of her time.

## Noncash Contributions: Donations Less Than $500

For each single contribution of at least $250 but not exceeding $500, the taxpayer must have all the documentation described for noncash contributions less than $250. In addition, the organization's written acknowledgement must state whether the taxpayer received any goods or services in return and a description and good faith estimate of any such items.

## Noncash Contributions: Donations of More Than $500

If a taxpayer's total deduction for all noncash contributions for the year is over $500, he must also file Form 8283, *Noncash Charitable Contributions.* [50] If any single donation is valued at over $5,000, the taxpayer must also get an appraisal.

## *Special $500 Rule for Donated Vehicles, Boats, and Airplanes

Special rules apply to any donation of a vehicle, boat, or airplane. If the taxpayer donates a vehicle to a charity and the taxpayer claims a deduction of more than $500, the taxpayer can only deduct the smaller of:
- The gross proceeds from the sale of the vehicle, or
- The vehicle's fair market value on the date of the contribution.

Form 1098-C shows the gross proceeds from the sale of the vehicle. If the taxpayer does not attach Form 1098-C, the maximum value that can be taken for a vehicle donation is $500. Vehicles that are not in working condition may have zero donation value.

---

[50] A Treasury Department audit report says that too many taxpayers are failing to comply with the requirements for noncash donations. The report says that hundreds of thousands of taxpayers claim noncash charitable donations of more than $500, but are not submitting a Form 8283 as required. The IRS is going to start flagging these returns and asking taxpayers to send in the missing forms before they can receive the charitable deduction.

> **Example:** Kevin donates his used motorcycle to his church fundraiser. The FMV ("Blue Book" value) of the motorcycle is $2,500. The church sells the motorcycle 60 days later; the organization sends Kevin a Form 1098-C showing the proceeds from the sale of the donated item. The church was only able to sell the motorcycle for $1,700. Therefore, Kevin may only deduct $1,700 on his Schedule A (the smaller of the FMV or the gross proceeds from the sale). He must attach a copy of Form 1098-C, *Contributions of Motor Vehicles, Boats, and Airplanes*, to his tax return.

## *Exceptions to the $500 Rule for Donated Vehicles

There are two exceptions to the strict rules regarding vehicle donations:

- **Exception 1:** If the charity takes the vehicle for its own use, the taxpayer can deduct the vehicle's FMV.
- **Exception 2:** If the charity gives or sells the vehicle directly to a needy person, the taxpayer generally can deduct the vehicle's FMV at the time of the contribution.

# Deductible Volunteering Expenses

A taxpayer may deduct expenses incurred while away from home performing services for a charitable organization only if there is no significant element of personal pleasure in the travel. However, a deduction will not be denied simply because the taxpayer enjoys providing services to a charitable organization. The taxpayer is still allowed to take a charitable contribution deduction for the expenses if he is on-duty in a genuine and substantial sense throughout the trip.

The IRS does not allow a taxpayer to deduct a monetary "value" of the hours he spends volunteering.

> **Example:** Charles volunteered for the Boy Scouts in 2012. He was the den leader and regularly paid out-of-pocket expenses for travel, gas, and parking while performing duties and picking up supplies on behalf of the Scouts. Charles was not paid for his work. Charles may deduct his out-of-pocket costs related to the volunteer work, but he may not take a deduction for the value of his time.

> **Example:** Francine regularly volunteers at her local animal shelter. She uses her own car to travel back and forth to the shelter. She is not reimbursed for mileage. Francine also fosters kittens on behalf of the shelter. She pays for food and other supplies out-of-pocket while she is fostering the kittens. Once the kittens are old enough for adoption, she returns them to the animal shelter so that they may be adopted by the public. Francine may deduct her mileage and her out-of-pocket costs as a charitable contribution.

## Deductible Contributions and the 50% Limit

There are limits to the amounts that can be claimed as a deductible donation. A taxpayer may not take a deduction for charitable contributions that exceed 50% of his adjusted gross income. In other words, if a taxpayer had $40,000 in gross income in 2012, the maximum he could deduct as a charitable contribution in 2012 would be $20,000 (50% of AGI). Any amounts that are disallowed by this limit may be carried forward to a future year (explained later in this unit.)

There is a reduced limit of 30% or 20% that applies to certain organizations. This means that for certain nonprofit organizations, a taxpayer's contribution cannot exceed either 30% or 20% of his AGI.

Examples of 50% limit organizations include churches, hospitals, most schools, state or federal government units, and animal welfare organizations. Also included are corporations, trusts, or foundations organized solely for charitable, religious, educational, scientific, or literary purposes, or to prevent cruelty to children or animals, or to foster certain national or international amateur sports competition.

# Organizations Subject to the 30% Limit

Certain organizations only qualify for the "30% limit." This means that the deductible amount of the contribution cannot exceed 30% of the taxpayer's AGI. A 30% limit applies to the following organizations:

- Veterans organizations
- Fraternal societies (such as Knights of Columbus or Elks)
- Nonprofit cemeteries

In addition, the 30% limit applies in the following cases:

- Gifts for the actual use of any organization (such as the donation of a table that the organization uses for itself)
- Any gift of appreciated property (such as stocks)

Appreciated property, also called capital gain property, may be given to an organization that is normally a 50% organization, such as a church. However, capital gain property is subject to either a 30% or 20% limit, regardless of the organization type that actually receives the donation.

> **Example:** Howard's adjusted gross income is $50,000. During the year, he gave appreciated stocks with an FMV of $15,000 to his synagogue, which is a 50% limit organization. Howard also gave $10,000 cash to a veteran's organization. The $15,000 gift of capital gain property is subject to the special 30% limit, even though it was given to a religious organization. The $10,000 gift is subject to the other 30% limit. However, both gifts are fully deductible by Howard because neither is more than the 30% limit that applies ($15,000 in each case), and together they are not more than the 50% limit of Howard's AGI ($50,000 x 50% = $25,000).

# Appreciated Property and the 20% Limit

The 20% limit applies to all gifts of appreciated property to qualified organizations that are not 50% organizations.

**Example:** Vincent's adjusted gross income is $23,000. During the year, he gave appreciated stocks with an FMV of $10,000 to his fraternal society, Kiwanis, which is a 30% limit organization. Vincent makes no other donations during the year. The $10,000 donation of capital gain property (the stocks) is subject to the special 20% limit because it is capital gain property that was donated to a 30% limit organization. The donation is not fully deductible by Vincent, because it exceeds 20% of his AGI ($23,000 x 20% = $4,600). Therefore, the maximum deduction for charitable contributions that he can take is limited to $4,600, and he must carry over the remaining $5,400 to a future tax year.

Any contributions made by the taxpayer and carried over to future years retain their original character. For example, contributions made to a 30% organization are always subject to the 30% limit of AGI.

A donor can choose to deduct gifts of long-term appreciated property under a 50% of AGI limit rather than the 30% or 20% limit. As a trade-off, however, the donor's deduction for the long-term appreciated property will be limited to its cost basis instead of its FMV.

## Nonqualified Types of Donations

There are some expenses that do not qualify as charitable deductions, even if the amounts are given to a qualified charity or organization. Amounts that may not be deducted include contributions to political candidates; blood donated to a blood bank or the Red Cross; the cost of raffle, bingo, or lottery tickets, even if the amounts go to a qualified charity; and part of a contribution that benefits the taxpayer, such as the FMV of a meal eaten at a charity dinner.

**Example:** Bill goes to a local church fundraiser. His church is a qualified organization. The fundraiser includes a bingo game, with all the proceeds going to the church. Bill spends $200 on bingo cards, but does not win anything. Even though the $200 went to the church, the cost of the bingo game is not considered a charitable gift and is therefore not deductible.

## Charitable Contribution Carryovers

A carryover is simply an amount that a taxpayer is unable to deduct in the current year. Charitable contributions are subject to a five-year carryover period. The taxpayer can deduct the unused contribution for the next five years until it is used up, but not beyond that time.

In 2012, appreciated real property donated to charity for conservation purposes can be carried forward for 15 years.

> **Example:** Louise owns 200 acres of wetlands. She decides to donate the property to the Wildlife Conservation Society, a 501(c)(3) organization. The property is then used for wildlife conservation and research only. This is a qualified conservation contribution eligible for a 15-year carryover.

The 30% of AGI limitation also has been increased to 50% for qualified conservation contributions (100% for farmers and ranchers.)

# Summary: Certain Itemized Deductions

## Medical and Dental Expenses

Deductible medical and dental expenses are reported and calculated on Schedule A. Qualified medical and dental expenses are expenses the taxpayer paid during the tax year for himself, his spouse, and his dependents.

## Taxes

Deductible taxes are reported on Schedule A. Taxpayers can deduct the following:

1. State and local income taxes
2. State, local, or foreign real estate taxes
3. State and local personal property tax payments

## Deductible Mortgage Interest

Deductible mortgage interest is reported on Schedule A. The taxpayer should receive Form 1098, *Mortgage Interest Statement*, which shows the deductible amount of interest he paid during the tax year. Only taxpayers who are legally liable for the debt can deduct the interest. Taxpayers can treat amounts paid in 2012 for qualified mortgage insurance as home mortgage interest. The deduction is limited to $1 million for married filers and $500,000 for single.

## Charitable Deductions

Qualified charitable contributions are reported on Schedule A. Taxpayers may deduct cash donations, fair market value of used goods, and unreimbursed volunteer and travel expenses that relate directly to the services the taxpayer provided for the qualifying organization. Any donation over $250 requires a receipt from the organization. Any noncash donation over $500 must be reported using IRS Form 8283, *Noncash Charitable Contributions*. If any single noncash donation is valued over $5,000, the taxpayer must also get an appraisal.

# Unit 7: Questions

1. Which of the following taxes can taxpayers deduct on Schedule A?

A. Federal income tax.
B. Real estate tax.
C. Tax on alcohol and tobacco.
D. Foreign sales taxes.

**The answer is B.** Only the real estate taxes are deductible. Taxpayers can deduct real estate tax on Schedule A as an itemized deduction. ###

2. Angie and Sheldon file a joint return and claim their two children as dependents. They have an adjusted gross income of $95,400. Last year the family accumulated $6,620 in unreimbursed medical and dental expenses that included the following:

1. Prescription eyeglasses for Angie $320
2. Prescription contacts for Sheldon $1,000
3. Sheldon's smoking-cessation program $5,300

The total of Sheldon and Angie's deductible medical expenses is _____.

A. $6,620.
B. $6,300.
C. $5,620.
D. $0.

**The answer is D.** Angie and Sheldon cannot deduct any of their medical expenses. Only the portion of total medical expenses that exceeds 7.5% of the taxpayer's AGI is deductible. The total of Angie and Sheldon's medical expenses, $6,620, is less than $95,400 x 7.5% = $7,155. ###

3. Which of the following is a deductible medical expense?

A. Liposuction.
B. Premiums for life insurance.
C. Prescription hearing aids.
D. Cost of child care while a parent is in the hospital.

**The answer is C.** Only the cost of the hearing aids is a deductible medical expense. Life insurance premiums, child care, and nonprescription medicines are not deductible. ###

4. All of the following are deductible medical expenses except _____.

A. Transportation for medical care.
B. Transportation to a medical conference related to the chronic disease of a dependent.
C. Smoking-cessation programs.
D. Nonprescription nicotine gum and patches.

**The answer is D.** Taxpayers may deduct transportation related to medical care. The cost of smoking programs and prescription drugs is also deductible. However, over-the-counter medicines are not deductible as medical expenses. ###

5. Max and Wendy are both 30 years old and file jointly for 2012. They decide not to itemize their deductions. Max is legally blind. What is their standard deduction amount in 2012?

A. $8,700.
B. $11,900.
C. $13,050.
D. $13,350.

**The answer is C.** The answer is figured as follows: ($11,900 + $1,150) on their Form 1040. Max is blind, so he and Wendy are allowed an additional $1,150 as a standard deduction amount. Their standard deduction is $13,050. ###

6. Which of the following taxpayers must either itemize deductions or claim zero as their deduction?

A. Mindy, who files a joint return with her husband.
B. Leslie, who claims two dependents and files Form 1040.
C. Pearl, whose itemized deductions are more than the standard deduction.
D. Gabe, whose wife files a separate return and itemizes her deductions.

**The answer is D.** Married taxpayers who file separately and whose spouses itemize deductions must either claim "0" as their deduction or itemize their deductions. ###

7. All of the following factors determine the amount of a taxpayer's standard deduction except _____.

A. The taxpayer's filing status.
B. The taxpayer's adjusted gross income.
C. Whether the taxpayer is 65 or older, or blind.
D. Whether the taxpayer can be claimed as a dependent.

**The answer is B.** The standard deduction amount depends on the taxpayer's filing and dependent status, and whether the taxpayer is blind or at least 65 years old. It is not based on the taxpayer's income. ###

8. Sara and James are both 25, and they have been married for two years. What is their standard deduction in 2012?

A. $11,900.
B. $8,700.
C. $5,950.
D. $950.

**The answer is A.** Sara and James may take the standard deduction for married couples who file jointly, which is $11,900 in 2012. ###

9. Brenda is 22, single, and recently graduated from college. She has no dependents. She provides all of her own support. What is her standard deduction in 2012?

A. $950.
B. $3,700.
C. $5,950.
D. $8,700.

**The answer is C.** Brenda is single, with no dependents. Her standard deduction is $5,950. ###

10. Which of the following taxpayers is *required* to itemize deductions?

A. Sophie, who has one dependent child.
B. Andrea, who wants to deduct the alimony she paid to her ex-husband.
C. Gabrielle, whose itemized deductions are more than the standard deduction.
D. Samir, who is a nonresident alien.

**The answer is D.** A nonresident or dual-status alien during the year (who is not married to a U.S. citizen or resident) must itemize deductions. He cannot choose the standard deduction. The other taxpayers listed are not required to itemize their deductions but may elect to do so. ###

11. All of the following are deductible medical expenses except _____.

A. Elective cosmetic surgery.
B. Lactation supplies.
C. Legal abortion.
D. Prescription birth control pills.

**The answer is A.** Elective cosmetic surgery is not a deductible medical expense. All the other expenses listed are acceptable as deductible medical expenses. ###

12. All of the following home improvements may be itemized and deducted as medical expenses except _____:

A. The cost of installing porch lifts and other forms of lifts.
B. The cost of lowering cabinets to accommodate a disability.
C. The cost of making doorways wider to accommodate a wheelchair.
D. The cost of an elevator costing $4,000 that adds $5,000 to the FMV of the home.

**The answer is D.** The deduction for capital improvements is limited to the excess of the actual cost of the improvements over the increase in the fair market value of the home. Since the elevator adds value to the home, it cannot be deducted as a medical expense. ###

13. Which of the following items is not a deductible medical expense?

A. Dental implants to replace broken or missing teeth.
B. Over-the-counter aspirin.
C. Guide dog expenses for a blind person.
D. Prescription contact lenses.

**The answer is B.** The cost of medical items such as false teeth, prescription eyeglasses or contact lenses, laser eye surgery, hearing aids, crutches, wheelchairs, and guide dogs for the blind or deaf are all deductible medical expenses. Over-the-counter medicines are not deductible. ###

14. Justin had the following medical expenses in 2012:

• $450 for contact lenses
• $800 for eyeglasses
• $9,000 for a broken leg, of which $8,000 was paid for by his insurance
• $200 for prescription drugs
• $1,900 for a doctor-prescribed back brace
• $200 for child care while in the hospital

What is his medical expense deduction before the imposition of the 7.5% income limit?

A. $1,900.
B. $4,350.
C. $4,550.
D. $12,350.

**The answer is B**. His medical expense deduction before limitations is $4,350 ($450 + $800 + $200 + $1,900 +$1,000). The babysitting is not deductible, even though it was incurred while Justin was obtaining medical care. The amount reimbursed by insurance is not deductible. ###

15. Jesse is in the process of adopting a child. In 2012, the child lived with Jesse, and he provided all of the child's support. However, the adoption is not final. Which of the following statements is true?

A. Jesse can include medical expenses that he paid before the adoption becomes final, if the child qualified as his dependent when the medical services were provided or paid.
B. Jesse cannot claim the medical expenses because the adoption is not final.
C. Jesse must save his receipts and, once the adoption becomes final, he may amend his tax return.
D. A taxpayer may only claim medical expenses for a biological child or a step-child.

**The answer is A**. Jesse can include medical expenses that he paid before the adoption becomes final, so long as the child qualified as a dependent when the medical services were provided or paid. ###

16. Which of the following is a deductible medical expense?

A. Acupuncture for back pain.
B. Karate lessons for an overweight person.
C. Marriage counseling.
D. Teeth whitening.

**The answer is A**. In this instance, only acupuncture qualifies as an IRS-allowed medical expense. Medical care expenses must be primarily to alleviate or prevent a physical or mental defect or illness. They do not include expenses that are merely beneficial to general health, such as vitamins, gym classes, or vacations. ###

17. Dora's AGI is $40,000. She paid medical expenses of $3,500. Taking into account the AGI limit, how much can Dora deduct on her Schedule A?

A. $0.
B. $500.
C. $2,313.
D. $2,500.

**The answer is B.** Dora can deduct only $500 of her medical expenses because that is the amount that exceeds 7.5% of her AGI. Dora's AGI is $40,000, 7.5% of which is $3,000. ###

18. Which of the following taxes can taxpayers deduct on Schedule A?

A. Local sales taxes.
B. Fines for speeding.
C. Social Security taxes.
D. Homeowners' association fees.

**The answer is A.** In 2012, taxpayers have the option of claiming state and local sales taxes as an itemized deduction instead of claiming state and local income taxes (a taxpayer cannot claim both). Taxpayers may deduct sales taxes on Schedule A. The other expenses listed are not deductible as taxes on Schedule A. ###

19. Which of the following expenses are deductible on Schedule A?

A. Stamp taxes.
B. Parking ticket obtained while getting emergency medical care.
C. Drivers' license fees.
D. Personal property taxes paid on a speedboat.

**The answer is D.** Only the property taxes paid on the boat are deductible. These are also called "DMV fees." Parking tickets and fines are never deductible. Drivers' license fees and stamp taxes are not deductible. ###

20. Ryan is having money troubles and agrees to sell his home to Janie. Janie agrees to pay all the delinquent real estate taxes on the residence, totaling $2,000. How must Janie treat the property tax payment of $2,000?

A. Janie may deduct the taxes as an itemized deduction on her Schedule A.
B. Janie may not deduct the taxes. She must add the taxes paid to her basis in the property.
C. The taxes may be prorated and deducted over the life of her loan.
D. Janie may deduct the taxes paid as an adjustment to income.

**The answer is B.** Janie can only deduct the property taxes that are legally imposed on her. She cannot deduct property taxes because she was not the legal owner of the property when the taxes were imposed. Property taxes paid during a purchase may be added to the buyer's basis if the taxes are for the time period that the property was owned by the seller. ###

21. Which of the following taxes is not deductible on Schedule A?

A. Property tax on a vacation home.
B. Special assessments to improve the sidewalks.
C. DMV fees based on the vehicle's value.
D. Property taxes paid on a home in Mexico.

**The answer is B.** The assessment to improve sidewalks is not deductible. Many states, cities, and counties also impose local benefit taxes for improvements to property, such as assessments for streets, sidewalks, and sewer lines. These taxes cannot be deducted, but they can be added to the property's basis. ###

22. For a tax to be deductible, all of the following must be true except _____.

A. The tax must be imposed during the tax year.
B. The taxpayer must be legally liable for the tax.
C. The tax must be paid during the tax year.
D. The tax must be paid by the taxpayer.

**The answer is A.** Taxpayers can deduct tax imposed during a *prior* year, so long as the taxes were paid during the current tax year. ###

23. Christopher and Angie file a joint return. During the year, they paid:

- $5,000 in home mortgage interest
- $600 in credit card interest
- $4,000 interest on an auto loan
- $3,000 loan interest on an empty lot that was purchased for building a home

How much can Christopher and Angie report as deductible interest?

A. $0.
B. $5,000.
C. $8,000.
D. $8,600.

**The answer is B.** Only their home mortgage interest ($5,000) is deductible as interest on Schedule A. The other types of interest are all personal interest. Personal interest is not deductible. Interest paid on a plot of land is not deductible as mortgage interest, even if the taxpayer later decides to build a home on the property. Only the interest that is secured by an actual home (not land) would be deductible as mortgage interest. ###

24. Nathaniel owns a home, and he also has a cabin in the mountains that he maintains. The cabin sat empty all year. Which of the following statements is true?

A. Only the mortgage interest and property tax on his main home is deductible.
B. Both the mortgage interest and property tax on his main home and the cabin are deductible.
C. The mortgage interest on both homes is deductible, but the property tax on the cabin is not.
D. The mortgage interest and property tax on his main home is deductible, and the property tax on the cabin is deductible. Any mortgage interest on the second home is not deductible.

**The answer is B.** Both the mortgage interest and property tax on his main home and the second residence are deductible. The mortgage interest on a second home is deductible, even if the taxpayer did not use the home during the year. ###

25. For the mortgage interest deduction, which of the following choices would qualify as a home?

A. An empty lot where the taxpayer plans to build his main home.
B. A sailboat with a camp stove and no bathroom.
C. A vacation cabin without running water.
D. An RV with a small kitchen, bathroom, and sleeping area.

**The answer is D.** A qualified home includes a house, condominium, cooperative, mobile home, house trailer, boat, or similar property that has sleeping, cooking, and toilet facilities. ###

26. Harvey refinanced his home and paid closing costs in 2012. He used the proceeds from the refinance to put on a new roof and also to pay off one of his credit cards. He paid the following fees:

- $400 Loan origination fee (points)
- $500 Home appraisal fee
- $45 Document prep fee
- $60 Loan closing fee
- $70 Title insurance

How much of the fees Harvey paid to the bank for the loan is fully deductible in 2012?

A. $0.
B. $400.
C. $900.
D. $945.
E. $1,005.

**The answer is A.** Harvey may not fully deduct any of the expenses listed because the home loan is a refinance, not a purchase. Deductible fees are limited to home mortgage interest and certain real estate taxes. Points that represent interest on a refinancing are generally amortized over the life of the loan. Fees that are not associated with the acquisition of a loan (other than fees representing interest for tax purposes) generally only affect the basis of the home. Fees related to the acquisition of a loan, such as a credit report fee, are not deductible. ###

27. Ingrid is single with the following income and expenses:
- Wages $70,000
- Interest income $3,000
- Mortgage interest paid $24,000
- Investment interest expense $5,000
- Personal credit card interest $3,400
- Car loan interest $1,200
- Late fees on her mortgage $50

What is Ingrid's total allowable deduction for interest expense on her Schedule A?
A. $24,000.
B. $27,000.
C. $27,050.
D. $32,400.

**The answer is C.** The answer is: $24,000 + $3,000 + $50 = $27,050. The deduction for investment interest expense is limited to investment income. Late fees paid on a qualifying mortgage are deductible as interest. The remaining amount of interest expense must be carried over to the next tax year and may be used to offset income in future tax years. The credit card interest is not deductible. ###

28. Alexander and Melinda are married and file jointly. They have the following interest expenses in the current tax year. How much deductible interest do they have after limitations?

•$10,000 in mortgage interest on a main home
•$2,000 in mortgage interest on a second home
•$4,600 in interest on a car loan
•$600 in credit card interest
•$3,000 in margin interest expense
•$2,400 in investment income

A. $10,000.
B. $12,000.
C. $14,400.
D. $15,000.

**The answer is C**. The answer is figured as follows: $10,000 + $2,000 + $2,400 = $14,400. The mortgage interest on both homes is deductible. The interest on the auto loan and credit cards is not deductible. The margin interest expense is deductible, but limited to the amount of investment income, which is $2,400. Investment interest is deductible by individuals only to the extent of investment income. The remaining investment interest expense may be carried over to a future tax year. ###

29. All of the following are deductible charitable contributions that Larissa made to a qualifying battered women's shelter except _____.

A. Fair market value of the used kitchen appliances, in good condition, she donated to the shelter.
B. $35 of the $50 admission Larissa paid for a shelter fundraising dinner. (The fair market value was $15.)
C. Fair market value of the hours Larissa spent staffing the shelter.
D. Larissa's transportation costs for driving to and from her shift at the shelter.

**The answer is C.** Larissa cannot deduct the value of her volunteer hours. The value of a person's time and service is never deductible. ###

30. Which taxpayer is required to fill out Form 8283 and attach it to his or her return?

A. Abu, who made a single cash contribution of $650 to a qualified organization.
B. Hunter, whose deductible cash contributions totaled $550.
C. Marilyn, whose noncash contributions totaled $250.
D. Debra, whose noncash contributions totaled $600.

**The answer is D.** Debra would be required to fill out Form 8283, *Noncash Charitable Contributions*, and attach it to her return. That is because any noncash donation over $500 must be described on Form 8283. ###

31. Julia made the following contributions last year:

•$600 to St. Martin's Church (The church gave her a receipt)
•$32 to the SPCA
•$40 to a family whose house burned
•$50 for lottery tickets at a fundraiser
•$100 for playing bingo at her church
•Furniture with an FMV of $200 to Goodwill

The amount that Julia can claim as deductible cash contributions is _____.

A. $672.
B. $632.
C. $72.
D. $32.

**The answer is B.** Julia's donations to her church and to the SPCA are her only deductible cash contributions. Lottery tickets and bingo (or any type of gambling) are not charitable contributions, even if the proceeds go to a qualifying organization. The donation of furniture to Goodwill is not a cash contribution, and therefore would not be included in the calculation. Noncash contributions are reported separately from cash contributions. ###

32. Amelia donates $430 in cash to her church. What is required on the receipt to substantiate the donation correctly for IRS recordkeeping requirements?

A. The reason for the contribution.
B. Amelia's home address.
C. The amount of the donation.
D. Amelia's method of payment.

**The answer is C.** A taxpayer can claim a deduction for a contribution of $250 or more only if he has a receipt or acknowledgment from the qualified organization. The receipt must include:

- The amount of cash contributed
- Whether the qualified organization gave the taxpayer any goods or services in return
- A description and good faith estimate of the value of any goods or services provided in return by the organization (if applicable)

A receipt for the donation must also show the amount, the date, and the name of the organization that was paid. ###

33. Lindy donates her used car to a qualified charity. She bought it three years ago for $15,000. A used car guide shows the FMV for this type of car is $5,000. Lindy's friend, Buck, offered her $4,500 for the car a week ago. Lindy gets a Form 1098-C from the organization showing the car was sold for $1,900. How much is Lindy's charitable deduction?

A. $15,000.
B. $5,000.
C. $4,500.
D. $1,900.

**The answer is D.** Lindy can only deduct $1,900 for her donation. This is because she is only allowed to take the lesser of the car's FMV or the amount for which the charity was able to sell the car. Since the car only sold for $1,900, that is the amount of the donation, regardless of its Blue Book value. ###

34. Oscar donated a nice leather coat to a thrift store operated by his church. He paid $450 for the coat three years ago. Similar coats in the thrift store sell for $50. What is Oscar's charitable deduction?

A. $0.
B. $50.
C. $400.
D. $450.

**The answer is B.** Oscar's donation is limited to $50. Generally, the FMV of used clothing and household goods is far less than their original cost. For used clothing, a taxpayer should claim as the value the price that buyers actually pay in used clothing stores, such as consignment or thrift shops, or at garage sales. ###

35. Laney pays $105 for a ticket to a church dinner. All the proceeds go to the church. The ticket to the dinner has an FMV of $20, the cost of the dinner. At the dinner, Laney buys $35 worth of raffle tickets, which the church is selling as a fundraiser. She does not win any raffle prizes. What is Laney's deductible charitable contribution to her church?

A. $85.
B. $120.
C. $140.
D. $195.

**The answer is A.** To figure the amount of Laney's charitable contribution, she must subtract the value of the benefit received ($20) from the total payment ($105). Therefore, Laney can deduct $85 as a charitable contribution to the church. The cost of raffle tickets or other wagering activity is never deductible as a charitable contribution. ###

36. Deductions to the following organizations are subject to the 50% limitation on deductible contributions:

A. Churches.
B. Hospitals.
C. Fraternal societies such as the Kiwanis and the Lions Club.
D. Both A and B.

**The answer is D.** The 50% limit applies to the total of all charitable contributions made during the year. This means that the deduction for charitable contributions cannot exceed 50% of a taxpayer's AGI. A 30% limit applies to veterans' organizations, fraternal societies, nonprofit cemeteries, and certain private non-operating foundations. ###

37. Nancy donates $300 in cash to her local food bank. What type of documentation is required for her donation?

A. No documentation.
B. A canceled check.
C. A self-prepared statement.
D. A receipt for the donation showing the amount, date, and who was paid.

**The answer is D.** A taxpayer can claim a deduction for a contribution of $250 or more only if he has an acknowledgment or receipt of the contribution from the charity. The receipt must reflect the amount, date, and the name of the organization that was paid, plus a statement regarding whether any goods or services were given to the taxpayer. ###

38. Vera and Jack are married and file jointly. They contributed $15,000 in cash from their savings to their synagogue during 2012. They also donated $3,000 to a private foundation that is a nonprofit cemetery organization. A 30% limit applies to the cemetery organization. Their adjusted gross income for 2012 was $30,000. Vera and Jack's deductible contribution for 2012 and any carryover to next year is:

A. $18,000 with zero carryover to next year.
B. $15,000 with $2,100 carryover to next year.
C. $7,500 with $2,100 carryover to next year.
D. $15,000 with $3,000 carryover to next year.

**The answer is D.** Vera and Jack cannot deduct more than $15,000, which is 50% of their income of $30,000. The remaining amount must be carried forward to a future tax year (five years for most charitable deductions.) ###

39. During a fundraising auction at his local church, Lyle pays $600 for a week's stay at a beachfront hotel, where he stays during a vacation in August. He intends to make the payment as a contribution, and all the proceeds go to help the church. The FMV of the stay is $590. What is Lyle's charitable contribution?

A. $0.
B. $10.
C. $590.
D. $600.

**The answer is B.** Lyle can only deduct $10, because he received the benefit of staying at the property. Only the excess contribution over the FMV of the item qualifies as a charitable contribution. ###

40. Summer is a youth group leader who supervises teens on a weekend retreat. She is responsible for overseeing the setup of the trip and enjoys the activities she supervises during the retreat. She also oversees breaking down the campsite and helps transport the group home. Which of the following statements is true?

A. Summer may not deduct her travel expenses because she enjoyed the retreat. Therefore, it is a vacation and is not deductible.
B. Summer may deduct her out-of-pocket expenses, including travel expenses.
C. Summer may deduct only the travel expense to and from the campsite.
D. None of the above.

**The answer is B.** A taxpayer may claim a charitable contribution deduction for out-of-pocket expenses incurred while away from home performing services for a charitable organization only if there is no significant element of personal pleasure in the travel. However, a deduction will not be denied simply because the taxpayer enjoys providing services to a charitable organization. The taxpayer is still allowed to take a charitable contribution deduction for the expenses if he is on-duty in a genuine and substantial sense throughout the trip. Since Summer had substantial supervisory and leadership duties throughout the trip, her out-of-pocket expenses, including travel costs, are deductible. ###

41. Julio spent the entire day attending his human rights organization's regional meeting as a chosen delegate. He spent $50 on travel to the meeting and $25 on materials for the meeting. In the evening, Julio went to the theater with two other meeting attendees. He spent $50 on movie tickets. The charity did not reimburse Julio for any of his costs. How much can Julio deduct as a charitable expense?

A. $25.
B. $50.
C. $75.
D. $150.

**The answer is C.** Julio's charitable contribution is $75 ($50 + $25 = $75). He can claim his travel and meeting expenses as charitable contributions, because they are directly related to his charitable activities. However, he cannot claim the cost of the evening at the theater, as those are personal entertainment costs. ###

42. Ted pays a babysitter $100 to watch his children while he does volunteer work at the Red Cross. He also has $50 in transportation expenses, of which $10 was reimbursed by the organization. What is Ted's deductible expense?

A. $0.
B. $40.
C. $50.
D. $150.

**The answer is B.** Only Ted's transportation costs are deductible ($50 - $10 reimbursement = $40). A taxpayer cannot deduct payments for child care expenses as a charitable contribution, even if they are necessary so he can do the volunteer work. ###

43. In March 2012, Sonia volunteers for 15 hours in the office of a local homeless shelter. The full-time receptionist is paid $10 an hour to do the same work Sonia does. Sonia makes $15 per hour as a cashier at her regular job. She also has $16 in out-of-pocket expenses for bus fare to the shelter. How much can Sonia deduct on her taxes as a charitable contribution?

A. $16.
B. $150.
C. $225.
D. $241.

**The answer is A.** A taxpayer cannot deduct the "value" of his time or services as a charitable deduction. However, a volunteer may deduct out-of-pocket expenses and the costs of gas and oil or transportation costs for getting to and from the place where he volunteers. Sonia cannot use the standard mileage rate because she did not use her own car for transportation. ###

44. All of the following are nonprofit organizations. However, not all of them qualify for deductible contributions. Sam donated to each nonprofit listed. What is his total qualified deduction for 2012?

Amount Organization
$100      Methodist church
$120      County animal shelter
$75       Salvation Army
$25       Red Cross
$50       Political contribution
$300      Chamber of Commerce
$670      Total Contributions

A. $320.
B. $370.
C. $220.
D. $670.

**The answer is A.** The contributions to the political organization and the Chamber of Commerce are not deductible on Schedule A. The deduction is figured as follows: ($100 + $120 + $75 + $25 = $320). ###

45. Ali participated in a fundraising raffle event for his local mosque. All the money collected by the mosque, a qualified organization, went to feed the homeless. Ali purchased $300 in bingo cards and won movie tickets valued at $60. What is Ali's charitable deduction?

A. $0.
B. $60.
C. $240.
D. $300.

**The answer is A.** Ali may not deduct any amount as a contribution. Deducting the cost of raffle, bingo, or lottery tickets is specifically prohibited by IRS Publication 17, even if the money goes to a qualified charity. The cost of raffle, bingo, or lottery tickets is never deductible as a charitable contribution. ###

46. Martin contributes to many organizations. In 2012, he donates $5,000 in cash to his church and $4,000 to his local Chamber of Commerce. He also contributes land with a fair market value of $16,000 to his church. Martin has a basis of $5,000 in the land. His taxable income for the year is $45,000. What is the maximum amount he can deduct for charitable contributions?

A. $9,000.
B. $18,500.
C. $22,500.
D. $25,000.

**The answer is B.** The contribution to the Chamber of Commerce is not a deductible contribution. The $5,000 contribution in cash is fully deductible, but gifts of appreciated property are subject to a maximum deduction of 30% of the taxpayer's adjusted gross income. However, charitable gifts of appreciated property held long-term are subject to a lower deductibility ceiling: 30% of AGI, with a five-year carryover of any excess deduction. So, Martin figures his charitable contribution as follows:

($45,000 x 30%) =          $13,500
($5,000 + $13,500) =         $18,500
Carryover = $2,500
($16,000 - $13,500 =      $2,500) ###

47. In 2012 Henry experienced numerous health problems. As a result, Henry and his wife Marie incurred the following medical expenses:

| | |
|---|---|
| Physician and hospital fees | $10,000 |
| Dental and orthodontic fees | $5,000 |
| Medical and dental insurance premiums | $12,000 |
| Eyeglasses and contact lenses | $1,000 |
| Health club dues | $1,000 |
| Prescription medications | $3,000 |
| Nonprescription drugs and medicines | $1,000 |

They also drove 3,000 miles in connection with medical visits, and incurred parking and toll charges of $100. The insurance premiums were paid through Henry's employer-sponsored health insurance plan and were not reported as income in box 1 of his Form W-2. Henry and Marie had adjusted gross income of $100,000 in 2012. What is the amount of their medical expense deduction for the year on Schedule A?

A. $33,000.
B. $19,790.
C. $12,290.
D. $33,790.

**The answer is C.** The insurance premiums are not deductible because they were paid through an employer-sponsored health insurance plan and were not reported in box 1 of Form W-2. Neither health club dues nor nonprescription medicines (except for insulin) are deductible.

The deductible costs listed total $19,100, and the 3,000 miles driven in connection with medical visits can be deducted at a standard mileage rate of $.23, or $690. Deductibility of the resulting total of $19,790 is limited to the amount in excess of 7.5% of adjusted gross income, or $7,500, so the amount of their medical expense deduction calculated on Schedule A would be $12,290.  ###

Supporting calculations:

Deductible expenses:

| | |
|---|---|
| Physician and hospital fees | $10,000 |
| Dental and orthodontic fees | $5,000 |
| Eyeglasses and contact lenses | $1,000 |
| Prescription medications | $3,000 |
| Parking and tolls | $100 |
| Mileage at standard mileage rate of $.23 | $690 |
| **Total deductible expenses** | **$19,790** |

| | |
|---|---|
| Adjusted gross income | $100,000 |
| 7.5% limit | ($7,500) |
| Limitation ($19,750-$7,500) | |
| Medical expense deduction on Schedule A | $12,290 |

48. All of the following statements regarding home equity debt are correct except:
A. There is a $150,000 limit on the amount of debt that can be treated as home equity debt for purposes of the mortgage interest deduction.
B. The taxpayer does not have to use the home equity loan on improvements to the home for it to be eligible as deductible interest.
C. The debt must not exceed the property's fair market value.
D. Both B and C.

**The answer is A.** The limit on the amount of debt that can be treated as home equity debt for purposes of the mortgage interest deduction is $100,000, not $150,000. ###

49. In 2012, Remy had the following transactions from which she earned interest:

1. Interest of $700 from a certificate of deposit that matured in September.

2. Upon maturity of the first CD, she invested the proceeds in a second certificate with a maturity in March 2013. As of December 31, this certificate has accrued interest of $400.

3. She loaned $2,000 to a family member who repaid the loan and related interest of $120 with a check dated December 31 that Remy received on January 4, 2013.

What is the amount of taxable interest income that Remy must report for the year?

A. $1,100.
B. $1,220.
C. $700.
D. $820.

**The answer is C.** The interest earned on the first certificate was received upon maturity, and was therefore taxable in 2012. The accrued interest on the second certificate would have been subject to penalty if the certificate had been canceled prior to maturity, and was therefore not taxable. Remy did not have constructive receipt of the interest paid on the loan until 2013, and it was therefore not taxable in 2012. ###

# Unit 8: Other Itemized Deductions

**More Reading:**
Publication 561, *Determining the Value of Donated Property*
Publication 587, *Business Use of Your Home*
Publication 547, *Casualties, Disasters, and Thefts*
Publication 529, *Miscellaneous Deductions*

In this unit, we continue our look at deductions that taxpayers can take on their 1040 tax returns. We start with deductible nonbusiness casualty losses, which are reported on Schedule A. Casualty losses related to a business (including self-employed businesses that are reported on Schedule C and Schedule F) are treated differently.

## Casualty Losses

A casualty is the damage, destruction, or loss of property resulting from an identifiable event that is sudden, unexpected, or unusual. Examples include a car accident, fire, earthquake, flood, vandalism, or theft.

Losses that do not meet this definition and are thus not deductible include:

- Damage done by pets
- Slow insect damage to trees, clothing, or household items, such as termite or moth damage
- Arson
- Lost property
- Progressive deterioration ("normal wear and tear")
- Losses in real estate value from market fluctuations
- Accidental breakage of china, dishes, or other items during regular use

A taxpayer must have proof of the casualty or theft in order to deduct it. The taxpayer must also prove that the loss was actually caused by the event. Specifically, the taxpayer must be able to prove:

- The type of casualty loss (car accident, fire, storm, etc.) and the date of occurrence
- That the taxpayer was the legal owner of the property, or at least legally liable for the damage (such as leased property where the lessee was responsible for damage)
- Whether insurance reimbursement exists

**Example:** Gregory rents a car from Reliable Rentals, Inc. He declines renter's insurance and signs a contract stating he will be responsible for any damage. The rental car is stolen and now Gregory is responsible for paying back Reliable Rentals. Gregory's car insurance does not have rental car coverage, so he is liable for the full amount. Gregory may deduct the loss as a casualty loss, subject to the applicable rules.

Personal casualty losses are subject to the "Single Event Rule." This means that events closely related in origin are considered a single event. For example, it is a single casualty when the damage comes from two or more closely related causes, such as wind and flood damage from the same storm. A single casualty may also damage two or more pieces of property, such as a hailstorm that damages both a taxpayer's home and his car parked in the driveway.

# Nonbusiness Casualty Loss Limits ($100 & 10% Rule)

Each personal casualty or theft loss is limited to the excess of the loss over $100. In addition, a 10%-of-AGI limit applies to the net loss. The "$100 Rule" and "10% Rule" only apply to nonbusiness casualty losses, not to business property losses.

## 1. The $100 Rule

After a taxpayer has figured the casualty loss on personal-use property, he must reduce that loss by $100. This reduction applies to each total casualty or theft loss. It does not matter how many pieces of property are involved in a single event; the taxpayer only has to reduce the losses for each event by $100.

> **Example:** A fire damaged Dick's house in January, causing $3,000 in damage. In September, storm damaged his house again, causing $5,000 in damage. Dick must reduce each loss by $100.

> **\*Note:** If a taxpayer has *more than one* casualty loss during the year, he must reduce each loss by $100 separately. Then the taxpayer must reduce the total of all losses by 10% of adjusted gross income.

## 2. The 10% Rule

The taxpayer must reduce the total of all personal casualty losses on personal-use property by 10% of his AGI. This rule does not apply to a net disaster loss within a federally declared disaster area.

Married couples filing jointly with a loss from the same event are treated as if they were one person, with the $100 Rule and 10% Rule being applied only one time.

## Reporting a Casualty Loss or Gain

Taxpayers use Form 4684, *Casualties and Thefts*, to report a gain or loss from a personal casualty. The taxpayer may claim a deductible loss on personal-use property only if he itemizes deductions.

Sometimes taxpayers will have a gain from casualty losses because the insurance reimbursement will exceed their basis. However, if a taxpayer has a gain on damaged property, he can postpone reporting the gain if the insurance reimbursement is spent to restore the property.

Gain may also be postponed by buying replacement property within a specified period of time. The replacement period begins on the date the property was damaged, destroyed, or stolen, and ends two years after the close of the first tax year in which any part of the gain is realized. For a main home or its contents located in a federally declared disaster area, the replacement period is generally four years, rather than two. [51] For victims of Hurricane Katrina and certain other extreme disaster areas, the replacement period has been extended to five years, assuming the property is purchased in the same area.

For disaster area losses, taxpayers may choose to deduct the loss on the previous year's tax return, rather than in the year the disaster loss occurred. This may result in a lower tax for that year, often producing or increasing a cash refund.

For casualty losses in general, this is how the taxpayer determines his deduction:

1. Calculate the *lesser* of the FMV or adjusted basis of the item prior to the loss.
2. Subtract any payments/reimbursements from insurance.
3. Subtract $100 for each event (2012 limit).
4. Subtract 10% of the taxpayer's AGI.

---

**Example:** Many years ago, Al bought a vacation cottage for $18,000. A storm destroyed the cottage, now valued at $250,000. Al received $146,000 from his insurance company. He had a gain of $128,000 ($146,000 – $18,000 basis). Al spent the full $146,000 to rebuild his cottage. Since he used the insurance proceeds to rebuild his cottage, he can postpone reporting or recognizing the gain until the cottage is sold.

---

## Decrease in FMV from a Casualty Loss

Casualty losses are deductible only for actual damage caused to a property. The cost of cleaning up or making repairs after a casualty is not included. Nor is a decline in market value of property in or near a casualty area.

---

**Example:** In 2012, Nicole purchased a condo for $200,000. Two months after the purchase, a hurricane destroyed five other properties on her block. A resulting appraisal showed that all of the properties within a five-mile radius had declined in fair market value by 15% because people were afraid to purchase homes in "hurricane territory." The reduction in the home's FMV is not a deductible casualty loss.

---

## Insurance Reimbursements

Taxpayers can deduct qualified casualty losses to their homes, household items, and vehicles. A taxpayer may not deduct casualty and theft losses that are covered by insurance unless he files a claim for reimbursement. The taxpayer must reduce his casualty loss by the amount of the insurance reimbursement. If the taxpayer decides not to file an insurance claim but has a deductible, he may still claim the amount of the insurance deductible, since that amount would not have been covered by the policy anyway.

---

[51] More detailed information about replacement property can be found in Unit 12, *Nonrecognition Property Transfers.*

**Example:** Sonny has a $750 deductible on his car insurance. He has a car accident in 2012, incurring $6,000 of damage. The insurance company pays Sonny for the damage minus the $750 deductible. The amount of Sonny's casualty loss is based solely on his deductible. Sonny's actual casualty loss is only $650 ($750 – $100).

**Example:** Caitlyn has homeowners' insurance. In 2012, a small fire causes $8,000 in damage to her home. She does not want her insurance premium to go up, so she declines to file a claim and pays for the damage out-of-pocket. Her insurance policy carries a $1,500 deductible. Caitlyn cannot deduct the loss because she declined to file an insurance claim. However, she is allowed to deduct $1,500, the amount of the deductible, because her insurance would not have covered that amount in any case.

A taxpayer does not have to reduce his casualty loss by insurance payments received to cover living expenses in the following two situations:

- When a taxpayer loses use of his main home because of a casualty.
- When government authorities do not allow a taxpayer access to his main home because of a casualty or a threat of one.

However, if these insurance payments are more than the temporary increase in his living expenses, a taxpayer must include the excess in his income. This is not required if the casualty occurs in a federally declared disaster area. None of those insurance payments are taxable.

The taxable part of the insurance payment should be included in income for the year the taxpayer gains use of his main home, or, if later, for the year the taxable part of the insurance payment is received.

**Example:** Olivia's main home was damaged by a tornado in August 2010. After repairs were made, she moved back into her home in November 2011. She received insurance payments in 2010 and 2011 that were $1,500 more than the temporary increase in her living expenses during those years. Olivia includes this amount in income on her 2011 Form 1040. In 2012, she receives another $500 to cover her living expenses in 2010 and 2011. She must include that payment on her 2012 tax return.

## Rules for Determining Fair Market Value and Adjusted Basis

A casualty loss is limited to the lesser of the FMV of the property, or the property's adjusted basis right before the loss. The cost of replacement property is not part of a casualty or theft loss.

**Example:** Don purchased an antique vase at a garage sale for $600. Later, he discovered that the vase was actually a rare collectible and its FMV was $20,000. The vase was stolen two months later during a robbery. Don's casualty loss is limited to the $600 he paid for it, which is his basis in the property. Don cannot claim a casualty loss deduction for $20,000, the value of the item.

> **Example:** Raquel bought a new leather sofa four years ago for $3,000. In April, a fire destroyed the sofa. Raquel estimates that it would now cost $5,000 to replace it. However, if she had sold the sofa before the fire, she probably would have received only $900 for it because the sofa was already four years old. Raquel's casualty loss is $900 (still subject to the $100 and 10% rules), the FMV of the sofa before the fire. Her loss is not $3,000 (her basis) and it is not $5,000 (the replacement cost).

## Theft Losses

A theft loss may be deducted in the year that the theft is discovered. It does not matter when the theft actually occurred. Qualifying theft losses include:

- Blackmail
- Burglary
- Embezzlement
- Extortion
- Kidnapping for ransom
- Larceny
- Robbery
- Mail fraud

The taking of property must be illegal under the law of the state where it occurred, and it must have been done with criminal intent. However, a taxpayer does not have to show a conviction for theft.

If a taxpayer takes a deduction for stolen property and the property is later recovered by the police, he must report the recovery as income in the year the property is recovered. However, he must only report the amounts that actually reduced tax in an earlier year.

## Nondeductible Losses

**Decline in value of stock:** A taxpayer may not deduct the decline in value of stock as a casualty loss, even if it is related to accounting fraud. There is an exception for Ponzi scheme losses, which may be deducted as capital losses.

**The cost of insurance:** The cost of insurance or other protection is not deductible as a casualty loss. This rule applies to nonbusiness assets only.

> **Example:** Jordan pays for renter's insurance to cover the furniture and appliances in his home from theft or other disaster losses. Jordan may not deduct the cost of the renter's insurance as a casualty loss.

> **Example:** Sydney is self-employed and owns a clothing boutique. She pays for hazard insurance on the boutique. Sydney may deduct the cost of the insurance on her shop as a regular business expense.

# Business Casualty Losses

A business-related casualty loss is treated very differently than a personal casualty loss. Business casualty losses may be tested on either Part 1 or Part 2 of the exam. This is because a business loss may affect a self-employed taxpayer, as well as an investor who owns rental units.

If income-producing property (such as rental property) is subject to a casualty loss, the amount of the taxpayer's loss is the adjusted basis in the property minus any salvage value and minus any insurance or other reimbursement received.

The loss is figured as follows:

| The taxpayer's adjusted basis in the property |
| :---: |
| MINUS |
| Any salvage value |
| MINUS |
| Any insurance reimbursement |

**Example:** Mario is a self-employed florist who owns his own shop. A utility van he uses for floral deliveries was involved in an accident. Mario had purchased the van for $70,000. The accumulated depreciation on the van prior to the accident was $40,000. He disposed of the van for $500 (salvage value of the scrap metal.) Mario's insurance company reimbursed him $20,000. His casualty loss is determined as follows:

| | |
| :--- | :--- |
| Acquisition cost | $70,000 |
| Less accumulated depreciation | ($40,000) |
| Adjusted basis of van | $30,000 |
| Minus salvage value | ($500) |
| Initial loss from accident | $29,500 |
| Minus insurance reimbursement | ($20,000) |
| **Amount of casualty loss** | **$9,500** |

# Miscellaneous Itemized Deductible Expenses

There are numerous other deductions taxpayers may take on their tax returns, with these miscellaneous expenses divided into two important categories:

- Miscellaneous expenses subject to the 2% of AGI limit, and
- Miscellaneous expenses deductible in full (not subject to the 2% AGI limit).

## Miscellaneous Expenses Subject to the 2% Limit

A taxpayer may deduct certain expenses as miscellaneous itemized deductions on Schedule A. The taxpayer may only claim the amount that exceeds 2% of his AGI. There are many common types of these miscellaneous expenses subject to the 2% limit, including many expenses an employee may incur.

**Example:** Andy's AGI is $45,000, and he has $1,100 in miscellaneous deductible work-related expenses. He must first figure out the 2% limit before he can start deducting these expenses (2% X $45,000 = $900). He can therefore deduct only $200 of those expenses ($1,100 - $900 = $200). Andy adds this amount to his Schedule A as an itemized deduction.

Investment expenses are allowed as a deduction if the expenses are directly connected with the production of investment income. Examples include investment counseling fees and the rental of a safe deposit box to keep investment documents. Investment expenses are included as a miscellaneous itemized deduction on Schedule A and are allowable only after applying the 2% limit.

Expenses related to a hobby are deductible, but only up to the amount of hobby income. A "hobby" is not considered a business because it is not carried on to make a profit.

# Legal Fees

Many legal expenses are not deductible for individual taxpayers, such as the cost of attorney fees for drafting a will. But certain legal expenses are deductible, if they are incurred when a taxpayer is attempting to produce or collect taxable income, such as advice related to collecting alimony.

A taxpayer cannot deduct legal fees and court costs for getting a divorce. But he may deduct legal fees paid for tax advice in connection with a divorce and legal fees to obtain alimony. In order to be deductible, the tax advice fees must be separately stated on the attorney's bill. In addition, a taxpayer may deduct fees paid to appraisers, actuaries, and accountants for services in determining the correct tax or in helping to get alimony. A taxpayer can deduct fees for legal advice on federal, state, and local taxes of all types, including income, estate, gift, inheritance, and property taxes, even if the advice is related to a divorce. If an attorney's legal fee includes amounts for tax advice and other tax services, the taxpayer must be able to prove the expense was incurred for tax advice and not for some other legal issue.

**Example:** The lawyer handling Jenna's divorce consults another law firm, which handles only tax matters, to obtain information on how the divorce will affect her taxes. Since Jenna consulted with the second law firm specifically to discuss tax matters, she can deduct the part of the fee paid to the second firm and separately stated on her bill, as an itemized deduction on Schedule A, subject to the 2% limit.

**Example:** The lawyer handling Mack's divorce uses the firm's tax department for tax matters related to his divorce. Mack's statement from the firm shows the part of the total fee for tax matters. This is based on the time required, the difficulty of the tax questions, and the amount of tax involved. Mack can deduct this part of his bill as an itemized deduction on Schedule A, subject to a 2% limit.

A taxpayer can claim deductible legal fees by claiming them as miscellaneous itemized deductions subject to the 2%-of-AGI limit.

> **Example:** Betty pays an attorney $4,500 for handling her divorce. She also pays an additional $1,500 fee for services in collecting alimony that her former husband refuses to pay. Betty can deduct the fee for collecting alimony ($1,500), subject to a 2% limit, if it is separately stated on the attorney's bill. The $4,500 divorce fee is not deductible.

## Unreimbursed Employee Business Expenses

An employee may deduct certain work-related expenses as itemized deductions. These expenses are first reported on Form 2106, *Employee Business Expenses*, and the amount is transferred to Schedule A. The taxpayer can deduct only unreimbursed employee expenses that are:

- Paid or incurred during the tax year,
- For carrying on the business of being an employee, and
- Ordinary and necessary.

An expense does not have to be required to be deductible. However, it must be a common expense that would be accepted in the taxpayer's trade or profession.

The following are examples of unreimbursed employee expenses that may be deductible:

- Business liability insurance premiums
- Malpractice insurance
- Depreciation on an asset the employer requires for work
- Dues to professional societies
- Subscriptions to professional journals
- Expenses of looking for a new job in the taxpayer's present occupation
- Legal fees related directly to a job
- Licenses and regulatory fees
- Tax counseling, preparation, and assistance
- Union dues
- Work clothes and uniforms (if required and not suitable for everyday use)
- Tools and supplies used for work
- Educator expenses
- Work-related education
- Home office or part of a home used regularly and exclusively in the taxpayer's work
- Travel, transportation, meals, and lodging related to the taxpayer's work
- Employee meals and entertainment

An employee may deduct unreimbursed business-related meals and entertainment expenses he has for entertaining a client, customer, or another employee. The limit on deductible meals and entertainment is 50% (the same for self-employed taxpayers and businesses). The taxpayer must apply the "50% limit" *before* applying the 2% of AGI limit. The taxpayer can deduct meals and entertainment expenses only if they meet the following tests:

- The main purpose of the meal or entertainment was the active conduct of business,
- The taxpayer conducted business during the entertainment period, and
- The taxpayer had more than a general expectation of some other specific business benefit at a future time.

## Deductible Employee Travel Expenses

An employee may not deduct commuting expenses, which are the expenses incurred when going from a taxpayer's home to his main workplace. However, there are numerous instances where an employee may deduct mileage or other travel expenses relating to his employment. Deductible employee travel expenses include:

- Getting from one work location to another in the course of business
- Visiting clients or customers
- Going to a business meeting away from the regular workplace
- Traveling from a first job to a second job in the same day
- Getting from a taxpayer's home to a temporary workplace

Any amounts reimbursed by the employer are not deductible by the employee.

## Conventions: Special Rules

A taxpayer may deduct the cost of travel and attendance to conventions in the U.S. or the "North American area," including Canada and Mexico[52]. For cruises, there is a $2,000 annual cap on deductions, or $4,000 if filing jointly and both spouses went on qualifying cruise ship conventions. The IRS imposes strict substantiation requirements for taxpayers attempting to use this deduction.

A deduction is not allowed for conventions focused exclusively on investments or financial planning.

## Tax Home and Work Location

A taxpayer's "tax home" is his principal place of work, *regardless of where he actually lives*. A taxpayer's tax home is used to determine if travel expenses are deductible.

Travel and meal expenses are considered deductible if the taxpayer is traveling away from his *tax home*, which is determined based on the following two factors:

- The travel is away from the general area or vicinity of the taxpayer's tax home.

---

[52] The IRS maintains a list of these countries, many of which are tourist meccas and may not normally be associated with being in the "North American area." Examples include Aruba, Jamaica, Costa Rica, Barbados, Bermuda, Panama, the Marshall Islands, and the Netherlands Antilles. (Revenue Ruling 2011-26).

- The trip is long enough or far away enough that a taxpayer cannot reasonably be expected to complete the roundtrip without sleep or rest.

This does not necessarily mean that a taxpayer needs to stay overnight at the destination in order to deduct the expense. For example, it may mean that an individual has an all-day meeting and needs to get a few hours of sleep in a hotel before driving home.

Once a taxpayer has determined that he is traveling away from his *tax home*, he can deduct "ordinary and necessary" expenses incurred while traveling on business Examples of deductible travel expenses while a taxpayer is away from home include:

- The cost of getting to a business destination (air, rail, bus, car, ferry, etc.)
- Meals and lodging while away from home
- Taxi fares
- Dry cleaning and laundry
- Use of a car while at the business location
- Computer rental fees
- Baggage charges, including shipping samples and display materials to the destination
- Tips on eligible expenses

## Multiple work locations

If a taxpayer has *more than one* place of business or work, the "tax home" must be determined using several factors. The following facts should be used to determine which one is the main place of business or work:

- The total time ordinarily spent in each place
- The level of business activity in each place
- Whether income from each place is significant

The most important consideration is the length of time spent at each location. If a taxpayer regularly works in more than one place, his tax home is the general area where the main place of business or work is located. If a taxpayer has more than one place of business, then his tax home is his main place of business.

---

**Example:** Gary is a marketing consultant who lives with his family in Chicago, but works full-time in Milwaukee where he stays in a hotel and eats in restaurants. Gary returns to Chicago every weekend. He may not deduct any of his travel, meals, or lodging expenses in Milwaukee because that is his tax home. Gary's travel on weekends to his family home in Chicago is not for work, so these expenses are also not deductible.

---

If a person does not have a regular place of business because of the nature of his work, then his tax home can be the place where he lives.

**Example:** Seville is a truck driver who lives in Tucson, Arizona with his family. Seville is employed by a trucking firm that has its main terminal in Phoenix. At the end of his long trucking runs, Seville returns to his home terminal in Phoenix and spends one night there before returning home. Seville cannot deduct any expenses he has for meals and lodging in Phoenix or the cost of traveling from Phoenix to Tucson. This is because Phoenix is Seville's "tax home" (Publication 463).

There are special rules for temporary work assignments. When a taxpayer is working away from his main place of business and the job assignment is temporary, his *tax home* does not change. The taxpayer can deduct his travel expenses because the job assignment is of a temporary nature, and therefore, the travel is considered business-related.

**Note:** A temporary work assignment is any work assignment that is expected to last for *one year or less*. Travel expenses paid or incurred in connection with a temporary work assignment away from home are deductible. However, travel expenses paid in connection with an *indefinite* work assignment are *not deductible*. Any work assignment over one year in duration is considered *indefinite*. A taxpayer cannot deduct travel expenses at a work location if it is realistically expected that he will work there for more than one year.

**Example**: Terry is a construction worker who lives and works primarily in Los Angeles. He is also a member of a trade union that helps him get work. Because of a shortage of jobs, Terry agrees to work at a construction site in Fresno. The Fresno job lasts ten months. Since the job lasts less than one year, the Fresno job is considered *temporary* and Terry's tax home is still in Los Angeles. Therefore, Terry's travel expenses are deductible since he was traveling away from his tax home for business or work. Terry can deduct travel expenses, including meals and lodging, while traveling between his temporary place of work and his tax home in Los Angeles.

There is a special rule for military personnel. Members of the armed forces on a permanent duty assignment overseas are not considered to be "traveling away from home."

Therefore, members of the military cannot deduct their travel expenses for meals and lodging while on permanent duty assignment. However, military personnel that are permanently transferred from one duty station to another may be able to deduct their moving expenses as an adjustment to income.

# Office in the Home

If a taxpayer has an office in his home that qualifies as a principal place of business, he can deduct daily transportation costs between the home office and another work location in the same trade or business. These are not commuting expenses, because commuting expenses are never deductible. However, the travel between a home office to a business location would be considered deductible travel.

In order to qualify as a home office, the space must be used exclusively and regularly:

- As the taxpayer's principal place of business, or
- As a place to meet with patients or clients in the normal course of your business, or
- In any connection with a business where the business portion of the home is a separate structure not attached to the home.

**Example:** Vince is a self-employed bookkeeper who works exclusively out of his home office. He has many clients. Vince travels from his home office directly to his clients' locations and performs his bookkeeping services on-site. Vince does not have any other office. In this case, the travel from his home office to his clients' locations is deductible as business mileage.

**Example:** Martha is a part-time tax preparer. During tax season, she uses her study to prepare tax returns. She also uses the study to exercise on her treadmill. The room is not used exclusively in Martha's profession, so she cannot claim a deduction for the business use. Also, since the space does not qualify as a bona-fide home office, then the travel from her home office to another business location (such as a client's office or home) would not be deductible.

## Calculating the Home Office Percentage

The home office deduction depends on the percentage of the home that is used for business. A taxpayer can use any reasonable method to compute business percentage, but the most common methods are to:

- Divide the area of the home used for business by the total area of the home, or
- Divide the number of rooms used for business by the total number of rooms in the home if all rooms in the home are about the same size.

Taxpayers may not deduct expenses for any portion of the year during which there was no business use of the home.

**Example:** Lillian is a self-employed bookkeeper, and she has a qualified home office. The entire square footage of her home is 1,200 square feet. Her home office is 240 square feet, so her home office percentage is 20% (240 ÷ 1,200) of the total area of her home. Her business percentage is 20%.

**Example:** Glenn is a tool salesman who is on the road most of the time, and his home is the only fixed location for selling tools. Glenn regularly uses the right half of his basement for storage of inventory and product samples. The expenses for the space are deductible as an employee-related home office expense.

## Job Search Expenses

A taxpayer may deduct job search expenses, subject to the 2% of AGI limit, if the expenses relate to the same profession. Expenses incurred can be deducted even if the taxpayer does not find a new job.

If the job search qualifies, the taxpayer can deduct costs for using an employment agency or career counselor, and for traveling to interviews. The taxpayer may also deduct the cost of printing, preparing, and mailing resumes.

The following expenses are not deductible:

- Job search expenses for a new occupation
- Living expenses incurred during a period of unemployment between the ending of the last job and a new period of employment
- A taxpayer looking for a new job the first time

## Job-Related Education

The cost of courses designed to maintain or improve the skills needed for a present job (or required by an employer or the law) is deductible as an employee business expense. The taxpayer may also choose to take an education credit. The education must meet at least one of the following tests:

- The education must maintain or improve skills that are required for the taxpayer's current line of work
- The education must be required by law or by the taxpayer's employer as a condition of his employment

If a taxpayer has a regular job and then enrolls in work-related education courses on a temporary basis, he can also deduct the round-trip costs of transportation between his home and school. This is true regardless of the location of the school, the distance traveled, or whether the taxpayer attends school on non-work days.

In some cases, a taxpayer may be able to take an education credit for his education expenses, so may choose between the credit and the miscellaneous itemized deduction, whichever produces a lower tax.

## Deductible Uniforms

The cost of uniforms and other special work clothes required by an employer can be deducted as work-related expenses. The uniforms must not be suitable for everyday use. The taxpayer may also deduct the cost of upkeep, including laundry and dry cleaning bills.

Examples of employees who may deduct their uniforms include delivery workers, firefighters, health care workers, law enforcement officers, letter carriers, professional athletes, and transportation workers (air, rail, bus, etc.) Musicians and entertainers can deduct the cost of theatrical clothing and accessories that are not suitable for everyday wear. An employee can deduct the cost of protective clothing, such as safety shoes or boots, safety glasses, hard hats, and work gloves.

Full-time active-duty military personnel cannot deduct the cost of their uniforms. However, they may be able to deduct the cost of insignia, shoulder boards, and related items.

## Nondeductible Expenses

The IRS has a lengthy list of expenses that cannot be deducted. These are just a sample of expenses that are not allowed:

- Lunch with coworkers
- Meals while working late
- Club dues
- Lost or misplaced cash or property
- Hobby losses
- Residential telephone line
- Home security system
- Home repairs, insurance, and rent
- Wristwatches
- Personal legal expenses
- Losses from the sale of a home, furniture, or personal car
- Brokers' commissions
- Burial or funeral expenses, including the cost of a cemetery lot
- Check-writing fees
- Fees and licenses, such as car licenses, marriage licenses, and dog tags
- Fines and penalties, such as parking tickets
- Investment-related seminars
- Life insurance premiums
- Personal disability insurance premiums

## *Miscellaneous Deductions (Not Subject to the 2% Limit)*

There are also some expenses that are not subject to the 2% limit. A taxpayer can fully deduct on Schedule A the expenses that fall under this category, without regard to any percentage of income limits.

The expenses that are not subject to the 2% rule are:

1. Gambling losses to the extent of gambling winnings. The full amount of a taxpayer's gambling winnings is reported on line 21 of his Form 1040. Gambling losses are deducted on Schedule A, up to the total amount of gambling winnings. Taxpayers must have kept a written record of their losses.

> *Note: Gambling losses in excess of winnings are not deductible. The full amount of winnings must be reported as income, and the losses (up to the amount of winnings) may be claimed as an itemized deduction.

2. Work-related expenses for individuals with a disability that enable them to work, such as attendant care services at their workplace.

> **Example:** Erin has a visual disability. She requires a large screen magnifier at work in order to see well enough so she can perform her work. Erin purchased her screen magnifier for $550. She may deduct the cost of the screen magnifier as an itemized deduction not subject to the 2% floor.

3. Amortizable premium on taxable bonds: If the amount a taxpayer pays for a bond is greater than its stated principal amount, the excess is called a "bond premium." If this occurs, the excess is treated as a miscellaneous itemized deduction that is not subject to the 2% limit.

4. Casualty or theft losses from *income-producing* property: A taxpayer can deduct a casualty or theft loss as a miscellaneous itemized deduction not subject to the 2% limit if the damaged or stolen property was income-producing property (property held for investment, such as stocks, bonds, gold, silver, vacant lots, and works of art).

5. A taxpayer can deduct the federal estate tax attributable to income "in respect of a decedent" that the taxpayer includes in gross income. Income in respect of a decedent is income that a deceased taxpayer would have received had the death not occurred and which was not properly includable in the decedent's final income tax return.

# Unit 8: Questions

1. Alfred lives in Baltimore where he has a seasonal job for eight months each year and earns $25,000. He works the other four months in Miami, also at a seasonal job, and earns $9,000. Where is Alfred's tax home?

A. Miami.
B. Baltimore.
C. Alfred is a transient for tax purposes.
D. Alfred has no tax home.

**The answer is B.** Baltimore is Alfred's main place of work because he spends most of his time there and earns most of his income there. Therefore, Baltimore is Alfred's tax home for IRS purposes. ###

2. Brad is working on a temporary work assignment in another city. He is not sure how long the assignment will last. He travels overnight every week. So far, the work assignment has lasted 11 months in 2012, and Brad has incurred $800 in travel expenses and $300 in meal expenses. What is his deductible expense for this activity in 2012?

A. $0.
B. $800.
C. $950.
D. $1,100.

**The answer is A.** Brad cannot deduct any of the expenses, because travel expenses paid in connection with an indefinite work assignment are not deductible. ###

3. All of the following may be claimed as miscellaneous itemized deductions except _____.

A. Unreimbursed commuting expenses to and from work.
B. Professional society or union dues.
C. Expenses of looking for a new job.
D. Work-related expenses for individuals with a disability.

**The answer is A.** The expenses of commuting to and from work are not deductible expenses. ###

4. Felicity is a self-employed midwife who has a home office. Felicity's principal place of business is in her home, although she does not meet with clients in her home. Instead, she goes out to her clients' homes and performs her duties on-site. Which of the following statements is true?

A. Felicity can deduct the cost of round-trip transportation between her home office and her clients' place of business.
B. Felicity cannot deduct the cost of round-trip transportation between her home office and her clients' homes, but she may deduct the transportation costs from her clients' homes to other business locations.
C. Felicity does not have a qualified home office, because she does not meet clients in her home.
D. None of the above.

**The answer is A.** Felicity can deduct daily transportation costs between her home office and a client's location. Felicity does not have to meet with clients in her home in order for her home office to qualify as her principal place of business. The transportation costs between two work locations are considered a deductible travel expense. ###

5. Patrice's antique Persian rug was damaged by a new kitten before it was housebroken. Patrice estimates the loss at $4,500. Her AGI for the year is $50,000. How much of the casualty loss may she deduct?

A. $0.
B. $4,500.
C. $3,000.
C. $2,900.

**The answer is A.** A casualty loss is not deductible if the damage is caused by a family pet. Because the damage was neither unexpected nor unusual, the loss is not deductible as a casualty loss. ###

6. Megan, an engineer, maintains a residence in Denver, Colorado where her employer has a permanent satellite office. In 2012, Megan's employer enrolls her in a ten-month executive training program at their corporate offices in Santa Clara, California. Megan will attend classroom training in Santa Clara and do temporary work assignments throughout the United States, but she does expect to return to work in Denver after she completes her training.

Every Monday she flies to Santa Clara and stays in the city the entire week. She maintains a small, one-bedroom apartment in Santa Clara and incurs all the ordinary and necessary expenses in the upkeep of the apartment. She returns to Denver on the weekends to spend time with family and attend to her personal affairs from her Denver residence. Where is Megan's "tax home" for 2012?

A. Santa Clara, California.
B. Denver, Colorado.
C. Neither, because Megan is a transient for tax purposes.
D. Both, because Megan spends time in both places.

**The answer is B.** Her tax home is still in Denver, because her work assignment is temporary. For IRS purposes, a work assignment is temporary if it is expected to last for one year or less. Since Megan is going to be away for only ten months, her tax home remains in Denver. Travel expenses paid or incurred in connection with a temporary work assignment away from home are deductible. ###

7. Eli purchased a used car for $11,000 in 2012. He forgot to purchase auto insurance, and three months later he totaled his car in an auto accident. The car's FMV on the date of the accident was $10,000. He was able to sell the car to a salvage yard for $300. Eli's AGI for 2012 was $50,000. What is Eli's deductible loss?

A. $0.
B. $4,200.
C. $4,600.
D. $9,700.

**The answer is C.** This is a nonbusiness casualty loss, so Eli must first reduce his loss by $100 and then 10% of his AGI. The answer is calculated as follows:

| Basis: | $10,000 |
|---|---|
| Insurance | $0 |
| Salvage value | ($300) |
| Statutory reduction | ($100) |
| 10% of AGI | ($5,000) |
| Deductible Loss | $4,600 |

Eli's deductible casualty loss on Schedule A is $4,600. ###

8. Joshua's adjusted gross income is $20,000. Determine which expenses he would include in the total for his miscellaneous itemized deductions.

**Expense Description:**
Income tax preparation fee $100
Safe deposit box rental (to store bonds) $75
Life insurance premiums $600
Home security system $175
Loss on the sale of a personal vehicle $1,800
Investment journals and newsletters $250
Investment advisory fees $200
Attorney fees for preparation of a will $1,000

What is the total of Joshua's qualified miscellaneous itemized expenses (**before** the application of any AGI limits)?

A. $2,400.
B. $1,225.
C. $800.
D. $625.

**The answer is D.** The deductible expenses are the income tax preparation fee ($100); the safe deposit box rental ($75); the investment journals and newsletters ($250); and the investment advisory fees ($200). Therefore, his total deduction before application of the 2% floor is $625. ###

9. Brady's garage caught fire in 2012. The garage is not attached to his primary residence. Brady estimates the property damage at $6,000. He declines to file an insurance claim because he fixes the damage himself. Brady pays $3,000 for the cost of the materials. He estimates the value of his labor to be approximately $2,800. His insurance company has a $1,000 deductible for any casualty loss claim filed. What is Brady's deductible casualty loss before any deductions or income limitations?

A. $0.
B. $1,000.
C. $3,000.
D. $6,000.

**The answer is B.** If a taxpayer's property is covered by insurance, he cannot deduct a loss unless he files an insurance claim for reimbursement. However, if the taxpayer declines to file an insurance claim, the IRS limits eligible casualty losses to the amount that is not normally covered by insurance, such as the amount of the insurance deductible. ###

10. Isaac's home was damaged by a tornado. He had $90,000 worth of damage, but $80,000 was reimbursed by his insurance company. Isaac's employer had a disaster relief fund for its employees. Isaac received $4,000 from the fund and spent the entire amount on repairs to his home. What is Isaac's deductible casualty loss before applying the deduction limits?

A. $0.
B. $4,000.
C. $6,000.
D. $10,000.

**The answer is C.** Isaac's casualty loss before applying the deduction limits is $6,000. Isaac must reduce his unreimbursed loss ($90,000 - $80,000 = $10,000) by the $4,000 he received from his employer. Isaac's casualty loss before applying the deduction limits is $6,000 ($10,000 - $4,000). ###

11. All of the following may be claimed as miscellaneous itemized deductions except _____.

A. Funeral expenses.
B. Union dues.
C. Laundry costs for uniforms.
D. Investment expenses.

**The answer is A.** Funeral expenses are not deductible as a miscellaneous itemized deduction. All of the other expenses listed are deductible as itemized deductions on Schedule A. ###

12. All of the following miscellaneous itemized deductions are subject to the 2% of AGI limit except _____.

A. Tax preparation fees.
B. Union dues.
C. Investment expenses.
D. Gambling losses to the extent of gambling winnings.

**The answer is D.** Gambling losses to the extent of gambling winnings are not subject to the 2% AGI limit. ###

13. Kim uses her home office while she works as a translator for an online translating company. Kim meets the requirements for deducting expenses for the business use of her home. Her home office is 480 square feet and her home is 2,400 square feet. What is Kim's business use percentage in order to figure her allowable deduction?

A. 5%.
B. 10%.
C. 15%.
D. 20%.

**The answer is D.** Kim uses 20% of her home for business. Her office is 20% (480 ÷ 2,400) of the total area of her home. Therefore, her business percentage is 20%. ###

14. Simon's AGI is $75,000. Therefore, the first_____ of miscellaneous employee work-related expenses is not deductible.

A. $1,000.
B. $1,500.
C. $5,625.
D. Some other amount.

**The answer is B.** Simon's employee work-related expenses are subject to the 2% limit of adjusted gross income. Therefore, Simon must figure his deduction on Schedule A by first subtracting 2% of his AGI (75,000 x 2% = $1,500) from the total amount of these expenses. ###

15. Marissa works as a tax preparer for A+ Tax Services. She was hired as a preparer three years ago, but this year her employer changed his educational requirements. Now all the tax preparers are required to take three additional courses in order to keep their current positions. Marissa incurred the following expenses when she took these courses:

$100 Required supplies
$550 Tuition
$120 Required books
$50 Credit card interest from paying tuition
$65 Bus passes to and from school
$885 Total educational expenses

What is Marissa's deductible work-related educational expense on her Schedule A before the 2% limitation?

A. $550.
B. $670.
C. $835.
D. $885.

**The answer is C.** Marissa may deduct all the costs as work-related educational expenses, with the exception of the credit card interest, which is a personal expense and not deductible. ###

16. Which of the following expenses does not qualify as a deductible transportation expense?

A. Getting from one client to another in the course of a taxpayer's business or profession.
B. Commuting expenses.
C. Traveling overseas to sign a business contract with a foreign supplier.
D. Going to a business meeting out-of-state.

**The answer is B.** A taxpayer can include in business expenses amounts paid for transportation primarily for and essential to business or trade. A taxpayer cannot deduct personal commuting expenses, no matter how far his home is from his regular place of work. ###

17. Which of the following will qualify for a deduction on Schedule A as an employee business expense?

A. The employer reimburses expenses under a tuition reimbursement (nontaxable) program.
B. Taking classes that maintain or improve skills needed in the taxpayer's present work.
C. Taking classes that are required by a taxpayer's employer or the law to keep his present salary, status, or job. The required education must serve a bona fide business purpose to the taxpayer's employer.
D. Both B and C.

**The answer is D.** Both B and C are correct. A taxpayer can deduct the costs of qualifying work-related education as business expenses. Choice "A" is incorrect because any amounts that are reimbursed by an employer cannot be deducted by the taxpayer. ###

18. During the year, Leon paid $350 to have his tax return prepared. He also paid union dues of $450 and paid an attorney $3,000 to draft his will. What is Leon's miscellaneous itemized deduction on his Schedule A before the 2% limitation?

A. $350.
B. $450.
C. $800.
D. $3,800.

**The answer is C.** The attorney fees for drafting the will are not deductible. The tax preparation fees and union dues are deductible and subject to a 2% of AGI floor. ###

19. Connor is deaf. He purchased a special device to use at work so he can identify when his phone rings. He paid for the device out-of-pocket, and his employer did not reimburse him. How should Connor report this on his tax return?

A. Connor may deduct the purchase as an itemized deduction, not subject to the 2% floor.

B. Connor may deduct the purchase as an itemized deduction, subject to the 2% floor.

C. Connor may not deduct the purchase because he is not totally disabled.

D. Connor may not deduct the purchase because he is not self-employed.

**The answer is A.** Connor may deduct the expenses for the special device as an impairment-related work expense. The deduction is not limited. If a taxpayer has a physical or mental disability that limits employment, he can choose to deduct the expense as a miscellaneous itemized deduction, not subject to the 2%-of-income floor.###

20. Abby has the following income and losses in 2012:

$45,000 in wages
$10,000 in gambling winnings
$13,000 in gambling losses
$1,500 in attorney fees for a divorce

How should these transactions be treated on her tax return?

A. Report $55,000 in taxable income and $10,000 in miscellaneous itemized deductions on Schedule A, not subject to the 2% floor.

B. Report $53,000 in taxable income and $13,000 in miscellaneous itemized deductions, subject to the 2% floor.

C. Report $55,000 in taxable income and $13,000 in miscellaneous itemized deductions on Schedule A, subject to the 2% floor.

D. Report $45,000 in taxable income and $14,500 in miscellaneous itemized deductions on Schedule A, not subject to the 2% floor.

**The answer is A.** The full amount of income must be reported on Form 1040 ($45,000 + $10,000 = $55,000). The gambling losses are deductible only up to the amount of gambling winnings; a taxpayer must report the full amount of gambling winnings on Form 1040. The taxpayer then may deduct gambling losses on Schedule A (Form 1040). Gambling losses are not subject to the 2% of income limitation, but taxpayers cannot report more gambling losses than they do gambling winnings. Attorney fees for a divorce are not deductible, (but separate legal advice related to collecting alimony is). ###

21. Brooke had adjusted gross income of $20,000 in 2012. Her home sustained damage from a storm, and she incurred a loss of $3,000. Her home insurance policy had a deductible of $2,500 for this type of loss, so she elected not to file a claim.

Based upon the information provided, what is the amount of casualty loss Brooke can deduct for the year?

A. $900.
B. $3,000.
C. $2,000.
D. $400.

**The answer is D.** Because the property was covered by insurance and Brooke did not file a claim, the casualty loss deduction is limited to the amount of the insurance deductible, as this amount would have been her out-of-pocket cost if a claim had been filed. This amount is further subject to a reduction of $100 and limited to the net amount that exceeds 10% of adjusted gross income.

**Supporting calculations:**

| | |
|---|---|
| Loss from storm | $3,000 |
| Limited to amount of deductible | $2,500 |
| Less $100 threshold | ($100 ) |
| Loss after $100 limit | $2,400 |
| Adjusted gross income | $20,000 |
| Multiply by 10% limit | $2,000 |
| Casualty loss deduction ($2,400-$2,000) | $400 |

22. If a taxpayer's home was destroyed in a flood and the area was later declared a federally declared disaster area, how long would the taxpayer typically have to purchase replacement property?

A. One year.
B. Two years.
C. Four years.
D. Five years.

**The answer is C.** In most casualty losses, taxpayers have two years to purchase a replacement for damaged or destroyed property. But in the case of most federally declared disaster areas, the period is usually four years. In certain extreme cases, including those taxpayers affected by Hurricane Katrina, the replacement period has been extended to five years. ###

23. Enrique and Crystal had adjusted gross income of $75,000 in 2012 and incurred the following miscellaneous expenses:

| | |
|---|---|
| Homeowners' association dues | $1,000 |
| Fine from homeowners' association for violation of bylaws | $100 |
| Loss from burglary of their home | $9,000 |
| Tax preparation fees | $250 |

Based upon the information provided, what is the amount of expenses they can deduct for 2012?

A. $1,750.
B. $10,250.
C. $1,350.
D. $1,400.

**The answer is D.** Neither the homeowners' association dues nor the fine are deductible. The tax preparation fees did not exceed 2% of adjusted gross income, and therefore are not deductible. The amount of the burglary loss, less $100, that exceeds 10% of adjusted gross income is deductible as a casualty loss.

**Supporting calculations:**

| | |
|---|---|
| Loss from theft | $9,000 |
| Less $100 threshold | ($100) |
| Loss after $100 limit | $8,900 |
| Adjusted gross income | $75,000 |
| Multiply by 10% limit | $7,500 |
| Casualty loss deduction ($8,900--$7,500) | $1,400 |

24. All of the following statements are true except:

A. A taxpayer may deduct job-related expenses, subject to the 2% of AGI limit.
B. Job search costs, such as the use of an employment agency, are deductible expenses.
C. The job search does not have to result in a new job for the taxpayer in order for his expenses to be deductible.
D. A taxpayer may deduct expenses related to the search for a job in a new occupation.

**The answer is D.** For job search expenses to be deductible, they must relate to the taxpayer's existing occupation. A taxpayer may not deduct expenses if they are connected with the search for a job in a brand new field. ###

25. Wes had a fire in his garage in 2012 that destroyed his car and two beautiful oriental rugs. He had recently bought the car for $30,000. The FMV of the car just before the fire was $27,500. Its FMV after the fire was $500 (scrap value.) He had purchased the rugs for $2,500, and their FMV just before the fire was $5,000. Wes's insurance company reimbursed him a total of $24,000. Wes's AGI in 2012 was $70,000. What is his casualty loss deduction?

A. 0.
B. $3,500.
C. $1,000.
D. $900.

**The answer is A.** Wes does not have a deductible casualty loss. Since the fair market value of the car was lower than its cost, it is used as the starting point to determine his loss. Net of the salvage value, he had a loss of $27,000 on the car. His loss on the rugs is limited to his original cost since it was lower than FMV. Thus he had total losses of $29,500 before the insurance reimbursement, and a net loss of $5,500. After subtracting the $100 deduction, he had potentially deductible losses of $5,400. However, his deduction is limited to the amount of the losses that exceeds 10% of his AGI, or $7,000. ###

| Calculations | Car | Rugs |
| --- | --- | --- |
| Basis for the casualty loss | $27,000 | $2,500 |
| Insurance reimbursement | | $24,000 |
| Net loss after insurance reimbursement ($29,500 - $24,000) | | $5,500 |
| Subtract $100 | | $5,400 |
| AGI X 10% ($70,000 X 10%) | | $7,000 |
| Allowable casualty loss | | $0 |

# Unit 9: Tax Credits

> **More Reading:**
> Publication 972, *Child Tax Credit*
> Publication 503, *Child and Dependent Care Expenses*
> Publication 596, *Earned Income Credit*
> Publication 970, *Tax Benefits for Education*
> Publication 514, *Foreign Tax Credit for Individuals*

A tax credit directly reduces tax liability, which means it is usually more valuable than a tax deduction of the same dollar amount. It is important to understand this distinction for the EA exam. A tax deduction will reduce income that is subject to tax, but a tax credit will actually reduce tax *liability*—the amount the taxpayer is required to pay the IRS.

In some cases, such as with the Earned Income Credit, a tax credit is refundable. This can create a tax refund—even if the taxpayer does not owe any tax. There are two types of tax credits:

- **Nonrefundable credits**
- **Refundable credits**

## Nonrefundable Tax Credits

A nonrefundable tax credit reduces tax liability dollar-for-dollar. It can cut the amount a taxpayer owes to zero but not beyond that, which means that any remaining credit will not be refunded to the taxpayer.

Most tax credits are nonrefundable, and some of the most common are:

- Child and Dependent Care Credit
- Child Tax Credit
- American Opportunity Credit (partially refundable but very restricted, so is nonrefundable for most taxpayers)
- Lifetime Learning Credit
- Retirement Savings Contributions Credit
- Residential energy credits
- Adoption Credit (refundable in 2010 and 2011, but nonrefundable again for 2012)

## Refundable Tax Credits

A refundable tax credit is a credit that can produce a tax refund even if the taxpayer does not owe any tax. Refundable tax credits that can reduce tax liability below zero include the following:

- Credit for Excess Social Security Tax or Railroad Retirement Tax Withheld
- Additional Child Tax Credit
- Earned Income Credit

# Child and Dependent Care Credit

The Child and Dependent Care Credit allows a taxpayer a credit for a percentage of child care expenses for children under age 13 and disabled dependents of any age. This is a nonrefundable credit for child care expenses that allow taxpayers to work or to seek work. The credit offsets regular tax and the alternative minimum tax.

Under the American Taxpayer Relief Act of 2012, the credit has increased to $3,000 for one child and $6,000 for two or more children.

The credit ranges from 20% to 35% of qualifying expenses, depending on a taxpayer's income. Taxpayers with AGI of $43,000 or more are allowed a credit of only 20% of qualifying expenses. However, the credit is not phased out at higher income levels.

A taxpayer must pass five eligibility tests in order to qualify for this credit:

- Qualifying person test
- Earned income test
- Work-related expense test
- Joint return test
- Provider identification test

## Qualifying Person Test

For purposes of this credit, a qualifying person is:

- A dependent child under the age of 13
- A spouse who is physically or mentally unable to care for himself or herself
- Any other dependents who are unable to care for themselves

**Example:** Samuel paid someone to care for his wife, Janet, so he could work. Janet is permanently disabled and requires an in-home care aide. Samuel also paid to have someone prepare meals for his 12-year-old daughter, Jill. Both Janet and Jill are qualifying persons for the credit.

Only a custodial parent may take the Child and Dependent Care Credit.

## The Earned Income Test

Both the taxpayer and his or her spouse if married must have earned income during the year in order to qualify for this credit. This generally means both spouses must work. The credit is not available to MFS filers.

The taxpayer's spouse is treated as having earned income for any month he or she is:

- A full-time student, or
- Disabled

> **Example:** Jessica and Quincy are married. Quincy worked full-time as a custodian in 2012. Jessica attended school full-time from January 1 to June 30. She was unemployed during the summer months and did not attend school the rest of the year. Jessica should be treated as having earned income for the six months she attended school full-time.

## Work-Related Expense Test

Child and dependent care expenses must be work-related to qualify for this credit, meaning a taxpayer must be working or searching for work. Expenses incurred so that a spouse may do volunteer work or take care of personal business, or for a married couple to go on a "date night" do not qualify.

> **Example:** Patsy is a stay-at-home mom who volunteers several hours a week at a local autism information hotline. Her husband works full-time as a school vice-principal. They pay a babysitter to stay with their young daughter during the hours Patsy volunteers. The couple does not qualify for the dependent care credit because the babysitting expense is not work-related. Since Patsy does not have a job, is not disabled, and is not a full-time student, the child care expenses are ineligible.

> **Example:** Darcy's four-year-old son attends a daycare center while she works three days a week. The daycare charges $150 for three days a week and $250 for five days a week. Sometimes Darcy pays the extra money so she can run errands on her days off. However, this extra charge is not a qualifying expense. Darcy's deductible expenses are limited to $150 a week, the amount of her work-related daycare expense.

The following kinds of expenses qualify for the Child and Dependent Care Credit:

- Education: Preschool or other programs below the level of kindergarten; before or after-school care of a child in kindergarten or above
- Care outside the home for a child under 13 or a care center for a disabled dependent
- Transportation for a care provider to take a qualifying person to or from a place where care is provided
- Fees and deposits paid to an agency or preschool to acquire child care
- Household services, if they are at least partly for the well-being and protection of a qualifying person

> **Example:** Roger's 10-year-old child attends a private school. In addition to paying for tuition, Roger pays an extra fee for before and after-school care so he can be at work during his scheduled hours. Roger can count the cost of the before and after-school program when figuring the credit, but not the cost of tuition.

**Example:** Emily is single and her elderly mother, Lorraine, is her dependent. Lorraine is completely disabled and must be in an adult daycare so she does not injure herself. Emily pays $8,000 per year for Lorraine to be in the adult daycare. Emily may take the dependent care credit, because Lorraine is disabled and incapable of self-care.

Examples of child care expenses that do not qualify include:

- Tuition costs for children in kindergarten and above
- Summer school or tutoring programs
- The cost of sending a child to an overnight camp (but day camps generally do qualify)
- The cost of transportation not provided by a care provider
- A forfeited deposit to a daycare center (since it is not for care and so is not a work-related expense)

**Example:** Ellie is divorced and has custody of her 12-year-old daughter, Destiny, who takes care of herself after school. In August, Ellie spends $2,000 to send Destiny to an overnight camp for two weeks. She also sends Destiny to a Girl Scout day camp for a week in July while Ellie is working. The cost of the Girl Scout camp is $75. Ellie may only count the $75 toward the child care credit because the cost of sending a child to an overnight camp is not considered a work-related expense. Next summer, when Destiny turns 13, she will no longer be a qualifying child under the rules of this credit.

Care expenses do not include amounts paid for food, clothing, education, or entertainment. Small amounts paid for these items, however, can be included if they are incidental and cannot be separated from the cost of care.

**Example:** Krista takes her three-year-old child to a nursery school that provides lunch and educational activities as part of its program. The meals are included in the overall cost of care, and they are not itemized on her bill. Krista can count the total cost when she figures the credit.

Payments for child care will not qualify for the credit if made to a family member who is either:

- The taxpayer's own child under age 19
- Any other dependent listed on the taxpayer's tax return

Taxpayers may combine costs for multiple dependents. For example, if a taxpayer pays daycare for three qualifying children, the $6,000 limit does not need to be divided equally among them.

**Example:** Alec has three children. His qualifying daycare expenses for his first child are $2,300. His qualifying expenses for his second child are $2,800, and the expenses for his last child are $900. Alec is allowed to use the total amount, $6,000, when figuring his credit.

> **Example:** Diego and Valeria both work and have three children. They have $2,000 in daycare expenses for their son, Miguel; $3,000 for their son, Marcelo; and $4,000 for their daughter, Cecilia. Although their total child care expenses are $9,000, they may only use the first $6,000 as their basis for the Child and Dependent Care Credit.

> **Example:** Lori is a single mother with a dependent child, Noah, who is five years old. Lori takes Noah to daycare five days per week so she can work. Lori makes $46,000 in wages and spends $5,200 per year on daycare for Noah. The maximum that Lori can claim as a dependent care credit is $3,000 since she only has one qualifying child, even though her actual expenses exceed that amount.

## Joint Return Test

The joint return test specifies that married couples who wish to take the credit for child and dependent care must file jointly. However, a married taxpayer can be "considered unmarried" for tax purposes if he qualifies for head of household filing status. Taxpayers who file separately are not eligible for this credit.

In the case of divorced or separated taxpayers, only the custodial parent is allowed to take the Child and Dependent Care Credit.

## Provider Identification Test

This test requires that taxpayers provide the name, address, and Taxpayer Identification Number of the person or organization who provided the care for the child or dependent.

If a daycare provider refuses to supply identification information, the taxpayer may still claim the credit. He must report whatever information he has (such as the provider's name and address) and attach a statement to Form 2441, *Child and Dependent Care Expenses,* explaining the provider's refusal to supply the information.

# Child Tax Credit and Additional Child Tax Credit

Taxpayers with income below certain threshold amounts may claim the Child Tax Credit to reduce income tax for each qualifying child under the age of 17.

- **Child Tax Credit:** This is a *nonrefundable* credit of up to $1,000 per qualifying child. Taxpayers whose tax liability is zero cannot take the Child Tax Credit because there is no tax to reduce. However, taxpayers may be able to take the additional Child Tax Credit, which is refundable, even if their tax liability is zero.

- **Additional Child Tax Credit:** This is a *refundable* credit that may result in a refund even if the taxpayer does not owe any tax. Taxpayers who claim the Additional Child Tax Credit must claim the Child Tax Credit as well, even if they do not qualify for the full amount.

The Child Tax Credit is reduced if the taxpayer's modified adjusted gross income is above the threshold amounts shown below:

- Married filing jointly: $110,000
- Single, head of household, or qualifying widow(er): $75,000
- Married filing separately: $55,000

The credit is phased out incrementally as the taxpayer's income increases. The credit is reduced by $50 for each $1,000 of MAGI that exceeds the threshold amounts listed above.

In addition, the Child Tax Credit is limited by the amount of income tax and any alternative minimum tax owed.

**Example**: Cordell and Roxana file jointly and have two children who qualify for the Child Tax Credit. Their MAGI is $86,000 and their tax liability is $954. Even though their AGI is less than the threshold limit of $110,000, they can only claim $954, reducing their tax to zero. Because Cordell and Roxana cannot claim the maximum Child Tax Credit of $1,000, they may still be eligible for the additional Child Tax Credit.

**Example:** Clint files as head of household and has three children who qualify for purposes of the Child Tax Credit. His MAGI is $54,000 and his tax liability is $4,680. Clint is eligible to take the full credit of $1,000 per child ($3,000) because his MAGI is less than $75,000 and his tax liability is greater than $3,000.

## Definition of a Qualifying Child for the Child Tax Credit

To be eligible to claim the Child Tax Credit, the taxpayer must have at least one qualifying child. To qualify, the child must:

- Be claimed as the taxpayer's dependent.
- Meet the relationship test: must be the son, daughter, adopted child, stepchild, foster child, brother, sister, stepbrother, stepsister, or a descendant of any of them (for example, a grandchild, niece, or nephew).
- Meet the age criteria: *under* the age of 17 at the end of the year.
- Not have provided over half of his or her own support.
- Have lived with the taxpayer for more than six months of the tax year.[53]
- Be a U.S. citizen, U.S. national, or resident of the U.S. Foreign-born adopted children will qualify if they lived with the taxpayer all year, even if the adoption is not yet final.

**Example:** Ed's son, Jeff, turned 17 on December 31, 2012. He is a citizen of the United States and has a valid SSN. According to the Child Tax Credit rules, he is not a qualifying child because he was not under the age of 17 at the end of 2012.

---

[53] There are special rules for children of divorced or separated parents, as well as children of parents who never married. In some cases the noncustodial parent may be entitled to claim the dependency exemption for a child and thus the Child Tax Credit and additional Child Tax Credit.

> **Example:** Laura's adopted son, Nash, is 12. He is a United States citizen and lived with Laura for the entire tax year. Laura provided all of her son's support. Nash is a qualifying child for the Child Tax Credit because he was under the age of 17 at the end of the tax year; he meets the relationship requirement; he lived with Laura for at least six months of the year; and Laura provided his complete support.

## Additional Child Tax Credit

The Additional Child Tax Credit is for certain individuals who do not qualify for the full amount of the nonrefundable Child Tax Credit. Since the Additional Child Tax Credit is *refundable*, it can produce a refund even if the taxpayer does not owe any tax.

Like the Child Tax Credit, the Additional Child Tax Credit allows eligible taxpayers to claim up to $1,000 for each qualifying child after subtracting the allowable amount of Child Tax Credit. For taxpayers with earned income over $3,000, the credit is based on the lesser of:

- 15% of the taxpayer's taxable earned income that is more than $3,000, or
- The amount of unused Child Tax Credit (caused when tax liability is less than the allowed credit).

> **Example**: May and Dmitri have two qualifying children, a MAGI of $66,000, and a tax liability of $850. Because their tax liability is less than the full amount of the Child Tax Credit, they may be able to take the additional Child Tax Credit of up to $1,150 ($2,000 - $850).

In 2012, the IRS changed Form 8812 for the Additional Child Tax Credit to Schedule 8812. The schedule is now used to report both the Child Tax Credit and the Additional Child Tax Credit.

# The Adoption Credit

In 2012, a maximum nonrefundable credit of up to $12,650 per child can be taken for qualified expenses paid to adopt a child. For a special needs child, the credit is allowed even if the taxpayer does not have any adoption expenses.

The Adoption Credit phases out ratably between $189,710 and $229,710. The phase-out ranges are the same for all taxpayers regardless of filing status.

If a taxpayer receives employer-provided adoption benefits that are excluded from income, he may still be able to take the Adoption Credit. However, the exclusion and the credit cannot be claimed for the same expense.

Since the Adoption Credit is nonrefundable, any unused credit may be carried forward for five years.

Qualified adoption expenses are directly related to the adoption of a child. These include:

- Adoption fees
- Court costs
- Attorney fees
- Travel expenses related to the adoption
- Re-adoption expenses to adopt a foreign child

Qualified adoption expenses do not include:

- Illegal adoption expenses
- A surrogate parenting arrangement
- The adoption of a spouse's child
- Any amounts that were reimbursed by an employer or any other organization

An eligible child is:

- Under 18 years old, or
- Disabled of any age.

Until the adoption becomes final, a taxpayer may take the credit in the year after expenses were paid. Once the adoption becomes final, a taxpayer can take the credit in the year the expenses were paid.

**Special needs child:** A taxpayer may claim the full credit regardless of actual expenses paid or incurred. A special needs child is defined in the following ways:

- A United States citizen or resident.
- A state has determined the child cannot or should not be returned to his or her parents' home.
- A state has determined that the child will not be adopted unless assistance is provided to the adoptive parents.

In making the determination about special needs, a state may take into account the following factors: a child's ethnic background and age; whether he is a member of a minority or sibling group; and whether he has a physical, mental, or emotional handicap.

**Example:** Noel and Cassie adopt a special needs child, and the adoption is finalized in 2012. Their actual adoption expenses are $7,500. They are still allowed to take the full $12,650 credit in 2012.

**Unsuccessful adoptions:** A taxpayer who has attempted to adopt a child but is unsuccessful is still eligible for the Adoption Credit. Expenses are combined when there are multiple attempts to adopt, or when another adoption attempt is successful and finalized.

**Foreign child:** If the eligible child is from a foreign country, the taxpayer cannot take the Adoption Credit unless the adoption becomes final. A foreign child is defined as a child who was not a citizen or resident of the United States at the time the adoption effort began.

# Education Credits in General

There are two education credits available that are based on qualified expenses a taxpayer pays for postsecondary education (college):

- The American Opportunity Credit[54]
- The Lifetime Learning Credit

There are general rules that apply to these credits, as well as specific rules for each. For example, taxpayers may take education credits for themselves, their spouse, and their dependents who attended an eligible educational institution during the tax year. Eligible educational institutions include colleges, universities, vocational schools, or community colleges. Taxpayers can claim payments that were prepaid for the academic period that begins in the first three months of the next calendar year.

---

**Example:** Tom paid $1,500 in December 2012 for college tuition for the spring semester that begins in January 2013. Tom can deduct the $1,500 education credit on his 2012 return, even though he will not start college until 2013.

---

A taxpayer cannot claim education credits if he:

- can be claimed as a dependent on someone else's tax return
- files as married filing separately
- has AGI above the limit for the taxpayer's filing status
- or his spouse was a nonresident alien for any part of the tax year[55]

To claim the credit for a dependent's education expenses, the taxpayer must claim the dependent on his return, but he does not necessarily have to pay for all of the dependent's qualified education expenses.

In some circumstances, eligible students may claim education credits for themselves even if their parents actually paid the qualified tuition and related expenses. This would be the same tax treatment as if the parent had given the student a gift.

If a taxpayer does not claim an exemption for a dependent who is an eligible student, the student may claim the American Opportunity or Lifetime Learning Credit on his own return, if the situation applies.[56]

---

[54] The American Opportunity Credit was scheduled to expire in 2012, but was retroactively extended by the American Taxpayer Relief Act of 2012.

[55] In a case when one spouse is a U.S. citizen or a resident alien and the other spouse is a nonresident alien, the taxpayers may elect to treat the nonresident spouse as a U.S. resident. If the taxpayers make this choice, both spouses are treated as residents for income tax purposes and for withholding purposes.

[56] This concept is covered in more detail in Publication 970, with various examples.

> **Example:** Cathy has a 19-year-old son named Trent who is her dependent and a full-time college student. Trent's grandmother paid his tuition directly to the college. For purposes of claiming an education credit, Cathy is treated as receiving the money as a gift and paying for the qualified tuition and related expenses. Since Cathy claims Trent as a dependent, she may still claim an education credit. Alternatively, if Trent claims himself on his own return and his mother does not, he might be able to claim the expenses as if he paid them himself.

If a taxpayer has education expenses for more than one student, he can take the American Opportunity Credit and the Lifetime Learning Credit on a per student basis. This means that a taxpayer may claim the American Opportunity Credit for one student and the Lifetime Learning Credit for another student on the same tax return.

> **Example:** Reed pays college expenses for himself and his dependent daughter, who is 18. Reed goes to graduate school, and he qualifies for the Lifetime Learning Credit. His daughter is an undergraduate, and she qualifies for the American Opportunity Credit. He can choose to take both credits on his tax return because he has two eligible students, his daughter and himself.

## Qualified Education Expenses

Qualified education expenses are tuition and required related expenses.

> **Example:** Elias is a college senior who is studying to be a dentist. This year, in addition to tuition, he pays a fee to the university for the rental of the dental equipment he is required to use in the program. Elias's equipment rental fee is a qualified education expense.

Expenses that do not qualify include:

- Room and board
- Medical expenses, including student health fees
- Insurance
- Transportation or personal, living, or family expenses

Any course of instruction or other education involving sports, games, or hobbies is not a qualifying expense *unless* the course is part of the student's degree program.

Tuition expenses are reported to the taxpayer on Form 1098-T, *Tuition Statement*, issued by the school.

Qualified education expenses must be reduced by the amount of any tax-free educational assistance received, such as Pell grants, tax-free portions of scholarships, and employer-provided educational assistance.

> **Example:** Faith received Form 1098-T from the college she attends. It shows that her tuition was $9,500 and that she received a $1,500 tax-free scholarship. Her maximum qualifying expenses for the education credit would be $8,000 ($9,500 - $1,500).

> **Example:** In 2012, Jacqueline paid $3,000 for tuition and $5,000 for room and board at her university. She was also awarded a $2,000 tax-free scholarship and a $4,000 student loan. To qualify for the education credit, she must first subtract the tax-free scholarship from her tuition, her only qualified expense. A student loan is not considered tax-free educational assistance because it must be paid back, so it is not income. To calculate her education credit, Jacqueline only had $1,000 in qualified expenses ($3,000 tuition - $2,000 scholarship).

# The American Opportunity Credit (AOC)

The American Opportunity Credit (AOC) allows taxpayers to claim a credit of up to $2,500 based on qualified tuition and related expenses paid for each eligible student. The credit covers: 100% of the first $2,000, and 25% of the second $2,000 of eligible expenses. This credit applies *per student*, up to the amount of tax.

In 2012, under certain conditions, 40% of the AOC is refundable, which means the taxpayer can receive up to $1,000 even if no taxes are owed. [57] Requirements for the AOC are as follows:

- **Degree requirement:** The student must be enrolled in a program that leads to a degree, certificate, or other recognized educational credential.
- **Workload:** The student must take at least one-half of the normal full-time workload for at least one academic period beginning during the tax year.
- **No felony drug conviction:** The student must be free of any felony conviction for possessing or distributing a controlled substance.
- **First four years of education:** Only undergraduate education is eligible. A student in graduate school does not qualify for this credit. The credit can only be claimed for four tax years for one student.

The credit phases out for joint filers with income between $160,000 and $180,000 and for single filers with income between $80,000 and $90,000. Couples with income above $180,000 and single filers with income above $90,000 do not qualify.

If a student does not meet all of the conditions for the American Opportunity Credit, he may still be able to take the Lifetime Learning Credit.

---

[57] Because of specific age restrictions, an American Opportunity Credit claimed on a college student's return generally will not be refundable if the student is under age 24. This means, for practical purposes, the credit is nonrefundable for the vast majority of taxpayers.

# Lifetime Learning Credit

The Lifetime Learning Credit is a nonrefundable tax credit of 20% of up to $10,000 of qualified tuition and fees paid during the tax year. The maximum credit is $2,000 per taxpayer. This amount is per tax return, not student. A family's maximum credit is the same regardless of the number of qualified students.

Requirements for the Lifetime Learning Credit are as follows:

- **No workload requirement:** A student is eligible no matter how many or how few courses he takes.
- **Non-degree courses eligible:** A student qualifies if he is simply taking a course to acquire or improve job skills.
- **All levels of postsecondary education:** A student may be an under-graduate, graduate, or professional degree candidate.
- **Unlimited number of years:** There is no limit on the number of years for which the credit can be claimed for each student.

**Example:** Roland attends Creek Community College after spending six months in prison for a felony cocaine conviction. He paid $4,400 for the course of study, which included tuition, equipment, and books required for the course. The school requires that students pay for books and equipment when registering for courses. The entire $4,400 is an eligible educational expense under the Lifetime Learning Credit. Roland does not qualify for the American Opportunity Credit because he has a drug conviction.

**Example:** Lai works full-time and takes one course a month at night school. Some of the courses are not for credit, but she is taking them to advance her career. The education expenses qualify for the Lifetime Learning Credit, but not for the American Opportunity Credit.

For 2012, the phase-out for the Lifetime Learning Credit for single filers is between $52,000 and $62,000. For joint filers, the phase-out is between $104,000 to $124,000.

If a taxpayer does not qualify for either of these education credits, he may still qualify for the tuition and fees deduction (as an adjustment to income, covered in Unit 6), which can reduce the amount of taxable income by up to $4,000. However, a taxpayer cannot claim the tuition and fees deduction in the same year that he claims either of the education credits. A taxpayer must choose to take *either* the tax credit or the deduction, and should consider which provides the greatest tax benefit.

# Earned Income Credit

The Earned Income Credit (EIC) is also known as the earned income tax credit (EITC)[58], and it is frequently tested on the EA exam. The EIC is a fully refundable federal income tax credit for lower income people who work and who have earned income under a certain threshold.[59]

## Rules for Qualifying for the Earned Income Credit

There are very strict rules and income guidelines for the EIC. To claim the EIC, a taxpayer must meet all of the following tests:

- Must have a valid Social Security Number. Any qualifying child must also have a valid SSN.
- Must have earned income from wages or self-employment.
- Passive income must not exceed $3,200 in 2012.
- Filing status cannot be MFS.
- Must be a U.S. citizen or legal resident all year (or a nonresident alien married to a U.S. citizen or resident alien filing MFJ).
- Cannot be a dependent of another taxpayer.

## Qualifying Income for the EIC

Only earned income such as wages qualifies for the EIC. Qualifying earned income also includes:

- Tips
- Union strike benefits
- Net earnings from self-employment

For purposes of the EIC, earned income does not include the following:

- Social Security benefits
- Workfare payments
- Alimony or child support
- Pensions or annuities
- Unemployment benefits

**\*Note:** Inmate wages do not qualify as earned income when figuring the Earned Income Credit. This includes amounts for work performed while in a prison work release program or in a halfway house.

---

[58] The IRS uses both terms. For consistency's sake, we refer to this credit as the Earned Income Credit (EIC), but you should be familiar with the other terminology as well.

[59] Legislation in 2009 increased the EIC to 45% for families with three or more children, and increased the beginning point of the phase-out range for joint filers (regardless of the number of children) to lessen the marriage penalty. The American Taxpayer Relief Act of 2012 extended these provisions through 2017.

Income that is excluded from tax is generally not considered earned income for the EIC. However, nontaxable combat pay is an exception, if the taxpayer elects to treat it as earned income.

Passive income from investments does not qualify as earned income for the EIC. Investment income includes taxable interest and dividends, tax-exempt interest, capital gain net income, and income from residential rental property. In 2012, any amount of investment income above $3,200 disqualifies a taxpayer from claiming the EIC.

## Taxpayers Without a Qualifying Child

Low-income taxpayers without children may still qualify for the EIC in certain cases, but the rules are stricter and the amount of the credit is less.

Any taxpayer with a qualifying child may claim the EIC without any age limitations, but a taxpayer *without* a child can only claim the EIC if all of the following tests are met:

- Must be at least age 25, but under 65, at the end of the year (if married, either spouse can meet the age test)
- Must live in the United States for more than half the year
- Must not qualify as a dependent of another person
- Cannot file Form 2555 (related to foreign earned income exclusions[60])

# *EIC Thresholds and Limitations*

## 2012 Tax Year

Earned income and adjusted gross income must each be less than:
- $45,060 ($50,270 MFJ) with three or more qualifying children
- $41,952 ($47,162 MFJ) with two qualifying children
- $36,920 ($42,130 MFJ) with one qualifying child
- $13,980 ($19,190 MFJ) with no qualifying children

---

**Example:** Graham is single and his AGI is $39,000. He has one qualifying child. Graham cannot claim the EIC because his AGI exceeds the income threshold for single filers.

---

The amount of the Earned Income Credit varies between a maximum of $475 for a taxpayer with no qualifying children up to a maximum of $5,891 for married taxpayers with three or more children.

---

[60] Taxpayers who do not exclude their foreign income from their gross income (by filing Form 2555 or Form 2555-EZ) may still be eligible for the EIC.

## Qualifying Child Tests for the EIC

The definition of a "qualifying child" for purposes of the EIC is stricter than it is for the dependency exemption. In order to qualify for the EIC, the taxpayer's qualifying child must meet the following four tests:

1. **Relationship Test**
2. **Age Test**
3. **Residency Test**
4. **Joint Return Test**

# Relationship Test for EIC

The child must be related to the taxpayer in the following ways:

- Son, daughter, stepchild, eligible foster child, adopted child, or a descendant of any of them (for example, a grandchild), or
- Brother, sister, half-brother, half-sister, stepbrother, stepsister, or a descendant of any of them (for example, a niece or nephew).

**Example:** Rusty is 31 and takes care of his younger sister, Colleen, who is 16. He has taken care of her since their parents died five years ago. Colleen is Rusty's qualifying child for purposes of the EIC.

An adopted child is always treated as a taxpayer's own child. An eligible foster child must be placed in the taxpayer's home by an authorized placement agency or by court order.

In the case of a foreign adoption, special rules apply. To claim the EIC, the taxpayer must have a valid SSN. Any qualifying child listed on Schedule EIC also must have a valid SSN. An ATIN number is not sufficient. However, the taxpayer can elect to amend the tax return once an SSN is granted and the adoption is final.

## Age Test for EIC

In order to qualify for the EIC, the child must be:

- Age 18 or younger, or
- A full-time student, age 23 or younger, or
- Any age, if permanently disabled.

In addition, the qualifying child must be younger than the taxpayer claiming him, unless the child or person is permanently disabled.

**Example:** Garth, age 45, supports his older brother, Jeremiah, age 56. Jeremiah, who is mentally challenged and permanently disabled, lives with Garth. In this case, Jeremiah meets the criteria to be Garth's qualifying child for purposes of the EIC.

### Residency Test and Joint Return Test

The qualifying child (dependent) may not file a joint return with a spouse, except to claim a refund.

> **Example:** Margaret's 18-year-old son and his 18-year-old wife had $800 of interest income and no other income. Neither is required to file a tax return. Taxes were taken out of their interest income due to backup withholding, so they file a joint return only to get a refund of the withheld taxes. The exception to the joint return test applies, so Margaret's son may still be her qualifying child if all the other tests are met.

For the residency test, the child must have lived with the taxpayer in the United States for more than half of 2012. U.S. military personnel stationed outside the United States are considered to meet the residency test for purposes of the EIC.

A child who was born or died in 2012 meets the residency test for the entire year if the child lived with the taxpayer the entire time he or she was alive in 2012.

> **Example:** Tawanda gave birth to a baby boy in March 2012. The infant died one month later. The child would still be a qualifying child for purposes of the EIC because he meets the other tests for age and relationship.

## EIC Fraud and Penalties

Taxpayers who improperly claim the EIC with a reckless or intentional disregard of the rules cannot take the credit for the next two years. Those who fraudulently claim the EIC may be banned from taking the credit for ten years.

Tax professionals face significant due diligence requirements in preparing EIC claims for their clients. A $500 penalty per failure is imposed on any preparer who fails to meet these requirements. For a more detailed discussion of the EIC, see Part 3 (Representation) of the EA PassKey Review.

## Retirement Savings Contributions Credit (Saver's Credit)

Qualified individuals are allowed a nonrefundable credit of up to $1,000 ($2,000 MFJ) for eligible contributions to an IRA or an employer-sponsored retirement plan. The amount of the credit is the eligible contribution multiplied by the credit rate, based on filing status and AGI.

To be eligible for this credit,[61] a taxpayer must be at least 18 years old, and must not be a full-time student or claimed as a dependent on another person's return. In 2012, modified AGI cannot be more than:

- $57,500 for married filing jointly
- $43,125 for head of household
- $28,750 for single, married filing separately, or qualifying widow(er)

---

[61] The IRS also refers to this credit as the "Saver's Credit," so either term may be used on the EA exam.

> **Example:** Truman is 24 and earns $32,000 during the year. He is single and contributes $3,000 to his 401(k) plan at work. Truman is not eligible for the credit because his income exceeds the threshold limit of $28,750.

The taxpayer must have made voluntary contributions to a qualified retirement plan, including traditional IRAs and Roth IRAs; tax-exempt employee-funded pension plans; elective deferrals to 401(k) plans; and voluntary after-tax contributions to any qualified retirement plan or IRA.

Most workers who contribute to traditional IRAs already deduct all or part of their contributions. The Saver's Credit is in addition to these other deductions.

When figuring the credit, a taxpayer generally must subtract the amount of distributions received from his retirement plans from the contributions he has made. This rule applies to distributions received in the two years before the year the credit is claimed; the year the credit is claimed; and the period after the end of the credit year but before the due date, including extensions, for filing the return for the credit year.

> **Example:** Rashid and Angela filed joint returns in 2010 and 2011, and plan to do so in 2012 and 2013. Rashid received a taxable distribution from a qualified plan in 2010 and a taxable distribution from an eligible deferred compensation plan in 2011. Angela received taxable distributions from a Traditional IRA in 2012 and tax-free distributions from a Roth IRA in 2013 before April 15. Rashid contributes to an IRA in 2012, and he and Angela qualify for the credit. Their modified adjusted gross income in 2012 is $53,000, below the Saver's Credit income limit. Rashid and Angela must reduce the amount of their qualifying contributions in 2012 by the total of the distributions they receive in 2010, 2011, 2012, and 2013.

The Saver's Credit amount can be as low as 10% or as high as 50% of a maximum annual contribution of $2,000 per person, depending on filing status and AGI.

# Foreign Tax Credit

The nonrefundable Foreign Tax Credit is designed to relieve taxpayers of the double tax burden that occurs when their foreign source income is taxed by both the U.S. and the foreign country.

U.S. citizens and resident aliens are eligible for the Foreign Tax Credit. Nonresident aliens are not eligible. Foreign tax paid is usually reported to the taxpayer by the financial institution on Form 1099-INT or Form 1099-DIV.

Four tests must be met to qualify for the credit:

- The tax must be imposed on the taxpayer.
- The taxpayer must have paid (or accrued) the tax.
- The tax must be a legal and actual foreign tax liability.
- The tax must be an income tax.

Taxpayers may claim the credit on line 47 of Form 1040 if, among other conditions, all foreign income is passive income and total taxes paid do not exceed $300

($600 MFJ). If the tax paid exceeds $300 ($600 MFJ), then taxpayers must file Form 1116, *Foreign Tax Credit*, in order to claim the credit.

---

**Example:** Yusuf and Fatima are married and file jointly. They own a number of foreign stocks, and their Form 1099-DIV shows foreign tax paid of $590. The couple is not required to complete Form 1116, because their foreign taxes are less than $600.

---

**Example:** Colette is a shareholder of a French corporation. She receives $300 in earnings from the corporation. The French government imposes a 10% tax ($30) on Colette's earnings. She must include the gross earnings ($300) in her income. The $30 of tax withheld is a qualified foreign tax for purposes of the Foreign Tax Credit.

---

In most cases, it is to the taxpayer's advantage to take the Foreign Tax Credit since a credit directly reduces tax liability. However, taxpayers have the option to itemize foreign taxes as "Other Taxes" on Schedule A. They may choose either the deduction or the credit, whichever gives them the lowest tax, for all foreign taxes paid. Taxpayers cannot claim both the deduction and the tax credit on the same return. However, a taxpayer may alternate years, taking a credit in one year and a deduction in the next year.

Taxpayers also may not claim the Foreign Tax Credit for taxes paid on any income that has already been excluded from income using the foreign earned income exclusion or the foreign housing exclusion.

---

**\*Note:** Do not confuse the Foreign Tax Credit and the foreign earned income exclusion. The foreign earned income exclusion allows a portion of foreign earned income to be completely excluded from income, so it is not taxed. The Foreign Tax Credit adds the taxpayer's foreign income to his taxable income and then *reduces* the U.S. tax by the credit amount. The foreign earned income exclusion only applies to income that is earned while a taxpayer is living and working overseas. The Foreign Tax Credit applies to any type of foreign income, including investments.

---

Certain taxes do not qualify for the Foreign Tax Credit, including interest or penalties paid to a foreign country, taxes imposed by countries involved with international terrorism,[62] and taxes on foreign oil or gas extraction income.

The Foreign Tax Credit is nonrefundable, and the taxpayer is allowed a one-year carryback and a ten-year carryforward of any unused credit.

The Foreign Tax Credit cannot be more than the taxpayer's total U.S. tax liability multiplied by a fraction. The limit on this credit is figured by calculating the total tax liability multiplied by a fraction made up of total foreign income divided by total income from foreign and U.S. sources.

---

[62] The list of terrorist nations includes Cuba, the Sudan, and North Korea— a full list of excluded nations is published in Publication 514, *Foreign Tax Credit for Individuals.*

> **Example:** Harold's total tax liability is $1,000. In 2012, he made $20,000 from foreign-based investments, along with another $60,000 from U.S. sources. To figure the limit on the Foreign Tax Credit, Harold must take his total foreign income ($20,000) and divide it by the total income from all sources ($20,000 + $60,000). This gives Harold a fraction of .25, which is multiplied by his total tax liability ($1,000 x .25 = $250). This is the limit on his Foreign Tax Credit.
>
> (Foreign Source Taxable Income ÷ Worldwide Taxable Income) X
> (U.S. Income Tax before Credit = FTC Limitation.)

# Residential Energy Credits

Taxpayers who purchase certain qualified energy-efficient improvements for their main home may be allowed a nonrefundable tax credit. There are two types of residential energy credits:

- Residential Energy Efficient Property Credit
- Nonbusiness Energy Property Credit

Both are nonrefundable credits that are calculated and claimed on IRS Form 5695, *Residential Energy Credits.*

**Nonbusiness Energy Property Credit:** Taxpayers may claim this credit for energy efficient property placed in service in 2012. The credit is equal to 30% of the cost of the following property:

- Solar energy systems (water heating and electricity)
- Fuel cells
- Small wind energy systems
- Geothermal heat pumps

No credit is allowed for equipment used to heat swimming pools or hot tubs. The credit is allowed for new construction as well as improvements to existing homes located in the United States.

**Residential Energy Efficient Property Credit:** The credit is equal to 10% of the cost of qualified energy efficient improvements to existing homes, plus 100% of the cost of any residential energy property costs paid or incurred in 2012.[63] Various credit amounts are given for qualified fans; furnaces and hot water boilers; electric heat pumps; biomass fuel stoves; central air conditioners; and certain types of water heaters. The total combined amount of credit that can be claimed is $500 for all tax years after 2005, or a combined $200 limit for exterior windows after 2005.

---

[63] The American Taxpayer Relief Act of 2012 retroactively reinstated this credit for 2012 and extended it through 2013.

# Additional Individual Taxpayer Energy Credits

The IRS also allows credits for other energy-related expenses:

- **Plug-in Electric Motorcycles and 3-Wheeled Vehicles:** A 10% individual income tax credit. Under revisions to the credit, golf carts and other low-speed vehicles do not qualify.[64]

- **Alternative Fuel Vehicle Property:** A 30% credit for the cost of installing qualified clean-fuel vehicle refueling property at a taxpayer's principal residence. The credit is limited to $1,000 per taxable year for nonbusiness taxpayers.[65]

# Other Credits

A number of other credits are not widely used (or widely tested on the EA exam) because they are limited to certain individuals, or for certain types of asset purchases.

- **Mortgage Interest Credit:** Provides a nonrefundable credit to low-income homeowners who hold qualified mortgage credit certificates issued by local or state governments.

- **Health Coverage Tax Credit:** Provides a refundable credit for certain taxpayers who receive pension benefits from the Pension Benefit Guaranty Corporation. The credit pays 72.5% of qualified health insurance premiums for eligible individuals and their families.

- **Credit for Excess Social Security Tax:** Refunds workers who overpay their tax for Social Security, which usually happens when an employee is working two jobs and both employers withhold Social Security tax. If the taxpayer's withholding for Social Security tax exceeds the annual maximum, he can request a refund of the excess amount. This also applies to overpaid Railroad Retirement taxes.

- **Credit for the Elderly or Disabled:** This credit applies only to taxpayers 65 or older or taxpayers under 65 who retired on permanent disability. This nonrefundable tax credit has such strict income limitations that few taxpayers qualify for it.

- **Credit for Prior Year Alternative Minimum Tax:** This credit is available if a taxpayer paid AMT generated by deferral items in a prior year. It can only be used to the extent that regular tax exceeds the tentative minimum tax.

---

[64] Retroactively reinstated and amended for 2012.

[65] Retroactively reinstated for 2012 and extended through 2013.

# Unit 9: Questions

1. All of these taxpayers contributed to their employers' 401(k) plan. Which taxpayer qualifies for the Retirement Savings Contributions Credit based on his or her adjusted gross income?

A. Ed, who is single and has an adjusted gross income of $35,200.
B. Sybil, who is married filing jointly and has an adjusted gross income of $55,000.
C. Bert, who is married filing separately and has an adjusted gross income of $30,600.
D. Carl, who is a qualifying widower and has a modified AGI of $29,000.

**The answer is B.** Sybil qualifies for the credit because her AGI is under $57,500, which is the threshold limit for married filing jointly. Taxpayers who file as single, qualifying widow(er), or married filing separately (such as Ed, Carl, and Bert) cannot qualify if they have an AGI that exceeds the AGI limits. ###

2. Gail's earned income from wages is $7,000. She has interest income of $3,250. She is single and has a valid Social Security Number. She does not have any dependents. Which of the following statements is true?

A. Gail qualifies to claim the Earned Income Credit.
B. Gail does not qualify for the Earned Income Credit.
C. Gail qualifies for the Earned Income Credit and the Child Tax Credit.
D. None of the above.

**The answer is B.** Gail does not qualify for the EIC because her investment income exceeds $3,200 for 2012. ###

3. For purposes of the EIC, which of the following types of income are considered "earned income"?
A. Alimony.
B. Interest and dividends.
C. Workfare payments.
D. Household employee income reported on Form W-2.

**The answer is D.** Household employee income is considered earned income, because it is a type of wages. Alimony, workfare payments, and interest and dividends are not considered earned income for purposes of the EIC. ###

4. Orlando is a university senior who is studying to be an optometrist. Which of the following expenses is a qualifying expense for the American Opportunity Credit?

A. The rental of the vision equipment he is required to use in this program.
B. Student health fees.
C. Room and board.
D. A physical education course not related to his degree program.

**The answer is A.** Because Orlando's equipment rental fee must be paid to the university as a condition for enrollment, it is considered a qualified related expense. Qualified tuition and related expenses do not include insurance or medical expenses (student health fees), room and board, transportation, or similar personal, living, or family expenses even if the fees must be paid to the institution as a condition of enrollment or attendance, or any course of instruction or other education involving sports, games, or hobbies, *unless* the course is part of the student's degree program. ###

5. Which of the following would be a qualifying child for purposes of the Child Tax Credit?

A. An 18-year-old dependent who is a full-time student.
B. A six-year-old nephew who lived with the taxpayer for seven months.
C. A child actor who is 15 years old and provides over half of his own support.
D. A foster child who has lived with the taxpayer for four months.

**The answer is B**. A nephew that lived with the taxpayer for seven months may qualify. In order to qualify for the Child Tax Credit, the taxpayer must have a qualifying child who lived with him for more than six months and who is under the age of 17. The child cannot have provided more than half of his own support. ###

6. Beatrice has three dependent children, ages 2, 12, and 18, who live with her. Assuming she meets the other criteria, what is the maximum Child Tax Credit she can claim on her 2012 tax return?

A. $0.
B. $1,000.
C. $2,000.
D. $3,000.

**The answer is C.** Beatrice can claim $2,000 as a maximum credit, or $1,000 for each qualifying child. For purposes of this credit, she only has two qualifying children, because one of her dependents is already over 17 and therefore no longer eligible for the credit. ###

7. Scott is 43 and unmarried. Scott's half-brother, Hayden, turned 16 on December 30, 2012. Hayden lived with Scott all year, and he is a U.S. citizen. Scott claimed Hayden as a dependent on his return. Which of the following is true?

A. Hayden is a qualifying child for the Child Tax Credit.
B. Hayden is not a qualifying child for the Child Tax Credit.
C. Hayden is not a qualifying child for the Child Tax Credit because siblings do not qualify.
D. Hayden only qualifies for the Child Tax Credit if he is a full-time student.

**The answer is A.** Hayden is a qualifying child for the Child Tax Credit because he was under age 17 at the end of 2012. Siblings can be qualifying children for purposes of this credit. ###

8. Which of the following statements regarding the Foreign Tax Credit is correct?

A. The Foreign Tax Credit is a refundable credit.
B. The Foreign Tax Credit is available to U.S. citizens and nonresident aliens.
C. Taxpayers may choose to take a deduction for foreign taxes paid rather than the Foreign Tax Credit.
D. Taxpayers can choose to claim both a deduction and a tax credit for foreign taxes paid, so long as the taxes were paid to different countries.

**The answer is C.** Taxpayers have the option to itemize foreign taxes on Schedule A. They may choose either the deduction or the credit, whichever gives them the lowest tax, for all foreign taxes paid. Taxpayers cannot choose to claim both the deduction and a tax credit on the same return. ###

9. The Lifetime Learning Credit is different from the American Opportunity Credit. However, they do share some of the same requirements. Which of the following requirements is true for both education credits?

A. There is no limit to the number of years the credits can be claimed.
B. Expenses related to housing are allowed as qualified education expenses.
C. The credits are available for only the first two years of postsecondary education.
D. To be eligible for either of the education credits, taxpayers must use any filing status other than married filing separately.

**The answer is D.** Taxpayers who use the filing status of married filing separately are not eligible to claim either the American Opportunity or Lifetime Learning Credits. ###

10. All of the following items are deductible as education-related expenses for the Lifetime Learning Credit except:

A. Required books.
B. On-campus child care in order to attend class.
C. Tuition.
D. Required fees.

**The answer is B.** Daycare is not a qualifying education expense. For purposes of the Lifetime Learning Credit, qualified education expenses are tuition and certain related expenses required for enrollment or attendance at an eligible educational institution. ###

11. Which of the following individuals is eligible for the American Opportunity Credit?

A. Garrett, who is enrolled full-time as a postgraduate student pursuing a master's degree in biology.
B. Lucy, who is taking a ceramics class at a community college.
C. Doug, who was convicted of a felony for distributing a controlled substance.
D. Beth, who is taking three-quarters of the normal full-time course load required for a computer science associate's degree program and who attended classes the entire school year in 2012.

**The answer is D.** Beth is eligible for the American Opportunity Credit because she is taking at least one-half of the normal full-time workload for her course of study for at least one academic period beginning in 2012. Graduate courses do not qualify, and courses that do not lead to a degree, certificate, or other recognized credential also do not qualify for this educational credit. Persons with felony drug convictions are ineligible for this credit. ###

12. In 2012, what is the maximum amount of the American Opportunity Credit?

A. $2,500 per tax return.
B. $2,500 per student.
C. $2,000 per tax return.
D. $1,000 per student.

**The answer is B.** In 2012 the maximum credit is $2,500 per student. The credit is *per* student *per* year, and the taxpayer's family may have more than one eligible student per tax return. ###

13. What is the maximum amount of the Lifetime Learning Credit in 2012?

A. $2,000 per student.
B. $2,500 per student.
C. $1,000 per student.
D. $2,000 per tax return.

**The answer is D.** The maximum credit is $2,000 per tax return. The credit is allowed for 20% of the first $10,000 of qualified tuition and fees paid during the year. The credit is per tax return, not per student, so only a maximum of $2,000 can be claimed each year, no matter how many qualifying students a taxpayer may have. ###

14. Samira and Rishi are married and file jointly. Their daughter, Chetana, was enrolled full-time in college for all of 2012. Samira and Rishi obtained a loan in 2012 and used the proceeds to pay for Chetana's tuition and related fees. They repaid the loan in 2013. When will they be entitled to claim an education credit?

A. They cannot claim an education credit.
B. 2013.
C. 2012.
D. Both 2012 and 2013.

**The answer is C.** Samira and Rishi are eligible to claim an education credit for the year 2012. The credit should be calculated for the year in which the taxpayer paid the expenses, not the year in which the loan is repaid. ###

15. Edwin is a professional bookkeeper. He decides to take an accounting course at the local community college in order to improve his work-related skills. Edwin is not a degree candidate. Which educational credit does he qualify for?

A. The American Opportunity Credit.
B. The College Saver's Credit.
C. The Lifetime Learning Credit.
D. The Mortgage Interest Credit.

**The answer is C.** Edwin qualifies for the Lifetime Learning Credit. He does not qualify for the American Opportunity Credit because he is not a degree candidate and because his course work-load does not meet the requirements. The "College Saver's Credit" does not exist. The Mortgage Interest Credit is not an education credit. ###

16. In 2012, Tyrone paid $5,000 of his own funds to cover all of the cost of his college tuition. Tyrone also received a Pell grant for $3,000 and a student loan for $2,000, which he used for housing costs and books. For purposes of figuring an education credit, what are Tyrone's total qualified tuition and related expenses?

A. $10,000.
B. $7,000.
C. $5,000.
D. $2,000.

**The answer is D.** The total qualified tuition payments are the net of the $5,000 tuition minus the grant of $3,000, which equals $2,000. The $3,000 Pell grant is tax-free, so it is not a qualified tuition and related expense and must be deducted from his overall qualifying costs. ###

17. Based on the Child and Dependent Care Credit rules, which of the following individuals meets the eligibility test for a qualifying person?

A. Jeremy, 5, who is taken care of by his mother at home all day.
B. Virgil, 21, a full-time student supported by his parents.
C. Leroy, 80, who lives at home with his son but is not disabled.
D. Leanne, 52, who is unable to care for herself and is married to Jake, an employed construction worker.

**The answer is D.** Leanne meets the qualifying person test because she is the spouse of someone who works, and she is unable to care for herself. ###

18. What is the maximum amount of the adoption tax credit for 2012?

A. $10,150.
B. $11,650.
C. $12,550.
D. $12,650.

**The answer is D.** The maximum credit for 2012 is $12,650 *per child*. If a taxpayer adopts two children, he will be eligible for the full credit on each child. The credit phases out for taxpayers with MAGI between $189,710 and $229,710. ###

19. Geraldine placed a $250 deposit with a preschool to reserve a place for her three-year-old child. Later, she changed jobs and was unable to send her child to that particular preschool, so she forfeited the deposit. She later found another preschool and had $4,000 in qualifying daycare costs. Which of the following is true?

A. The forfeited deposit is not deductible.
B. The forfeited deposit is deductible.
C. The forfeited deposit is a deduction on Schedule A.
D. Geraldine may deduct the deposit because she took her child to another preschool.

**The answer is A.** The forfeited deposit is not for actual child care, and thus it is not a work-related expense. A forfeited deposit is not actually for the care of a qualifying person, so it cannot be deducted as a child care expense and does not qualify for the Child and Dependent Care Credit. ###

20. Brett and Amy paid daycare for their three-year-old son so they could work. Their child care expenses were $3,000 in 2012. Amy also paid a deposit of $100 to the daycare and an enrollment fee of $35. Brett was reimbursed for $1,200 by his flexible spending account at work. How much of the child care expenses can they use to figure their Child and Dependent Care Credit?

A. $1,800.
B. $1,900.
C. $1,935.
D. $3,135.

**The answer is C.** Their child care expenses are figured as follows: ($3,000 + $100 + $35) - $1,200 = $1,935. If a taxpayer has a reimbursement under a flexible spending account, those amounts are pre-tax. Taxpayers cannot use reimbursed amounts to figure this credit. Fees and deposits paid to an agency or a daycare provider are qualifying expenses if the taxpayer must pay them in order to receive care. Only a forfeited deposit would be disallowed. ###

21. Nina pays for daycare for each of the following individuals so she can work. All of the following are qualifying individuals for purposes of the Child and Dependent Care Credit except:

A. Nina's husband, who is totally disabled.
B. Nina's son, age 13, who is Nina's dependent.
C. Nina's nephew, age 12, who is also Nina's dependent.
D. Nina's niece, who is 35, lived with her all year, and is completely disabled.

**The answer is B.** Nina's son does not qualify, because he is over the age limit for the credit. To qualify for the Child and Dependent Care Credit, the qualifying person must be under the age of 13 or completely disabled. ###

22. All of the following are qualified expenses for purposes of the Child and Dependent Care Credit except_____:

A. $500 payment to a grandparent for child care while the taxpayer is gainfully employed.
B. $300 payment to a daycare while the taxpayer is looking for employment.
C. $500 child care expense while the taxpayer obtains medical care.
D. $600 in daycare expense for a disabled spouse while the taxpayer works.

**The answer is C.** Child care costs to obtain medical care are not a deductible expense. Deductible daycare costs must be work related and for a child under 13, a disabled dependent, or a disabled spouse of any age. Child care so that the taxpayer can volunteer, obtain medical care, run errands, or do other personal business is not qualifying child care. ###

23. Which of the following expenses is not a qualified expense for purposes of the Adoption Credit?

A. Court costs.
B. Re-adoption expenses to adopt a foreign child.
C. Attorney fees for a surrogate arrangement.
D. Travel expenses.

**The answer is C.** The cost of a surrogate is not a qualified adoption expense. Qualified adoption expenses are expenses directly related to the legal adoption of an eligible child. These expenses include adoption fees, court costs, attorney fees, travel expenses (including amounts spent for meals and lodging) while away from home, and re-adoption expenses to adopt a foreign child. ###

24. Austin is a U.S. citizen who is adopting a foreign child. His income in 2012 was $31,000. The adoption is almost final, and he has an ATIN for the child. The child lived with Austin all year. Which of the following is true?

A. Austin can claim the Earned Income Credit because his child is a qualifying child.
B. Austin's income is too high to claim the Earned Income Credit in 2012.
C. Austin cannot claim the Earned Income Credit in 2012, but he can elect to amend his tax return once an SSN is granted and the adoption is final.
D. The Earned Income Credit is not applicable to foreign-adopted children.

**The answer is C.** To claim the EIC, the taxpayer must have a valid SSN issued by the Social Security Administration. Any qualifying child listed on Schedule EIC also must have a valid SSN. An ATIN is not sufficient for purposes of the EIC. However, the taxpayer can elect to amend the tax return once an SSN is granted and the adoption is final. ###

25. To qualify for the Earned Income Credit, which of the following is true?

A. The taxpayer must have a dependent child.
B. The taxpayer must be a U.S. citizen or legal U.S. resident all year.
C. The taxpayer's filing status can be MFS if the taxpayer does not live with his or her spouse.
D. The taxpayer's only income may be from Social Security benefits.

**The answer is B.** The taxpayer must be a U.S. citizen or legal resident all year. Taxpayers do not need to have a dependent child in order to qualify for the Earned Income Credit; however, the EIC is greatly increased if the taxpayer has a qualifying child. Single taxpayers who are low-income may still qualify for the credit. A taxpayer cannot claim the EIC if his filing status is MFS. A taxpayer must have earned income to qualify for the EIC; Social Security benefits do not qualify. ###

26. For those claiming the Earned Income Credit in 2012, the taxpayer's interest or investment income must be _____ or less.

A. $2,950.
B. $3,100.
C. $3,200.
D. $4,000.

**The answer is C.** For purposes of the EIC, interest or investment income must be $3,200 or less. ###

27. Monty and Belinda are married and living together. Monty earned $12,000 and Belinda earned $9,000 in 2012. They have two minor children and have decided to file MFS tax returns, each claiming one child as a dependent. Which statement is true?

A. They can both qualify for the Earned Income Credit on their MFS tax returns.
B. Based on the information, they may qualify for the EIC on a joint tax return.
C. Monty can file single and qualify for the EIC.
D. Belinda can file as head of household and claim the credit.

**The answer is B.** Since Monty and Belinda are married and live together, they can choose to file a joint return or each may choose to file separately. A taxpayer cannot qualify for the EIC on a MFS return, so Monty and Belinda must file jointly in order to claim the credit. ####

28. Which of the following filing conditions would not prevent an individual from qualifying for the Earned Income Credit for the year 2012?

A. MFS filing status.
B. A taxpayer with a qualifying child who is 23 and a full-time student.
C. Investment income of $3,300.
D. A taxpayer who is 68 years old without a qualifying child.

**The answer is B.** All the other choices are disqualifying for purposes of the EIC. At the end of the tax year, the child must be under age 19, or under age 24 and a full-time student, or any age and disabled. ###

29. The Nonbusiness Energy Property Credit can be used for very specific energy systems or improvements to a taxpayer's main home or main home under construction. Which of the following items is not a qualifying item for purposes of the credit?

A. Solar energy systems.
B. Geothermal heat pumps.
C. Small wind energy systems.
D. Energy-efficient windows.

**The answer is D.** The Nonbusiness Energy Property Credit is a credit of 30% of the costs of solar energy systems, fuel cells, small wind energy systems, and geothermal heat pumps. There is no dollar limit on this credit. Energy-efficient windows do not qualify for this credit, but they may for the Residential Energy Property Credit, which applies to certain other energy-efficient improvements installed in a taxpayer's primary residence. ###

30. Couples who file jointly may be eligible to deduct up to _____ per year for contributions to an IRA under the Retirement Savings Contributions Credit?

A. $500.
B. $1,000.
C. $2,000.
D. $5,000.

**The answer is C.** MFJ taxpayers are allowed a nonrefundable credit of up to $2,000 for eligible contributions to an IRA or an employer-sponsored retirement plan. The credit is $1,000 per year for single filers. ###

31. Generally, which is more beneficial to taxpayers when it comes to reducing income tax liability: a nonrefundable credit, a refundable credit, or a deduction?

A. A nonrefundable credit.
B. A refundable credit.
C. A deduction.
D. All are equally beneficial in reducing income tax liability.

**The answer is B.** A refundable credit is not limited by an individual's tax liability. It can provide a taxpayer a refund even if he has zero tax liability. An example is the Earned Income Credit. ###

32. Arlene is single. She has a sixteen-year-old grandson who lived with her from May through December of 2012. She provided 90% of his support and he provided the other 10%. Arlene's MAGI was $85,000 in 2012. Calculate the amount of her Child Tax Credit.

A. $250.
B. $500.
C. $1,000.
D. She is not entitled to the credit because a grandson is not a qualifying child for purposes of the child care credit.

**The answer is B.** Arlene is entitled to claim the Child Tax Credit because her grandson is a qualifying child for purposes of the credit: she provided more than half of his support, he is under 17, and he lived with her for more than half the year. However, Arlene cannot take the full $1,000 credit for her grandson because her income is above $75,000, the threshold for single, head of household, and qualifying widow(er) filers. The credit is reduced by $50 for each $1,000 of MAGI that exceeds the threshold amount. Thus, Arlene's credit is reduced by $500 (10 X $50). ###

33. Zoe attends Valley Oaks College full-time, pursuing an undergraduate degree in business. Because she changed majors in her junior year, she is now in her fifth year of college. She has a $4,000 Pell grant for the 2012 school year. Her parents have taken the American Opportunity Credit for Zoe the past four years. Calculate the amount her parents can claim for the AOC in 2012 given the following expenses for Zoe's education:

- Tuition: $15,000
- Room and board: $12,000
- Medical insurance: $1,000

A. $0.
B. $2,000.
C. $2,500.
D. $4,800.

**The answer is A.** Zoe does not qualify for the AOC because she is in her fifth year of college and her parents have already claimed the credit the prior four years. If she had been eligible for the credit, she would have had $11,000 in eligible expenses. Room and board and medical insurance are not qualified expenses for the AOC, and tuition must be reduced by any tax-free scholarships, such as the Pell grant. The AOC is a maximum credit of $2,500 per student (100% of the first $2,000 of eligible expenses and 20% of the next $2,000). Zoe would qualify for the Lifetime Learning Credit. ###

34. What is the maximum amount a taxpayer can deduct on qualified improvements to his main home under the Residential Energy Efficient Property Credit?

A. No maximum limit.
B. $5,000.
C. $1,000.
D. $500.

**The answer is D.** The total combined credit is $500 for all tax years after 2005. ###

35. In 2012, Dylan and Hannah adopt a special needs child who is completely disabled. Their adoption expenses are $7,000, and their travel expenses related to the adoption are $1,200. Their modified AGI for 2012 is $175,000. What is their maximum Adoption Credit in 2012?

A. $7,000.
B. $8,200.
C. $12,650.
D. None of the above.

**The answer is C.** Dylan and Hannah can take the full Adoption Credit because they adopted a special needs child. There is a special rule for taxpayers who adopt special needs children. The full amount of the Adoption Credit is still allowed, even if the taxpayer does not have qualified adoption expenses. ###

# Unit 10: Basis of Property

| More Reading: |
|---|
| **Publication 551,** *Basis of Assets* |
| **Publication 544,** *Sales and Other Dispositions of Assets* |

## Understanding Basis

Almost everything a taxpayer owns and uses for personal purposes, pleasure, or investment is a capital asset. Examples include:

- A main home or vacation home
- Furniture
- Antiques
- A car or boat
- Stocks or bonds (except when held for sale by a professional securities dealer)
- Gold, silver, coins, etc. (except when they are held for sale by a professional dealer)

The tax treatment of these assets varies based on whether the asset is personal-use, business property, or investment property.

When capital assets are sold, the difference between the asset's basis and the selling price is a **capital GAIN** or a **capital LOSS**.

In order to correctly calculate capital gains and losses, you must first understand the concept of "basis" and "adjusted basis." The basis of the asset is usually its cost.

"Cost basis" is the amount of money invested into a property for tax purposes. Usually this is the cost of the item when it is purchased. However, there are some instances in which basis is different than the cost of the item. Basis is figured in another way when property is acquired by gift or inheritance. The cost basis of an asset can include:

- Sales taxes charged during the purchase
- Freight-in charges
- Installation and testing fees
- Delinquent real estate taxes that are paid by the buyer of a property
- Legal and accounting fees

All of these costs are added to an asset's basis. They are not deductible as an expense, whether or not the asset is business-use or personal-use.

**Example:** Raoul purchases a new car for $15,000. The sales tax on the vehicle is $1,200. He also pays a delivery charge to have the car shipped from another dealership to his home. The freight charge is $210. Therefore, Raoul's basis in the vehicle is $16,410 ($15,000 + $1,200 + $210).

**Example:** Hilda is a self-employed writer. She purchases a new printer for her home office. The printer costs $540, with an additional $34 for sales tax. Therefore, Hilda's basis in the item is $574 ($540 + $34).

In order to correctly report a capital gain or loss, a taxpayer needs to identify:

- The asset's **basis** (or adjusted basis):
  - **Basis** is the original cost of the asset.
  - **Adjusted basis** includes original cost plus any increases or decreases to that cost (such as commissions, fees, depreciation, casualty losses, and insurance reimbursements.)
- The asset's **holding period**:
  - Short-term property is held one year or less.
  - Long-term property is held more than one year.
- The proceeds from the sale.

## Basis of Real Property (Real Estate)

The basis of real estate usually includes a number of costs in addition to the purchase price. If a taxpayer purchases real property (a house, a tract of land, a building), certain fees and other expenses automatically become part of the cost basis. This also includes real estate taxes the seller owed at the time of the purchase, if the real estate taxes were paid by the buyer.

**Example:** Tara sells Lawrence a home for $100,000. She is unemployed and has fallen behind on her property tax payments. Lawrence agrees to pay the delinquent real estate taxes as a condition of the sale. The delinquent property tax at the time of purchase totaled $3,500. The IRS does not allow a taxpayer to deduct property taxes that are not his legal responsibility. Therefore, Lawrence must add the property tax to his basis. Lawrence's basis in the home is $103,500 ($100,000 + $3,500).

If a property is constructed rather than purchased, the basis of the property includes the expenses of construction. This includes the cost of the land, building permits, payments to contractors, lumber, and inspection fees. Demolition costs and other costs related to the preparation of land must be added to the basis of the land.

**Example:** Wanda purchases an empty lot to build her home. The lot costs $50,000. She also pays $2,800 for the removal of tree stumps before construction can begin. There is also an existing concrete foundation on the lot that Wanda dislikes, so she has the foundation demolished and removed in order to build a new foundation. The demolition costs are $6,700. All of these costs must be added to the basis of the land (not the basis of the building). Therefore, Wanda's basis in the land is $59,500 ($50,000 + $2,800 + $6,700).

## Adding Settlement Costs to Basis

Generally, a taxpayer must include settlement costs for the purchase of property in his basis. The following fees are some of the closing costs that can be included in a property's basis:

- Abstract fees
- Charges for installing utilities
- Legal fees (including title search and preparation of the deed)
- Recording fees
- Surveys
- Transfer taxes
- Owner's title insurance

Also included in a property's basis are any amounts the seller legally owes that the buyer agrees to pay, such as back taxes or interest, recording or mortgage fees, charges for improvements or repairs, and sales commissions. A taxpayer cannot include fees incidental to getting a loan.

## *How to Figure Adjusted Basis*

Before figuring gain or loss on a sale or exchange, a taxpayer usually must make increases or decreases to the basis of the property. The result is the **adjusted basis**.

**Example:** Brian buys a house for $120,000. The following year, he paves the driveway, which costs him $6,000. Brian's *adjusted basis* in the home is now $126,000 ($120,000 original cost + $6,000 in improvements).

**Example:** Whitney purchases a commercial washing machine for her pet grooming business. The washer costs $1,230, with an additional $62 in sales tax and freight and installation charges of $96. Whitney receives a manufacturer's rebate check for $300 several weeks later. Her basis in the washer is figured as follows:

| | |
|---|---|
| Cost: | $1,230 |
| Sales tax: | $62 |
| Installation: | $96 |
| Rebate: | ($300) |
| **Basis:** | **$1,088** |

## Basis "Other Than" Cost

There are times when a taxpayer cannot use *cost* as the basis for property. In these cases, the fair market value or the adjusted basis of the property can be used. Below are some examples of when an asset's basis will be something other than cost.

### Property Received in Exchange for Services

If a taxpayer receives property in payment for services, he must include the property's FMV in income, and this becomes his basis in the property. If two people agree on a cost beforehand and it is deemed reasonable, the IRS will usually accept the agreed-upon cost as the asset's basis.

> **Example:** Cassidy is an EA who prepares tax returns for a long-time client named Katie. Katie then loses her job and cannot pay Cassidy's bill, which totals $450. Katie offers Cassidy an antique vase in lieu of paying her invoice. The fair market value of the vase is approximately $520. Cassidy agrees to accept the vase as full payment on Katie's delinquent invoice. Cassidy's basis in the vase is $450, the amount of the invoice that was agreed upon by both parties.

## Basis After Casualty and Theft Losses

If a taxpayer has a casualty loss, he must decrease the basis of the property by any insurance proceeds. A taxpayer may increase the basis in the property by the amount spent on repairs that restore the property to its pre-casualty condition.

> **Example:** Ira paid $5,000 for a car several years ago. It was damaged in a flood, so he spends $3,000 to repair it. He does not have flood insurance on the car. Therefore, his new basis in the car is $8,000 ($5,000 + $3,000).

Remember, after a casualty loss, insurance reimbursements decrease basis, while out-of-pocket repairs increase basis.

## Assumption of a Mortgage or Loan

If a taxpayer buys property and assumes an existing mortgage on it, the taxpayer's basis includes the amount paid for the property plus the amount owed on the mortgage. The basis also includes the settlement fees and closing costs paid for buying the property. Fees and costs for getting a loan on the property (points) are not included in a property's basis.

> **Example:** Sondra buys a building for $20,000 cash and assumes a mortgage of $80,000 on it. Therefore, her basis is $100,000.

## Basis Adjustments after an Involuntary Conversion

An involuntary conversion occurs when a taxpayer *involuntarily* gives up, sells, or exchanges property. This might happen after a disaster, such as a house fire, drought, or a flood. Involuntary conversions may also occur after casualties, thefts, or the condemnation of property. If a taxpayer receives replacement property as a result of an involuntary conversion, the basis of the replacement property is figured using the basis of the converted property. A taxpayer may also have to figure gain if the amount of the insurance reimbursement exceeds his basis of the asset.

> **Example:** Joy receives insurance money of $8,000 for her shed, which was destroyed by an earthquake. Joy's basis in the shed was $6,000. She uses $6,000 to purchase a new shed. Joy needs to recognize a $2,000 gain, since she realized a gain of $2,000 from the conversion ($8,000 - $6,000) and only used $6,000 of the $8,000 insurance proceeds to replace the shed.

# Basis of Securities

A taxpayer's basis in securities (stocks or bonds) is usually the purchase price, plus any additional costs, such as brokers' commissions. In order to compute gain or loss on a sale, taxpayers must provide their basis in the sold property. The basis of stock is usually its cost, but basis can also include other fees.

When a taxpayer sells securities, the investment company will send Form 1099-B, *Proceeds from Broker and Barter Exchange Transactions,* showing the gross proceeds of the sale. Form 1099-B does not usually include how much taxpayers paid; they must keep track of this information themselves. If taxpayers cannot provide their basis, the IRS will deem it to be zero.

Many taxpayers own shares of stock they bought on different dates or for different prices. This means they own more than one block of stock. Each block may differ from the others in its holding period (long-term or short-term), its basis (amount paid for the stock), or both.

In directing a broker to sell stock, the taxpayer may specify which block, or part of a block, to sell; this is called *specific identification*. The specific identification method requires good recordkeeping; however, this method simplifies the determination of the holding period and the basis of the stock sold, giving the taxpayer better control and versatility in handling an investment. If the taxpayer cannot identify the specific block at the time of sale, shares sold are treated as coming from the earliest block purchased; this method is called First In, First Out (FIFO).[66]

---

**FIFO example:**

Tia bought 50 shares of stock of Coffee Corp. in 2005 for $10 a share. In 2006, Tia bought another 200 shares of Coffee Corp. for $11 a share. In 2008, she bought 100 shares for $9 a share. Finally, in 2012, she sells 130 shares. She cannot identify the exact shares she disposed of, so she must use the stock FIFO method to figure the basis of the shares that she sold. Tia figures her stock basis as follows:

### Shares purchased

| Year | # of shares | Cost per share | Total cost |
|------|-------------|----------------|------------|
| 2005 | 50 | $10 | $500 |
| 2006 | 200 | $11 | $2,200 |
| 2008 | 100 | $9 | $900 |

**The basis of the stock that Tia sold is figured as follows:**

| | |
|---|---|
| 50 shares (50 × $10) balance of stock bought in 2005 | $500 |
| 80 shares (80 × $11) stock bought in 2006 | $880 |
| Total basis of stock sold in 2012 | $1,380 |

---

[66] Specific identification and First In, First Out (FIFO) are also common inventory methods that are used by businesses. You will learn more about how these inventory methods are used by businesses in Part 2 of the EA exam course books.

**Example:** Amber buys two blocks of 400 shares of stock (800 shares total), the first in May 2010 for $11,200 and the second in June 2011 for $11,600. In September 2012, she sells 400 shares for $11,500 without specifying which block of shares she is selling. Because Amber did not specify a block of shares at the time of sale, the sold shares are treated as coming from the earliest block purchased. Since the basis and holding period defaults to the original block of shares, Amber realizes a long-term gain of $300 ($11,500 - $11,200).

## Adjusted Basis of Securities

Events that occur after the purchase of the stock can require adjustments (increases or decreases) to the per share basis of stock. The original basis per share can be changed by events such as stock dividends, stock splits, and dividend reinvestment plan (DRIP) accounts.

- **Stock dividends** are additional shares that companies grant to their shareholders. These additional shares increase the taxpayer's ownership so the original basis is spread over more shares, which decreases the basis per share.
- **Stock splits** occur when a corporation distributes more stock to its existing stockholders as a way to bring down the market price of its stock. For example, in a "2-for-1" stock split, a corporation issues one share of stock for every share outstanding. This then decreases the basis per share by half. The original basis of $200 for 100 shares becomes $200 for 200 shares. (The total basis does not change; only the basis per share of stock changes.)

**Example:** Victoria pays $1,050 for 100 shares of Jolly Ice Cream stock, plus a broker's commission of $50. Her basis in the 100 shares is $1,100 ($1,050 cost + $50 broker's commission). Therefore, the original cost basis *per share* is $11 ($1,100/100). Victoria receives 10 *additional* shares of stock as a nontaxable stock dividend. Her $1,100 basis must be spread over 110 shares (100 original shares plus the 10-share stock dividend). Adding 10 shares means her basis per share decreases to $10 ($1,100/110).

### Basis after a Stock Split (Stock Dividend)

The way to figure basis after a stock split or a stock dividend is to divide the taxpayer's adjusted basis of the old stock between the shares of the old stock and the new stock. For example, this means that if the old stock was priced at $10 per share, after the split each share would be worth $5. This is because the corporation's assets did not increase, only the number of outstanding shares.

Stock acquired in a nontaxable stock dividend or stock split has the same holding period as the original stock. If the original stock has a long-term holding period, stock received in a nontaxable stock dividend also has a long-term holding period. For example, if the original stock has a holding period of three months, the new stock immediately has a three-month holding period

A stock dividend and a stock split usually are not taxable events.

But after a stock split, a taxpayer needs to recalculate his basis for the newly acquired shares. The new basis per share is the total cost of the shares divided by the new share count.

**Example:** Sean bought 100 shares of MaxiWin Corp. for $50 per share. Sean's cost basis is $50 x 100 shares or $5,000. In 2012, MaxiWin issues a stock dividend, and Sean receives 100 additional shares of stock. Therefore, his new basis in each individual stock is $25 = ($5,000 ÷ [100+100]).

In rare cases, a stock dividend may be taxable. A taxable stock dividend occurs most often when shareholders have the option to receive cash or other property *instead* of stock. The holding period for stock received as a *taxable* stock dividend begins on the date of distribution.

## Restricted Stock

If stock is granted to a taxpayer but is subject to restrictions, then the taxpayer does not have to report any income until the stock is either granted or sold (when it is taxable depends on the circumstances).

Restricted stock is stock that has been granted to a taxpayer (usually an employee of a company) that is nontransferable and subject to certain conditions, such as termination of employment or failure to meet certain performance targets. Stock-based compensation generally consists of either transferring stock or issuing stock options to an employee (or independent contractor) as part of a compensation package. Stock is considered transferred only if the employee has the risks and benefits of an owner of the stock.

Generally, restricted stock is not eligible for capital gains treatment, and the entire amount of the vested stock must be reported as ordinary income in the year of vesting. The amount that must be reported as ordinary income is calculated by subtracting the exercise price of the stock from the fair market value of the stock on the date of vesting. The difference is then reported as ordinary income by the shareholder.

If the shareholder decides to hold the stock and sell at a later date, then the difference between the sale price and the fair market value on the date of vesting is then reported as a capital gain or loss.

**Example:** Natasha is a sales executive working for Borgnini Corp. As part of her compensation package, she receives a restricted stock grant of 2,000 shares. The restriction on the stock is lifted once she reaches certain sales targets. At the end of the year, Natasha reaches her sales goals, and the stock is vested. On her grant date, Borgnini stock is trading at $15 per share. Natasha decides to declare the stock at vesting, so she must report $30,000 (2,000 shares X $15 per share) as ordinary income.

# Stock Options

Companies often grant stock options to their employees as an incentive. Stock options are not stock but merely the option to purchase stock at a later date. There are two types of stock options, and they have very different tax treatment.

## Incentive Stock Options (ISO)

An incentive stock option allows an employee to purchase stock at a pre-established price (exercise price) that may be below the actual market price on the date of exercise. The tax advantage with an ISO is that income is not reported when the option is granted or when the option is exercised. Income is only reported once the stock is ultimately sold. However, the bargain element, representing the difference between the exercise price and the market value of the stock on the exercise date, is considered a tax preference item for AMT purposes. The employee's basis in the stock is the actual amount paid at exercise plus any amount paid for the option itself.

## Nonqualified Stock Options (NQSO)

A nonqualified stock option also allows an employee to purchase stock at a pre-established price (exercise price). However, the difference between the exercise price and the market value of the stock on the exercise date must be recognized as ordinary income in the year the option is exercised. The employee's basis in the stock is the market value of the stock at exercise (which was used to determine his tax liability) plus any amount paid for the option itself.

## Basis of Property Transferred From a Spouse (or Former Spouse)

The basis of property transferred by a spouse (or former spouse if the transfer is incident to divorce) is the same as the spouse's adjusted basis. Generally, there is no gain or loss recognized on the transfer of property between spouses or former spouses if the transfer is because of divorce. This rule applies even if the transfer was in exchange for cash, the release of marital rights, the assumption of liabilities, or other considerations.

---

**Example:** Before they divorced, Demi and Zachary jointly owned a home that had a basis of $50,000 and an FMV of $250,000. When they divorced last year, Demi transferred her entire interest in the home to Zachary as part of their property settlement. Zachary's basis in the interest received from Demi is her adjusted basis in the home. His total basis in the home is their joint adjusted basis ($50,000).

---

**Example:** Margot and Thornton divorced in 2012. Thornton owns stocks with a fair market value of $350,000 and a basis of $200,000. Pursuant to the divorce decree, Thornton transfers all of the stocks to his former spouse. The stock transfer is treated as a nontaxable transfer; therefore, no gain or loss is recognized by either party. Margot's basis in the stock is $200,000.

## Basis of a Nonbusiness Bad Debt

There are two kinds of bad debts—business and nonbusiness. If someone owes a taxpayer money that he cannot collect, he has a bad debt. To deduct a bad debt, the taxpayer must have a basis in it—that is, the taxpayer must have already included the amount in income or must have already loaned out the cash.

Taxpayers must prove that they have taken reasonable steps to collect the debt and that the debt is worthless. A debt becomes worthless when it is certain that the debt will never be paid. It is not necessary to go to court if the taxpayer can show that a judgment from the court would be uncollectible. A partially worthless debt is not deductible. The taxpayer may take a bad debt deduction only in the year the debt becomes worthless, but a taxpayer does not have to wait until the debt comes due, if there is proof that the debt is already worthless (for example, if the debtor dies or declares bankruptcy).

**Example:** In January 2012, Stephanie loans her friend Jed $14,000 to buy a car. Jed signs a note and promises to pay the entire debt back with interest by December 31, 2012. Jed has a bad car accident in June 2012 and cannot pay his debts so he files for bankruptcy. Stephanie does not have to wait until the debt comes due. The bankruptcy means the loan has become worthless, since there is no longer any chance the amount owed will be paid. Stephanie can take the deduction for nonbusiness bad debt.

For a legitimate bad debt to be deductible, the intent of the loan must be genuine. If a taxpayer lends money to a relative or friend with the understanding that it will not be repaid, it is considered a gift and not a loan. There must be a true creditor-debtor relationship between the taxpayer and the person or organization that owes the money.

## Loan Guarantees

A *loan guarantee* is not a true debtor-creditor relationship. If a taxpayer simply guarantees a debt (by cosigning on the loan) and the debt becomes worthless, the taxpayer cannot take a bad debt deduction. There must be a profit motive in order for the loan to qualify as a true debtor-creditor relationship.

**Example:** Lucas and Jason are co-workers. Lucas, as a favor to Jason, co-signs on an auto loan at their local credit union. Jason does not pay the loan and declares bankruptcy. Lucas is forced to pay off the note in order to maintain his credit. However, since he did not enter into a formal guarantee agreement to protect an investment or to make a profit, Lucas cannot take a bad debt deduction.

When minor children borrow from their parents, there is no genuine debt, and bad debt cannot be deducted.

A legitimate nonbusiness bad debt is reported as a short-term capital loss on Schedule D (Form 1040). It is subject to the capital loss limit of $3,000 per year, or $1,500 if a taxpayer files MFS.

# Basis of Inherited Property

The basis of an asset is generally its cost. However, in the case of inherited assets, heirs typically use a "stepped up" basis. It does not matter what the deceased person actually paid for the asset. The basis of inherited property is generally the FMV of the property on the date of the decedent's death. This means that when the property is sold, the gain will be calculated based on the change in value from the date of death.

This typically results in a beneficial tax situation for anyone who inherits property because the taxpayer generally gets an increased basis. However, there are cases in which this rule can work against taxpayers. Although most property such as stocks, collectibles, and bonds increase in value over time, there are also instances in which the value of the property's value drops. This would create a "stepped-down" basis.

| |
|---|
| **Example #1:** Sasha's uncle bought 300 shares of Harrison Foods stock many years ago for $500. Sasha inherited the Harrison stock when her uncle died. On the date of her uncle's death, the value of the stock was $9,000. Therefore, Sasha's basis in the stock is $9,000. She later sells the stock for $11,000. She has a capital gain of $2,000 ($11,000 - $9,000). |
| **Example #2:** With the same facts as above, if Sasha were to sell the stock for $8,000, she would have a capital loss of $1,000. |
| **Example #3**: Sasha's aunt also bought 100 shares of stock many years ago for $10,000. Sasha inherited the stock when her aunt died. On the date of her aunt's death, the value of the stock was $150. Therefore, Sasha's basis in the stock is $150. She later sells the stock for $150. She cannot report a loss on the stock. That is because the basis of the stock was stepped-down for tax purposes. |

Usually, the basis of an estate is determined on the date of death. However, there is a special rule that allows the personal representative of the estate to elect a different valuation date. If the executor makes this election, the valuation date is six months *after* the date of death. For assets disposed within six months after death, the value at the date of disposition is used. This election is made in order to reduce the amount of estate tax that must be paid. In order to elect the alternative valuation date, the estate value and related estate tax must be less than they would have been on the date of the taxpayer's death.

If a federal estate tax return (Form 706) does not have to be filed for the deceased taxpayer, the basis in the beneficiary's inherited property is the FMV value at the date of death,[67] and the alternate valuation date does not apply.

If a taxpayer inherits property, the capital gain or loss on any later disposition of that property is always treated as a long-term capital gain or loss. This is true regardless of how long the beneficiary actually held the property. The taxpayer is con- considered to have held the inherited property for more than one year even if he disposes of the property less than one year after the decedent's death.

# Basis of Property Received as a Gift

The basis of property received as a gift is determined differently than property that is purchased. The taxpayer must know the adjusted basis of the property just before it was gifted, its fair market value, and the amount of gift tax paid on it, if any, by the giver (donor).

Generally, the basis of gifted property is the same in the hands of the donee as it was in the hands of the donor. This is called a "transferred basis." For example, if a taxpayer gives his son a car and the taxpayer's basis in the car is $2,000, the basis of the vehicle remains $2,000 for the son. However, in cases where the donor pays gift tax, the amount of gift tax paid that is attributable to appreciation of the property's value while the donor held it is added to his basis.

**Example:** Alicia's father gives her 50 shares of stock. The FMV of the stock is currently $1,000. Her father has an adjusted basis in the stock of $500. Alicia's basis in the stock, for purposes of determining gain on any future sale, is $500 (transferred basis).

## Figuring Basis on a Gift

If the FMV of the gifted property is **less** than the donor's adjusted basis (including any gift tax paid on appreciation while the donor held the property), the donee's basis for gain is the same as the donor's adjusted basis. If the donee reports a loss on the sale of gifted property, his basis is the lower of the donor's adjusted basis or the fair market value of the property on the date of the gift.

The sale of gifted property can also result in no gain or loss. This happens when the sale proceeds are *greater* than the gift's FMV but *below* the donor's basis.

**Example:** Charlie's grandmother, Leslie, bought 20 shares of Ford stock many decades ago. Her basis in the stock is $1,000, and thus Charlie's transferred basis is also $1,000. At the time of the gift, the stock has an FMV of $7,500. During the year, Charlie sells the stock for $7,500. He must report a taxable gain of $6,500. The answer is determined as follows: ($7,500 sale price - $1,000 basis = $6,500 capital gain).

---

[67] Most estates are not subject to the estate tax and are not subject to the requirement to file an estate tax return. A filing is required for estates with combined gross assets and prior taxable gifts exceeding a basic exclusion amount ($5,120,000 in 2012.) Detailed information about estate and gift taxes may be found in Unit 15, *Estate and Gift Taxes*.

**Example:** Hugh gives his nephew, Russell, a gift of 500 shares of stock. Hugh's basis in the stock is $1,000, meaning Russell's transferred basis is also $1,000. However, the FMV at the time of the gift is only $900 because the stock has lost some value. Russell sells the stock two months later for $940. Russell does not have any gain or loss for tax purposes. This is because Russell's basis for determining gain is $1,000. However, Russell's basis for determining loss is $900 (the FMV at the time of the gift). This is an example of a sale of gifted property resulting in no gain or loss. This happens when the sale ($940) is above the gift's FMV ($900) but below the donor's basis ($1,000).

**Example:** Benny's Aunt Roberta bought 100 shares of IBM stock when it was at $92. Roberta's basis for the 100 shares is $9,200. Roberta then gives the stock to Benny when it is selling at $70 and has an FMV of $7,000. In this case, Benny has a "dual basis" in the stock. He has one basis for purposes of determining a gain, and a different basis for determining a loss. Here are three separate scenarios that help illustrate how the gain or loss would be calculated when Benny sells the gifted stock:

**Scenario #1:** If Benny sells the stock for more than his aunt's basis, he will use Roberta's basis to determine his amount of gain. For example, if he sells the stock for $11,000, he will report a gain of $1,800 ($11,000 - $9,200).

**Scenario #2:** If Benny sells the stock for less than the FMV of the stock at the time of the gift ($7,000 in the example), he must use that basis to determine the amount of his loss. For example, if the stock continues to decline and Benny eventually sells it for $4,500, he can report a loss of $2,500 ($7,000 - $4,500).

**Scenario #3:** If Benny sells the stock for an amount between the FMV and the donor's basis, no gain or loss will be recognized. For example, if Benny sells the stock for $8,000, there will be no gain or loss on the transaction.

The holding period for a gift is treated differently than the holding period for inherited and purchased property. If a taxpayer receives a gift of property, then the holding period includes the donor's holding period. This concept is also known as "tacking on" the holding period.

**Example:** Florence gives her niece, Marion, an acre of land. At the time of the gift, the land had an FMV of $23,000. Florence's adjusted basis in the land was $20,000. Florence held the property for six months. Marion holds the land for another seven months. Neither held the property for over a year. However, Marion may "tack on" her holding period to her aunt's holding period. Therefore, if Marion were to sell the property, she would have a long-term capital gain or loss, because jointly they held the property for thirteen months, which is over one year.

# Holding Period (Short-Term or Long-Term)

When a taxpayer disposes of investment property, he must determine his holding period in order to figure gain or loss. Holding periods vary based on whether the property was purchased, inherited, or acquired as a gift.

The holding period determines whether any capital gain or loss was a short-term or long-term capital gain or loss. This is very important, because long-term capital gains rates are given more beneficial tax treatment.

If a taxpayer holds investment property for more than one year, any capital gain or loss is *long-term* capital gain or loss. If a taxpayer holds property for one year or less, any capital gain or loss is *short-term* capital gain or loss.

| |
|---|
| **Long-term= More than one year** |
| **Short-term= One year or less** |

To determine how long a taxpayer has held an investment property, he should begin counting on the date *after* the day he acquires the property. The day the taxpayer disposes of the property is part of the holding period.

**Example:** Nicky bought 50 shares of stock on February 5, 2011 for $10,000. She sells all the shares on February 5, 2012 for $20,500. Nicky's holding period is not more than one year, and so she has a short-term capital gain of $10,500. The short-term gain is taxed at ordinary income rates. A long-term gain is taxed at preferential tax rates. If Nicky had waited one more day, she would have received long-term capital gain treatment on her gains, and it would have saved her on income taxes.

**Example:** Stuart bought 100 shares of Castlebarry Corp. stock on October 1, 2011 for $1,200. To determine his holding period, Stuart must start counting his holding period on October 2, 2011 (the day *after* the purchase). He sells all the stock on October 2, 2012 for $2,850. Stuart's holding period has been over one year, and therefore, he will recognize a long-term capital gain of $1,650 ($2,850 - $1,200).

Stock acquired as a stock dividend (also called a stock split) has the same holding period as the original stock owned.

**Example:** On September 10, 2009, Jamal bought 500 shares of Felton Software stock for $1,500, including his broker's commission. On June 6, 2012, Felton Software distributes a 2% nontaxable stock dividend (10 additional shares). Three days later, Jamal sells all his Felton Software stock for $2,030. Although Jamal owned the 10 shares he received as a nontaxable stock dividend for only three days, all the stock has a long-term holding period. Because he bought the stock for $1,500 and then sold it for $2,030 more than a year later, Jamal has a long-term capital gain of $530 on the sale of the 510 shares.

# Unit 10: Questions

1. On February 11, 2012, Henry bought 1,000 shares of Greenbrae Corporation stock for $4 each, plus paid an additional $70 for his broker's commission. What is Henry's basis in the stock?

A. $1,000.
B. $4,000.
C. $4,070.
D. None of the above.

**The answer is C.** Henry's basis in the stock is $4,070 ([1,000 X $4] = $4,000 + $70). ###

2. Brigit purchased 1,000 shares of Free Drive, Inc. on January 3, 2012. The original basis in the 1,000 shares of stock she purchased was $5,100, including the commission. On August 14, 2012, she sold 500 shares for $3,300. What is the adjusted basis of the stock she sold?

A. $5,100.
B. $2,550.
C. $3,300.
D. $3,255.

**The answer is B.** Brigit's original basis in the total stock was $5,100, which is $5.10 per share, so her basis in the 500 shares she sold is 500 X $5.10, or $2,550. ###

3. Tariq bought two blocks of 400 shares of stock. He purchased the first block in April 2008 for $1,200 and the second block in March 2012 for $1,600. In June of 2012, he sold 400 shares for $1,500 without specifying which block of shares he was selling. Tariq's sold stock represents a _____.

A. Short-term loss of $100.
B. Short-term gain of $300.
C. Long-term loss of $100.
D. Long-term gain of $300.

**The answer is D.** The basis and holding period would automatically default to the original block of shares, so Tariq realized a long-term gain of $300. ###

4. Consuela bought 40 shares of Giant Corporation for a total purchase price $1,540. She also paid a $20 broker's commission on the purchase. What is her initial basis per share?

A. $39.
B. $38.50.
C. $1,560.
D. $77.

**The answer is A.** Consuela's initial basis for this stock is $1,560, or $39 per share ($1,560 ÷ 40 shares). Cost basis includes the amount paid for the stock and any commission paid on the purchase. ###

5. On March 10, 2009, Hans bought 500 shares of Merring Roadster stock for $1,500, including his broker's commission. On June 6, 2012, Merring distributed Hans a nontaxable stock dividend of 10 additional shares. Three days later, he sold all his stock for $2,030. What is the nature of his gain on all the shares sold?

A. Long-term capital gain of $530.
B. Long-term capital gain of $500, short-term gain of $30.
C. Short-term capital gain of $530.
D. None of the above.

**The answer is A.** Although Hans owned the 10 shares he received as a nontaxable stock dividend for only three days, all the stock has a long-term holding period. Because he bought the stock for $1,500 and then sold it for $2,030 more than a year later, Hans has a long-term capital gain of $530 on the sale of the 510 shares. ###

6. Deirdre bought 100 shares of stock of Around Pound Corporation in 2005 for $10 a share. In January 2006 Deirdre bought another 200 shares for $11 a share. In July 2006 she gave her son 50 shares. In December 2009 Deirdre bought 100 shares for $9 a share. In April 2012 she sold 130 shares. Deirdre cannot identify the shares she disposed of, so she must use the stock she acquired first to figure the basis. The shares Deirdre gave her son had a basis of $500 (50 × $10). What is the basis of the 130 shares of stock Deirdre sold in 2012?

A. $880.
B. $1,380.
C. $1,300.
D. $1,000.

**The answer is B.** If a taxpayer buys and sells securities at various times in varying quantities and she cannot adequately identify the shares sold, the basis of the securities sold is the basis of the securities acquired first (FIFO). Deirdre figures the basis of the 130 shares of stock she sold as follows:

| 50 shares (50 × $10) | |
|---|---|
| Balance of stock from 2005: | $500 |
| 80 shares (80 × $11) | |
| Stock bought in January 2006: | $880 |
| **Total basis of stock sold** | **$1,380** |

###

7. Julian owned one share of common stock that he bought for $45. The corporation distributed two new shares of common stock for each share held. Julian then had three shares of common stock. What is Julian's new basis for each share?

A. $5.
B. $45.
C. $15.
D. $135.

**The answer is C.** Julian's basis in each share is $15 ($45 ÷ 3). If a taxpayer receives a nontaxable stock dividend, divide the adjusted basis of the old stock by the number of shares of old and new stock. The result is the taxpayer's basis for each share of stock. ###

8. Claire owned two shares of common stock. She bought one for $30 in 2007 and the other for $45 in 2008. In 2012, the corporation distributed two new shares of common stock for each share held (a "2-for-1" stock split). Claire had six shares after the distribution. How is the basis allocated between these six shares?

A. All six shares now have a basis of $12.50.
B. Three shares have a basis of $10 each and three have a basis of $15 each.
C. The shares are valued at $45 each.
D. Some other amount.

**The answer is B.** The shares now are valued as follows: three with a basis of $10 each ($30 ÷ 3), and three with a basis of $15 each ($45 ÷ 3). If a taxpayer receives a nontaxable stock dividend, he must divide the adjusted basis of the old stock by the number of shares of old and new stock. The result is the taxpayer's basis for each share of stock. ###

9. On her one-year anniversary at her new job, Faith's employer gave her restricted stock with the condition that she would have to return it if she did not complete a full five years of service with her company. Her employer's basis in the stock was $16,000, and its FMV is $30,000. How much should she include in her income for the current year, and what would be her basis in the stock?

A. Income of $16,000; basis of $30,000.
B. Income of $10,000; basis of $30,000.
C. Income of $30,000; basis of $16,000.
D. Faith would not report any income or have any basis in the stock until she has completed five years of service.

**The answer is D.** The stock is restricted, so Faith does not have constructive receipt of it. She should not report any income until she receives the stock without restrictions. Constructive receipt does not require physical possession of the item of income. However, there are substantial restrictions on the stock's disposition because Faith must complete another four years of service before she can sell or otherwise dispose of the stock. ###

10. Stephen purchases a truck for $15,000 to use in his carpentry business. He puts $5,000 down in cash and finances the remaining $10,000 with a five-year loan. He then pays taxes and delivery costs of $1,300. He also pays $250 to install a protective bedliner. What is Stephen's basis for depreciation in the truck?

A. $6,550.
B. $10,000.
C. $16,550.
D. $16,300.

**The answer is C.** Stephen's basis in the truck is the cost of both acquiring the property and preparing the property for use. Therefore, his basis is figured as follows: ($15,000 + $1,300 + $250) = $16,550. Any funds that are borrowed to pay for an asset are also included in the basis. ###

11. Mackenzie purchases an empty lot for $50,000. She pays $15,000 in cash and finances the remaining $35,000 with a bank loan. The lot also has a $4,000 lien against it for unpaid property taxes, which she also agrees to pay. Which statement below is correct?

A. Mackenzie's basis in the property is $50,000, and she may deduct the property taxes on her Schedule A as property taxes paid.
B. Mackenzie's basis in the property is $19,000.
C. Mackenzie's basis in the property is $54,000.
D. Mackenzie's basis in the property is $46,000.

**The answer is C.** Her basis is figured as follows: ($50,000 + $4,000 = $54,000). Mackenzie may not deduct the delinquent property taxes on her Schedule A. This is because any obligations of the seller that are assumed by the buyer increase the basis of the asset, and are not currently deductible. Since Mackenzie did not legally owe the property taxes but she still agreed to pay them, she must add the property tax to the basis of the property. ###

12. Marilyn won the lottery and then made personal loans to several friends. The loans were a true debtor-creditor relationship but not business related. She could not collect on many of these loans. How does Marilyn report these transactions?

A. The losses from the uncollectible loans are not deductible, since they were personal loans.
B. The losses are deductible as nonbusiness bad debt on Schedule D.
C. The losses are deductible as a business expense on Schedule C.
D. The losses are deductible on Schedule A as casualty losses.

**The answer is B.** A nonbusiness bad debt is reported as a short-term capital loss on Schedule D. It is subject to the capital loss limit of $3,000 per year. ###

13. Conrad purchased Blue-Chip Corporation stock in 2009 and sold it in 2012. In 2012, he also traded in a copy machine that he had been using in his business since 2008 for a new model. On December 15, 2012, Conrad's mother gifted him 35 shares of Energy Corp. stock that she had held for five years. Conrad sold the gifted stock two weeks after he received it from his mother. What is the holding period for all these assets?

A. All short-term.
B. Blue-Chip stock and copy machine are long-term and Energy Corp. stock is short-term.
C. All the stocks are long-term; the copy machine is short-term.
D. All are long-term.

**The answer is D.** All the property is long-term property. If a taxpayer holds investment property for more than one year, any capital gain or loss is a long-term capital gain or loss. If a taxpayer holds a property for one year or less, any capital gain or loss is a short-term capital gain or loss. If a taxpayer receives a gift of property, then the holding period includes the donor's holding period. Since Conrad's mother had already held the stock for a few years, it would receive long-term treatment in Conrad's possession. ###

14. When trying to determine the holding period for investment property, which of the following is important?

A. The cost of the property.
B. In the case of gifted property, the amount of the gift.
C. The date of acquisition.
D. The amount realized in the transaction.

**The answer is C.** To determine the holding period, a taxpayer must begin counting on the day after the acquisition date. If a taxpayer's holding period is not more than one year, the taxpayer will have a short-term capital gain or loss. The amount realized in the transaction has no bearing on the holding period. ###

15. For Mother's Day on May 13, 2012, Jonathon gives his mother, Caryna, a classic 1963 Corvette. Jonathon had purchased the car for $50,000 on January 4, 2012 and then worked for several months restoring it. At the time of his gift, the car's FMV was $63,000.

Although Caryna enjoys driving the Corvette, she dislikes its poor gas mileage and decides she would rather have a new Prius. She sells the Corvette on March 15, 2013 for $65,000. What is the nature of Caryna's gain or loss?

A. Short-term loss.
B. Short-term capital gain.
C. Long-term loss.
D. Long-term capital gain.

**The answer is D.** Even though Caryna owned the Corvette for less than a year, she has a long-term capital gain. That is because the time Jonathon owned the car—three months—is "tacked on" to Caryna's holding period of ten months. If a taxpayer receives a gift of property, the holding period includes the donor's holding period. ###

16. Esteban installs artificial turf at a client's home at a cost of $1,500. After the installation, his client, Andie, receives a foreclosure notice and is unable to pay Esteban's bill. She has a goldendoodle show dog that just had puppies. The FMV of each puppy is $1,800. Esteban loves animals and decides to take one of the puppies as full payment on Andie's delinquent bill. What is Esteban's basis in his new dog?

A. $0.
B. $300.
C. $1,500.
D. $1,800.

**The answer is C.** If a taxpayer receives property in payment for services, he must include the property's FMV in income, and this becomes his basis. However, if two people agree on a cost beforehand and it is deemed reasonable, the IRS will usually accept the agreed-upon cost as the asset's basis. ###

17. On July 1, 2012 Miletech Corporation granted 1,000 non-qualified stock options to an executive with an option price of $23 per share. On December 31, 2012, the executive exercised all of his options when the market price per share was $43. What is the basis of his stock and what amount should be included on his Form W-2 as income in 2012?

A. Basis $23,000; income $0.
B. Basis $43,000; income $20,000.
C. Basis $0; income $0.
D. None of the above.

**The answer is B.** The basis of the stock would be the value on December 31, 2012 (1,000 x $43 = $43,000). The options were issued at an option price of $23 which means that $20,000 ($43 - $23 = $20 x 1,000 = $20,000), representing the difference between his exercise price and the stock's value at exercise, must be included in his W-2 for 2012. When the stock is later sold, the taxpayer would recognize gain or loss equal to the difference between his sales proceeds and the $43,000 basis in the stock. ###

18. On June 1, 2012, Pham Software Corporation granted 500 incentive stock options to an executive with an option price of $25. On December 31, 2012, the executive exercised all of his options when the market price per share was $50. What is the basis of his stock and how much should be included on his Form W-2 as income for 2012?

A. Basis $12,500; income $0.
B. Basis $0; income $0.
C. Basis $12,500; income $12,500.
D. Basis $12,500; income $25,000.

**The answer is A.** For incentive stock options, the basis in the stock is based on the actual price per share paid upon exercise of the options. Any increase in value attributable to the difference between the exercise price and the value at the date of exercise is not recognized until the stock is sold. However, the taxpayer may need to make an adjustment for alternative minimum tax (AMT) purposes of $12,500 (500 x $25 = $12,500) for the bargain element. When the stock is sold, income will be recognized for the difference between the option price and the value on the date of the sale. ###

# Unit 11: Capital Gains and Losses

> **More Reading:**
> Publication 550, *Investment Income and Expenses*
> Publication 544, *Sales and Other Dispositions of Assets*
> Publication 537, *Installment Sales*

The sale of assets—whether they are securities, such as stocks, or personal property, such as a main home—will result in a capital gain or loss. Learning how to calculate capital gains and losses is essential to understanding how property transactions are taxed.

Losses from the sale of personal-use property, such as a main home, furniture, or jewelry, are not deductible.

> **Example:** Liam owns a Subaru that he uses to commute to work, run errands, and take on weekend ski trips. He purchased the car four years ago for $20,500. In 2012, he sells the car for $12,000. Liam cannot claim a loss from the sale of the car since it is his personal-use vehicle.

> **Example:** Mason sold his personal computer to his friend for $750. Mason paid $5,000 for the computer five years ago. Mason used the computer to play games, surf the Internet, and pay bills on-line. He did not use the computer for business. Mason cannot deduct a loss on the sale of his personal computer.

Property held for personal use only, rather than for investment, is a capital asset, and a taxpayer must report a gain from its sale as a capital gain.

> **Example:** Priscilla collects antique coins as a hobby. She is not a professional dealer. Two years ago, Priscilla gets lucky and purchases an antique Roman coin for $50. In 2012, she is offered $1,000 for the coin, and she promptly sells it. Priscilla has a taxable capital gain and she must report it on her tax return.

The capital gains tax rate depends on the holding period, type of asset, and the taxpayer's ordinary income bracket.

Capital gains and deductible capital losses are reported on Schedule D (Form 1040), *Capital Gains and Losses.* Additional detail on certain transactions is first reported on Form 8949, *Sales and Other Dispositions of Capital Assets*.

## *Noncapital Assets*

Assets held for business-use or created by a taxpayer for purposes of earning revenue (author's writings, copyrights, inventory, etc.) are considered *noncapital* assets. Gains and losses from the sale of business property are reported on Form 4797, *Sales of Business Property*, and in the case of individual taxpayers, the amounts flow through to Form 1040, Schedule D. [68]

---

[68] See Publication 544, *Sales and Other Dispositions of Assets,* for additional information on the sale of business property. Gains and sales of business property are covered more in Book 2.

**Example:** Tony is a sole proprietor of a fitness club. He also owns stock in a few companies as an investment. In 2012, Tony sold used fitness equipment from his club in order to make room for new equipment. Since the fitness equipment was business property, the sale of these assets is reported on Form 4797, *Sales of Business Property.* Also during the year, Tony sold some Google stock at a substantial profit. He has a capital gain on the stock and must report the sale on Schedule D.

The following assets are noncapital assets:

- Inventory or any property held for sale to customers
- Depreciable property used in a business, even if it is fully depreciated
- Real property used in a trade or business, such as a commercial building or a residential rental
- Self-produced copyrights, transcripts, manuscripts, drawings, photographs, or artistic compositions
- Accounts receivable or notes receivable acquired by a business
- Stocks and bonds held by professional securities dealers
- Business supplies
- Commodities and derivative financial instruments

Unlike capital assets, many noncapital asset losses may be deducted as business expenses.

**Example:** Michael is a self-employed fisherman who reports his income and loss on Schedule F. In 2012, he sells some of his commercial fishing equipment, which was business-use only. The fishing equipment is a noncapital asset, and the sale must be reported on Form 4797, *Sales of Business Property.* Also during the year, Michael sells his vacation home and has a substantial loss on the sale. Unlike the fishing equipment, the vacation home is a capital asset, and since it is personal-use only, Michael cannot deduct the loss on the sale.

## *The $3,000 Loss Limit and Loss Carryovers*

Capital losses are always netted against capital gains. However, there is an exception for stock losses. *Up to $3,000* in excess capital losses is deductible against ordinary income in a tax year ($1,500 for taxpayers filing MFS). The allowable loss is referred to as the capital loss deduction limit. Unused losses are carried over to later years.

The carryover losses are combined with the gains and losses that actually occur in the next year. Short-term and long-term capital loss carryovers are reported on Schedule D.

The carryover retains its character as either long-term or short-term. A long-term capital loss carried over to the next tax year will reduce that year's long-term capital gains before it reduces that year's short-term capital gains.

**Example:** Arthur purchased stock two years ago for $16,000. The stock declines in value, and he finally sells the stock in 2012 for $12,000. Arthur has a $4,000 long-term capital loss. He also has $30,000 in wages in 2012. He may claim $3,000 of his long-term capital loss against his ordinary income, thereby lowering his gross income to $27,000 ($30,000 - $3,000). The remainder of the long-term capital loss must be carried forward to a future year ($1,000 carryover).

Unused losses may be carried over year after year until they are all deducted. There is no limit on how many times a capital loss can be carried over during the taxpayer's life.

## Determining Capital Gain or Loss

A taxpayer determines gain or loss on a sale or trade of stock or property by comparing the amount realized with the adjusted basis of the property.

- GAIN: If the taxpayer realizes more than the adjusted basis of the property, the difference is a gain.
- LOSS: If the taxpayer realizes less than the adjusted basis of the property, the difference is a loss.

**Example:** Nadine purchased 50 shares of Hammaker Corporation stock five years ago for $5,000. Then, two years ago, she purchased 750 shares of Shelby Ironworks stock for $8,200. In 2012, Nadine sells all her stock. Her Hammaker stock sold for $2,000, which means she had a loss. Her Shelby stock sold for $13,000, which means she had a gain. All of Nadine's gains and losses are long-term, because she held all her stock for more than one year. Her long-term loss and long-term gain are netted against each other to figure her net capital gain. Nadine's gains and losses are figured as follows:

| Stock | Basis | Sale Price | Gain (or loss) |
|-------|-------|-----------|----------------|
| Hammaker | $5,000 | $2,000 | ($3,000) |
| Shelby | $8,200 | $13,000 | $4,800 |
| **Net Capital Gain** | | | **$1,800** |

There are many instances in which a taxpayer may have a realized gain that is not a taxable event.

A "recognized" gain or loss is the actual amount that must be included in income (or deducted from income) for tax purposes.

If a taxpayer sells securities through a broker during the year, he should receive Form 1099-B, *Proceeds from Broker and Barter Exchange Transactions*, by January 31 following the end of the tax year. This statement shows the gross proceeds from the sale of securities. The IRS also receives a copy of Form 1099-B from the broker. If Form 1099-B does not include the basis, the taxpayer must provide this information; otherwise, the IRS will deem the basis to be zero. (Any broker fees should be added to the basis, not deducted from the proceeds.)

327

> **Example:** Corbin receives Form 1099-B showing a net sales price of $1,200 on the sale of 600 shares of Kominski Corporation. He bought the stock six years ago and sold it on September 25, 2012. His basis in Kominski, including commission, is $1,455. He has an overall loss on the stock, which he will report on Schedule D.

The sale and income (or loss) must be reported in the year the security is sold, regardless of when the taxpayer receives the proceeds from the stock sale.

## Worthless and Abandoned Securities

Taxpayers may choose to "abandon" securities. Stocks, stock rights, and bonds (other than those held for sale by a securities dealer) that became worthless during the tax year are treated as though they were sold on the last day of the tax year. The taxpayer reports the loss as if he sold the shares for zero dollars on the last day of the taxable year.

This rule is helpful for a taxpayer who has a security that has declined in value so much that he wishes to take a loss on it rather than retain ownership.

> **Example:** Reginald owned 500 shares of WorldCom stock. The company files for bankruptcy and the bankruptcy court extinguishes all rights of the former shareholders. Reginald learns of the bankruptcy court's decision in December 2012. Rather than wait for a formal notice from the court, Reginald chooses to abandon his WorldCom securities, knowing that his shares are worthless. He takes a capital loss on his 2012 tax return, reflecting the value of his worthless shares as "zero."

To abandon a worthless security, a taxpayer must permanently surrender all rights to it and receive no consideration in exchange.

> **\*Note:** Worthless securities get special tax treatment. Unlike other losses, a taxpayer is allowed to amend a tax return up to seven years prior in order to claim a loss from worthless securities. This is more than double the usual three-year statute of limitations for amending returns.

## Capital Gain Distributions and Mutual Funds

A mutual fund is a regulated investment company generally created by pooling funds of investors to allow them to take advantage of a diversity of investments and professional management. Mutual funds often sell profitable investments at certain times throughout the year.

Form 1099-DIV reports capital gain distributions from the mutual fund. Profits of these sales are reported to the shareholders as capital gain distributions. If taxpayers (shareholders) decide to sell any of their shares in the mutual fund itself, Form 1099-B will be issued. The taxable gain or loss from the sale or exchange of the taxpayer's shares in a mutual fund is reported on Form 1040, Schedule D.

What makes these types of distributions unusual, however, is that capital gain distributions are *always* taxed at long-term capital gains tax rates, *no matter how long* a taxpayer has personally owned shares in the mutual fund.

# Qualified Small Business Stock (Section 1244)

There is a special type of stock called section 1244 small business stock (also called qualified small business stock or QSBS). QSBS is stock in qualifying domestic corporations that is subject to special tax rules that are favorable to the shareholder. Congress allows special treatment for this type of stock in order to spur investment in domestic corporations.

Qualified small business stock must be from a C corporation with gross assets of $50 million or less.

Losses on small business stock are considered ordinary losses rather than capital losses and any gain on a 1244 stock is a capital gain. This means that the losses are not subject to the capital loss limit ($3,000 per year), but gains are still given favorable capital gains rates. The amount that can be deducted as an ordinary loss is $50,000 for single filers and $100,000 for joint filers. Ordinary losses are more favorable to the taxpayer because he can deduct this loss against his ordinary gross income.

In order to qualify, the shareholder must be an individual or partnership; other entities such as corporations do not qualify for this specialized treatment.

Only the *original purchaser* of the stock can claim an ordinary loss. So, if this stock is inherited or gifted to another person, the special treatment for losses also does not apply.

Losses from the sale of section 1244 stock are reported on Form 4797, *Sales of Business Property*.

## *Special Rule: Excluded Gains on Small Business Stock*

Gains on qualified small business stock are also given preferential treatment:

- A taxpayer generally can exclude up to 50% of the gain from the sale or trade of qualified small business stock held for more than five years.
- For stock acquired after September 27, 2010 and before January 1, 2014,[69] the exclusion is 100%. The amount of gain eligible for the exclusion is limited to the greater of 10 times the taxpayer's basis in the stock or $10 million of gain from stock in that corporation.

**Example:** On December 15, 2012, Lenore purchases 100 shares of Button Makers USA, a domestic corporation with $20 million in annual revenue. The stock is qualified small business stock. Lenore must wait until December 16, 2017 to sell the stock in order to receive the 100% exclusion from gain.

---

[69] This time period was extended from January 1, 2012 to January 1, 2014 by the American Taxpayer Relief Act of 2012.

Gains from qualified small business stock are reported on Schedule D (Form 1040).

# Wash Sales and Disallowed Losses

A wash sale occurs when an investor sells a losing security to claim a capital loss, only to repurchase it again for a bargain. This used to be a common investor strategy until the IRS implemented a 30-day wash sale rule in which a taxpayer cannot recognize a loss on an investment if that investment was purchased within 30 days of sale (before or after the sale.)

A taxpayer cannot deduct losses from sales of securities in a wash sale. A wash sale is when a taxpayer sells securities and then turns around and:

- Buys identical securities,
- Acquires substantially identical securities in a taxable trade, or
- Acquires a contract or option to buy identical securities.

> **Example:** Carlos sells 1,000 shares of Granger Corporation stock on December 4, 2011 and takes a loss of $3,200. Carlos has seller's remorse, and on January 2, 2012 he buys back 1,000 shares of Granger stock. Because of the IRS wash sale rules, all of the $3,200 loss is disallowed. He cannot take the loss until he finally sells those repurchased shares at some later time. He must add the disallowed loss to the basis of the newly-purchased shares, resulting in an increase to the basis.

The wash sale rule time period actually lasts a total of 61 calendar days: the 30 days before the sale is made, the 30 days after the sale is made, and the day of the sale. To claim a loss as a deduction, the taxpayer needs to avoid purchasing the same stock (or similar security) during the wash sale period. For a sale on July 31, for example, the wash sale period includes all of July and August.

If a taxpayer's loss was disallowed because of the wash sale rules, he must add the disallowed loss to the basis of the new stock or securities. The result is an increase in the taxpayer's basis in the new stock or securities. This adjustment postpones the loss deduction until the disposition of the new stock or securities.[70]

For purposes of the wash sale rules, securities of one corporation are not considered identical to securities of another corporation. This means that a person can sell shares in one corporation and then purchase shares in a different corporation, and this will not trigger a wash sale. In order for a wash sale to apply, the shares must be identical.

Similarly, "preferred" stock of a corporation is not considered identical to the common stock of the same corporation.

---

[70] Wash sale rules do not apply to trades of commodity futures contracts and foreign currencies. The rules also do not apply to dealers in stocks or securities.

If the number of shares of identical securities a taxpayer buys within 30 days is either more or less than the number of shares sold, the taxpayer must determine the particular shares to which the wash sale rules apply. A taxpayer does this by matching the shares bought with an equal number of the shares sold. A taxpayer must match the shares bought in the same order that he bought them, beginning with the first shares purchased.

> **Example:** Chelsea bought 100 shares of Sarbella Pharmaceuticals stock on September 24, 2011. On February 3, 2012, she sold those shares at a $1,000 loss. On February 10, 2012, Chelsea bought 100 shares of identical Sarbella stock. Since she *repurchased* identical shares ten days after selling the stock, she cannot deduct her $1,000 loss. She must add the disallowed loss to the basis of the 100 shares she bought on February 10. This is a wash sale.

It is considered a wash sale if a taxpayer sells stock and his spouse then repurchases identical stock within 30 days. This is true even if the spouses file separate tax returns.

## Installment Sales

An installment sale is a sale of property in which at least one payment is to be received after the tax year in which the sale occurs. If a taxpayer sells property and receives payments over a number of years, he is allowed to use the installment method in order to defer tax by only reporting gains as each installment is received.

A taxpayer's total gain on an installment method is generally the amount the selling price of the property sold exceeds the adjusted basis in that property.

Each payment on an installment sale typically consists of the following three parts:

- Interest income
- Return of the adjusted basis in the property
- Gain on the sale

In each year the taxpayer receives a payment, he must include both the interest part and the part that is his gain on the sale. The taxpayer does not include in income the part that is the return of basis in the property. Basis is the amount of the taxpayer's investment in the property for investment purposes.

A certain percentage of each payment (after subtracting interest, which is reported as ordinary income) is reported as installment sale income. The percentage is called the gross profit percentage[71] and is figured by dividing the gross profit from the sale by the contract price.

---

[71] You may be required to figure gross profit percentage for either Part 1 or Part 2 of the EA exam using a set of figures provided. Gross profit percentage is commonly used in business to measure a company's performance.

A taxpayer must calculate his installment sale income by using the following formula:

---

**Figuring Adjusted Basis and Gross Profit Percentage**

1. Enter the selling price for the property: _____

2. Enter the adjusted basis for the property: _____

3. Enter the selling expenses: _____

4. Enter any depreciation recapture: _____

5. Add lines, 2, 3 and 4. This is the adjusted basis for installment sale purposes. _____

6. Subtract line 5 from line 1. This is the gross profit. _____ (If zero or less, there is no gain, and a taxpayer cannot use the installment method.)

7. Enter the contract price for the property._____

8. Divide line 6 by line 7. This is the gross profit percentage.

---

The selling price is the FMV of the property, any existing mortgage or debt the buyer pays or assumes, and any selling expenses the buyer pays.

If the installment sale includes any income due to depreciation recapture, it is reported as ordinary income in the year of the sale.

---

**Example:** Ernesto sells property in an installment sale at a contract price of $6,000. His gross profit is $1,500. The gross profit percentage on the sale is 25% ($1,500 ÷ $6,000). After subtracting interest, Ernesto reports 25% of each payment, including the down payment, as installment sale income. The remainder (balance) of each payment is the tax-free return of the property's basis.

---

**Example:** In 2011, Chloe sells an empty lot with a basis of $40,000 for $100,000. Her gross profit is $60,000. She receives a $20,000 down payment and the buyer's note for $80,000. The note provides for four annual payments of $20,000 each, plus 8% interest, beginning in 2012. Chloe's gross profit percentage is 60%. She must report a gain of $12,000 on each payment received.

---

If the taxpayer decides not to use the installment method, he must report all the gain in the year of the sale. Installment sale rules do not apply to property that is sold at a loss.

The installment method cannot be used for publicly traded securities, such as stocks and bonds. This means that a taxpayer is forced to report gain on the sale of securities in the year of the sale, regardless of whether the proceeds are received until the following year.

---

**Example:** Dillon owns 500 shares of stock, which he sells at a gain on December 29, 2012. Dillon does not receive the proceeds until January 15, 2013. Dillon is required to report the capital gain on the sale of the stock on his 2012 tax return. He cannot delay reporting the gain, and the sale is not considered an installment sale.

---

Installment sales are allowed to related parties (covered next). However, if a taxpayer sells property to a relative and the relative later sells or disposes of the property within two years of the original sale, the taxpayer will lose the benefit of installment reporting.

---

**Example:** Lou sells a plot of land to his daughter, Melanie. The sale price is $25,000, and Lou realizes a profit on the sale of $10,000. Melanie agrees to pay in five installments of $5,000. A year later, Melanie sells the property to another person. Lou must report the entire profit of $10,000 on the sale, even though he may not have received all the installment payments. The installment method is disallowed on this related party sale, because the property was disposed of before the two-year holding period.

---

No gain or loss is recognized on the transfer of an installment obligation between a husband and wife if the transfer is incident to a divorce.

Installment sales are reported on Form 6252, *Installment Sale Income*, which is attached to Form 1040. A taxpayer may also be required to complete Schedule D or Form 4797.

# Related Party Transactions and Capital Losses

Special rules apply to related-party transactions, which are business deals between two parties who are joined by a special relationship. If a taxpayer sells capital assets to a close family member or to a business entity that the taxpayer controls, he may not receive all the benefits of the capital gains tax rates, and he may not be able to deduct his losses. The related party transactions were put into place to prevent related persons and entities from shuffling assets back and forth and taking improper losses.

## 50% Control Rule

If a taxpayer controls more than 50% of a corporation or partnership, then any property transactions between the taxpayer and the business would be subject to related party transaction rules.

In general, a loss on the sale of property between related parties is not deductible. When the property is later sold to an unrelated party, gain is recognized only to the extent it is more than the disallowed loss. If the property is later sold at a loss, the loss that was disallowed to the related party cannot be recognized.

If a taxpayer sells or trades property at a loss (other than in the complete liquidation of a corporation), the loss is not deductible if the transaction is between the taxpayer and the following related parties:

- Members of immediate family, including a spouse, siblings or half-siblings, ancestors, or descendants (children, grandchildren, etc.). *Note: For purposes of this rule, uncles, aunts, nephews, nieces, cousins, stepchildren, stepparents, in-laws, and ex-spouses are not considered related parties.

- A partnership or corporation that the taxpayer controls. A taxpayer "controls" an entity when he has more than 50% ownership in it. This also includes partial ownership by other family members.
- A tax-exempt or charitable organization controlled by the taxpayer or a member of his family.
- Losses on sales between certain closely related trusts or business entities controlled by the same owners.

> **Example:** Hillary buys stock from her brother, Clyde, for $7,600. Clyde's cost basis in the stock is $10,000. He cannot deduct the loss of $2,400 because of the related-party transaction rules. Later, Hillary sells the same stock on the open market for $10,500, realizing a gain of $2,900. Hillary's reportable gain is $500 (the $2,900 gain minus the $2,400 loss not allowed to her brother).

> **Example:** Vicky purchases stock from her father for $8,600. Her father's basis in the stock is $11,000. Vicky later sells the stock on the open market for $6,900. Her recognized loss is $1,700 (her $8,600 basis minus $6,900). Vicky cannot deduct the loss that was disallowed to her father.

In the case of a related party transaction, if a taxpayer sells multiple pieces of property and some are at a gain while others are at a loss, the gains will generally be taxable while the losses cannot be used to offset the gains.

# Summary: Capital Gains

1. Almost everything a taxpayer owns and use for personal purposes, pleasure, or investment is a capital asset.

2. Taxpayers must report all capital gains, but not all capital losses are deductible. A taxpayer may only deduct capital losses on investment property, not on personal-use property.

3. The tax rates that apply to net capital gain are generally lower than the tax rates that apply to other income. For 2012, the maximum capital gains rate for most people is 15%. For lower-income individuals, the rate may be 0% on some or all of the net capital gain. Rates of 25% or 28% may apply to special types of net capital gain.

4. If capital losses exceed capital gains, a taxpayer may deduct the excess on his tax return to reduce other income, such as wages, up to an annual limit of $3,000 ($1,500 if MFS).

## Holding Period

- Short-term property is held one year or less.
- Long-term property is held more than one year.

Long-term capital gains are taxed at a lower rate than short-term gains, so it is always beneficial for a taxpayer to have a long-term holding period, rather than short-term.

## Stock Rules, Wash Sales, and Stock Splits

Stock acquired in a nontaxable stock dividend or stock split has the same holding period as the original stock owned.

A wash sale occurs when a taxpayer sells or otherwise disposes of stock or securities at a loss and within 30 days before or after the sale or disposition, the taxpayer buys identical stock or securities. Losses are disallowed on a wash sale.

# Unit 11: Questions

1. Norma sells an empty lot with an adjusted basis of $20,000. Her buyer assumes an existing mortgage on the property of $15,000 and agrees to pay Norma $10,000, with a cash down payment of $2,000 and then $2,000 every year (plus 12% interest) in each of the next four years. The selling price is $25,000. What is Norma's gross profit and gross profit percentage on the installment sale?

A. The gross profit is $5,000, and the gross profit percentage is 50%.
B. The gross profit is $10,000, and the gross profit percentage is 100%.
C. The gross profit is $15,000, and the gross profit percentage is 20%.
D. The gross profit is $5,000, and the gross profit percentage is 100%.

**The answer is A.** Norma's gross profit is $5,000, and the gross profit percentage is 50%. Her selling price is $25,000 ($15,000 existing mortgage + $10,000 payment over four years). Therefore, Norma's gross profit is $5,000 ($25,000 – $20,000 installment sale basis). The contract price is $10,000 ($25,000 – $15,000 mortgage). Her gross profit percentage is 50% ($5,000 ÷ $10,000). Norma must report half of each $2,000 payment received as gain from the sale. She must also report all interest received as ordinary income. ###

2. What is the maximum number of years a taxpayer can carry over an unused capital loss?

A. One year.
B. Two years.
C. Five years.
D. As many times as required to receive the entire deduction.

**The answer is D.** Unused capital losses may be carried over year after year until they are all deducted. There is no limit on how many times a loss can be carried over during the taxpayer's life. ###

3. Five years ago, Marsha bought 100 shares of stock. Her sale date was March 10, 2012. Marsha's original cost for the stock was $10,110, plus an additional $35 in broker's fees. When she sold the stock, she received gross proceeds of $8,859. What is the net gain or loss from this transaction?

A. $1,286 in long-term capital loss.
B. $1,286 in short-term capital loss.
C. $1,251 in long-term capital loss.
D. $1,251 in long-term capital gain.

**The answer is A.** The answer is figured as follows: The original basis is increased by the broker's commission. Therefore, Marsha's adjusted basis is $10,145 ($10,110 + $35). The gross proceeds from the sale are $8,859, which is subtracted from the basis, resulting in a long-term capital loss of $1,286 ($10,145 - $8,859).

4. Gianna purchased 200 shares of stock on January 2, 2012 for $1,000. She sold all the shares on December 31, 2012 for $2,500. On January 3, 2013, the stocks were delivered and payment was submitted to Gianna's account. How should this sale be reported?

A. $1,500 long-term gain on her 2012 return.
B. $1,500 short-term gain on her 2012 return.
C. $1,500 long-term gain on her 2013 return.
D. $1,500 short-term gain on her 2013 return.

**The answer is B.** The sale and income must be reported in the year the security is sold, regardless of when the proceeds were received. She held the shares for less than one year, so her gain is short-term. Therefore, Gianna has a short-term gain that must be reported on her 2012 tax return. ###

5. Ruben bought 100 shares of stock on October 1, 2011 when the share price was $26. He then sold them for $20 a share on October 1, 2012. How should this trade be reported, and what is the nature of Ruben's gain or loss?

A. Ruben has a short-term capital loss of $600.
B. Ruben has a long-term capital loss of $500.
C. This is a wash sale.
D. This is a short-term loss of $500.

**The answer is A.** Ruben has a short-term capital loss of $600 = (100 shares X $26) - (100 shares X $20). Ruben's holding period was not more than one year, which means that the loss must be treated as a short-term capital loss. To determine holding period, begin counting on the date *after* the date the taxpayer acquires the property. ###

6. Tahir purchased 100 shares in Foresthill Mutual Fund in April 2012 for $750. He received a capital gain distribution of $120 in 2012. The $120 was reported to him on Form 1099-DIV. How should this be reported on his tax return?

A. Tahir must reduce his stock's basis by $120.
B. Tahir must report the $120 as interest income.
C. Tahir must report the $120 as a long-term capital gain.
D. Tahir must report the $120 as a short-term capital gain.

**The answer is C.** Mutual funds frequently distribute capital gains to shareholders. Capital gain distributions for mutual funds are always taxed at long-term capital gain tax rates, no matter how long a taxpayer has actually held the mutual fund shares. ###

7. Fred bought ten shares of Jixi Corporation stock on October 1, 2011. He sold them for a $7,000 loss on October 1, 2012. He has no other capital gains or losses. He also has $20,000 of wage income. How must Fred treat this transaction on his tax return?

A. Fred may deduct the $7,000 as a long-term capital loss on his 2012 return.
B. Fred may deduct the $7,000 as a short-term capital loss on his 2012 return.
C. Fred may deduct $3,000 as a short-term capital loss to offset his wage income on his 2012 return. The remaining amount, $4,000, must be carried over to future tax years.
D. Fred may not offset any of his wage income, so the entire loss must be carried over to future tax years.

**The answer is C.** Fred has a short-term loss because he did not hold the stock for over one year. He may deduct $3,000 of the loss in 2012, netting against his wage income. The remaining amount, $4,000, must be carried over to future tax years. The carryover retains its character as either long-term or short-term. ###

8. Melissa purchased 1,000 shares of Devil Foods Company stock in 2010 at $10 per share. She sold 900 shares on January 15, 2012 at $9 per share, resulting in a $900 loss. Melissa's husband, Alex, purchased 900 shares on February 10, 2012. Alex and Melissa keep their finances separate and will file MFS in 2012. Which of the following is true?

A. Melissa may deduct the $900 capital loss on her tax return.
B. Melissa has a wash sale and her loss is not deductible.
C. Alex may deduct the loss on his separate tax return.
D. None of the above.

**The answer is B.** The loss is disallowed. Melissa has a wash sale, because her spouse repurchased identical securities within 30 days. It does not matter if they file MFS. If a taxpayer sells stock and her spouse then repurchases identical stock within 30 days, the taxpayer has a wash sale. ###

9. Nikhil's adjusted basis in 500 shares of Edico Corporation was $2,550. If Nikhil sold 500 shares for $3,300, then what is his reported sales price for the shares and the resulting gain or loss?

A. $3,300 sales price and $750 gain.
B. $3,300 sales price and $700 gain.
C. $3,255 sales price and $750 gain.
D. $2,550 sales price and $750 loss.

**The answer is A.** The sales price is $3,300, which is $750 more than the adjusted basis of the shares. ###

10. Kevin paid $1,200 for 100 shares of stock last year. He also paid his broker a $75 fee on the purchase of his stock. A few months later, Kevin sold the stock. His Form 1099-B shows $925 as the gross proceeds from the sale. What is the amount Kevin will report as his sales price?

A. $850.
B. $925.
C. $1,000.
D. $1,275.

**The answer is B.** The sales price of the stock always remains the same. The sales price (or gross proceeds) is never adjusted. The broker's commission is instead added to the stock's basis. ###

11. Dorian purchased 1,000 shares of Hometown Mutual Fund on February 15, 2009 for $15 per share. On January 31, 2012, he sold all his shares for $3.75 per share. He also earned $45,000 in wages in 2012. He has no other transactions during the year. How should this transaction be reported on his tax return?

A. Dorian has a short-term capital loss of $11,250. He will be allowed to offset $11,250 of his wage income with the capital loss.
B. Dorian must carry over the entire loss to a future tax year and offset capital gains.
C. Dorian may take a $3,000 capital loss on his 2012 tax return and the remainder of the losses will carry forward to subsequent years.
D. Dorian may take a $5,000 capital loss on his 2012 tax return and the remainder of the losses will carry forward to subsequent years.

**The answer is C.** Dorian cannot deduct all his stock losses in the current year. Dorian may take a $3,000 capital loss on his 2012 tax return and the remainder of the losses will carry forward to subsequent years. ###

12. Kayla's cost basis was $2,400 for 600 shares of stock she purchased in December 2009 and then sold in September 2012. She sold the 600 shares for $4,400 and paid a $100 broker's commission. Her broker reported the gross proceeds of $4,400 on Form 1099-B. What was the sales price for the shares and the amount and type of capital gain or loss?

A. $4,400 sales price and $2,000 short-term gain.
B. $4,400 sales price and $1,900 long-term gain.
C. $4,500 sales price and $2,100 short-term gain.
D. $4,500 sales price and $1,900 long-term gain.

**The answer is B.** The sales price was $4,400, which was $1,900 more than the adjusted basis of $2,500 ($2,400 cost + $100 commission) of the shares. ###

13. Colin purchased 100 shares of Entertainment Digital Media stock for $1,000 on December 1, 2010. He sold these shares for $750 on December 22, 2011. Colin has seller's remorse, and on January 19, 2012 he repurchases 100 shares of Entertainment stock for $800. Which of the following statements is true?

A. Colin may report his capital losses from the first sale of stock.
B. Colin has a reportable loss in 2011, and a taxable gain in 2012.
C. Colin may not deduct his stock losses and must add the disallowed loss to his basis.
D. Colin may report a $250 capital loss in 2012.

**The answer is C.** Because Colin bought substantially identical stock, he cannot deduct his loss of $250 on the sale. However, he may add the disallowed loss to the cost of the new stock to obtain his adjusted basis in the new stock. This is called the "wash sale rule." ###

14. If taxpayers cannot provide their basis in a property and the property is later sold, the IRS will deem the basis to be _____.

A. Zero.
B. Fair market value.
C. Actual cost.
D. Average cost.

**The answer is A.** In order to compute gain or loss on a sale, taxpayers must provide their basis in the sold property. The basis on property is usually its cost. If taxpayers cannot provide their basis in the property, the IRS will deem the basis to be zero. ###

15. Gerardo has 100 shares of Wild Fishery stock, which he purchased five years ago for $1,500. In May 2012, Wild Fishery issues a nontaxable stock dividend of 50 additional shares. Gerardo sells 60 shares on December 25, 2012. What is his adjusted basis in these 60 shares?

A. $500.
B. $600.
C. $900.
D. $2,250.

**The answer is B.** Gerardo's basis in the original stock was $1,500 for 100 shares, so his original basis per share was $15 ($1,500/100). The addition of 50 shares means Gerardo's basis per share *decreased* to $10 per share ($1,500/150). Therefore, Gerardo's basis in the 60 shares he sold in December is $600 ($10 adjusted basis per share X 60). ###

16. All of the following statements are true about related party transactions except:

A. If a taxpayer controls more than 50% of a corporation or partnership, then any property transactions between the taxpayer and business would be subject to the related party transaction rules.
B. Typically, a loss on the sale of property between related parties is not deductible.
C. The related party transaction rules apply to spouses, siblings and half-siblings, grandchildren, uncles, and aunts.
D. Installment sales are allowed to related parties, but if the property is sold within two years of the original sale, the installment method and its tax benefits will be disallowed.

**The answer is C.** Related party transaction rules do not apply to uncles, aunts, nieces, nephews, cousins, stepchildren, stepparents, and in-laws. ###

17. Oliver operates an electronics repair business as a sole proprietorship. In 2012, Oliver sold property that was acquired for use in the business for $15,000. The purchase price of the property was $12,000, and Oliver had claimed depreciation of $3,000 related to the property. He accepted a down payment of $5,000 from the buyer, along with a note requiring additional payments of $2,500 plus interest in each of the next four years.

Based upon the information provided, what amount of taxable income will result from the installment sale of this property in 2012?

A. Capital gain of $1,000 and ordinary income of $3,000.

B. Capital gain of $5,000 and ordinary income of $1,000.

C. Capital gain of $2,000.

D. Capital gain of $1,000 and ordinary income of $1,000.

**The answer is A.** The amount of depreciation deducted for the property ($3,000) is recaptured and reported in 2012 as ordinary income. This amount is added back to the adjusted basis of $9,000 to determine the adjusted basis for the installment sale ($12,000). This amount is subtracted from the total proceeds of the sale ($15,000) to determine the gross profit of $3,000, which derives a gross profit percentage of 20%. This percentage is applied to the portion of proceeds received in 2012 ($5,000) to determine the amount of capital gain recognizable this year. ###

Supporting calculations:

| | |
|---|---|
| Original purchase price | $12,000 |
| Less depreciation deductions | ($3,000) |
| Adjusted basis at date of sale | $9,000 |
| Depreciation recapture | $3,000 |
| Adjusted basis for installment sale | $12,000 |
| Proceeds of sale | $15,000 |
| Gross profit | $3,000 |
| Gross profit percentage 20% | |
| Proceeds in 2012 | $5,000 |
| Capital gain to be recognized | $1,000 |

# Unit 12: Nonrecognition Property Transactions

| **More Reading:** |
|---|
| **Publication 523, *Selling Your Home*** |
| **Publication 544, *Sales and Other Dispositions of Assets*** |

Nonrecognition property transactions are transactions in which a taxpayer sells or exchanges property without any tax consequences. Some of these transactions are nontaxable, some are tax deferred, and some are considered nontaxable exchanges.

The three most common transactions that result in nonrecognition treatment are:

- Sale of a primary residence (section 121, excluded gain)
- Like-kind exchanges (section 1031 exchange)
- Involuntary conversions (section 1033 exchange)

In some cases, these transactions are partially taxable.

# Sale of Primary Residence (Section 121)

In many cases, a taxpayer may exclude the gain from the sale of a primary residence. Up to $250,000 of gain may be excluded for single filers and up to $500,000 for joint filers. Generally, if the taxpayer can exclude all of the gain, it is not even necessary to report the sale. If all or part of the gain is taxable, then the sale must be reported on Schedule D.

A loss on the sale of a primary residence cannot be deducted.

The section 121 exclusion only applies to a "main home" and not to rental properties, vacation homes, or second homes. A taxpayer's main home is the residence where he lives most of the time. It does not have to be a traditional house. The main home can be a:

- House
- Houseboat
- Mobile home
- Cooperative apartment
- Condominium

In order to qualify as a "home," it must have sleeping, kitchen, and bathroom facilities.

> **Example:** Wayne owns and lives in a house in the city. He also owns a beach house, which he uses only during the summer. The house in the city is his main home; the beach house is not. Wayne sells the beach house and has $100,000 in gain. The gain cannot be excluded, because the beach house is not his primary residence.

# Eligibility Requirements for the Section 121 Exclusion

To be eligible for the exclusion, taxpayers must:

- Have sold the home that has been their main home
- Meet "ownership" and "use" tests
- Not have excluded gain in the two years prior to the current sale of their home

## *The Ownership Test and Use Test*

To meet the *ownership* and *use tests,* during the five-year period ending on the date of the sale the taxpayer must have:

- Owned the home for at least two years (the ownership test), and
- Lived in the home as his main home for at least two years (the use test).

---

**Example:** For the past six years, Lindsay lived with her parents in the home her parents owned. On September 1, 2011, she bought the house from her parents. She continued to live there until December 14, 2012 when she sold it because she wanted a bigger house. Lindsay does not meet the requirements for exclusion. Although she *lived* in the property as her main home for more than two years, she did not *own* it for the required two years. Therefore, she does not meet both the ownership and use tests.

---

The required two years of ownership and use do not have to be continuous. Taxpayers meet the tests if they can show that they owned and lived in the property as their main home for either 24 full months or 730 days (365 x 2) during the five-year period.

---

**Example:** In 2004, Carter lived in a rented apartment. The apartment building was later changed to a condominium, which he bought on December 1, 2009. In 2010, Carter became ill, and on April 14 of that year he moved into his daughter's home. On July 10, 2012, while still living in his daughter's home, Carter sold his condo. He can exclude all the gain on the sale because he meets the ownership and use tests. His five-year period is from July 11, 2007 to July 10, 2012 (the date he sold the condo). He owned the condo from December 1, 2009 to July 10, 2012 (over two years). He lived there from July 11, 2007 (the beginning of the five-year period) to April 14, 2010 (over two years).

---

Ownership and use tests can be met during different two-year periods. However, a taxpayer must meet both tests during the five-year period ending on the date of the sale.

---

**Example:** Irene bought and moved into a house in July 2008. She lived there for 13 months and then moved in with her boyfriend and kept her house vacant. They broke up in January 2011. She moved back into her own house in 2011 and lived there for 12 months until she sold it in July 2012. Irene meets the ownership and use tests because during the five-year period ending on the date of sale, she owned the house for four years and lived in the house for a total of 25 months.

---

Short, temporary absences, even if the property is rented during those absences, are still counted as periods of use. Short absences include vacations and trips. Longer breaks, such as a one-year sabbatical, do not.

> **Example:** Katarina bought her home on February 1, 2009. Each year, she left her home for a four-month summer vacation. Katarina sold the house on March 1, 2012. She may exclude up to $250,000 of gain. The vacations are short temporary absences and are still counted toward her periods of use.

# Married Homeowners

The ownership and use tests are applied somewhat differently to married homeowners. Married homeowners can exclude gain of up to $500,000 if they meet all of the following conditions:

- They file a joint return.
- *Either* spouse must meet the ownership test (only one is required to own the home).
- Both spouses must meet the use test.
- Neither spouse must have excluded gain in the two years before the current sale of the home.

If either spouse does not satisfy all these requirements, the couple cannot claim the maximum $500,000 exclusion.

> **Example:** Leigh sells her main home in June 2012, and she has $350,000 of gain. She marries Kelly in September 2012. Leigh meets the ownership and use tests, but Kelly does not. Leigh can exclude up to $250,000 of gain on her 2012 tax return, whether she files MFJ or MFS. The $500,000 exclusion for joint returns does not apply in this case because Kelly does not meet the use test.

> **Example:** Robert owns a home that he has lived in continuously for eight years. In June 2009, he marries Annabel. She moves in with her husband and they both live in the house until December 1, 2012 when the house is sold. Robert meets the ownership test and the use test. Annabel meets the use test, because only Robert is listed as the owner of the property. On a jointly filed return, they may still claim the maximum $500,000 exclusion because they both meet the use test, and Robert meets the ownership test.

An unmarried couple who own a home and live together may take the $250,000 exclusion individually on their separate returns if they qualify for the use and ownership tests. Sometimes this exclusion also applies to family members who own a home and live together.

> **Example:** Greta and Sydney are twin sisters. They are both widowed and decide to purchase a home and live together. If they were to later sell the home, then the ownership and use tests would apply to them as well. Each sister would be able to claim an exclusion of up to $250,000 for their portion of the sale on their individual returns.

## Deceased Spouses and Home Sales

There are special rules regarding the section 121 gain when a taxpayer's spouse dies. A taxpayer is considered to have owned and lived in a home during any period of time when the spouse owned and lived in it as a main home (provided that the taxpayer did not remarry before the date of sale). In effect, the holding period is "tacked on" for surviving spouses.

An unmarried surviving spouse may exclude up to $500,000 of gain if he or she sells the home within two years of the spouse's death.

> **Example:** Alice has owned and lived in her home for the last seven years. She marries William in April 2012, and he moves into the home with her. Alice dies six months later, and William inherits the property. He does not remarry. William sells the home on December 1, 2012. Even though William did not own or live in the house for two years, he meets the test requirements because his period of ownership and use includes the period that Alice owned and used the property before her death. William may qualify to exclude up to $500,000 of the gain because of the special rule that applies to surviving spouses.

This exclusion also applies to a home that is transferred by a spouse if the transfer is part of a divorce. In the case of a divorce, the receiving spouse is considered to have owned the home during any period of time that the transferor owned it.

### Five-Year Test Period Suspension for Military Personnel

Taxpayers can choose to have the five-year test period for ownership and use suspended during any period the homeowner (or spouse if married) served on "qualified official extended duty" as a member of the armed services or Foreign Service of the United States, as an employee of the intelligence community, or as a member of the Peace Corps. This means that the taxpayer may be able to meet the two-year use test even if he and/or his spouse did not actually live in the home during the normal five-year period required of other taxpayers.

Taxpayers qualify if they serve at a duty station at least 50 miles from their main home or live in government quarters under government order. Taxpayers are considered to be on extended duty when they are called to active duty for more than 90 days or for an indefinite period.

> **Example**: Luis bought a home in 2001 and lived in it for two-and-a-half years. Beginning in 2005, he was on qualified official extended duty in the U.S. Army, and left the home vacant. He sold his home in 2012 and had a $12,000 gain. Luis would not normally meet the use test in the five-year period before the sale. However, he can disregard those six years, because of the special exclusion for military taxpayers.

This extension of time can also apply to taxpayers who have recently left the military.

### Exception to the "Use Test" for the Disabled

There is an exception to the use test if, during the five-year period before the sale of the home, the taxpayer becomes physically or mentally unable to care for himself. The taxpayer must have owned and lived in the home for at least one year.

Under this exception, the taxpayer is still considered to have lived in the home during any time that he is forced to live in a medical facility, including a nursing home, because of medical reasons.

# Qualifying for a Reduced Exclusion

Taxpayers who owned and used a home for less than two years (meaning they do not meet the ownership and use tests) may be able to claim a reduced exclusion under certain conditions. These include selling the home due to a change in place of employment, health, or unforeseen circumstances.

## Unforeseen Circumstances

The IRS will accept that a home sale has occurred primarily because of unforeseen circumstances if any of the following events occur during the taxpayer's period of use and ownership of the residence:

- Death or divorce.
- Health reasons (for a spouse, child, or other related person, such as a father, sibling, etc. The related person does not have to be a dependent in order for the special circumstances to qualify for the exclusion.)
- Unemployment or a job change. (The "job related" exclusion qualifies if the new job is at least 50 miles farther than the old home was from the former place of employment. If there was no former place of employment, the distance between the new place of employment and the old home must be at least 50 miles.)
- Multiple births resulting from the same pregnancy.
- Damage to the residence resulting from a disaster, or an act of war or terrorism.
- Involuntary conversion of the property.

The circumstances may involve the taxpayer, his spouse, a co-owner, or a member of the taxpayer's household. The regulations also give the IRS the discretion to determine other circumstances as unforeseen. For example, the IRS Commissioner determined that the September 11, 2001 terrorist attacks were an "unforeseen circumstance."

---

**Example:** Justin purchased his new home in Mississippi in June 2011, but shortly after he moved in he lost his job. He found a new job in North Carolina and sold his house in April 2012. Because the distance between Justin's new place of employment and his former home is at least 50 miles, the sale satisfies the conditions of the distance safe harbor. Justin's sale of his home is due to a change in place of employment, and he is entitled to claim a reduced exclusion of gain from the sale.

---

# How to Figure the Reduced Exclusion

The reduced exclusion amount equals the full $250,000 or $500,000 (for married couples filing jointly) multiplied by a fraction. The numerator is the shorter of:

- The period of ownership that the taxpayer owned and used the home as a principal residence during the five-year period ending on the sale date, or
- The period between the last sale for which the taxpayer claimed the exclusion and the sale date for the home currently being sold.

The denominator is two years, or the equivalent in months or days. The amount of the reduced exclusion is figured by determining the number of days the taxpayer actually owned and used the property, divided by either 730 days (two years) or 24 months (two years).

---

**Example:** Carrie purchases her home on January 1, 2012 for $350,000. Her mother is diagnosed with terminal cancer, and Carrie must move to care for her. Even though Carrie does not claim her mother as a dependent, the move still qualifies as an unforeseen circumstance. Carrie sells her home on May 1, 2012 for $430,000, realizing a gain of $80,000. She qualifies for the reduced maximum exclusion, and part of her gain is nontaxable. She owned and occupied the home for 121 days (January 1 to May 1). She may exclude $41,438 ($250,000 X [121 ÷ 730]). Therefore, Carrie's taxable gain is $38,562 ($80,000 - $41,438). This amount would be a short-term capital gain since she owned the house for less than one year.

---

**Example:** Sabrina, a single taxpayer, lived in her principal residence for one full year (365 days) before selling it at a $400,000 gain in 2012. She qualifies for the reduced exclusion because she is pregnant with triplets (multiple births exclusion). Sabrina can exclude $125,000 of gain ($250,000 X [365 ÷ 730]).

---

# Land Sale Only and Adjacent Lots

If a taxpayer sells the land on which his main home is located but not the house itself, he cannot exclude the gain. Similarly, the sale of a vacant plot of land with no house on it does not qualify for the Section 121 exclusion.

---

**Example:** Theresa purchases an empty lot in 2008 for $90,000, intending to build her dream home. The construction was delayed and her house was never completed. In December 2012, Theresa sells the land for $150,000. She owned the property for more than a year, so she has $60,000 of long-term capital gain. None of the gain can be excluded from income, because there is no residence on the property.

---

If a taxpayer sells a vacant lot that is *adjacent to his main home*, he may be able to exclude the gain from the sale under certain circumstances. Gain from the sale of vacant land that was used as part of the principal residence may be excluded if the land sale occurs within two years before or after the sale of the home.

The sale of the land and the sale of the home are treated as one sale for purposes of the exclusion.

# Figuring the Gain or Loss on a Home Sale

The following are used to figure the gain or loss on the sale of a home:

- Selling price
- Amount realized
- Basis
- Adjusted basis

**Selling Price:** The selling price is the total amount the taxpayer received for his main home. It includes money, all notes, mortgages, or other debts taken over by the buyer as part of the sale, and the fair market value of any other property or services that the seller received. Real estate sales proceeds are reported on Form 1099-S, *Proceeds From Real Estate Transactions*. If a taxpayer does not receive a Form 1099-S, he must figure basis by using sale documents and other records.

**Amount Realized:** The amount realized is the selling price minus selling expenses, which include commissions, advertising fees, legal fees, and loan charges paid by the seller, such as points.

**Basis:** The basis in a home is determined by how the taxpayer *obtained* the home. For example, if a taxpayer purchases a home, the basis is the cost of the home. If a taxpayer builds a home, then the basis is the building cost plus the cost of land. If a taxpayer receives a home through an inheritance or gift, the basis is either its FMV or the adjusted basis of the home.

**Example:** Eve is single. She sells her home for $350,000 in 2012. She purchased the home twenty years ago for $50,000 and has lived in it continuously since then. She pays $4,000 in seller's fees to sell the home. Her amount realized in the sale is $346,000 ($350,000 - $4,000 = $346,000). Her basis is subtracted from her amount realized in order to figure her gain: ($346,000 - $50,000 basis) = $296,000. Eve's gain is $296,000, but she qualifies for a section 121 exclusion because she meets the ownership and use tests. Therefore, she may exclude up to $250,000 of her gain from tax. Her taxable gain is figured as follows: ($296,000 gain - $250,000 section 121 exclusion) = $46,000 in long-term capital gain. If the selling price or amount realized is $250,000 or less ($500,000 or less if filing jointly), there is no need to figure the realized gain, assuming the ownership and use tests are met.

If the taxpayer inherited the home, the basis is its FMV on the date of the decedent's death, or the later alternate valuation date chosen by the representative for the estate.

**Adjusted Basis:** The *adjusted basis* is the taxpayer's basis in the home increased or decreased by certain amounts. Increases include additions or improvements to the home. In order to be considered a basis *increase*, an addition or improvement must have a useful life of more than one year (example: putting on a new roof or an additional bedroom). Repairs that simply maintain a home in good condition are not considered improvements and should not be added to the basis of the property. Decreases to basis include deductible casualty losses, credits, and product rebates.

**Formula for figuring adjusted basis:**

**Basis + Increases - Decreases = Adjusted Basis**

**Example:** Immanuel purchased his home years ago for $125,000. In 2012, Immanuel added another bedroom to the property. The cost of the addition was $25,000. This *increased* the house's basis. Immanuel's adjusted basis is therefore $150,000.

If the *amount realized* is more than the adjusted basis of the property, the difference is a gain, and the taxpayer may be able to exclude all or part of it. If the amount realized is less than the adjusted basis, the difference is a nondeductible loss.

**Example:** Pete sold his main home for $275,000. His selling expenses were $10,000. The amount realized on Pete's sale is $265,000 (selling price minus selling expenses). He purchased his home ten years ago for $180,000. Therefore, his gain on the sale of the house is $85,000 ($265,000 - $180,000). If Pete meets the ownership and use tests, he can exclude all the gain from the sale of his home, and the sale does not have to be reported on his tax return.

Proceeds from the sale of a main home that meets the ownership and use tests must be reported *only* if the taxpayer has a gain on the sale that is not fully covered by the exclusion. Gain from the sale of a home that is not the taxpayer's main home will generally have to be reported as income.

In both cases, the nonexcludable gain is taxable gain and must be reported on Schedule D. If the home was used for business purposes or as rental property, the gain is reported on Form 4797, *Sales of Business Property*.

If the taxpayer owns a home for one year or less, the gain is reported as a short-term capital gain. If the taxpayer owns the home for more than one year, the gain is reported as a long-term capital gain.

The fees and costs for obtaining a mortgage are not deductible and cannot be included in a home's basis. These costs include items such as termite inspections or title fees that would be required regardless of whether a taxpayer was financing the purchase. Points may be deducted as mortgage interest on Schedule A. The IRS defines points as prepaid interest paid by a home buyer at closing in order to obtain a mortgage or a lower interest rate.

If a taxpayer took depreciation deductions because he used his home as a rental or for other business purposes, he cannot exclude the part of the gain equal to any deductible depreciation. Section 121 applies only to the *nonbusiness* portion of a home.

---

**Example:** Erica lives in one side of a duplex she owns and rents out the other side. Both units are the same size. She purchased the duplex in 2004 for $200,000. In 2012, Erica sells the duplex for $340,000 for a total gain of $140,000. Since only half of the duplex counts as her primary residence, she would have to split the gain based on the portion of the property that qualifies as her main home. Under section 121, Erica may exclude one half of the gain ($70,000). The other $70,000 is long-term capital gain that she has to report. Erica also has the option to reinvest the proceeds from her rental property sale into a new property by executing a section 1031 exchange.

---

# Like-Kind Exchanges (Section 1031 exchange)

A section 1031 "like-kind" exchange occurs when similar business property is exchanged. If a taxpayer trades business or investment property for similar property, he does not have to pay tax on the gain or deduct any loss until he disposes of the property he received. To qualify for nonrecognition treatment, the exchange must meet all of the following conditions:

- The property must be business or investment property. A personal residence does not qualify.
- The property must not be "held primarily for sale" (such as inventory).
- Securities such as stocks and bonds do not qualify for like-kind exchange treatment.

353

- Partnership interests do not qualify for like-kind exchange treatment.
- There must be an *actual exchange* of property (the exchange for cash is treated as a sale, not an exchange).
- The property to be received must be identified in writing within 45 days after the date of transfer of the property given up.

The replacement property must be received by the earlier of:

- The 180th day after the date on which the original property was given up in the trade, or
- The due date, including extensions, for the tax return for the year in which the transfer of the property relinquished occurs.

Taxpayers report like-kind exchanges to the IRS on Form 8824, *Like-Kind Exchanges*.

# Rules Regarding Acceptable Like-Kind Exchanges

To qualify as a section 1031 exchange, the property must be "like-kind" property, such as the trade of real estate for real estate or personal property for personal property.

Real properties are generally acceptable as like-kind exchanges regardless of whether the properties are improved or unimproved. For instance, the exchange of a store building for farmland would be an acceptable trade.

The property also must be the same "class" of property. For example, the exchanges of an apartment building for an office building and a panel truck for a pickup truck qualify as trades of "like" property. However, the exchange of a semi-truck for a plot of land would not qualify as a section 1031 exchange, even if both properties were business properties.

> **Example:** Casey exchanges a private jet with an adjusted basis of $400,000 for an office building valued at $375,000. Private property (the jet) cannot be exchanged with real property (the building). Casey would not qualify for section 1031 treatment.

The trade of a piece of factory machinery for a factory building is not a qualifying exchange; nor is the trade of equipment or business property that is used within the United States with that used outside the United States, as the two are not considered "like" property.

Under the same rule, real estate located *inside* the United States and real estate located *outside* the United States is not "like property" and does not qualify for section 1031 treatment.

A taxpayer cannot deduct a loss in a section 1031 transaction.

# Unacceptable and Disallowed Trades

The following types of property will not qualify for section 1031 treatment:

- Livestock of different sexes
- Securities, bonds, stocks, or notes
- Currency exchanges
- The exchange of partnership interests

# What is "Boot"?

Although the Internal Revenue Code itself does not use the term "boot," the term is frequently used to describe property that is not "like-kind" property. The receipt of "boot" will cause a realized gain on an otherwise nontaxable exchange.

Usually this occurs when two people exchange property that is unequal in value, so one party pays cash, or "boot," to make up the difference.

The exchange is still valid, but the taxpayer who receives boot may have to recognize a taxable gain. Boot received can be offset by qualified costs paid during the transaction.

> **Example:** Sloan wishes to exchange his rental property in a 1031 exchange. His relinquished rental property has an FMV of $60,000 and an adjusted basis of $30,000. Sloan's replacement property has an FMV of $50,000, and he also receives $10,000 in cash as part of the exchange. Sloan, therefore, has a realized gain of $30,000 on the actual exchange, but he is required to pay tax on only $10,000—the cash (boot) received in the exchange. The rest of his gain is deferred until he sells or disposes of the property at a later date.

The fair market value of the boot is recognized as taxable gain.

Sometimes boot is recognized when two people exchange property that is subject to a liability. Liabilities on property are "netted" against each other. The taxpayer is treated as having received boot only if he is relieved of a greater liability than the liability he assumes.

This is also called "debt reduction boot," and it occurs when a taxpayer's debt on the replacement property is less than the debt on the relinquished property. "Debt reduction boot" most often occurs when a taxpayer is acquiring a less valuable or expensive property.

# Basis of Property Received in a Like-Kind Exchange

The basis of the property received is generally the adjusted basis of the property transferred.

> **Example:** Judy has a rental house with an adjusted basis of $70,000. In 2012, she trades the rental house for an empty lot with an FMV of $150,000. Judy's basis in the lot is $70,000, which is the adjusted basis of her previous property.

**Example:** Adrian exchanges rental real estate (adjusted basis $50,000, FMV $80,000) for another rental property (FMV $80,000). No cash was exchanged in the transaction. Adrian's basis in the new property is the same as the basis of his old property ($50,000). Basis is increased by any amount that is treated as a dividend, plus any gain recognized on the trade. Basis is decreased by any cash received and the FMV of any other (additional) property received.

**Example:** Peyton bought a new diesel truck for use in her catering business. She paid $43,000 cash, plus she traded in her old truck for $13,600. The old truck cost $50,000 two years ago. Peyton took depreciation deductions of $39,500 on the old vehicle. Even though she deducted depreciation of $39,500, the $3,100 gain on the exchange ($13,600 trade-in allowance minus her $10,500 adjusted basis) is not reported because the gain is postponed under the rules for like-kind exchanges.

The basis of any other or additional property received is its fair market value on the date of the trade. The taxpayer is taxed on any gain realized, but only up to the amount of the money and the fair market value of the "unlike" (or boot) nonqualified property received.

## Property Plus Cash

If a taxpayer trades property and also pays money for it, the basis of the property received is the basis of the property given up, increased by any additional money paid.

**Example:** Jorge trades a plot of land (adjusted basis $30,000) for a different plot of land in another town (FMV $70,500). He also pays an additional $4,000 in cash. Jorge's basis in the new land is $34,000: his $30,000 basis in the old land plus the $4,000 additional money he paid.

## Section 1031 Exchanges Between Related Parties

Like-kind exchanges are allowed between related parties and family members. However, if *either* party disposes or sells the property within two years after a 1031 exchange, the exchange is usually disqualified; any gain or loss that was deferred in the original transaction must be recognized in the year the disposition occurs.

For purposes of this rule, a "related person" includes close family members (spouses, siblings, parents, and children). There are some exceptions to this two-year rule:

- If one of the parties originally involved in the exchange dies, the two-year rule does not apply.
- If the property is subsequently converted in an involuntary exchange (such as a fire or a flood), the two-year rule does not apply.
- If the exchange is genuinely not for tax avoidance purposes, the subsequent disposition will generally be allowed.

Exchanges between related parties get close scrutiny by the IRS because they are often used by taxpayers to evade taxes on gains.

# Involuntary Conversions (Section 1033)

An involuntary conversion occurs when a taxpayer's property is damaged, destroyed, or condemned, and the taxpayer then receives an award, insurance money, or some other type of payment. The property must be converted, beyond the taxpayer's control, as a result of:

- Theft, destruction, or other disaster,
- Condemnation, or
- Threat of condemnation.

Gain or loss from an involuntary conversion of property is usually recognized for tax purposes unless the property is a main home. A taxpayer reports the gain or deducts the loss in the year the gain or loss is realized. A taxpayer cannot deduct a loss from an involuntary conversion on personal-use property unless the loss resulted from a casualty or theft.

However, under section 1033, a taxpayer can avoid reporting gain on an involuntary conversion by receiving or investing in property that is similar to the converted property. If insurance proceeds or some other source produces a gain on the exchange, tax can be deferred by reinvesting the proceeds in property similar to the property that was subject to the involuntary conversion.

**Example:** Denise owns a residential rental with an adjusted basis of $50,000. It is destroyed by a hurricane in 2012. Her property is insured, so the insurance company gives Denise a check for $100,000, which is the FMV of the home. Denise buys a replacement rental property six months later for $100,000. Her realized gain on the involuntary conversion is $50,000 ($100,000 insurance settlement minus her $50,000 basis). However, Denise does not have to recognize any taxable gain because she reinvested all the insurance proceeds in another, similar property. This is an example of a qualified 1033 exchange.

## The Replacement Period

The replacement period for an involuntary conversion generally ends two years after the end of the first tax year in which any part of the gain is realized.

**Example:** Barney owns a dog grooming business. On September 1, 2012, a flood destroys a storage shed filled with his grooming supplies. Barney's insurance company reimburses him for the entire loss. Barney has until December 31, 2014 to replace the shed and supplies using the insurance proceeds. Barney is not required to report the insurance proceeds on his 2012 tax return. So long as Barney reinvests all the insurance proceeds in the replacement property, he will not have any gain.

Real property that is held for investment or used in a trade or business is allowed a three-year replacement period. The replacement period is four years for livestock that is involuntarily converted because of weather-related conditions.

If a main home is damaged or destroyed and is in a federally-declared disaster area, the replacement period is extended to four years. Certain other extreme disaster areas, including Hurricane Katrina, the May 2007 Kansas storms and tornadoes, and the Midwestern area disasters of 2008, have a five-year replacement period, but only if the replacement property is purchased in the same area.

| Property type | Replacement period |
|---|---|
| Most property except those noted below. | Two years |
| Real property that is held for investment or business use. This includes residential rentals, office buildings, etc. | Three years |
| Sale of livestock due to weather-related conditions. | Four years |
| Property in federally-declared disaster area | Four to five years |

If a taxpayer reinvests in replacement property similar to the converted property, the replacement property's basis is the same as the converted property's basis on the date of the conversion. The taxpayer will have a carryover basis in the new property. Essentially, the taxpayer's basis in the new property will be its cost, reduced by any gain realized on the old property that was not recognized.

The basis may be *decreased* by the following:

- Any loss a taxpayer recognizes on the involuntary conversion
- Any money a taxpayer receives that he does not spend on similar property

The basis is *increased* by the following:

- Any gain a taxpayer recognizes on the involuntary conversion
- Any cost of acquiring the replacement property

**Example:** Paula paid $100,000 for a rental property five years ago. After factoring in her depreciation deductions, her adjusted basis in the property is $75,000 at the beginning of 2012. The property is insured for $300,000 and is destroyed by fire in June 2012. On December 15, 2012, Paula receives a $300,000 payment from her insurance company. She reinvests all the insurance proceeds, plus $5,000 more of her own savings, into a new rental apartment building. She qualifies to defer all of her gain. Her basis in the new rental property is $80,000 ($75,000 + $5,000 of her additional investment).

> **Example:** Franco owns an apartment building in Oklahoma with a basis of $250,000. Franco receives an insurance settlement of $400,000 after the building is destroyed by a tornado. A year later, Franco decides to purchase another apartment building in Wisconsin for $380,000. Franco's realized gain on the involuntary conversion is $150,000 ($400,000 - $250,000 basis). Franco must recognize $20,000 of gain, because he received an insurance payment of $400,000, but only spent $380,000 on the replacement property ($400,000 - $380,000). His basis in the new property is $250,000, which is calculated as the cost of the new property in Wisconsin minus the deferred gain ($380,000 - $130,000 = $250,000). If Franco had used all the insurance proceeds and invested it in the new property, he would not have to report any taxable gain.

## Condemnations

A condemnation is a type of involuntary conversion. Condemnation is the process by which private property is seized from its original owner for public use. The property may be taken by the government or by a private organization that has the legal power to seize it.

The owner generally receives a condemnation award (money or property) in exchange for the property that is taken. A condemnation is like a forced sale, the owner being the seller and the government being the buyer.

> **Example:** The federal government informs Trevor that his farmland is being condemned to make it into a public park. Trevor goes to court to try to keep his property. The court decides in favor of the government, which takes Trevor's property and pays him $400,000 in exchange. Trevor's basis in the farmland was $80,000. He decides not to purchase replacement farmland. Therefore, he has a taxable event, and $320,000 would need to be recognized as income ($400,000 - $80,000 = $320,000). If Trevor were to purchase replacement property with the condemnation award, he would have a nontaxable section 1033 exchange.

A condemnation award is the money that is paid for the condemned property. Amounts taken out of the award to pay debts on the property are considered paid to the taxpayer and are included in the amount of the award.

> **Example:** The state condemned Gabriel's property in order to build a light rail system. The court award was set at $200,000. The state paid Gabriel only $148,000 because it paid $50,000 to his mortgage company and $2,000 in accrued real estate taxes. Gabriel is considered to have received the entire $200,000 as a condemnation award.

The time period for replacing condemned property is the same as other qualified section 1033 exchanges—two years after the end of the first tax year in which any part of the gain on the condemnation is realized. For business-use property, the replacement period is three years instead of two.

**Example:** Joel owns a pool hall. In February 2012, the building is condemned by the city because of the discovery of asbestos in the building. He receives his condemnation award in May 2012. He has until December 31, 2015 to replace the condemned pool hall with a similar building.

## *Condemnation of a Primary Residence*

If a taxpayer has a gain because his main home is condemned, he can generally exclude the gain as if he had sold the home under the section 121 exclusion. Single filers can exclude up to $250,000 of the gain and joint filers up to $500,000.

**Example:** Lane and Candace are married and file jointly. They paid $100,000 for their home ten years ago. The house is insured for $700,000. Their home is destroyed by a mudslide in 2012, so they receive an insurance payment of $700,000. They have a realized gain on the conversion of $600,000 ($700,000 - $100,000). But $500,000 of the gain is excluded under section 121, leaving $100,000 as taxable long-term capital gain. They may also choose to reinvest the insurance proceeds under the rules for involuntary conversions and defer all the gain.

# Summary:
# Nonrecognition Property Transactions

### Section 121: Sale of Primary Residence

To be eligible for the exclusion, taxpayers must meet the following conditions during the five-year period ending on the date of the sale:

- The home sold had to be their main home where they lived most of the time.
- They had to own the home for at least two years (the ownership test)
- They had to live in the home as their principal residence for at least two years (the use test)
- They must not have excluded gain in the two years before the current sale of the home

The required two years of ownership/use do not have to be continuous. The maximum that can be excluded is $250,000 or $500,000 for MFJ.

### Section 1031: Like-Kind Exchanges

Section 1031 exchanges only apply to business properties such as real estate, but not to exchanges of inventory, stocks, bonds, or partnership interests. Livestock of different sexes does not qualify as "like kind" property; nor does property used in the United States and property used outside the United States.

The property to be received must be identified within 45 days after the date of transfer of the property given up. The replacement property must be received by the earlier of:

- The 180th day after the date on which the original property was given up in the trade, or
- The due date, including extensions, for the tax return for the year in which the transfer of the property relinquished occurs.

## Section 1033: Involuntary Conversions

An involuntary conversion occurs when a taxpayer's property is destroyed, stolen, condemned, or disposed of under the threat of condemnation, and the taxpayer receives property or money in payment, such as insurance or a condemnation award.

The gain on an involuntary conversion can be deferred if insurance or condemnation proceeds are reinvested in another property. The taxpayer's basis in the new property is its cost, reduced by any gain realized on the old property that was not recognized.

# Unit 12: Questions

1. Erik sold his home for $275,000. His selling expenses were $10,000. What is the amount realized on this sale?

A. $265,000.
B. $275,000.
C. $285,000.
D. Some other amount.

**The answer is A.** The amount realized on Erik's sale is $265,000, the selling price minus selling expenses. ###

2. Isaiah lived in and owned his home for fifteen months. In 2012, he decides to move in with his new girlfriend, so he sells his home for $285,000. His adjusted basis in the home is $160,000. What is the amount and nature of his taxable gain on the sale?

A. $0 (the gain is excluded under section 121).
B. $160,000 short-term capital gain.
C. $125,000 long-term capital gain.
D. $125,000 short-term capital gain.

**The answer is C.** Since he does not meet the ownership or use tests, he cannot exclude any of his gain under section 121. The correct answer is $125,000, which is the result of subtracting the adjusted basis in the home from the amount realized ($285,000- $160,000 = $125,000). Since he owned the property for more than a year, his gain is taxed as a long-term capital gain. ###

3. Ariana bought her principal residence for $250,000 on May 3, 2011. She sold it on May 3, 2012 for $400,000 because she wanted to move to Hawaii. What is the amount and character of her gain?

A. Long-term ordinary gain of $650,000.
B. Long-term capital gain of $150,000.
C. Short-term ordinary gain of $250,000.
D. Short-term capital gain of $150,000.

**The answer is D.** Ariana owned the home for one year or less, so the gain is reported as a short-term capital gain. She must start counting her holding period after the date of purchase. ###

4. Lucille owns a home in the Vail ski area (the "ski home"). She stays at the ski home most weekends and spends the entire months of December, January, and February there. When she is not at the ski home, she lives in a four-room apartment that she rents in Denver. For over half the year, she lives in Denver. What is Lucille's primary residence for purposes of the section 121 exclusion?

A. Her ski home in Vail.
B. Her apartment in Denver.
C. She is considered a transient for tax purposes.
D. None of the above.

**The answer is B.** Lucille's main home is her rental apartment in Denver because she lives there most of the time. If she were to sell the ski home, she would not qualify for the section 121 exclusion on the sale because it is a vacation home and not her primary residence. ###

5. Heather, a single woman, bought her first home in June 2002 for $350,000. She lived continuously in the house until she sold it in July 2012 for $620,000. Which of the following is true?

A. Heather may exclude up to $250,000 in gain. The remaining amount must be reported and will be taxed as a long-term capital gain.
B. Heather may exclude all the gain. There is no amount that needs to be reported.
C. Heather may not exclude any of the gain.
D. Heather may exclude $250,000 in gain. The remaining amount must be reported as a short-term capital gain.

**The answer is A.** Heather may exclude the maximum amount of gain ($250,000) from the sale of her home. Her gain is $270,000 ($620,000 - $350,000). Her taxable gain is $20,000 ($270,000 gain - $250,000 exclusion). The $20,000 taxable gain must be reported as a long-term capital gain. ###

6. Mitchell purchased his primary residence for $350,000 on January 1, 2009. On January 3, 2012, he sells the home for $320,000, incurring a loss of $30,000. How is this transaction reported?

A. Mitchell has a short-term capital loss that can be reported on Schedule D.
B. Mitchell cannot deduct any loss from the sale of his home.
C. Mitchell has a long-term capital loss that can be reported on Schedule D.
D. Mitchell has a deductible casualty loss.

**The answer is B.** If a taxpayer has a loss on the sale of a primary residence, he cannot deduct it on his return. Losses from the sale of a main home are never tax-deductible. ###

7. All of the following would generally be acceptable as "unforeseen circumstances" for a taxpayer to take a reduced exclusion on the sale of his primary residence except _____:

A. The home is condemned by the city.
B. A legal separation.
C. The birth of twin girls.
D. Moving to another state to be closer to grown children.

**The answer is D.** The move to be closer to grown children would not qualify. All of the following events would be qualifying events in order to claim a reduced exclusion from a premature sale:

• A divorce or legal separation.
• A pregnancy resulting in multiple births.
• Serious health reasons. (The person who is sick does not need to be the taxpayer's dependent).
• The home is sold after being seized or condemned (such as by a government agency).
• A move due to a new job or new employment.

If any of these exceptions apply, the taxpayer may figure a reduced exclusion based on the number of days he owned and lived in the residence. ###

8. Geoff sold his main home in 2012 at a $29,000 gain. He meets the ownership and use tests to exclude the gain from his income. However, he used one room of the home for business in 2010 and 2011. His records show he claimed $3,000 in depreciation for a home office. What is Geoff's taxable gain on the sale, if any?

A. $0.
B. $1,000.
C. $2,000.
D. $3,000.

**The answer is D.** Geoff can exclude $26,000 ($29,000 - $3,000) of his gain. He has a taxable gain of $3,000. He must report the gain from depreciation recapture. If a taxpayer took depreciation deductions because he used his home for business purposes or as a rental property, he cannot exclude the part of the gain equal to any depreciation allowed as a deduction. ###

9. Bob and Grace were married in January 2008. They purchased their first home in March 2008 for $150,000. In February 2012, Bob and Grace legally separated, and the court granted Grace total ownership of the home as part of the divorce settlement. The divorce became final in June 2012, and the fair market value of the home at the time of the transfer was $370,000. Grace sells the house on December 23, 2012 for $480,000. What is Grace's taxable gain in the transaction?

A. $0.
B. $80,000.
C. $120,000.
D. $210,000.

**The answer is B.** Special rules apply to divorced taxpayers. Grace meets the ownership and use tests, and the basis in the property remains the same. Transfers related to a divorce are generally nontaxable, and the fair market value of the property at the time of the divorce has no bearing on the taxable outcome. The gain is figured as follows:

| Original cost | $150,000 |
|---|---|
| Sale price | $480,000 |
| Total realized gain | $330,000 |
| Sec. 121 exclusion | ($250,000) |
| Taxable gain | $80,000 |

Since she owned the property for longer than one year, the taxable portion of Grace's gain would be reported as a long-term capital gain. ###

10. Alfred and Kay are married and file jointly. They owned and used a home as their principal residence for 15 months. Alfred got a new job in another state and they sold their home in order to move for the new employment opportunity. What is the maximum amount that can be excluded from income under the rules regarding a reduced exclusion?

A. $22,727.
B. $250,000.
C. $312,500.
E. $500,000.

**The answer is C**. In this case, a reduced exclusion is available, even though the taxpayers did not live in the home for two full years. They qualify for a reduced exclusion because Alfred is moving for a change in employment. In this case, their maximum reduced exclusion is $312,500 [$500,000 x (15 months/24 months)]. The reduced exclusion applies when the premature sale is primarily due to a move for employment in a new location. ###

11. Shane and Phyllis move after living in their home for 292 days, because Phyllis became pregnant with triplets and they needed a larger home. The gain on the sale of the home is $260,000. Since they have lived there for less than two years but meet one of the exceptions, what is the actual amount of their reduced exclusion? (Two years=730 days)

A. $60,000.
B. $200,000.
C. $260,000.
D. $500,000.

**The answer is B.** The couple has an exclusion of $200,000 (292/730 multiplied by the $500,000 exclusion available for married taxpayers). The remaining $60,000 would be considered taxable capital gain income and would be reported on Schedule D. This move qualifies for the reduced exclusion, because multiple births from the same pregnancy are considered a health-related move. ###

12. Regina bought a house for $189,000 in July 2008. She lived there continuously for 13 months and then moved in with her boyfriend. They later separated, and Regina moved back into her own house in 2011 and lived there for 12 months until she sold it in July 2012 for $220,000. What is the amount and nature of her gain?

A. Regina has no taxable gain, because the sale qualifies for a section 121 exclusion.
B. $31,000 long-term capital gain.
C. $31,000 short-term capital gain.
D. $30,000 long-term capital gain.

**The answer is A.** This sale qualifies for section 121 treatment. Regina meets the ownership and use tests because during the five-year period ending on the date of sale, she owned the house for four years and lived in it for a total of 25 months. The gain is not taxable and does not need to be reported. ###

13. Jonah exchanged a rental building for another rental building. He had a basis of $16,000, plus he had made $10,000 in improvements prior to the exchange. He exchanged it for a building worth $36,000. Jonah did not recognize any gain from the exchange on his individual tax return. What is his basis in the new property?

A. $26,000.
B. $36,000.
C. $10,000.
D. $16,000.

**The answer is A.** The basis in the new building is the same as his basis in the old building, which was $16,000. The $10,000 in improvements is added to the $16,000, so the adjusted basis is $26,000. ###

14. Which of the following transactions do not qualify for a section 1031 like-kind exchange?

A. An exchange of a boutique in Manhattan for acres of farmland.
B. An exchange of an apartment building in New Mexico for an office building in Alaska.
C. An exchange of a business desk for a business printer.
D. An exchange of inventory for different inventory.

**The answer is D.** Inventory never qualifies for like-kind exchange treatment. The property must not be held "primarily for sale," such as merchandise, retail stock, or inventory. Generally, real property exchanges will qualify for like-kind treatment, even though the properties themselves might be dissimilar. ###

15. Allen is a flight instructor. He trades in a small plane (adjusted basis $300,000) for another, larger plane (FMV $750,000) and pays $60,000 in an additional down payment. He uses the plane 100% in his flight instruction business. What is his basis in the new plane?

A. $300,000.
B. $360,000.
C. $690,000.
D. $750,000.

**The answer is B.** Allen's basis is $360,000: the $300,000 basis of the old plane plus the $60,000 cash paid. The fair market value of the property has no bearing on Allen's basis in the new property. ###

16. Bailey exchanges his residential rental property (adjusted basis $50,000, FMV $80,000) for a different rental property (FMV $70,000). What is Bailey's basis in the new property?

A. $50,000.
B. $70,000.
C. $80,000.
D. $100,000.

**The answer is A.** His basis in the new property is the same as the basis of the old ($50,000). The basis of the property received is the same as the basis of the property given up. ###

17. Katherine owns a yacht that she uses for personal use. Her purchase price was $150,000. The yacht is destroyed in a storm in 2012. Katherine collects $175,000 from her insurance company and promptly reinvests all the proceeds in a larger, new yacht, which costs her $201,000. What is her basis in the new yacht?

A. $175,000.
B. $176,000.
C. $201,000.
D. $226,000.

**The answer is B.** The answer is figured as follows: ($175,000-$150,000) = $25,000: deferred gain; ($201,000-$25,000) = $176,000: new basis in the asset. Since Katherine purchased replacement property, the basis of the replacement property is the cost of the new yacht ($201,000) minus her deferred gain ($25,000). ###

18. A tornado destroyed Bryant's primary residence home on July 15, 2010. He wants to replace the home using a section 1033 exchange for involuntary conversions. What is the latest year that Bryant can replace the property in order to defer any gain from the insurance reimbursement?

A. Bryant must make the election by December 31, 2012.
B. Bryant must make the election by July 15, 2013.
C. Bryant must make the election by July 15, 2012.
D. Bryant must make the election by December 31, 2014.

**The answer is A.** Bryant must acquire qualifying replacement property by December 31, 2012 (two years from the end of the gain year) in order for the involuntary conversion to be a qualified section 1033 exchange. If Bryant's home were in a federally declared disaster area, he could have four years to replace the property, assuming he purchases the replacement in the same area. ###

19. Christian owns an office building with a $400,000 basis. The building was destroyed by a fire in 2012, and Christian receives insurance money totaling $600,000. He purchases a new office building for $450,000 and then invests the rest of the insurance proceeds in stocks. Which of the following statements is true?

A. Christian has $200,000 in taxable gain he must recognize on his tax return.
B. Christian has $150,000 in taxable gain he must recognize on his tax return.
C. Christian does not have a taxable gain, because he reinvested all the proceeds in qualifying investment property.
D. Christian has $50,000 in taxable gain he must recognize on his tax return.

**The answer is B.** Christian's realized gain is $200,000 ($600,000 - $400,000) and his taxable gain is $150,000. He purchased another building for $450,000, so he may defer $50,000 of the gain under section 1033 for involuntary conversions. The remainder of the gain, $150,000 ($600,000 - $450,000), must be recognized because he did not reinvest all of the remaining proceeds into "like-kind" property. If Christian had reinvested all the proceeds in the new building, then his entire gain would have been deferred, and he would not have to pay taxes on any of the amount. ###

20. Aiden exchanges a residential rental in Las Vegas with a basis of $100,000 for an investment property in Miami Beach valued at $220,000 plus $15,000 in cash. What is Aiden's taxable gain on the exchange, and what is the basis of the new property in Miami Beach?

A. Taxable gain: $15,000; basis: $100,000.
B. Taxable gain: $0; basis: $235,000.
C. Taxable gain: $15,000; basis: $135,000.
D. Taxable gain: $15,000; basis: $220,000.

**The answer Is A.** Aiden's total realized gain on the exchange is $135,000 [$220,000 + $15,000] - $100,000 basis in the old property). Only the cash boot is taxable ($15,000). Aiden's basis in the new building is $100,000 (the original basis in the property he gave up.)

21. In 2012 Annalise sold her primary residence in Utah and moved to Iowa. She had purchased the house in 2000 for $200,000, and she sold it in 2012 for $550,000, net of selling expenses. During the time she lived in the house, she paid $25,000 for improvements and $15,000 for repairs.

Assuming that Annalise utilizes the maximum available exclusion, what amount would she report as taxable gain?

A. $100,000.
B. $60,000.
C. $75,000.
D. $0.

**The answer is C.** Annalise's adjusted basis in the house would be the total of her original purchase price of $200,000 and the $25,000 cost of improvements. The cost of repairs would not be considered in determining her adjusted basis. Therefore, her gain on the sale would be $325,000, or the excess of her net proceeds over her adjusted basis. As she met the requirements for ownership and use of the house as her primary residence, she would qualify for the maximum exclusion of $250,000 available to a single taxpayer, and the taxable portion of her gain would be $75,000. ###

| Purchase price of house | $200,000 |
|---|---|
| Cost of improvements | $25,000 |
| Adjusted basis | $225,000 |
| **Net proceeds of sale** | **$550,000** |
| | |
| Gain on sale | $325,000 |
| Exclusion for single taxpayer | ($250,000) |
| **Taxable gain** | **$75,000** |

# Unit 13: Rental and Royalty Income

| More Reading: |
|---|
| Publication 527, *Residential Rental Property* |
| Publication 550, *Investment Income and Expenses* |
| Publication 946, *How to Depreciate Property* |

## Rental Income

Rental income is income from the use or occupation of property, whether for residential or commercial use. Rental income is generally subject to income tax, but not to self-employment tax, except in the case of bona fide real estate professionals.

Property owners can deduct the expenses of managing, conserving, and maintaining their rental properties. Common expenses include:

- Mortgage interest and property taxes
- Advertising
- Expenses incurred from the time a property is made available for rent to when it actually rented
- Maintenance, repairs, and utilities
- Insurance

## Losses from Rental Real Estate: *Special $25,000 Rule*

Most rental income is passive income, meaning the taxpayer does not actively or materially participate in earning the income. "Nonpassive" activities are businesses or activities in which the taxpayer works on a regular, continuous, and substantial basis.

Usually, taxpayers cannot deduct losses from passive activities from their active income. However, there is an exception in the IRC for losses relating to rental real estate activities.

If a taxpayer *actively participates* in a rental real estate activity, he can deduct up to $25,000 of losses against nonpassive income.

The full $25,000 allowance is available for taxpayers whose MAGI is less than $100,000. For every $2 a taxpayer's MAGI exceeds $100,000, the allowance is reduced by $1. Once MAGI exceeds $150,000, the special allowance is no longer available.

**Example:** Philip and Susanne have wages of $98,000 and a rental loss of $26,800 in 2012. They manage the rental property themselves. Because they meet both the active participation and the gross income tests, they are allowed to deduct $25,000 of the rental loss. The loss offsets their active income (wages). The remaining amount over the $25,000 limit ($1,800) that cannot be deducted is carried over to the next year.

Suspended passive losses can be carried forward indefinitely and used in subsequent years against passive activity income. Suspended losses are also released when a property is eventually sold or disposed of.

---

**Example:** Hal and Sally file MFJ and have AGI of $140,000. They have $25,000 in losses from their home rental that they actively manage. Because they actively manage the rental property, they qualify for the deduction of up to $25,000 in losses against nonpassive income. Therefore, Hal and Sally's deduction is reduced by $20,000 (0.5 x ($140,000 - $100,000). They will be able to deduct $5,000 ($25,000 - $20,000) against nonpassive income. The additional $20,000 in losses is carried forward to the following year.

---

If a taxpayer is married and files a separate return, but lived apart from his spouse for the entire tax year, the taxpayer's special allowance for rental losses cannot exceed $12,500 (one-half of the $25,000 special limit).

If the taxpayer *lived with* his spouse at any time during the year and is filing MFS, the taxpayer cannot offset any active income with passive rental losses.

---

**Example:** In March 2012, Campbell and Michelle legally separate and Campbell moves out of their home into an apartment. They jointly own a residential rental. Campbell earned $40,000 in wages in 2012, and Michelle earned $33,000 in wages. Their jointly-owned rental generated a loss of $6,000 for the year. Michelle and Campbell both filed MFS and reported $3,000 ($6,000 ÷ 2) of rental loss on their returns. Although Campbell and Michelle meet the active participation rules and the gross income test, neither is allowed to deduct any of the rental losses because they did not live apart for the entire year, and they are filing MFS. The loss is considered a "suspended passive activity loss" and must be carried over for use in a future year.

---

## The Definition of "Active Participation"

To "actively participate," a taxpayer must own at least 10% of the rental property and make management decisions in a significant and bona fide way, such as approving new tenants and improvements to the property and establishing the lease and rental terms.

The concept of "active participation" is frequently litigated by the IRS.[72] The IRS expects taxpayers to be able to prove that they actively participated in the management of the rental. If the taxpayer is deemed to not have "actively participated," then rental losses are disallowed, and the taxpayer is not eligible for the special $25,000 loss allowance.

---

[72] Rules regarding active participation: Ref. IRC § 469(i), Reg. § 1.469-1T(e)(3).

# Reporting Rental Income and Losses

If a taxpayer is a cash-basis taxpayer, as are most individual taxpayers, he must report rental income when it is constructively received, i.e. available without restrictions.

If a property is strictly a rental property, the income and loss should be reported on Schedule E, *Supplemental Income and Loss*, which is filed along with IRS Form 1040.

## *Treatment of Advance Rent*

"Advance rent" is any amount received before the period that it covers. Advance rent must be included in income in the year it is received, regardless of the period covered.

> **Example:** Earl signs a ten-year lease to rent his commercial office building. In 2012, the first year of the lease, Earl receives $5,000 for the first year's rent in a lump sum (in advance) and $5,000 as rent for the last year of the lease. It does not matter that the advance rent covers the last year of the rental agreement. Earl cannot postpone recognition of the payment. He must recognize the full $10,000 on his 2012 tax return.

If a tenant pays the taxpayer to cancel a lease, the amount received for the cancellation is rental income. The payment is included in the year received regardless of the taxpayer's accounting method or the period for which the rental income is covered.

# Security Deposits

Security deposits are not considered taxable income, if the deposit is refundable to the tenant at the end of the lease. If the taxpayer (landlord) keeps the security deposit because the tenant did not live up to the terms of the lease or damages property, the retained deposit amount is recognized in the year the deposit is retained. If the security deposit is to be used as a final payment of rent, it is actually advance rent and not a security deposit.

# Property or Services In Lieu Of Rent

If a taxpayer (landlord) receives property or services instead of cash rents, the fair market value of the property or services must be recognized as rental income. Just like other barter exchanges, if the tenant and landlord agree in advance to a price, the agreed upon price is the fair market value unless there is evidence to the contrary.

> **Example:** Beth's tenant, Chris, is a professional chimneysweep. Chris offers to clean all of Beth's chimneys in her apartment building instead of paying three months' rent. Beth accepts Chris's offer. Beth must recognize income for the amount Chris would have paid for three months' rent. Then Beth may include that same amount as a business expense for repairing the rental property. This is the correct procedure for recognizing rental income from an exchange of services.

If a tenant pays any expenses, those payments are rental income and the landlord must recognize them as such. The landlord can then deduct the expenses as deductible rental expenses.

> **Example:** Rosetta owns an apartment building. While she is out of town, the furnace in the apartment building breaks down. Kerry, Rosetta's tenant, pays for the emergency repairs out-of-pocket. Kerry then deducts the furnace repair bill from his rent payment. Rosetta must recognize both the rent income and the amount Kerry paid for the repairs. Rosetta can then deduct the cost of the furnace repair as a rental expense.

# *Partial Rental Use*

Different rules apply to a property that is used partially for rental purposes and partially for personal use. "Minimal rental use" is when a taxpayer rents his actual home as a rental unit for a limited time.

If a taxpayer has a net profit from rental activity, he generally may deduct all of his rental expenses, including depreciation. However, if the taxpayer uses a rental property for personal use and later has a net loss on the rental activity, the deduction for rental expenses is limited, which means that the taxpayer cannot take a loss.

Taxpayers who use a property for both personal and rental purposes must divide their expenses properly. If an expense applies to both rental use and personal use, such as the heating bill for the entire house, the taxpayer must prorate the expense between the two. The taxpayer is allowed to use any reasonable method for dividing the expense, so long as it is applied consistently. The two most common methods for dividing expenses are:

- The number of rooms in the home, and
- The square footage of the home.

It may also be reasonable to divide the cost of some items (for example, the water bill) based on the number of people using the unit.

Another common situation is a duplex in which the landlord lives in one unit and rents out the other side. Certain expenses apply to the entire property, such as mortgage interest and real estate taxes, and must be split to determine rental and personal expenses.

> **Example #1:** Pablo rents a granny cottage attached to his house. The granny cottage is 12 × 15 feet, or 180 square feet. Pablo's entire house, including the attachment, is 1,800 square feet. Pablo can deduct as a rental expense 10% of any expense that must be divided between rental use and personal use. Pablo's 2012 heating bill for the entire house is $600, and therefore $60 ($600 × .10) is considered a rental expense. The balance, $540, is a personal expense that Pablo cannot deduct.

**Example #2:** Gillian owns a duplex. She lives in one half and rents the other half. Both units are the same size. Last year, Gillian paid a total of $10,000 mortgage interest and $2,000 real estate taxes for the entire property. Gillian can deduct $5,000 mortgage interest and $1,000 real estate taxes on Schedule E. Gillian can claim the other $5,000 mortgage interest and $1,000 real estate taxes attributable to her personal use on Schedule A as itemized deductions.

## *Limit on Deductions for Personal-Use Property*

Some property is rented out at certain times and used for personal use other times, such as a beach house rented for the summer. In this case, expenses must be allocated based on the number of days the property is used for each purpose.

When a taxpayer uses a dwelling both as a home and a rental unit, expenses must be divided between rental use and personal use. On personal-use property, if rental expenses exceed rental income, the taxpayer cannot use the excess expenses to offset income from other sources. The excess deductions can be carried forward to the next year and treated as rental expenses for the same property. Any expenses carried forward to the next year will be subject to any limits that apply for that year.

**Example:** Jack owns a vacation condo on Hilton Head Island. He uses it as a personal residence four months out of the year and rents it out to tenants the rest of the year. Since Jack uses the condo more than 15 days for personal use, the condo is considered a personal use dwelling. Jack's rental income is $5,000 in 2012, and his rental expenses are $7,000 because he had a tenant who damaged the property. Jack cannot deduct the full amount of rental expenses because the condo is still considered primarily a personal-use property for tax purposes. Jack may carry over the unused expenses and deduct them from future rental income.

## How to Figure Days of Personal Use

A taxpayer must figure the number of days he uses a rental for his personal use. It is considered usage "as a personal home" if he uses the rental unit for personal purposes greater than:

- Fourteen days, or
- 10% of the total days it is rented at a fair rental price.

A day of personal use is any day that the unit/home is used by any of the following persons:

- The taxpayer or any person who has ownership interest in the property.
- A member of the taxpayer's family (unless the family member pays a fair rental price and uses the property as a "main home.")[73]

---

[73] For this rental rule, "family" includes only spouses, children, parents, grandparents, grandchildren, siblings, and half-brothers and half-sisters.

- Anyone under an arrangement that allows for the use of some other dwelling unit (such as a housing swap).
- Anyone at less than a fair rental price.

## Days Used for Repairs and Maintenance

Any day that the taxpayer or other owners spend working on repairs and maintaining the property is not counted as a day of personal use. The main purpose of the stay must be to complete the repairs or maintenance. A day is not counted as personal use even if family members use the property for recreational purposes on the same day.

> **Example:** Corey owns a mountain cabin that he normally rents out to tenants. He spends a week there with his family, working on maintenance each day. His family members spend their time fishing and swimming. Corey's main purpose of being at the cabin that week is to do maintenance work. Therefore, he does not have to count the days as personal use.

> **Example:** Steve owns a rental condo in Hawaii. In March, Steve visits the unit to re-paint, replace the carpet, and repair damage done by the former tenant. He has records to prove all of the purchases and repairs. He is at the condo performing repairs for three weeks and stays at the condo during that time. None of his time at the condo is considered "personal use" time.

## Donated Rental Property

A taxpayer also "personally uses" a dwelling unit if:
- He donates the use of the unit to a charitable organization, and
- The organization sells the use of the unit at a fundraising event, and the purchaser of the unit uses the unit.

# *Exception: Minimal Rental Use, or the "15 Day Rule"

If a taxpayer rents his main home for *fewer* than 15 days (14 days or less), he does not have to recognize any of the income as taxable. This is called the "15 day rule." He also cannot deduct any rental expenses.

> **Example:** Brynn owns a condo on the Gulf Coast. It is her main home. While she was away on vacation, she rented her condo for 14 days and charged $100 per day, for a total of $1,400. She also had $320 in expenses during that time. Brynn does not report any of the income or expenses since the rental qualifies under the exception for minimal rental use.

## Rental Expenses and the "Placed in Service" Date

Rental property is "placed in service" when it is ready and available for rent. A taxpayer can begin to depreciate property and deduct expenses as soon as he places the property in service for the production of income.

A taxpayer cannot deduct any loss of rental income for the period a property is vacant. But if a taxpayer is actively trying to rent the property, he can deduct ordinary and necessary expenses as soon as the property is *made available* for rent.

**Example:** Rodrigo purchased a rental property in 2012. He made the property available for rent on March 1, 2012 by advertising the property in the local newspaper. Rodrigo finally found a tenant on June 1, 2012. Even though the rental was unoccupied from March to June, Rodrigo may still deduct the mortgage interest and other expenses related to the property. Expenses incurred while a property is vacant but available for rent are generally deductible.

## Expenses for a Rental Property That is Later Sold

If a taxpayer sells property originally held for rental purposes, he can deduct the ordinary and necessary expenses for managing, conserving, or maintaining the property until it is sold.

**Example:** Gerry owns a rental property and wants to sell it. It is currently vacant, and Gerry still must pay the utility bills and landscaping costs. Gerry is also paying mortgage interest and property taxes. Gerry can deduct these expenses from his rental income.

## *Converting a Primary Residence to Rental Use*

If a taxpayer changes a primary residence to rental use at any time other than the beginning of a tax year, he must divide yearly expenses, such as taxes and insurance, between rental use and personal use. A taxpayer can deduct as rental expenses only the portion that is for the part of the year the property was used or held for rental purposes. For depreciation purposes, the property is treated as being "placed in service" on the conversion date.

The taxpayer cannot deduct depreciation or insurance for the part of the year the property was held for personal use. However, the taxpayer can include the home mortgage interest, qualified mortgage insurance premiums, and real estate tax expenses for the part of the year the property was held for personal use as an itemized deduction on Schedule A (Form 1040).

## Figuring the Basis of a Converted Property

When a taxpayer converts a property from personal use to rental use, he figures the basis for depreciation using the *lesser* of:

- Fair market value (the price the property would sell for on the open market), or
- The home's adjusted basis on the date of the conversion.

# Depreciation Rules for Rental Property

Rental properties must be depreciated. Depreciation is an income tax deduction that allows a taxpayer to recover the cost of business-use property. It is an annual allowance for the wear and tear, deterioration, and/or obsolescence of the property. Most types of tangible property (except land and land improvements), such as buildings, machinery, vehicles, furniture, and equipment, are depreciable.

**Example:** In 2007, Lance purchased a home for $180,000. On the date of purchase, the assessed value of the land was $30,000. After living in the home for five years, Lance converted it to a rental property on April 1, 2012. Since land is not depreciated, Lance will include only the cost of the house when figuring the basis for depreciation. The basis of the house is $150,000 ($180,000 - $30,000). In 2012, the county assessor's office assigned the home an FMV of $185,000, of which $40,000 was for land and $145,000 for the house. The basis for depreciation on the house is the FMV on the date of change ($145,000), because it is less than Lance's adjusted basis ($150,000). Lance must use $145,000 as his basis for figuring depreciation on Schedule E.

A taxpayer may only deduct a certain amount of depreciation expense each year, and must claim the correct amount. If a taxpayer does not claim all the depreciation he was entitled to deduct, he must still *reduce his basis* in the property by the full amount of depreciation that he could have deducted. Regardless of whether the taxpayer chooses to deduct the depreciation on his current return, he will still be treated as if he had taken the allowable deduction, and the basis in the property must be reduced.

Three basic factors determine how much depreciation a taxpayer can deduct:

- Basis
- Recovery period for the property
- Depreciation method used

Raw land is never depreciated because land does not wear out, become obsolete, or get used up. The costs of clearing, grading, planting, and landscaping are generally all part of the cost of land and cannot be depreciated.

**Example:** Diane owns an empty lot she purchased for $50,000, and she plans to build an apartment complex on it. Diane pays an additional $15,000 to clear the property of trees and debris so she can begin construction. Diane's basis in the land is therefore $65,000 ($50,000 + $15,000). The cost of clearing the brush must be added to the basis of the land, and is not deductible or depreciable.

# Repairs vs. Improvements

A taxpayer can deduct the cost of repairs to rental property, but cannot deduct the cost of "improvements." A taxpayer recovers the cost of improvements by taking depreciation.

The taxpayer must separate the costs of repairs and improvements, and keep accurate records. The taxpayer will need to know the cost of improvements when the property is later sold, because improvements increase a property's basis.

A "repair" keeps a property in operating condition. It does not add to the value of a property or substantially prolong its life. Repainting a property inside or out, fixing gutters or floors, fixing leaks, plastering, and replacing broken windows are examples of repairs.

**Example:** Keith owns a rental home. A baseball broke a window, so he replaced it with an upgraded model—an insulated double-pane window that helps control heating and cooling costs. Even though this window is a substantial upgrade from the previous one, it is still considered a repair, because the old window was broken and needed to be replaced. If Keith had decided to replace all the windows, the upgrade would have been considered an "improvement," and Keith would have been required to depreciate the cost.

When a taxpayer makes an improvement to a rental property, the cost must be capitalized and depreciated. It cannot be deducted on the tax return as an expense. The capitalized cost is usually depreciated as if the improvement were separate property from the dwelling unit.

**Example:** Keith's rental property also has a bad roof leak, so he replaces the entire roof at a cost of $7,000. This is considered a substantial improvement and must be depreciated over time. Keith cannot expense the cost of the roof against current income.

## Examples of Improvements

An *improvement* adds to the value of property, prolongs its useful life, or adapts it to new uses. Improvements include the following items:

- Putting a recreation room in an unfinished basement
- Paneling a den, putting in a fireplace, or other major construction
- Adding another bathroom or bedroom
- Putting decorative grillwork on a balcony
- Erecting a fence
- Installing new plumbing or wiring
- Putting in new cabinets
- Putting on a new roof
- Paving a driveway or adding a garage

> **Example:** Glenna owns a rental home. In 2012, she spent $7,000 replacing the carpet, $2,540 to pave the driveway, and $350 to repair a cracked window. Only the window repair ($350) can be expensed on her 2012 tax return. The cost of the new carpet and the new driveway must be capitalized and depreciated over time.

## Repair vs. Capitalization Rule Changes

In December 2011,[74] the IRS released temporary regulations that will mean major changes in determining whether certain costs are repairs or improvements, and thus whether they need to be expensed or capitalized. Under the changes, an improvement is redefined as a cost involving:

- A betterment of the unit of property,
- A restoration of the unit of property, or
- An adaptation of the unit of property to a new or different use.

The new IRS improvement standards apply to the building structure and each of the building's major component systems separately. The guidelines divide a building into nine different structural components called "building systems," such as those for plumbing, heating and air conditioning, and electrical. The effects of a repair on a specific building system, rather than the building as a whole, must be evaluated under the new, narrower definition of an improvement. The result will be to make costs more difficult to classify as repairs, meaning the taxpayer will not be able to deduct them as expenses but will have to capitalize them instead.

For example, under current guidelines significant repairs to an elevator may "better" the elevator but would not be significant to the building as a whole, so the repair could be expensed. Under the new guidelines, the costs would be significant to the *elevator system* and would have to be capitalized.

The final regulations are still being revised, and the IRS announced in December 2012 that it was delaying full implementation until 2014.[75] For 2012, the IRS is giving taxpayers the choice of whether to use the current rules or to adopt the new ones.

## Depreciation Periods

The depreciation periods for business and rental property vary from three years to 20 years. Land improvements such as fences, bridges, and shrubbery must be depreciated over 15 or 20 years.

For property used in rental activities, a taxpayer must use the Modified Accelerated Cost Recovery System (MACRS), which is the required method of accelerated

---

[74] Federal Register, Dec. 27, 2011
[75] IRS Notice 2012-73.

asset depreciation in the United States. Under MACRS, all assets are divided into classes that dictate the number of years over which an asset's cost will be recovered.

Buildings are depreciated using the straight-line method. Residential real estate is recovered over 27.5 years, and commercial buildings are depreciated over 39 years. Residential real estate is any structure that at least 80% of the gross rental income of the building is derived from dwelling units (such as an apartment complex), or a common residential rental home.

All other real property is classified as "commercial nonresidential property" and must be depreciated over 39 years. An example is a factory building.

Only the building portion of the rental can be depreciated, so the value of the land must be separated from the value of the building. If a taxpayer is uncertain of the FMV of the land and the buildings, he may calculate the basis using the assessed values for real estate tax purposes.

**Example:** In 2012, Shannon buys a rental property for $200,000. It has an assessed value of $160,000, of which $136,000 is for the house and $24,000 is for the land. Shannon can allocate 85% ($136,000 ÷ $160,000) of the purchase price to the house and 15% ($24,000 ÷ $160,000) of the purchase price to the land. Therefore, her basis in the house is $170,000 (85% of $200,000) and her basis in the land is $30,000 (15% of $200,000). Shannon may use $170,000 as her basis for depreciation on the property.

**Example:** A residential rental building with a cost basis of $137,500 would generate depreciation of $5,000 per year ($137,500 / 27.5 years).

# MACRS Recovery Periods
## Depreciable Property Used in Rental Activities

| Class of Property | Items Included |
|---|---|
| 3-year property | Most computer software, tractor units, some manufacturing tools, and some livestock. |
| 5-year property | Automobiles, computers and peripheral equipment, office machinery (faxes, copiers, calculators, etc.), appliances, stoves, refrigerators. |
| 7-year property | Office furniture and fixtures, and any property that has not been designated as belonging to another class. |
| 15-year property | Depreciable improvements to land such as shrubbery, fences, roads, and bridges. |
| 20-year property | Farm buildings that are not agricultural or horticultural structures. |
| 27.5-year property | Residential rental property (residential rental homes, condos, etc.) |
| 39-year property | Nonresidential real estate, such as factory buildings. |

# Other Rental Property Expenses

There are many types of expenses that rental property owners may legitimately deduct. Examples include advertising, cleaning, maintenance, utilities, fire and liability insurance, taxes, interest, and commissions for the collection of rent. If a taxpayer buys a leasehold for rental purposes, he can deduct an equal part of the cost each year over the term of the lease.

## Travel Expenses Related to Rental Property

A taxpayer can deduct the ordinary and necessary expenses of traveling away from home if the primary purpose of the trip is to collect rental income or to manage, conserve, or maintain his rental property.

> **Example:** Walt owns a rental property 200 miles from his home. Part of the rental home was damaged by fire. Walt travels to the property to inspect the damage and hire someone to do the repairs. His travel expenses are deductible as ordinary and necessary costs.

**Cannot Deduct Prepaid Insurance Premiums:** If a taxpayer pays an insurance premium on rental property for more than one year in advance, each year he can deduct the part of the premium payment that applies to that year. He cannot deduct the total premium in the year paid.

> **Example:** Connie owns a rental home. She receives a substantial discount from her insurance agent if she agrees to pay her hazard insurance two years in advance. Connie cannot deduct the full payment of the insurance in the year that she pays. She must prorate the insurance expense, even though she is a cash-basis taxpayer.

**Cannot Deduct Local Benefit Taxes:** Generally, a taxpayer cannot deduct charges for local benefits that increase the value of a property, such as charges for putting in streets, sidewalks, or water and sewer systems. These charges are non-depreciable capital expenditures that must be added to the basis of a property. A taxpayer can deduct local benefit taxes if they are for maintaining, repairing, or paying interest charges for the benefits.

# Not Rented for Profit

If a taxpayer is not renting a property to make a profit, he can deduct his rental expenses only up to the amount of his rental income. Losses cannot be deducted or carried forward to the next year if the expenses are more than the rental income for the year.

If a taxpayer's rental income is more than his rental expenses for at least three out of five consecutive years, he is presumed to be renting the property to make a profit. A taxpayer who is starting rental activity and does not have three years showing a profit may elect to have the presumption made after five years of rental experience.

## Exception for Real Estate Professionals

Real estate professionals are *exempt* from the passive activity rules if certain conditions are met. Rental activities in which real estate professionals materially participate during the year are not passive activities. A real estate professional may elect to treat his rental income as non-passive income. If the real estate professional elects this treatment, the rental income is subject to self-employment tax, and the taxpayer must file a Schedule C, rather than a Schedule E.

Real estate "dealers" are defined as those who are engaged in the business of selling real estate to customers with purposes of making a profit from those sales. The benefit of being classified as a "real estate professional" is that the taxpayer is treated like a Schedule C business and there is no limit on the amount of losses the taxpayer can claim on the activity. A taxpayer will qualify as a real estate professional for the tax year if he meets both of the following requirements:

- More than half of the services performed during the tax year are performed in real estate or real property businesses in which the taxpayer materially participates.
- The taxpayer performs more than 750 hours of services during the tax year in real property trades or businesses in which he materially participates.

Rental income received from the use of or occupancy of hotels, boarding houses, or apartment houses is included in self-employment income *if* the real estate professional provided services to the occupants.

Services are considered "provided to the occupants" if they are for the convenience of the occupants and not normally provided with the rental of rooms or space for occupancy only. Daily maid service, for example, is a service provided for the convenience of occupants, while heating, exterior lights, and the collection of trash are not.

## Royalty Income

Royalties from copyrights, patents, and oil, gas, and mineral properties are taxable as ordinary income. Royalty income is generally considered passive income and subject to the passive activity rules.

Royalties are payments that are received for the use of property. The most common types of royalties are for the use of copyrights, trademarks, and patents. Royalties are also paid by companies that extract minerals and other substances from the earth, such as oil or gas. Mineral property includes oil and gas wells, mines, and other natural deposits, such as geothermal deposits. Royalty income and expenses are reported on Schedule E, *Supplemental Income and Loss*.

**\*Exception:** There are special rules for taxpayers who are self-employed writers, artists, photographers, or inventors. In this case, the royalties are generated by a *self-created* copyright, trademark, or patent. Therefore, the royalties are reported as business income on Schedule C and are subject to self-employment tax.

Royalties from copyrights on literary, musical, or artistic works, and similar property, or from patents on inventions, are amounts paid for the right to use the property over a specified period of time. Royalties generally are based on the number of units sold, such as the number of books, tickets to a performance, or machines sold.

> **Example:** In 2012, Don's brother died. Don inherited a copyright from his brother who had written an instruction manual for woodworking. Don then leased the copyrighted material to schools and colleges for their use in the classroom. Since this was not a self-created copyright, the income is considered passive income. Don must report the income from this copyright on Schedule E.

# Unit 13: Questions

1. Thomas, who is single, owns a rental apartment building property. He actively participates in the rental activity by collecting rent and performing repairs. In 2012, Thomas had an overall loss of $29,000 on this rental activity and had no other passive income. His total income from wages is $60,000. How much of the rental loss may Thomas deduct on his 2012 return?

A. $0.
B. $6,000.
C. $25,000.
D. $29,000.

**The answer is C.** Thomas may deduct $25,000 in rental losses. The remaining amount, $4,000 ($29,000 - $25,000), must be carried over to the following year. ####

2. In 2012, Jane is single and has $40,000 in wages, $2,000 of passive income from a limited partnership, and $3,500 of passive losses from a rental real estate activity in which she actively participated. Which of the following statements is true?

A. $2,000 of Jane's $3,500 loss offsets her passive income. Jane may deduct the remaining $1,500 loss from her $40,000 wages.
B. Jane may not deduct the passive losses from her $40,000 in wages.
C. Jane may deduct any other losses.
D. Jane must carry over her losses to the subsequent tax year.

**The answer is A.** Jane may deduct the remaining $1,500 loss from her $40,000 wages. A taxpayer may deduct up to $25,000 per year of losses for rental real estate activities in which she actively participates. This special allowance is an exception to the general rule disallowing losses in excess of income from passive activities. ###

3. Which of the following costs incurred on rental property should be classified as a capital improvement and must be depreciated rather than expensed?

A. Replacing an entire deck.
B. Repairing a broken toilet.
C. Refinishing the existing wood floors.
D. Replacing a broken window pane.

**The answer is A.** The replacement of the deck would be considered a depreciable improvement. The other choices are repairs and may be deducted as current expenses. ###

4. Mike, a single taxpayer, had the following income and loss during the tax year:

- Salary $52,300
- Dividends $300
- Bank interest $1,400
- Rental losses ($4,000)

The loss came from a rental property that Mike owned. He advertised and rented the house to the current tenant himself. He also collected the rents and did the repairs or hired someone to do them. Which of the following statements is true?

A. Mike can claim the entire rental loss against his active income.
B. Mike cannot claim the rental loss because his income exceeds $50,000.
C. Mike cannot claim the rental loss because he is not a real estate professional.
D. Mike can claim $1,700 in rental losses and the remaining amount ($2,300) will be carried over to the following year.

**The answer is A.** Even though the rental loss is from a passive activity, Mike can use the entire $4,000 loss to offset his other income because he actively participated. If a taxpayer *actively participates* in a rental real estate activity, he can deduct up to $25,000 of losses against nonpassive income. This special allowance for rental activity is *an exception* to the general rule disallowing losses in excess of income from passive activities. ###

5. Gene signs a three-year lease to rent his business property. In December 2012, he receives $12,000 for the first year's rent and $12,000 as rent for the last year of the lease. He also receives $1,500 in 2012 as a refundable security deposit. How much of this income must Gene include in his 2012 tax return?

A. $1,500.
B. $12,000.
C. $24,000.
D. $25,500.

**The answer is C.** Gene must include $24,000 in his income in the first year. He must recognize all the advance rent as income immediately. The security deposit does not have to be recognized as income as it is refundable to the tenant. ###

6. Rosemary's home is used exclusively as her residence all year except for 13 days. During this time, Rosemary rents her home to alumni while the local college has its homecoming celebration. She made $3,000 in rental income and had $500 in rental expenses. Which of the following statements is true?

A. All of the rental income may be excluded.
B. Rosemary may exclude only $2,500 of the rental income.
C. Rosemary may deduct her rental expenses when she reports her rental income on Schedule E.
D. Rosemary must recognize $3,000 in rental income.

**The answer is A.** All the rental income may be excluded under the "15 day rule." This home is primarily personal use, and the rental period is disregarded, which means the IRS does not consider it a rental. The rental income is not taxable, and any of the rental expenses (such as utilities or maintenance costs) are considered nondeductible personal expenses. ###

7. Eric incurred the following expenditures in connection with his rental property. Which of them should be capitalized and depreciated?

A. New roof.
B. New kitchen cabinets.
C. New carpeting for all the bedrooms.
D. All of the above.

**The answer is D.** All of the property listed must be capitalized and depreciated. A taxpayer can deduct only the cost of repairs to his rental property. He cannot deduct the cost of improvements, but can recover the cost of improvements by taking depreciation over the life of the asset. ###

8. Terry purchased a heating, ventilating, and air conditioning (HVAC) unit for her rental property on December 15, 2012. It was delivered on December 28, 2012, and was installed and ready for use on January 2, 2012. When should the HVAC unit be considered "placed in service" for depreciation purposes?

A. December 15, 2012.
B. December 28, 2012.
C. January 1, 2012.
D. January 2, 2012.

**The answer is D.** The placed-in-service date is the date when an asset becomes available for use. In most cases, the placed-in-service date and the purchase date are the same, but that is not necessarily the case. Depreciation begins on the placed-in-service date. Since Terry did not actually have the HVAC unit in use until January 2, 2012, she must wait until 2012 to begin depreciating the unit. ###

9. Passive rental income and losses are reported on which IRS form?

A. Schedule E.
B. Schedule A.
C. Schedule C.
D. Schedule D.

**The answer is A**. Rental income and loss is reported on Schedule E, which is then attached to the taxpayer's Form 1040. Rental income is any payment received for the use or occupation of property, and is generally passive income. An exception exists for real estate professionals, who may report rental income on Schedule C. ###

10. Brian has a house in Arizona that is rented out for eight months each year. How many days can he use the house without losing income tax deductions?

A. As many days as he wants.
B. 14 days.
C. Zero days.
D. 24 days.

**The answer is D.** Brian can personally use his rental home the longer of 14 days or 10% of the time the rental was in use. The rental home was used for 240 days (30 x 8). Brian can use his rental home for 24 days (240 x 10%) with no impact in deducting expenses from his rental property. ###

11. In January 2012, Kimberly purchases a commercial office building and used office furnishings. The furnishings consist of chairs, desks, and file cabinets. The purchase price allocates $900,000 to the office building and $50,000 to the used office furnishings. According to the guidelines for MACRS depreciation, what recovery period must she use for the purchased items?

A. 27.5 years for the entire purchase (building and furnishings).
B. 39 years for the building and 5 years for the used office furnishings.
C. 15 years for the building and 5 years for the used office furnishings.
D. 39 years for the building and 7 years for the used office furnishings.

**The answer is D.** Commercial real estate is depreciated as 39-year property. The recovery period under MACRS for furniture is seven years. ###

12. Nick decides to convert his residence into rental property. He moves out of his home in May and starts renting it on June 1. He has $12,000 in mortgage interest on the home. How should Nick report his mortgage interest expense?

A. Nick can report $7,000 on Schedule E as interest expense and $5,000 on Schedule A as mortgage interest.
B. Nick should report the entire $12,000 on Schedule A.
C. Nick should report the entire $12,000 on Schedule E.
D. Nick can report $8,000 on Schedule E as interest expense and $4,000 on Schedule A as mortgage interest.

**The answer is A.** Nick must allocate his expenses between personal use and rental use. He can deduct as rental expenses seven-twelfths (7/12) of his yearly expenses, such as taxes and insurance. Starting with June, he can deduct as rental expenses the amounts he paid for items generally billed monthly, such as utilities. When figuring depreciation, he should treat the property as placed in service on June 1. ###

13. In 2012 Mimi has modified adjusted gross income of $120,000. She owns a rental house that has losses of $22,000 for the year. How much of the rental loss may she deduct on her tax return?

A. $0.
B. $11,000.
C. $15,000.
D. $22,000.

**The answer is C.** Mimi may only deduct $15,000 of the loss. The rental loss allowance is phased out when a taxpayer's MAGI is over $100,000. For every two dollars of income over $100,000, the rental loss allowance is reduced one dollar. The answer is figured as follows:

Mimi's income-MAGI threshold: ($120,000 - $100,000 = $20,000)
$20,000 X 50% = $10,000
$25,000 (normal rental allowance) - $10,000 = $15,000

$15,000 is the maximum in rental losses that Mimi can claim as a deduction. The remaining unused losses ($7,000) must be carried over to the following year. ###

14. Jake is a full-time freelance writer. He earns $23,000 in royalty income from one of his copyrighted books in 2012. He also has $4,000 in travel expenses related to the promotion of the book. How should this income be reported?

A. Jake must report $23,000 in taxable income on Schedule C.
B. Jake must report $23,000 in taxable income on Schedule E.
C. Jake must report $19,000 in taxable income on Schedule E.
D. Jake must report $19,000 in taxable income on Schedule C.

**The answer is D.** As a full-time writer, his royalty income is not considered passive income and therefore is subject to self-employment tax. Jake must report $19,000 in taxable income on Schedule C ($23,000 - $4,000 in expenses). ###

15. Aaron converts his basement level into a separate apartment with a bedroom, a bathroom, and a small kitchen. He rents the basement apartment at a fair rental price to college students on a 9-month lease (273 days). He figures that 10% of the total days rented at a fair rental price is 27 days (273 days X 10%). In June, Aaron's brothers stay with him and live in the basement apartment rent-free for 30 days. Which is the true statement?

A. Aaron may deduct all of his expenses for the converted basement apartment, as it is 100% rental use.
B. Aaron may not deduct any of his rental losses because the converted basement apartment is considered personal use.
C. Aaron must recognize imputed rental income from his brothers' use of the property, even if he did not actually receive it.
D. Aaron must divide his expenses between personal use and rental use, but he is still allowed to deduct losses from the property.

**The answer is B.** Since Aaron's family members use the basement apartment for free, this usage counts as personal use for Aaron. Therefore, the basement apartment is no longer considered a 100% rental unit. Aaron's personal use (the 30 days his family used it for free) exceeds the greater of 14 days or 10% of the total days it was rented (27 days). When a taxpayer uses a dwelling unit both as a home and a rental unit, expenses must be divided between rental use and personal use, and the taxpayer may not deduct rental expenses that exceed the rental income for that dwelling unit. Aaron's losses, if he has any, are not deductible. ###

16. In general, income from a residential rental property is subject to what kind of tax?

A. Income tax.
B. Income tax, Social Security tax, and Medicare tax.
C. Income tax and Social Security tax, but not Medicare tax.
D. Income tax and Medicare tax, but not Social Security tax.

**The answer is A.** In general, income from rental real estate is subject to income tax, but not to self-employment tax, with a rare exception for bona fide real estate dealers/brokers. ###

17. What is the depreciation period for residential rental property?

A. 20 years.
B. 22.5 years.
C. 27.5 years.
D. 39 years.

**The answer is C.** Residential rental property is depreciable over 27.5 years. ###

18. In 2012 Travis and Brittany moved to Canada. They decided to rent their house in California instead of selling it. They had purchased the home in 2006 for $500,000 and had paid $80,000 for various improvements through 2011. The purchase price of $500,000 was attributable to fair market values of $100,000 for the land and $400,000 for the house. Their new tenant paid a security deposit of $6,000 and moved in on July 1, 2012. The FMV of the property on July 1 was $525,000, comprised of $105,000 for the land and $420,000 for the house. The tenant then paid rent of $3,000 each month from July through December. Travis and Brittany incurred the following expenses in 2012 related to the house:

| | |
|---|---|
| Mortgage interest | $10,000 |
| Property taxes | $10,000 |
| Casualty insurance | $1,000 |

In addition, they paid $500 for repairs during December. Exclusive of depreciation expense, what was Travis and Brittany's taxable rental income for 2012?

A. $13,000.
B. $7,000.
C. $1,500.
D. $7,250.

**The answer is B.** Travis and Brittany must report six months of rental income at $3,000 per month, or $18,000, but the security deposit of $6,000 is refundable and therefore not recognized as income in 2012. They can deduct 6/12 of the amounts incurred for mortgage interest, property taxes, and casualty insurance, or $10,500, plus the $500 cost of repairs while the house was rented. Thus, their reportable net rental income before considering depreciation would be $7,000. ###

Supporting calculations:
**Taxable income:**

| | |
|---|---|
| Six months of rent (at $3,000) | 18,000 |

**Less deductible expenses:**

| | |
|---|---|
| Mortgage interest (for six months) | $5,000 |
| Property taxes (for six months) | $5,000 |
| Casualty insurance (for six months) | $500 |
| Repair cost | $500 |
| | |
| Expenses **before** depreciation | $11,000 |
| Rental income **before** depreciation | $7,000 |

19. Based upon the information in question 18, what is the amount of basis on which depreciation should be calculated for the rental period?

A. $400,000.
B. $480,000.
C. $580,000.
D. $420,000.

**The answer is D.** The basis for depreciation is the **lesser of** fair market value or the taxpayer's adjusted basis on the date the property was converted to rental use. The adjusted basis of the house on July 1, 2012 was $480,000 (original cost of $400,000 plus improvements of $80,000), but the FMV of $420,000 on the same date was lower. The basis of the land is not subject to depreciation. ###

Supporting calculations:

Adjusted basis of house:
| | |
|---|---|
| Cost | $400,000 |
| Improvements | $80,000 |
| Total adjusted basis | $480,000 |

| | |
|---|---|
| FMV on July 1, 2012 | $420,000 |

20. Tae-hyun acquired a residential rental property in 2012 for $1 million, paid an additional $100,000 to replace the roof, and paid $50,000 for repairs. The purchase price of the property was determined to be allocable as follows: 90% to the building and 10% to land. The property was placed in service in March.

Based upon the information provided, on what amount can Tae-hyun calculate and claim a depreciation deduction for this property?

A. $1,050,000.
B. $500,000.
C. $1,150,000.
D. $1,000,000.

**The answer is D.** The depreciable basis for the property is the sum of the purchase price less the portion attributable to non-depreciable land, or $900,000, plus the cost of improvements ($100,000), or a total of $1,000,000. The cost of repairs ($50,000) is separately deductible as a current expense, and does not affect the depreciation calculation.

Supporting calculations:

| | |
|---|---|
| Purchase price (less land cost) | $900,000 |
| Improvements (roof repair) | $100,000 |
| Depreciable basis | $1,000,000 |

21. Gabby owns a duplex. She lives in one half and rents the other. The property is condemned in order to add lanes to the interstate highway, and Gabby receives a condemnation settlement of $90,000. She originally paid $75,000 for the property and spent $15,000 for improvements prior to 2012. Through 2012, Gabby has claimed allowable depreciation deductions of $20,000 on the rental half of the property. She also incurred legal fees of $2,000 in connection with the condemnation settlement process. What amount of taxable gain or loss will Gabby report in 2012 as a result of the condemnation?

A. Taxable gain of $19,000.
B. Taxable gain of $18,000.
C. Taxable loss of $2,000.
D. Taxable loss of $22,000.

**The answer is A.** The gain and loss for the two portions of the property must be determined separately, as outlined in the following table. Gabby will have a taxable gain on the business portion of the property and the loss on the residential portion is not deductible. ###

|  | Residential Part | Business Part |
| --- | --- | --- |
| Condemnation award received | $45,000 | $45,000 |
| Minus legal fees | ($1,000) | ($1,000) |
| Net condemnation award | $44,000 | $44,000 |
| Adjusted basis: |  |  |
| Original cost, $75,000 | $37,500 | $37,500 |
| Improvements, $15,000 | $7,500 | $7,500 |
| Total | $45,000 | $45,000 |
| Minus depreciation | N/A | ($20,000) |
| Adjusted basis, business part | $0 | $25,000 |
| **Loss/Gain on property** | **($1,000)** | **$19,000** |

394

# Unit 14: Individual Retirement Arrangements

**More Reading:**
**Publication 590,** *Individual Retirement Arrangements (IRAs)*
**Publication 575,** *Pension and Annuity Income*

There are several types of IRA accounts, but in this unit, we will only discuss traditional IRAs and Roth IRAs since these are the two most common types of retirement accounts and the ones most heavily tested on Part 1 of the EA exam. Each IRA has different eligibility requirements.

**Traditional IRA:** A traditional IRA is the most common type of retirement savings plan. In most cases, taxpayers can deduct their traditional IRA contributions as an adjustment to income. Generally, amounts in a traditional IRA, including earnings and gains, are not taxed until distributed. If a taxpayer's income is too high, the taxpayer's contributions to his traditional IRA might not be deductible.

**Roth IRA:** A Roth IRA is a retirement account that features nondeductible contributions and tax-free growth. In other words, a taxpayer funds his Roth IRA with after-tax income, and the income then grows tax-free. When a taxpayer withdraws money from a Roth IRA, the withdrawal will not be subject to income tax. Not everyone can participate in a Roth IRA. There are strict income limits, and higher wage earners may be prohibited from participating in a Roth IRA account because of their income threshold.

**\*NOTE:** Only contributions to a traditional IRA are deductible as an adjustment to gross income. Roth IRA contributions are not deductible. Although contributions to a Roth IRA cannot be deducted, the taxpayer may still be eligible for the Retirement Savings Contributions Credit (the Saver's Credit), covered in Unit 9, *Tax Credits.*

**Example:** In 2012, Leo contributes $2,200 to a traditional IRA and $1,000 to a Roth IRA. The most Leo will be able to deduct as an adjustment to income is the $2,200 contribution to his traditional IRA. Roth IRA contributions are never deductible.

## Traditional IRA Rules

Not everyone can contribute to a traditional IRA. In addition, not everyone who contributes to a traditional IRA is allowed to deduct the contribution.

In order to make contributions to a traditional IRA:

1. The taxpayer must be *under* age 70½ at the end of the year.
2. The taxpayer must have qualifying nonpassive income, such as wages, salaries, commissions, tips, bonuses, or self-employment income. Investment and pension income do not count.
3. If a taxpayer's income is too high (and if either he or his spouse is covered by an employer plan), his deductible IRA contribution will be phased out.

> **\*Note:** For purposes of making an IRA contribution, taxable alimony and nontaxable combat pay count as qualifying nonpassive income. This allows taxpayers to build retirement savings in IRAs even if they rely on alimony income for support. This applies only to taxable alimony income and does not include child support payments.

> **Example:** Stan is an Army medic serving in a combat zone for all of 2012. Although none of his pay is taxable, it is still considered qualifying compensation for purposes of an IRA contribution.

IRAs cannot be owned jointly. However, a married couple who files jointly may choose to contribute to each of their IRA accounts, even if only one taxpayer has qualifying compensation.

This means that one taxpayer may choose to make an IRA contribution on *behalf* of his or her spouse, even if only one spouse had compensation during the year. Each spouse must have a separate IRA account.

> **Example:** Joaquin, 48, and Meg, 52, are married and file jointly. Joaquin works as a paramedic and makes $46,000 per year. Meg is a homemaker and has no income. Even though Meg has no taxable compensation, Joaquin may still contribute to her IRA account. Their combined maximum contribution for 2012 is $11,000. Joaquin may deposit $5,000, and Meg may deposit $6,000 because she is over 50 years of age.

Contributions can be made to a traditional IRA at any time on or before the due date of the return (not including extensions). For the 2012 tax year, a person may make an IRA contribution up until April 15, 2013.

This makes an IRA contribution a rare opportunity for tax planning because it can occur after the tax year has already ended. A taxpayer can even file his return claiming a traditional IRA contribution *before* the contribution is actually made. However, if a contribution is reported on the taxpayer's 2012 return but is not made by the deadline, the taxpayer must file an amended return.

> **Example:** Paul files his 2012 tax return on March 5, 2013. He claims a $4,000 IRA contribution on his tax return. Paul may wait as late as April 15, 2013 (the due date of the return) to make the IRA contribution for tax year 2012.

A taxpayer must have taxable income in order to contribute to an IRA, so a person whose only income is from self-employment and who shows an overall loss for the year would not be able to contribute. However, if the taxpayer has wages *in addition* to self-employment income, a *loss* from self-employment would not be subtracted from the taxpayer's wages when figuring total compensation.

> **Example:** Marcy is 45 and works part-time as an employee for a local library. She earns $10,000 in wages during 2012. She also works part of the year as a self-employed photographer. In 2012, her photography business has a loss of $5,400. Even though the taxpayer's *net income* for 2012 is only $4,600 ($10,000 wages − $5,400 loss from self-employment), her qualifying income for purposes of an IRA contribution is still $10,000, the amount of her wages. This means that Marcy can make a full IRA contribution of $5,000 in 2012.

"Compensation" for purposes of contributing to an IRA does not include passive income such as:

- Rental income
- Interest income
- Dividend and portfolio income
- Pension or annuity income
- Deferred compensation
- Income from certain partnerships
- Prize winnings or gambling income
- Items (except for nontaxable combat pay) that are excluded from income, such as foreign earned income and housing costs

Taxpayers cannot make IRA contributions that are greater than their qualifying compensation for the year. This means that if a taxpayer only has passive income for the year, he cannot contribute to an IRA at all.

> **Example:** Larry is 54 and wants to contribute to his traditional IRA. He is not a real estate professional, but he has $10,000 in passive rental income from residential rental properties. He also received $8,000 in interest income and has $3,000 in wages from a part-time job. The rental and interest income are passive income and are not considered "compensation" for purposes of funding his retirement account. Therefore, the maximum Larry can contribute to his traditional IRA is $3,000, the amount of his wage income.

## 2012 Traditional and Roth IRA Contribution Limits

**Under 50 years of age:**

- 2012 Contribution Limit: $5,000 per taxpayer
- Filing Jointly: $10,000

**50 years and over:**

- 2012 Contribution Limit: $6,000 per taxpayer
- Filing Jointly (Both 50 or older): $12,000

A taxpayer may choose to split his retirement plan contributions between a traditional IRA and a Roth IRA; however, the maximum contribution limits still apply. Although a person may have IRAs with several different financial institutions, for purposes of the contribution limits, tax law treats all of a taxpayer's IRAs as a single IRA.

> **Example:** Alan is 32. He has a traditional IRA at his regular bank and a Roth IRA through his stockbroker. Alan can contribute to both of his retirement accounts this year, but the combined contributions for 2012 cannot exceed $5,000. Alan decides to contribute $3,000 to his Roth IRA and $2,000 to his traditional IRA.

> **Example:** Naomi, 25, has only $3,000 in interest income in 2012. Naomi marries Carl during the year. In 2012, Carl has taxable wages of $34,000. He plans to contribute $5,000 to his traditional IRA. If he and Naomi file a joint return, each can contribute $5,000 to a traditional IRA. This is because Naomi, who has no qualifying compensation, can add Carl's compensation, reduced by the amount of his IRA contribution ($34,000 − $5,000 = $29,000), to her own compensation ($0) to determine her maximum contribution to a traditional IRA. Since they are filing a joint return, she can utilize Carl's qualifying compensation in order to contribute to her own traditional IRA. They both may contribute the maximum in 2012 ($5,000 each).

Even if they file a joint return, married taxpayers' combined IRA contributions cannot exceed their combined compensation, and neither spouse can contribute more than $5,000 (or $6,000 if 50 or older) to his or her own IRA.

> **Example:** Elliott and June are both age 49 and married. Elliott has $23,000 in pension income for the year. June has $13,000 in pension income and $7,000 in wages. Only June's wages count as qualifying compensation for purposes of IRA contributions. June may contribute the maximum to her IRA ($5,000). If they file jointly, Elliott can contribute $2,000 (equal to the remaining amount of June's qualifying compensation, $7,000 − $5,000 = $2,000).

Once again, a married couple cannot set up a "joint" IRA account. Each individual must have his or her own IRA, but married spouses may choose to make contributions to a spouse's IRA, up to the legal limit, if they file jointly. If taxpayers choose to file separately, then they must consider only their own qualifying compensation for IRA purposes.

> **Example:** Greg is 35, works full-time, and made $55,000 in 2012. His wife, Laverne, is 34, has a part-time job, and made $3,600 in 2012. They choose to file separately. Since they file MFS and Laverne only has $3,600 in compensation, she is limited to a $3,600 IRA contribution. Greg may contribute a full $5,000 to his own IRA account.

A taxpayer cannot claim the adjustment for an IRA contribution on Form 1040EZ; the taxpayer must use either Form 1040, Form 1040A, or Form 1040NR.

# Traditional IRA Phase-outs

## Phase-out Ranges for Deductibility

If the taxpayer (or his spouse) is not covered by an employer plan, he can take a deduction for traditional IRA contributions up to the smaller of:

- $5,000 ($6,000 if he is age 50 or older), or
- 100% of qualifying compensation.

However, the contribution will be phased out if either the taxpayer or his spouse (or both) are covered by a retirement plan at work.

## Phase-out Ranges When Covered by an Employer Plan

If a taxpayer (or his spouse) is covered by an employer retirement plan, the tax-deductible contribution to a traditional IRA is phased out at the following modified adjusted gross income (AGI) limits:

| Phase-outs for Taxpayers Covered by an Employer Plan | |
|---|---|
| Filing Status | Income Range |
| MFJ or QW | $92,000 - $112,000 |
| MFS (living with spouse) | $0 - $10,000 |
| Single, HOH, or MFS (living apart) | $58,000 - $68,000 |

| Phase-outs for Taxpayers Not Covered By An Employer Plan: | |
|---|---|
| Filing Status | Income Range |
| MFJ (spouse covered by employer plan) | $173,000 - $183,000 |
| MFS (spouse covered by employer plan) | $0 - $10,000 |
| Single, QW, HOH, or MFS (spouse not covered) | No limit |

If the taxpayer's modified AGI for the year is *below* the phase-out limits, the IRA contribution is fully tax-deductible. If modified AGI falls *within* the indicated income range, the IRA contribution is partially deductible. If modified AGI is *above* the indicated range, none of the IRA contribution is deductible.

> **Example:** Tamara is single and earned $95,000 in 2012. She is covered by a retirement plan at work, but she still wants to contribute to a traditional IRA. She is phased out for the deduction because her income exceeds the threshold for single filers. If she contributes to a traditional IRA in 2012, she must file Form 8606 to report her nondeductible contribution.

Married taxpayers who file MFS have a much lower phase-out range than those with any other filing status. However, if a taxpayer files a separate return and did not live with his or her spouse at any time during the year, the taxpayer is not treated as married for purposes of these limits, and the applicable dollar limit is that of a single taxpayer.

> **Example:** Don, age 43, is separated from his wife, although they are not divorced. They have lived in separate residences for the past three years. In 2012, Don earns $40,000 and files MFS. He is allowed to deduct his full IRA contribution of $5,000. This is because he did not live with his spouse at any time during the year, and therefore he is not subject to the lower IRA phase-out limits that normally apply to MFS filers.

# Rules for Deductibility of Traditional IRA Contributions

Separate limits apply to *contributions* to a traditional IRA and *the deductibility* of the contributions. Not everyone is allowed to deduct traditional IRA contributions. The deduction for contributions made to a traditional IRA depends on whether the taxpayer or his spouse is covered by an employer retirement plan and is also affected by income and filing status.

A taxpayer is permitted to have and contribute to a traditional IRA regardless of whether he or his spouse is covered by an employer retirement plan. However, if the taxpayer or his spouse is covered by an employer retirement plan, he may be entitled to only a partial deduction or no deduction at all.

If a taxpayer exceeds the income limits for making a fully tax-deductible contribution to a traditional IRA, the excess portion can still be made as a non-deductible or after-tax contribution. This means that, even though the full amount of the contribution may not be deductible, a taxpayer may still choose to contribute to his retirement on an after-tax basis. In either case, earnings will grow on a tax-deferred basis.

If a taxpayer makes nondeductible contributions to a traditional IRA, he must attach Form 8606, *Nondeductible IRAs*. Form 8606 reflects a taxpayer's cumulative nondeductible contributions, which is his tax basis in the IRA. If a taxpayer does not report nondeductible contributions properly, all future withdrawals from the IRA will be taxable unless the taxpayer can prove, with satisfactory evidence, that nondeductible contributions were made.

## Required Minimum Distributions

A person cannot keep funds in a traditional IRA indefinitely. Eventually they must be distributed. Traditional IRAs are subject to required minimum distributions (RMDs). When a retirement plan account owner reaches 70½ years of age, he is required to take a minimum distribution from the IRA every year. The amount is based on IRS tables.[76]

IRA owners are responsible for taking the correct amount of RMDs from their accounts on time every year. Failure to take an RMD can result in a penalty tax equal to 50% of the amount the taxpayer *should* have withdrawn, but did not. If the taxpayer

---

[76] An RMD is calculated for each account by dividing the balance of the IRA account by a life expectancy factor that the IRS publishes in tables within Publication 590, *Individual Retirement Arrangements (IRAs)*.

fails to take a required minimum distribution, he must file IRS Form 5329, *Additional Taxes on Qualified Plans*, to report the excise tax that applies as a result of the failure to take the RMD.

The first RMD must be taken by April 1 following the year the taxpayer turns 70½. The required minimum distribution for any subsequent year must be made by December 31.

A taxpayer must calculate the required minimum distribution for each year by dividing the IRA account balance at the end of the *preceding year* by the applicable distribution period per the IRS tables.

> **Example:** Dinah was born on October 1, 1941. She reaches age 70½ in 2012. Her first RMD must be paid by April 1, 2013. As of December 31, 2012, her IRA account balance was $78,000. Using IRS tables, the applicable distribution period for someone her age (71) is 26 years. Her required minimum distribution for 2012 is $3,000 ($78,000 ÷ 26). That amount must be distributed to her by April 1, 2013, in order to avoid the 50% excise tax.

When the owner of an IRA dies, different RMD rules apply to the beneficiary of the IRA. Generally, these rules depend upon whether:

- The owner's death occurred before or after the required beginning date for distributions,
- The beneficiary is an individual, and
- The beneficiary is the owner's spouse.

If the beneficiary of a traditional IRA is the owner's spouse, he or she is granted special treatment. Surviving spouses may "roll over" their deceased spouse's IRA into their own.

## Taxability of Distributions

Distributions from a traditional IRA are generally taxable in the year they are received, subject to the following exceptions:

- Rollovers
- Qualified charitable distributions
- Tax-free withdrawal of contributions
- Return on nondeductible contributions

## Withdrawal Penalty on Early Distributions

A taxpayer may withdraw funds at any time from a traditional IRA account. However, early withdrawals from a traditional IRA before age 59½ will generally be subject to an additional 10% tax, in addition to normal income tax on the distributed amount.

There are some exceptions to the general rule for early distributions, however. An individual may not have to pay the additional 10% tax in the following situations:

- The taxpayer has unreimbursed medical expenses that exceed 7.5% of adjusted gross income
- The distributions do not exceed the cost of the taxpayer's medical insurance
- The taxpayer is disabled
- The distributions are not more than qualified higher education expenses
- The distributions are used to buy, build, or rebuild a first home
- The distributions are used to pay the IRS due to a levy
- The distributions are made to a qualified reservist (an individual called up to active duty)

Even though these distributions will not be subject to the additional 10% tax, they will be subject to income tax at the taxpayer's normal rates.

Distributions that are properly rolled over into another retirement plan or account (other than conversions to a Roth IRA, as discussed further below) are generally not subject to either income tax or the 10% additional penalty. Taxpayers must complete a rollover within 60 days after the day they receive the distribution.

---

**Example:** Lauren, age 39, takes a $5,000 distribution from her traditional IRA account. She does not meet any of the exceptions to the 10% additional tax, so the $5,000 is an early distribution. Lauren must include the $5,000 in her gross income and pay income tax on it. She must also pay a 10% penalty tax on the early distribution. The penalty is $500 (10% × $5,000).

---

## Qualified Charitable Distribution (QCD)

A taxpayer who is 70½ or older may choose to make a qualified charitable contribution (QCD) of up to $100,000 ($200,000 for MFJ taxpayers) from his IRA to qualified charitable organizations. The amount of the QCD may be excluded from taxable income and may also be counted toward the taxpayer's RMD. The 2012 American Taxpayer Relief Act extended this tax-free treatment of distributions for charitable purposes through December 31, 2013, with the following special rule: For QCDs made during January 2013, taxpayers can elect to have the distribution deemed to have been made during 2012.

Further, taxpayers who took IRA distributions during December 2012 and contributed all or a portion of the distributions to eligible charities during January 2013 can elect to have these amounts treated as QCDs for 2012. With the exception of the provision described above that applies to December 2012 and January 2013, the IRA trustee must make the distribution directly to the qualified charity (the taxpayer cannot request a distribution and then donate the money later). Likewise, any tax withholdings on behalf of the owner from an IRA distribution cannot qualify as QCDs.

# Roth IRA Rules

Unlike a traditional IRA, none of the contributions to a Roth IRA are deductible, but the entire balance is generally tax-free at the time of withdrawal. However, distributions generally cannot be made until after a five-year holding period and after the taxpayer has reached age 59½. Further, income limits apply to Roth IRA contributions, which means high income earners may be prohibited from contributing to a Roth IRA. In 2012, the following income limit rules apply to Roth IRAs:

## 2012 Roth IRA Contribution Limits

| Filing Status | Full Contribution | Phase-out Range | No Roth IRA Allowed |
|---|---|---|---|
| Single, HOH filers[77] | Less than $110,000 | $110,000 - $125,000 | $125,000 or more |
| MFJ and QW filers | Less than $173,000 | $173,000 - $183,000 | $183,000 or more |
| MFS (lived with spouse) | N/A | $0 - $10,000 | $10,000 or more |

Anyone who earns income above the Roth threshold amount is not allowed to contribute or roll over into a Roth IRA.

The major differences between a Roth IRA and a traditional IRA are as follows:

- Contributions to a Roth IRA are not deductible by the taxpayer, and participation in an employer plan has no effect on the contribution limits.
- There are no required minimum distributions from a Roth IRA. A distribution is not required until a Roth IRA owner dies.
- Contributions to a Roth IRA can be made by persons who are over the age of 70½.

# IRA Rollovers in General

Generally, a "rollover" is a tax-free transfer from one retirement plan or account to *another* retirement plan or account. The contribution to the second retirement plan is called a "rollover contribution." If executed properly, *most* rollovers are nontaxable events. However, sometimes taxpayers will choose to convert a traditional IRA into a Roth IRA. In this case, the conversion will result in taxation of any previously untaxed amounts in the traditional IRA.

If a taxpayer receives an IRA distribution and wishes to make a rollover, he must complete the transaction by the 60th day after the day he receives the distribution from a traditional IRA account (or an employer's plan). The IRS may waive the 60-

---

[77] This phase-out range also applies to MFS taxpayers who did not live with their spouses at all during the year.

day requirement when the failure to do so would be inequitable, such as in the event of a casualty, disaster, or other event beyond the taxpayer's reasonable control.

If a taxpayer sells the distributed property (such as stocks distributed from an IRA) and rolls over *all the proceeds* into another traditional IRA or qualified retirement plan, no gain or loss is recognized. The sale proceeds (including any increase in value) are treated as part of the distribution and are not included in the taxpayer's gross income.

The IRS allows only one rollover per IRA account in a 12-month period. However, a trustee-to-trustee transfer (or "direct transfer") can be done more than once a year. A "trustee to trustee" transfer is when an IRA's current custodian (such as a bank) directly transfers the funds to a new custodian. The transfer is done between the two companies and the money never touches the taxpayer's hands.

Any taxable distribution paid from an employer-sponsored retirement plan is subject to a mandatory withholding of 20%, even if the taxpayer intends to roll it over later. If the taxpayer does roll it over and wants to defer tax on the entire taxable portion, he will be forced to add funds from other sources equal to the amount withheld. In order to avoid this, a taxpayer should always request a direct transfer—where the employer transfers the distribution directly to another eligible retirement plan. Under this option, the 20% mandatory withholding does not apply. It is called a "direct rollover" when a taxpayer has a check for his rollover funds made payable directly to his new retirement account.

> **Example:** On September 4, 2012, Adam begins a new job. He decides to transfer the balance of his traditional IRA account to his new employer's plan. Adam receives a total distribution from his IRA of $50,000 in cash and $50,000 in stock. On October 4, he rolls over the entire amount totaling $100,000 into his new employer's plan.

## Rollover after the Death of an IRA Owner

After the death of a traditional IRA owner, a surviving spouse can elect to treat the IRA as being his or her own by changing the ownership designation, or to "roll over" the IRA balance to his or her own IRA account or certain types of qualified retirement plans. Only spouses are allowed either of these options.

An IRA may not be rolled over into the account of any other family member or beneficiary after death. However, any amounts remaining in an IRA upon a taxpayer's death would be payable to beneficiaries and subject to tax upon receipt. After an IRA owner dies, the beneficiary can generally take distributions over his remaining life expectancy. The beneficiary's "life expectancy" is calculated by using the age of the beneficiary in the year following the year of the IRA owner's death. The IRS has tables for making these calculations.

> **Example:** Allison, 42, and Lorenzo, 53, are married. Allison dies in 2012, and at the time of her death she has $50,000 in her traditional IRA account. Lorenzo chooses to roll over the entire $50,000 into his own IRA account, thereby avoiding taxation on the income until he retires and starts taking distributions.

If a Roth IRA owner dies, and the sole beneficiary is the spouse, he or she can delay distributions until the owner would have reached 70 ½ or treat the IRA as his or her own. For other beneficiaries, the account balance must generally be distributed by the end of the fifth calendar year after the owner's death, or be paid as an annuity over the beneficiary's life expectancy beginning the year following the year of death.

## Conversion of a Traditional IRA to a Roth IRA

If a taxpayer wishes to convert his traditional IRA to a Roth IRA, he is required to pay federal income taxes on any pretax contributions, as well as any growth in the investment's value. Once the funds are converted to a Roth, all of the investment grows tax free, and funds can then be withdrawn on a tax-free basis.

> **Example:** Becky converted her traditional IRA to a Roth IRA in 2012. The traditional IRA had a balance of $100,000. The entire balance represents deductible contributions and earnings thereon that have not previously been taxed. She reports the amount of the balance that was converted as taxable income in 2012.

A Roth conversion is reported on Form 8606, *Nondeductible IRAs*. [78] Rules for Roth conversions are as follows:

- Taxpayers who decide to convert to a Roth must pay taxes on the amount they convert.
- Penalties apply if the taxpayer withdraws from the Roth within five years of the conversion
- Taxpayers can choose to do a partial conversion.

In the case of an inherited IRA, only an IRA inherited from a spouse may be converted to a Roth IRA. As a general rule, a taxpayer is allowed to treat an inherited IRA from his deceased spouse as his own IRA, which also includes the choice to do a Roth conversion. Non-spousal beneficiaries (for example, a child who inherits an IRA from a deceased parent) are not allowed to roll over or convert a traditional IRA to a Roth IRA.

## Excise Tax on Excess Contributions

If a taxpayer *accidentally* contributes more to his IRA than allowed, the excess contribution is subject to a 6% excise tax. The IRS will allow a taxpayer to *correct* an excess contribution if certain rules are followed. If he makes an excess contribution

---

[78] Under a special rule that applied only to 2010 conversions to a Roth IRA, taxpayers must generally include half the taxable income in their income in 2011 and half in 2012, unless they chose to include all of it in income on their 2010 return. Taxpayers who also received Roth distributions in either 2010 or 2011 may be able to report a smaller taxable amount for 2012.

that exceeds his yearly maximum or his qualifying compensation, the excess contributions (and all related earnings) must be withdrawn from the IRA before the due date (including extensions) of the tax return for that year. If a taxpayer corrects the excess contribution in time, the 6% penalty will apply only to the interest earned on the excess contribution. Contributions made in the year a taxpayer reaches 70½ are also considered excess contributions.

Each year that the excess amounts remain in the traditional IRA the taxpayer must pay a 6% tax. However, this tax can never exceed more than 6% of the combined value of all the taxpayer's IRA at the end of the tax year. In order to correct an "improper contribution" to an IRA, the taxpayer must withdraw the contribution and any earnings on that amount. Relief from the 6% excise penalty is available only if the following are true:

- The taxpayer must withdraw the full amount of the excess contribution on or before the due date (including extensions) for filing the tax return for the year of the contribution.
- The withdrawal must include any income earned that is attributable to the excess contribution.

Taxpayers must include the earnings on the excess contribution as taxable income, and that income is reported on the return for the year in which the withdrawal was made.

---

**Example:** Betsy is 66, self-employed, and also owns rental properties. She contributes the maximum amount of $6,000 to her traditional IRA in December 2012. She is very busy and her records are poor, so she files for an extension to prepare her tax return. When Betsy finally gives her records to her accountant, he discovers that her taxable income from self-employment is only $3,000. Her passive rental income is $18,000. Only the self-employment income counts as "compensation" for purposes of contributing to a traditional IRA, so Betsy has inadvertently made an excess contribution of $3,000. She must withdraw the excess contribution and any interest earned on it by the extended due date of her return or face an excise tax of 6%.

---

## Prohibited Transactions

Generally, a prohibited transaction is the improper use of a traditional IRA by the owner, a beneficiary, or a disqualified person (typically a fiduciary or family member). Types of prohibited transactions with a traditional IRA include:

- Borrowing money from it
- Selling property to it
- Using it as security for a loan
- Buying property for personal use with IRA funds

If a prohibited transaction occurs at any time during the year, the account ceases to be treated as an IRA and its assets are treated as if having been distributed as of the first day of the year. If the total fair market value as of that date is more than the basis in the IRA, the excess amount is reportable as taxable income. It may also be subject to the additional 10% tax on early distributions.

| Traditional IRA vs. Roth IRA | | |
|---|---|---|
| Issue | Traditional IRA | Roth IRA |
| **Age limit** | A person over 70½ cannot contribute. | No age limit. |
| **2012 contribution limits** | $5,000, or $6,000 if age 50 or older by the end of 2012. | $5,000, or $6,000 if age 50 or older by the end of 2012. |
| **Are contributions deductible?** | Usually, yes. Deductibility depends on AGI, filing status, and whether the person is covered by a retirement plan at work. | No. You can never deduct contributions to a Roth IRA. |
| **Filing requirements** | No filing requirement unless nondeductible contributions are made. | No filing requirement. |
| **Mandatory distributions** | A person must begin receiving required minimum distributions by April 1 of the year following the year he or she reaches age 70½. | No. There are no required distributions unless the IRA owner dies. |
| **How distributions are taxed** | Distributions from a traditional IRA are taxed as ordinary income. | Distributions from a Roth IRA are not taxed. |
| **Income limits** | No income limits. | There are income limits for contributions, but there are none that affect conversion of a traditional IRA to a Roth IRA. Taxes apply on the conversion. |

# Unit 14: Questions

1. Lucas, an unmarried college student working part-time, earns $3,500 in 2012. He also receives $500 in interest income and $4,000 from his parents to help pay tuition. What is his maximum IRA contribution in 2012?

A. $0.
B. $3,500.
C. $5,000.
D. $6,000.

**The answer is B.** His IRA contribution for 2012 is limited to $3,500, the total amount of his wages. The other income (the interest income and the gifted money from his parents) is not qualifying compensation for IRA purposes. ###

2. Vic, age 36 and single, is in the Marines. He has the following income in 2012:

$30,500 of nontaxable combat pay.
$2,100 of regular wages.
$4,600 of interest income.

What is the maximum amount of money that Vic can contribute to a traditional IRA?

A. $2,100.
B. $4,600.
C. $5,000.
D. $6,000.

**The answer is C.** Vic may contribute $5,000, the maximum contribution allowed for his age. That is because a taxpayer may elect to treat nontaxable combat pay as qualifying compensation for IRA purposes. The interest income is not considered compensation. ###

3. Celeste, who is 50 and single, worked for a telephone company in France and earned $48,500 for which she claimed the foreign earned income exclusion. In addition she earned $3,200 as an employee of an answering service while she was in the U.S. She also received alimony of $400 for the year. What is her maximum amount of allowable contribution to a traditional IRA for year 2012?

A. $3,200.
B. $3,600.
C. $5,000.
D. $6,000.

**The answer is B.** Foreign earned income and any other income that is excluded from tax (with the exception of nontaxable combat pay) is also excluded for IRA contribution purposes. Alimony of $400 and wages of $3,200 earned in the U.S. are considered compensation for purposes of an IRA contribution. ###

4. Rafael, 40, earns $26,000 in 2012. Although he is allowed to contribute up to $5,000 to his IRA, he only has enough cash to contribute $2,000. On May 15, 2013, Rafael expects to get a big bonus, and he wishes to make a "catch-up" contribution for 2012. Rafael filed a timely extension for his tax return. Which of the following statements is true?

A. Rafael can contribute an additional $3,000 in May 2013 for his 2012 tax year so long as he files his tax return by the extended due date.
B. Rafael cannot contribute an additional $3,000 after April 15, 2013.
C. Rafael can contribute an additional $3,000 in May 2013 for his 2012 tax year only if he files his return by April 15, 2013.
D. Rafael cannot make a 2012 contribution to his IRA after December 31, 2012.

**The answer is B.** Rafael cannot contribute an additional $3,000 after April 15, 2013, regardless of whether he files an extension. If contributions to a traditional IRA for the year were less than the limit, a taxpayer cannot contribute more after the original due date of the tax return to make up the difference. ###

5. Kristin, 42, is a full-time graduate student with $1,200 in wages. She marries Omar, 50, during the year. Omar has taxable compensation of $46,000 in 2012. What is the maximum they can contribute to their traditional IRA accounts in 2012 if they file jointly?

A. $1,200.
B. $6,200.
C. $10,000.
D. $11,000.

**The answer is D.** They can contribute $11,000 if they file jointly. Kristin can contribute $5,000, and Omar can contribute $6,000 because he is 50. Even though Kristin only has $1,200 in compensation, she can use Omar's compensation to determine her maximum contribution. ###

6. Jody is single, 51, and has the following compensation in 2012:

- $1,600 in annuity income
- $3,000 in wages
- $2,300 in alimony
- $3,000 in interest income
- $6,000 in rental income

What is the maximum amount that Jody can contribute to her traditional IRA in 2012?
A. $3,000.
B. $5,000.
C. $5,300.
D. $6,000.

**The answer is C.** Only Jody's wage income of $3,000 and the $2,300 in alimony qualify as compensation for purposes of an IRA contribution. The annuity income, rental income, and interest income are passive income and do not qualify. ###

7. Derek, age 62, is retired with $11,000 in interest income. He has no other taxable income in 2012. Derek marries Virginia, age 46, on March 26, 2012. Virginia has taxable compensation of $50,000 for the year. She plans to contribute $5,000 to a traditional IRA. How much can Derek contribute to an IRA?

A. $0.
B. $4,000.
C. $5,000.
D. $6,000.

**The answer is D.** Since Derek is over 50, if they file a joint return, he can choose to contribute $6,000 to an IRA. Even though Derek only has interest income, his wife has wage income. Each can contribute to a traditional IRA, even if only one spouse has qualifying compensation. ###

8. Colton, 49, and Molly, 52, are married and file jointly. They both work and each has a traditional IRA. In 2012, Molly earned $2,000 and Colton earned $50,000. If they file jointly, what is the maximum Molly can contribute to her IRA?

A. $2,000.
B. $5,000.
C. $6,000.
D. $12,000.

**The answer is C.** They can contribute up to $6,000 to Molly's IRA account because she is over 50 years old and can utilize Colton's earnings in order to make the maximum contribution. ###

9. An excess contribution to an IRA is subject to a tax. Which of the following is true?

A. The taxpayer will not have to pay the 6% tax on the excess contribution if he withdraws the excess contribution and any income earned on the excess contribution before the due date of the tax return for the applicable year, including extensions.
B. The 6% tax is due on both the excess contributions and any income earned on the excess contribution, even if the taxpayer withdraws the excess from the account.
C. A taxpayer will not have to pay the 6% tax if he withdraws the excess contribution and any income earned on the excess contribution before the due date of the tax return for the year, not including extensions.
D. A taxpayer will not have to pay the 6% on interest earned on the excess contributions so long as the taxpayer is disabled.

**The answer is A.** The taxpayer will not have to pay the 6% tax on the excess contribution if the excess contribution and any interest earned are withdrawn by the due date of his return, *including extensions*. If a taxpayer corrects the excess contribution in time, the 6% penalty will apply only to the interest earned on the excess contribution. ###

10. Elizabeth and Landon are 62 years old, married, and lived together all year. They both work and each has a traditional IRA. In 2012, Landon earned $4,000 in wages and $11,000 in annuity income. Elizabeth earned $52,000. They prefer to file separately. If they file separate returns, what is the maximum that Landon can contribute to his IRA?

A. $1,000.
B. $4,000.
C. $5,000.
D. $6,000.

**The answer is B.** As Landon is married and lived with his wife during the year but is filing separately, he can contribute no more than his $4,000 in wages, which is his only qualifying compensation for IRA purposes. ###

11. Preston and Ruby are 50 years old and married. They both work and each has a traditional IRA. In 2012, Preston earned $5,000 and Ruby earned $32,000. If they file jointly, what is the maximum they can contribute to their IRAs?

A. $5,000.
B. $6,000.
C. $10,000.
D. $12,000.

**The answer is D.** If married filing jointly, they can contribute up to $12,000 to all their IRAs. This is because they are over 50 and they each can make the maximum contribution of $6,000. ###

12. Frank, 72, and Sue, 61, are married and file jointly. In 2012, Frank earned $30,000 and Sue earned $5,000. If Frank and Sue file jointly, how much can they contribute to their traditional IRAs?

A. $5,000.
B. $6,000.
C. $11,000.
D. $12,000.

**The answer is B.** Only Sue can contribute to an IRA. Frank cannot contribute because he is over 70½ years old. However, Sue is over 50 and can utilize Frank's qualifying compensation in order to contribute the maximum of $6,000 to her IRA. ###

13. Miguel is 47. In 2012, he contributed $1,000 to a Roth IRA. He also wants to contribute to a traditional IRA account. What is the maximum he can contribute to a traditional IRA in 2012?

A. $0.
B. $3,000.
C. $4,000.
D. $5,000.

**The answer is C.** Assuming Miguel has sufficient qualifying compensation, he would be able to contribute $4,000; the 2012 maximum for contributions to all types of IRAs is $5,000 for taxpayers under 50. Taxpayers are allowed to have different types of IRA accounts, but the maximum contribution thresholds apply to their total contributions for the year. ###

14. Annette, age 40, and Gill, age 48, are married and file jointly. Annette is covered by a retirement plan at work, but Gill is not. In 2012, Annette contributed $2,000 to her traditional IRA and $3,000 to a traditional IRA for Gill. Annette has a modified AGI of $90,000; Gill has a modified AGI of $98,000. What is their allowable IRA deduction?

A. $5,000.
B. $3,000.
C. $2,000.
D. $0.

**The answer is D.** Annette and Gill's allowable IRA deduction is zero because their modified AGI is over the phase-out limit of $183,000 for 2012. However, they are still allowed to make nondeductible IRA contributions that would be reported on Form 8606. ###

15. Shari wants to roll over her retirement account to another bank. She received a distribution in 2012. How long does Shari have to complete the rollover in order to avoid income tax on the distribution?

A. 30 days.
B. 60 days.
C. Until the end of the year.
D. Until the due date of the return.

**The answer is B.** Shari has 60 days to complete the rollover. If she does not complete the rollover within 60 days, the distribution is treated as a taxable event and is subject to income tax in 2012. ###

16. Janelle plans to make a contribution to her traditional IRA. She files her 2012 tax return on March 1, 2013, claiming a deduction for her IRA contribution. However, she forgets to make the contribution in time and misses the deadline. What must Janelle do?

A. Janelle must file an amended return.
B. Janelle may claim the contribution as income in the following year.
C. Janelle must file an extension.
D. Janelle must pay an early withdrawal penalty.

**The answer is A.** If a contribution is reported on the 2012 return but is not made by the deadline, the taxpayer must file an amended return. IRA contributions must be made by the due date for filing the return, not including extensions. ###

17. David is 57 and he contributed $2,000 to his Roth IRA in 2012. What is the maximum he can contribute to a traditional IRA?

A. $0.
B. $3,000.
C. $4,000.
D. $5,000.

**The answer is C.** The 2012 maximum for contributions to all types of IRAs is $6,000 for taxpayers who are 50 or older. Since David is 57, and assuming he has sufficient qualifying compensation, he is allowed to contribute $4,000 to a traditional IRA in addition to the $2,000 contributed to the Roth IRA, for a combined total of $6,000. ###

18. Monica borrowed $100,000 and pledged the balance in her traditional IRA as security on the loan. At the beginning of 2012, the IRA had a balance of $70,000; at the time of the loan transaction, its balance was $80,000; and at the end of 2012, its balance was $75,000. Which of the following would result from this transaction?

A. Monica would have taxable income of $75,000.
B. Monica would have taxable income of $70,000.
C. Monica would have taxable income of $70,000.
D. Monica would have to pay an additional 10% penalty on her 2012 contribution to the IRA.

**The answer is B.** Pledging the IRA as security for a loan is considered a prohibited transaction that results in termination of the account's treatment as an IRA, and the FMV as of the beginning of the year is considered to be a taxable distribution. Assuming the entire balance of the account represented deductible contributions and earnings on them, Janelle would have had no basis in the account, and the entire $70,000 would be reportable as taxable income. ###

19. Which of the following is considered an excess contribution to an IRA?

A. A traditional IRA contribution made in the year a taxpayer reaches 70½.
B. A rollover to a Roth IRA.
C. A contribution made by a taxpayer who only has alimony income.
D. A Roth contribution made by a taxpayer who is 75.

**The answer is A.** Contributions to a traditional IRA made in the year a taxpayer reaches 70½ (and any later years) are considered excess contributions. In general, an excess contribution and any earnings on it are subject to an additional 6% tax if the taxpayer does not withdraw the contribution by the due date of the tax return, including extensions. ###

414

20. AJ was born on June 6, 1942. By what date must he take the first required minimum distribution from his traditional IRA?

A. April 1, 2012.
B. December 31, 2012.
C. December 31, 2013.
D. April 1, 2013.

**The answer is D.** The first required minimum distribution from a traditional IRA must be taken by April 1 of the year following the year in which the taxpayer turns 70½. AJ turned 70½ on December 6, 2012. ###

21. Doris is 58 years old and took a distribution of $8,000 from her traditional IRA in 2012. She had qualified higher education expenses of $6,000 during the year. What tax treatment would apply to the IRA distribution?

A. The entire distribution would be subject to regular tax plus the additional 10% applicable to early distributions.
B. The distribution would not be taxable.
C. A portion of the distribution ($2,000) would be subject to regular tax and the additional 10% applicable to early distributions would apply to the entire amount.
D. The entire distribution would be subject to regular tax and the additional 10% tax would apply to $2,000.

**The answer is D.** As Doris is not yet 59½, early distributions from her traditional IRA would typically be subject to the additional 10% tax. However, the additional tax would apply only to the extent that her distributions exceeded her qualified higher education expenses for the year. ###

# Unit 15: Estate and Gift Taxes

**More Reading:**
Publication 559, *Survivors, Executors, and Administrators*
Publication 950, *Introduction to Estate and Gift Taxes*

For Part 1 of the EA exam, you will be required to understand how estate and gift taxes affect individual taxpayers. For Part 2 of the exam, you will be tested on the treatment of estates as legal entities.

## Estates in General

For federal tax purposes, an estate is a separate legal entity that is created when a taxpayer dies. The deceased taxpayer's property may consist of items such as cash and securities, real estate, insurance, trusts, annuities, business interests, and other assets. A person who inherits property from an estate is not taxed on the transfer. Instead, the estate itself is responsible for paying any applicable taxes before the property is distributed. However, if the estate's assets are distributed to beneficiaries before applicable taxes are paid, the beneficiaries can be held liable for the tax debt, up to the value of the assets distributed.

## Requirements for the Personal Representative of an Estate

After a person dies, a personal representative, such as an executor named in his will or an administrator appointed by a court, will typically manage the estate and settle the decedent's financial affairs. If there is no executor or administrator, another person with possession of the decedent's property may act as the personal representative.

The personal representative is responsible for filing the final income tax return and the estate tax return, if required.

The personal representative is also responsible for determining any estate tax liability before the estate's assets are distributed to beneficiaries. The tax liability for an estate attaches to the assets of the estate itself, so if the assets are distributed to the beneficiaries before the taxes are paid, the beneficiaries may be held liable for the tax debt, up to the value of the assets distributed.

Either the personal representative or a paid preparer must sign the appropriate line of the return. Current IRS requirements require that the following tax returns be filed:

- The final income tax returns (Form 1040) for the decedent (for income received before death);
- Fiduciary income tax returns (Form 1041) for the estate for the period of its administration; (if necessary) and
- Estate Tax Return (Form 706), if the fair market value of the assets of the estate exceeds the applicable threshold for the year of death.

**Example:** James was unmarried when he died on April 20, 2012. His only daughter, Lillian, was named as the executor of his estate. James earned wages in 2012 before his death. Therefore, a final tax return is required for 2012. Lillian asks her accountant to help prepare her father's final Form 1040, which will include all the taxable income that James received in 2012 before his death. The accountant also helps Lillian with the valuation of her father's estate. After determining the fair market value of all her father's assets, they conclude that James's gross estate is valued at approximately $7 million. As this exceeds the threshold of $5,120,000 for 2012, an estate tax return (Form 706) is also required to be filed.

## The Final Income Tax Return (Form 1040)

The taxpayer's final income tax return is filed on the same form that would have been used if the taxpayer were still alive, but "deceased" is written after the taxpayer's name. The filing deadline is April 15 of the year following the taxpayer's death, just like regular tax returns.

The personal representative must file the final individual income tax return of the decedent for the year of death and any returns not filed for preceding years. If an individual died after the close of the tax year but before the return for that year was filed, the return for that year will not be the final return. The return for that year will be a regular return and the personal representative must file it.

**Example:** Stephanie dies on March 2, 2012. At the time of her death, she had not yet filed her 2011 tax return. She earned $51,000 in wages in 2011. She also earned $18,000 in wages between January 1, 2012 and her death. Therefore, Stephanie's 2011 and 2012 tax return must be filed by her representative. The 2012 return would be her final individual tax return.

On a decedent's final tax return, the rules for personal exemptions and deductions are the same as for any taxpayer. The full amount of the applicable personal exemption may be claimed on the final tax return, regardless of how long the taxpayer was alive during the year.

## Income In Respect of a Decedent

Income in respect of a decedent (IRD) is any taxable income that was earned but *not received* by the decedent by the time of death. IRD is not taxed on the final return of the deceased taxpayer. IRD is reported on the tax return of the person (or entity) that receives the income. This could be the estate, the surviving spouse, or another beneficiary, such as a child. Regardless of the decedent's accounting method, IRD is subject to income tax when the income is received.

IRD retains the same tax nature after death as if the taxpayer were still alive. For example, if the income would have been short-term capital gain to the deceased, it is taxed the same way to the beneficiary. IRD can come from various sources, including:

- Unpaid salary, wages or bonuses
- Distributions from traditional IRAs and employer-provided retirement plans
- Deferred compensation benefits
- Accrued but unpaid interest, dividends, and rent
- Accounts receivable of a sole proprietor

---

**Example:** Carlos was owed $15,000 in wages when he died. The check for these wages was not remitted by his employer until three weeks later and was received by his daughter and sole beneficiary, Rosalie. The wages are considered IRD, and Rosalie must recognize the $15,000 as ordinary income, the same tax treatment that would have applied for Carlos.

---

**Example:** Beverly died on April 30. At the time of her death, she was owed (but had not yet received) $1,500 in interest on bonds and $2,000 in rental income. Beverly's beneficiary will include $3,500 in IRD in gross income when the interest and rent are received. The income retains its character as passive interest income and passive rental income.

---

IRD is includible in the decedent's estate and subject to estate tax, and may also be subject to income tax if received by a beneficiary. Therefore, the beneficiary may take a deduction for estate tax paid on the IRD. This deduction is taken as a miscellaneous itemized deduction on Schedule A, and is not subject to the 2% floor, as are most other miscellaneous itemized deductions.

## IRS Form 1041, U.S. Income Tax Return for Estates and Trusts

An estate is a taxable legal entity that exists from the time of an individual's death until all assets have been distributed to the decedent's beneficiaries. Form 1041 is a fiduciary return used to report the following items for a domestic decedent's estate, trust, or bankruptcy estate:

- Current income and deductions, including gains and losses from disposition of the entity's property;
- A deduction for income that is either accumulated or held for future distribution or distributed currently to the beneficiaries; and
- Any income tax liability.

Current income would include IRD, if it was received by the estate rather than specific beneficiaries. As investment assets will usually continue to earn income after a taxpayer has died, this income, such as rents, dividends and interest, must be reported. Expenses of administering the estate can be deducted either from the estate's income on Form 1041 in determining its income tax, or from the gross estate on Form 706 in determining the estate tax liability, but cannot be claimed for both purposes.

Schedule K-1 is used to report any income that is distributed to each beneficiary and is filed with Form 1041, with a copy also given to the beneficiary.

The due date for Form 1041 is the fifteenth day of the fourth month following the end of the entity's tax year, but is subject to an automatic extension of five months if Form 7004 is filed. The tax year may be either a calendar or fiscal year, subject to the election made at the time the first return is filed. An election will also be made on the first return as to method (cash, accrual, or other) to report the estate's income.

Form 1041 must be filed for any domestic estate that has gross income for the tax year of $600 or more, or a beneficiary who is a nonresident alien (with any amount of income).

## The Gross Estate

The estate tax is a tax on the transfer of property from an individual's estate after his death. It applies to the taxable estate, which is the gross estate less certain deductions. The gross estate is based upon the fair market value of the taxpayer's property, which is not necessarily equal to his cost, and includes:

- The FMV of all tangible and intangible property owned by the decedent at the time of death.
- The full value of property held as joint tenants with the right of survivorship (unless the decedent and spouse were the only joint tenants)
- Life insurance proceeds payable to the estate, or for policies owned by the decedent, payable to the heirs.
- The value of certain annuities or survivor benefits payable to the heirs.
- The value of certain property that was transferred within three years before the decedent's death.

The gross estate does not include property owned solely by the decedent's spouse or other individuals. Lifetime gifts that are complete (so that no control over the gifts was retained) are not included in the gross estate.

## Deductions from the Gross Estate

Once the gross estate has been calculated, certain deductions (and in special circumstances, reductions to value) are allowed to determine the taxable estate. Deductions from the gross estate may include:

- Funeral expenses paid out of the estate.
- Administration expenses for the estate, including attorney's fees.
- Debts owed at the time of death.
- The marital deduction (generally, the value of the property that passes from the estate to a surviving spouse).
- The charitable deduction (generally, the value of the property that passes from the estate to a qualifying charity).

- The state death tax deduction (generally, any inheritance or estate taxes paid to any state).

The following items are not deductible from the gross estate:
- Federal estate taxes paid.
- Alimony paid after the taxpayer's death. These payments would be treated as distributions to a beneficiary.

Property taxes are deductible only if they accrue under state law prior to the decedent's death.

## The Marital Deduction

There are special rules and exceptions for transfers between spouses. The marital deduction allows spouses to transfer an unlimited amount of property to one another during their lifetimes or at death without being subject to estate or gift taxes.

To receive an unlimited deduction, the spouse receiving the assets must be a U.S. citizen, a legal spouse, and have outright ownership of the assets. The unlimited marital deduction is generally not allowed if the transferee spouse is not a U.S. citizen (even if the spouse is a legal resident of the United States). If the receiving spouse is not a U.S. citizen, assets transferred are subject to an annual exclusion, which is $139,000 in 2012.

## Basis of Estate Property

The basis of property inherited from a decedent is generally one of the following:
- The FMV of the property on the date of death.
- The FMV on an alternate valuation date, if elected by the personal representative.
- The value under a special-use valuation method for real property used in farming or another closely-held business, if elected by the personal representative.
- The decedent's adjusted basis in land to the extent of the value excluded from the taxable estate as a qualified conservation easement.

Property that is jointly owned by a decedent and another person will be included in full in the decedent's gross estate unless it can be shown that the other person originally owned or otherwise contributed to the purchase price. The surviving owner's new basis of property that was jointly owned must be calculated. To do so, the surviving owner's original basis in the property is added to the value of the part of the property included in the decedent's estate. Any deductions for depreciation allowed to the surviving owner on that property are subtracted from the sum.

If property is jointly held between husband and wife as tenants by the entirety or as joint tenants with the right of survivorship (if they were the only joint tenants), one-half of the property's value is included in the gross estate and there is a step-up in basis for that one-half. If the decedent holds property in a community property state, half of the value of the community property will be included in the gross estate of the decedent, but the entire value of the community property will receive a step-up in basis.

### Special Election for Decedent's Medical Expenses

Debts that were not paid before death, including medical expenses subsequently paid on behalf of the decedent, are liabilities of the estate and can be deducted from the gross estate on the estate tax return. However, if medical expenses for the decedent are paid out of the estate during the one-year period beginning with the day after death, the personal representative can alternatively elect to treat all or part of the expenses as paid by the decedent at the time they were incurred, and deduct them on the final tax return (1040) for the decedent.

### Estates and Credits

Estates are allowed some of the same tax credits that are allowed to individuals. The credits are generally allocated between the estate and the beneficiaries. However, estates are not allowed the credit for the elderly or the disabled, the Child Tax Credit, or the Earned Income Credit.

## Form 706: The Estate Tax Return

An estate tax return is filed using Form 706, *United States Estate (and Generation-Skipping Transfer) Tax Return.* After the taxable estate is computed, the value of lifetime taxable gifts is added to this number and the estate tax is computed. The tax is then reduced by the applicable credit amount. The applicable credit amount, formerly referred to as the unified credit, applies to both the gift tax and the estate tax applies to both the gift tax and the estate tax and it equals the tax on the basic exclusion amount.

For 2012, the basic exclusion amount is $5,120,000 and the related applicable credit amount is $1,772,800. Any portion of the applicable credit amount used against gift tax in a given year reduces the amount of credit that can be used against gift or estate taxes in later years. For estate tax purposes but not for gift taxes, the applicable credit amount may also include the tax applicable to the deceased spousal unused exclusion (DSUE). The DSUE is the unused portion of the decedent's predeceased spouse's estate that was not used against gift or estate tax liabilities. The predeceased spouse must have died on or after January 1, 2011 and the DSUE must have been reported on Form 706 filed on behalf of the first spouse's estate.

If required to be filed, the due date for Form 706 is nine months after the decedent's date of death. An automatic six- month extension may be requested by filing Form 4768. However, the tax is due by the due date and interest is accrued on any amounts owed that are not paid at that time.

The assessment period for tax is three years after the due date for a timely filed estate tax return. The assessment period is four years for transfers from an estate.

## The Generation-Skipping Transfer Tax (GST)

The generation skipping transfer tax (GST) may apply to gifts during a taxpayer's life or transfers occurring after his death, called bequests, made to "skip persons." A "skip person" is a person who belongs to a generation that is two or more generations *below* the generation of the donor. The most common scenario is when a taxpayer makes a gift or bequest to a grandchild.

The GST is assessed when a property transfer is made, including instances in which property is transferred from a trust. The GST tax is based on the amounts transferred to skip persons, after subtracting the allocated portions of the GST tax exemption. In 2012, the GST tax exemption is $5,120,000 and the GST tax rate is set at the maximum estate tax rate of 35%.

The GST is imposed separately and in addition to the estate and gift tax.

> **Example:** Patrick sets up a trust that names his adult daughter, Helene, as the sole beneficiary of the trust. In January 2012, Patrick dies, and the trust passes to Helene. However, later in the year, Helene also dies, and now the trust passes to her children (Patrick's grandchildren). Patrick's grandchildren are "skip-persons" for purposes of the GST, and the trust fund property may be subject to the GST.

Any *direct* payments that are made toward tuition or medical expenses are exempt from gift tax or GST.

> **Example:** Gordon wants to help support his grandchildren, but he wants to make sure that his gifts are not subject to gift tax, GST, or estate tax. So, in 2012, he offers to pay his grandchild's college tuition in full. Gordon writes a check directly to the college in the amount of $25,000. There is no tax consequence for this gift, and no reporting is required.

# The Gift Tax

The gift tax is imposed on the transfer of property by one individual to another and applies whether the donor intends the transfer to be a gift or not. Gift tax is always imposed on the donor, not the receiver, of the property. However, under special arrangements the donee may *agree* to pay the tax instead of the donor.

As discussed above, the estate tax and gift tax are subject to a combined basic exclusion amount ($5,120,000 in 2012) and use of any portion of this exclusion amount to reduce payment of gift taxes during a taxpayer's lifetime will reduce the amount available upon death to reduce applicable estate taxes. For 2012, the maximum gift tax rate is 35%.

Although any gift could potentially be a taxable gift, the following gifts are not taxable:

- Gifts that are not more than the annual exclusion. In 2012, the exclusion is $13,000 per person.
- Tuition or medical expenses paid for someone else, directly to the institution.
- Unlimited gifts to a spouse, so long as the spouse is a U.S. citizen.
- Gifts to a political organization for its use.
- Gifts to a qualifying charity.
- A parent's support for a minor child. This support is not considered a "gift" if it is required as part of a legal obligation, such as by a divorce decree.

Gift taxes are reported on Form 709, *United States Gift (and Generation-Skipping Transfer) Tax Return*. Form 709 is required for any of the following gifts:

- If the taxpayer gives more than the annual exclusion to at least one individual (except to a U. S. citizen spouse)
- If the taxpayer "splits gifts" with a spouse
- If a taxpayer gives a future interest[79] to anyone other than a U.S. citizen spouse

If the taxpayer's spouse is not a U.S. citizen, a gift tax return is required in the following instances:

- Any gifts totaling more than $139,000 (limit in 2012)
- A future interest of any value

If required, Form 709 is due by April 15, 2013. However, if the donor died during 2012, the filing deadline is the due date for his estate tax return (if earlier than April 15, 2013). Taxpayers who extend the filing of Form 1040 for six months using Form 4868 are deemed to have extended their gift tax return, if no gift tax is due with the extension. If gift tax is due, the tax payer must submit payment with a payment voucher. If the taxpayer does not extend Form 1040, the gift tax return can be extended separately.

| |
|---|
| **Example:** Earline gives her son, Dion, a gift of $13,000 in cash during the year. She also pays his college tuition, totaling $21,000. She writes the check directly to the college. Earline also pays for Dion's medical bills by issuing the check directly to his doctor's office. None of these gifts is taxable, and no gift tax return is required. |
| **Example:** Dave is single. In 2012, Dave gives his adult son, Noah, $15,000 to help start his first business. The money is not a loan, so Dave is required to file a gift tax return, since the amount exceeds the $13,000 annual exclusion amount. |

---

[79] A "future interest" is a gift that cannot be immediately used, possessed, or enjoyed.

## Gifts by Married Couples

Both the basic exclusion amount and the annual exclusion for gifts to individuals apply separately to each spouse, and each spouse must separately file a gift tax return if he or she made reportable gifts during the year. However, if a married couple makes a gift to another person, the gift can be considered as being one-half from one spouse and one-half from the other spouse. This is known as gift splitting. Gift splitting allows married couples to give up to $26,000 to a person without making a taxable gift. Both spouses must consent to split the gift. Married couples who split gifts must file a gift tax return, even if one-half of the split gift is less than the annual exclusion.

**Example:** Harold and his wife, Margie, agree to split gifts of cash. Harold gives his nephew, Mark, $21,000, and Margie gives her niece, Nicole, $18,000. Although each gift is more than the annual exclusion ($13,000), by gift splitting they can make these gifts without making a taxable gift. In each case, because one-half of the split gift is not more than the annual exclusion, it is not a taxable gift. However, the couple must file a gift tax return.

**Example:** Felicia gives her cousin, Jessie, $24,000 to purchase a new car. Felicia elects to split the gift with her husband, Rafael, and Rafael is treated as if he gave Jessie half the amount, or $12,000. Assuming they make no other gifts to Jessie during the year, the entire $24,000 gift is tax free. Since they have decided to split the gift, Jessie and Rafael are required to file gift tax returns.

## The Basis of Property Received as a Gift

For purposes of determining gain or loss on a subsequent disposition of property received as a gift, the taxpayer must consider:

- The gift's adjusted basis to the donor just before it was given to the taxpayer,
- The gift's FMV at the time it was given to the taxpayer, and
- Any gift tax paid actually paid on appreciation of the property's value while held by the donor (as opposed to gift tax offset by the donor's applicable credit amount).

When a taxpayer sells property received as a gift, he calculates gain based upon the donor's adjusted basis plus any gift tax paid on the donor's appreciation. If the same property were sold at a loss, the taxpayer's basis would be the lower of the donor's adjusted basis or the FMV at the time of the gift.

> **Example:** Darren's father gives him 20 shares of stock that are currently worth $900. Darren's father has an adjusted basis in the stock of $500. Darren's basis in the stock, for purposes of determining gain on any future sale of the stock, is $500. (This is the stock's transferred basis.)

Generally, the value of a gift is its fair market value on the date of the gift. However, the value of the gift may be less than its fair market value to the extent that the donee gives the donor something in return.

> **Example:** Donald sells his son, Jared, a house for $10,000. At the time of the gift, the fair market value of the house is $90,000. Donald has made a gift to his son of $80,000 ($90,000 - $10,000 = $80,000).

# Unit 15: Questions

1. Which of the following is not income in respect of a decedent?

A. Wages earned before death but still unpaid at the time of death.
B. Vacation time paid after death.
C. Taxable IRAs and retirement plans.
D. A royalty check that was received before death but not cashed.

**The answer is D.** Since the royalty check was received before the taxpayer died, it is not considered IRD income. Income in respect of a decedent is taxable income earned but not received by the decedent by the time of death. The fact that the royalty check was not cashed has no bearing on the nature of the income.

2. When is an estate tax return due?

A. Four months after the close of the taxable year.
B. Six months after the close of the calendar year.
C. Nine months after the date of death.
D. Twelve months after the date of death.

**The answer is C.** Estate tax returns are due nine months from the date of death, although the executor may request an extension of time to file.

3. Which of the following items is not an allowable deduction from the gross estate?

A. Debts owed at the time of death.
B. Medical expenses.
C. Funeral expenses.
D. Federal estate tax.

**The answer is D.** Federal estate tax is not deductible from the gross estate. All of the other items listed are allowable deductions from the gross estate.

4. The executor of Ophelia's estate is her sister, Elise. Elise decides to make a distribution of 100% of the estate's assets before paying the estate's income tax liability. Which of the following is true?

A. The beneficiaries of the estate can be held liable for the payment of the liability, even if the liability exceeds the value of the estate assets.
B. No one can be held liable for the tax if the assets have been distributed.
C. The beneficiaries can be held liable for the tax debt, up to the value of the assets distributed.
D. None of the above.

**The answer is C.** The tax liability for an estate attaches to the assets of the estate itself, so if the assets are distributed to the beneficiaries before the taxes are paid, the beneficiaries can be held liable for the tax debt, up to the value of the assets distributed.

5. Delia's estate has funeral expenses for the cost of her burial. How should the executor deduct these costs?

A. Funeral expenses are an itemized deduction on Form 1040.
B. Funeral expenses are deducted on Form 1041.
C. Funeral expenses are deducted on Form 706.
D. Funeral expenses cannot be deducted as an expense.

**The answer is C.** No deduction for funeral expenses can be taken on Form 1041 or Form 1040. Funeral expenses may only be claimed as a deduction from the gross estate on Form 706.

6. Duncan died in 2012. Following his death, the executor of his estate paid the following bills. Which of these is not an allowable deduction in determining Duncan's taxable estate?

A. Administration expenses.
B. State inheritance taxes.
C. Charitable contributions.
D. Alimony paid after the taxpayer's death.

**The answer is D.** Alimony paid after the taxpayer's death is not deductible from the gross estate. Deductions from the gross estate are allowed for:
•Funeral expenses paid out of the estate
•Administration expenses for the estate, including attorney's fees
•Debts owed at the time of death
•The marital deduction
•The charitable deduction
•The state death tax deduction

7. During December in each of the ten years prior to his death, Herman gave $30,000 to each of his two granddaughters. He also paid a total of $400,000 directly to Birchland College for their college tuition costs. When Herman died in June 2012, how much of his basic exclusive amount would he have used up as a result of these gifts to his granddaughters?

A. $600,000.
B. $1,000,000.
C. $340,000.
D. $400,000.

**The answer is C.** Each year's gift of $30,000 is reduced by the annual exclusion amount of $13,000, and a portion of Herman's basic exclusion amount must be used to avoid payment of gift tax on the excess amount of $17,000. Thus, over ten years, he uses a total of $170,000 for each granddaughter, or $340,000. Since the $400,000 was paid directly to Birchland College on behalf of the granddaughters, it is not subject to gift tax, and none of his basic exclusion amount must be used as a result of these additional gifts. It should be noted that his cash gifts to the granddaughters would also be subject to generation-skipping tax.

8. In general, who is responsible for paying the gift tax?

A. The estate.
B. The donor.
C. The receiver of the gift.
D. The executor.

**The answer is B.** The donor is generally responsible for paying the gift tax. ###

9. Donald's will provides that each of his ten grandchildren is to receive $1 million. Assuming that none of his GST exemption amount has previously been used in connection with gifts to the grandchildren or other skip persons, what portion of the total amount distributed to the grandchildren after his death in 2012 would be subject to GST?

A. $8,700,000.
B. $5,120,000.
C. $10,000,000.
D. $4,880,000.

**The answer is D.** The aggregate portion of his estate distributed to his grandchildren ($10 million) would be reduced by his exclusion amount for GST ($5,120,000) and the remainder of $4,880,000 would be subject to GST. ###

10. Dustin pays $15,000 in college tuition for his nephew, Rich, directly to Rich's college. Which of the following statements is correct?

A. The gift is taxable, and Rich must report the gift tax on his individual tax return (Form 1040).
B. The gift is not taxable, but Dustin must file a gift tax return.
C. The gift is taxable, and Dustin must file a gift tax return.
D. The gift is not taxable, and no gift tax return is required.

**The answer is D.** Tuition or medical expenses paid directly to a medical or educational institution for someone else are not included in the calculation of taxable gifts, and there is no reporting requirement. ###

11. In which case must a gift tax return be filed?

A. A married couple gives a gift of $13,000.
B. A married couple gives a gift of $15,000.
C. A single individual gives a gift of $4,000 to an unrelated person.
D. A wife gives a gift of $20,000 to her husband.

**The answer is B.** In order to make a gift to one individual in excess of the annual exclusion of $13,000 and avoid using any of their basic exclusion amounts, a married couple can use gift splitting. Gift splitting allows married couples to give up to $26,000 to a person without making a taxable gift ($13,000 from each spouse), but they are required to file a gift tax return. Gifts to a spouse generally do not require a tax return. ###

12. Shawn, a single taxpayer, has never been required to file a gift tax return. In 2012, Shawn gave the following gifts:

•$18,000 in tuition paid directly to a state university for an unrelated person.
•$13,500 paid to General Hospital for his brother's medical bills.
•$50,000 in cash donations paid to his city homeless shelter, a 501(c)(3).
•$15,000 as a political gift paid to the Libertarian Party (not a qualified charity).

Is Shawn required to file a gift tax return?

A. No.
B. Yes, because the donation to the political party is not an excludable gift.
C. Yes, because each of the gifts exceeded $13,000.
D. Yes, because the political gift is a reportable transaction.

**The answer is A.** None of the gifts is taxable, and no reporting is required. Tuition or medical expenses paid for someone directly to an educational or medical institution are not counted as taxable gifts. Nor are gifts to a political organization for its own use or gifts to a qualified charity. ###

13. In 2012, Jeffrey gives $25,000 to his girlfriend, Rachel. Which of the following statements is true?

A. The first $13,000 of the gift is not subject to the gift tax, but the remainder is subject to gift tax, and Rachel is responsible for paying it.
B. Rachel is required to file a gift tax return and pay tax on the entire gift.
C. Jeffrey is required to file a gift tax return, Form 709.
D. Jeffrey may choose to report the gift tax on Form 1040, Schedule A.

**The answer is C.** Jeffrey is required to file a gift tax return. Gift tax is paid by the donor, not the recipient, of the gift. The first $13,000 of the gift is not subject to gift tax because of the annual exclusion. The remaining $12,000 is a taxable gift. ###

14. All of the following gifts are excluded from the determination of the gift tax except:

A. A gift made to a political organization for its own use.
B. A cash gift given to a nonresident alien spouse of a U.S. citizen.
C. A medical bill paid directly to a hospital on behalf of a relative.
D. A gift made to a qualifying charity.

**The answer is B.** Although a full marital deduction is allowed for a spouse who is a U.S. citizen, a transfer of property to a noncitizen spouse is limited to $139,000 in 2012, and the excess amount would be subject to gift tax. ###

15. Alana had gifts totaling $28,000 in 2012 that were subject to gift tax. When is her gift tax return due?

A. March 15, 2013.
B. April 15, 2013.
C. June 15, 2013.
D. September 15, 2013.

**The answer is B.** Gift tax returns are typically due on April 15 of the following calendar year, and payment of the tax is also due then, although the filing may be subject to a six-month extension. If the donor died during 2012, the filing deadline is the due date for his estate tax return (if earlier than April 15, 2013). ###

16. Phil died in 2012. At the time of his death, he had assets of $4 million and liabilities of $500,000. He also had insurance policies in place that paid $1 million to his children.

Based upon the information provided, what is the taxable amount of Phil's estate that must be reported on Form 706?

A. $5 million.
B. $0.
C. $4 million.
D. $4.5 million.

**The answer is B.** The taxable amount of Phil's estate is $4.5 million. However, because this amount is less than the applicable exclusion amount of $5,120,000 for 2012, an estate tax return is not required to be filed.

Supporting calculations:

| | |
|---|---|
| Assets | $4,000,000 |
| Less liabilities | ($500,000) |
| Life insurance proceeds | $1,000,000 |
| Taxable estate | $4,500,000 |

###

# Index

# Also Available from PassKey Publications

## The Enrolled Agent Tax Consulting Practice Guide:

*Learn How to Develop, Market, and Operate a Profitable Tax and IRS Representation Practice*

ISBN-13: 978-0982266045
Available in Kindle and Nook editions and as a paperback

# About the Authors

Collette Szymborski is a certified public accountant and the managing partner of Elk Grove CPA Accountancy Corporation. She specializes in the taxation of corporations, individuals, and exempt entities. Elk Grove CPA also does estate planning.

Richard Gramkow is an enrolled agent with more than sixteen years of experience in various areas of taxation. He holds a master's degree in taxation from Rutgers University and is currently a tax manager for a publicly held Fortune 500 company in the New York metropolitan area.

Christy Pinheiro is an enrolled agent, registered tax return preparer, Accredited Business Accountant, and writer. Christy was an accountant for two private CPA firms and for the State of California before going into private practice. She is a member of the California Society of Enrolled Agents and CalCPA.